Frugal Innovation and Social Transitions in the Digital Era

Muhammad Nawaz Tunio
Mohammad Ali Jinnah University, Karachi, Pakistan

Atia Bano Memon
University of Sindh, Badin, Pakistan

A volume in the Advances in Human and Social
Aspects of Technology (AHSAT) Book Series

Published in the United States of America by
    IGI Global
    Information Science Reference (an imprint of IGI Global)
    701 E. Chocolate Avenue
    Hershey PA, USA 17033
    Tel: 717-533-8845
    Fax: 717-533-8661
    E-mail: cust@igi-global.com
    Web site: http://www.igi-global.com

Library of Congress Cataloging-in-Publication Data

Names: Tunio, Muhammad Nawaz, 1984- editor. | Memon, Atia Bano, 1984-
  editor.
Title: Frugal innovation and social transitions in the digital era /
  Muhammad Nawaz Tunio, and Atia Bano Memon, editors.
Description: Hershey, PA : Business Science Reference, 2022. | Includes
  bibliographical references and index. | Summary: "The objective of this
  book is through its contributed chapters that strive to find out and
  understand the social value of innovation, frugal innovation, and social
  innovation in society at local, national, and international levels"--
  Provided by publisher.
Identifiers: LCCN 2022027518 (print) | LCCN 2022027519 (ebook) | ISBN
  9781668454176 (hardcover) | ISBN 9781668454183 (paperback) | ISBN
  9781668454190 (ebook)
Subjects: LCSH: Organizational change. | Social change. | Technological
  innovations--Social aspects. | Diffusion of innovations--Social aspects.
Classification: LCC HD58.8 .F78 2022 (print) | LCC HD58.8 (ebook) | DDC
  658.4/06--dc23/eng/20220714
LC record available at https://lccn.loc.gov/2022027518
LC ebook record available at https://lccn.loc.gov/2022027519

This book is published in the IGI Global book series Advances in Human and Social Aspects of Technology (AHSAT) (ISSN: 2328-1316; eISSN: 2328-1324)

British Cataloguing in Publication Data
A Cataloguing in Publication record for this book is available from the British Library.

For electronic access to this publication, please contact: eresources@igi-global.com.

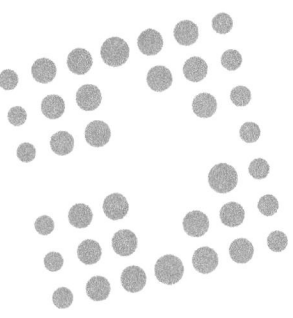

Advances in Human and Social Aspects of Technology (AHSAT) Book Series

Mehdi Khosrow-Pour, D.B.A.
Information Resources Management Association, USA

ISSN:2328-1316
EISSN:2328-1324

MISSION

In recent years, the societal impact of technology has been noted as we become increasingly more connected and are presented with more digital tools and devices. With the popularity of digital devices such as cell phones and tablets, it is crucial to consider the implications of our digital dependence and the presence of technology in our everyday lives.

The **Advances in Human and Social Aspects of Technology (AHSAT) Book Series** seeks to explore the ways in which society and human beings have been affected by technology and how the technological revolution has changed the way we conduct our lives as well as our behavior. The AHSAT book series aims to publish the most cutting-edge research on human behavior and interaction with technology and the ways in which the digital age is changing society.

COVERAGE

- Technology and Freedom of Speech
- Human-Computer Interaction
- End-User Computing
- Human Development and Technology
- Computer-Mediated Communication
- Technoself
- Technology Adoption
- Gender and Technology
- Cyber Behavior
- Technology Dependence

IGI Global is currently accepting manuscripts for publication within this series. To submit a proposal for a volume in this series, please contact our Acquisition Editors at Acquisitions@igi-global.com or visit: http://www.igi-global.com/publish/.

Titles in this Series

For a list of additional titles in this series, please visit: www.igi-global.com/book-series/advances-human-social-aspects-technology/37145

Handbook of Research on Implementing Digital Reality and Interactive Technologies to Achieve Society 5.0
Francesca Maria Ugliotti (Politecnico di Torino, Italy) and Anna Osello (Politecnico di Torino, Italy)
Information Science Reference • © 2022 • 731pp • H/C (ISBN: 9781668448540) • US $295.00

Exploring Ethical Problems in Today's Technological World
Tamara Phillips Fudge (Purdue University Global, USA)
Information Science Reference • © 2022 • 385pp • H/C (ISBN: 9781668458921) • US $240.00

Technological Influences on Creativity and User Experience
Joshua Fairchild (Creighton University, USA)
Information Science Reference • © 2022 • 305pp • H/C (ISBN: 9781799843542) • US $195.00

Machine Learning for Societal Improvement, Modernization, and Progress
Vishnu S. Pendyala (San Jose State University, USA)
Engineering Science Reference • © 2022 • 290pp • H/C (ISBN: 9781668440452) • US $270.00

The Digital Folklore of Cyberculture and Digital Humanities
Stamatis Papadakis (University of Crete, Greece) and Alexandros Kapaniaris (Hellenic Open University, Greece)
Information Science Reference • © 2022 • 361pp • H/C (ISBN: 9781668444610) • US $215.00

Multidisciplinary Perspectives Towards Building a Digitally Competent Society
Sanjeev Bansal (Amity University, Noida, India) Vandana Ahuja (Jaipuria Institute of Management, Ghaziabad, India) Vijit Chaturvedi (Amity University, Noida, India) and Vinamra Jain (Amity University, Noida, India)
Engineering Science Reference • © 2022 • 311pp • H/C (ISBN: 9781668452745) • US $270.00

Analyzing Multidisciplinary Uses and Impact of Innovative Technologies
Emiliano Marchisio (Giustino Fortunato University, Italy)
Information Science Reference • © 2022 • 275pp • H/C (ISBN: 9781668460153) • US $240.00

Handbook of Research on Applying Emerging Technologies Across Multiple Disciplines
Emiliano Marchisio (Giustino Fortunato University, Italy)
Information Science Reference • © 2022 • 548pp • H/C (ISBN: 9781799884767) • US $270.00

701 East Chocolate Avenue, Hershey, PA 17033, USA
Tel: 717-533-8845 x100 • Fax: 717-533-8661
E-Mail: cust@igi-global.com • www.igi-global.com

Table of Contents

Detailed Table of Contents

    Syed Haider Ali Shah, Bahria University, Pakistan
    Muhammad Jaffer, Bahria University, Pakistan
    Eman Zameer Rahman, Bahria University, Pakistan
    Arslan Asif, Bahria University, Pakistan

Understanding how frugal innovation supports social sustainability is necessary. Frugal innovation has strived to creatively address urgent societal issues while also creating income; it has had a tremendous influence on society. This essay's objective is to identify linkages between the ideas of social sustainability and cost-effective innovation. The objective of this book chapter is to identify linkages between the ideas of social sustainability and frugal innovation by reviewing the literature that is currently available in the field. This book will contribute by developing a link between these two concepts and will further expand our understanding of frugal innovation and social sustainability advancement while taking guidance from the sustainable development goals (SDGs), particularly those pertaining to social sustainability.

    Syed Haider Ali Shah, Bahria Business School, Bahria University, Pakistan
    Muhammad Jaffer, Bahria University, Pakistan
    Eman Zameer Rahman, Bahria University, Pakistan
    Syed Zeeshan Haider, Bahria University, Pakistan

The purpose of this book chapter is to highlight and to explore the frugal innovation phenomenon, whether it is global phenomena or local. Most importantly, the frugal innovation has different perspectives around the globe. Moreover, the role of digitalization is also crucial in the frugal innovation. How does digitalization impact the frugal innovation? The impact is boosting the frugal innovation or hindering the process of frugal innovation. The role of digitalization and globalization is impacting various business models and paving the way for the new products and services. It will be interesting to see the role of frugal innovation, the patterns of frugal innovation, the different trends of frugal innovation, and the impact on the society level. Some studies suggested that frugal innovation led to better competition and provided an environment for better products and services for consumers. This book chapter will explain the multiple perspectives, trends of frugal innovation, and its relation to the digitalization

Chapter 3

Syed Haider Ali Shah, Bahria Business School, Bahria University, Pakistan
Bushra Alvi, Bahria University, Pakistan
Zahir Ud Din, Bahria University, Pakistan
Bilal Arshad, Bahria University, Pakistan
Madiha Suhail, Bahria University, Pakistan
Saleh Ahmed Salem Alyafe, University of Malaya, Malaysia

The purpose of this book chapter is to highlight the different issues related to frugal innovation advancement, and how the advancement of the frugal innovation change and affect the social life, particularly the role in uplifting the standard of the living. Literature shows that there are some factors which need to be considered for frugal innovation. This area received a less attention from the researchers. The contribution of the book chapter will be elaborating different mechanisms which are affecting the growth and functions of organizations who are involve in the frugal innovation. The various definitions and multiple perspective regarding the frugal innovation will highlight the important elements for academia and practitioners to consider and conduct future research. This book chapter will highlight different components which will be helpful to the organization to involve in frugal innovation and make it a successful process by reviewing the literature.

Chapter 4

Ramakrishnan Vivek, Faculty of Management, Technological Campus, Sri Lanka
Mohsen Brahmi, University of Sfax, Tunisia
Yogarajah Nanthagopan, Faculty of Business Studies, Sri Lanka
Luigi Aldieri, University of Salerno, Italy

The chapter mainly highlights the impact of the COVID-19 pandemic on the global economy, utilizing macroeconomic concepts and describing how organizations around the world can use the strategic management technique of drawing up a PESTLE analysis to provide focused attention to each factor and macroeconomic party. This ultimately comprises the entire economy, with special attention being focused on the expansion of the environmental factor. The key problem discussed in the following research chapter was whether healthcare should be considered as a separate dimension under the environmental category in a PESTLE analysis. The methodology used involved gathering data from online journals relating to the relevant ministries of healthcare, and an extended review was conducted based on existing sources. The scenarios that unfolded as the pandemic first broke out, the policies imposed by the governments, and their shortcomings as policymakers were discussed, and the current day policies utilized to make sure the brunt of the pandemic doesn't boomerang again were analyzed.

Nosheen Rafiq, Bahria University, Pakistan
Syed Haider Ali Shah, Bahria Business School, Bahria University, Pakistan
Shahab Aziz, Bahria University, Pakistan
Afshan Sultana, University Malaya, Malaysia
Shams Ul Haq Khan, Bahria University, Pakistan
Zahir Ud Din, Bahria University, Pakistan
Muhammad Zeeshan Ahmed Sheikh, Bahria University, Pakistan
Ozair Ijaz Kiani, Bahria University, Pakistan

The chapter is about the role of frugal innovation and social sustainability in emerging nations and how it facilities the lives of people in developing countries. The development of any state depends upon the level of advanced technology, but all states are not in sound enough condition to use expensive technology to enhance quality of life. Therefore, such economies go towards the idea of frugal innovation where it offers 'low price' solutions that provide quality products and improves standard of living. This chapter focuses on how frugal innovation can provide latest technologies to people with limited resources. This chapter suggests the need of scientists and researchers and their leading role in order to enhance frugal innovation.

Samreen Fazal, Greenwich University, Karachi, Pakistan

HRM is a significant element of management that positively shapes the performance of SMEs. A plethora of literature studying HRM innovative practices deals with the impact of innovative HR practices encompassing workplace, behavioral, technological, and innovative leadership roles on the firms` efficient and innovative performance. These studies exhibit a substantial and positive influence of the innovative HR practices on the innovative performance driving innovation in firms particularly in SMEs. However, hitherto no prominent effort has been done predominantly in Pakistan to review and synchronize the extant knowledge in a composed manner. Therefore, the proposed chapter aims to consolidate, compile, and review the current literature associated with the innovative trends of HR practices in SMEs. In addition, it also seeks to offer a comprehensive HRM model to promote innovations in HRM practices. To sum up, this chapter will significantly contribute to the existing body knowledge based on HRM innovative practices in SMEs.

Nosheen Rafiq, Bahria University, Pakistan
Syed Haider Ali Shah, Bahria University, Pakistan
Rafia Amjad, Bahria University, Pakistan
Ozair Ijaz Kiani, Bahria University, Pakistan

The chapter is about the role of frugal innovation and how it improves overall quality of life in digital era. The development of any state depends upon the level of advanced technology, but all states are not in a sound enough condition to use expensive technology to enhance quality of life. Therefore, such economies go towards the idea of frugal innovation where it offers 'low price' solutions that provide quality products and improve standard of living. It also focuses on the idea of environmental protection as well. This chapter focuses on how frugal innovation can reduce the emission of carbon dioxide, wastage, excess usage of water, and participate in environmental sustainability. This chapter suggests the need of scientists and researchers and their leading role in enhancing frugal innovation

Leadership measures the ability to accomplish the set goal(s) due to the act of inspiring and motivating a group of your peers. Former United States president Dwight D. Eisenhower stated famously that "Leadership consists of nothing but taking responsibility for everything that goes wrong and giving your subordinates credit for everything that goes well." The Army's definition of leadership is "the process of influencing people by providing purpose, direction, and motivation while operating to accomplish the mission and improving the organization."

Innovation in education is pursuing knowledge that will support novel and distinctive ideas. We can describe the term 'innovation' in education as finding the most appropriate and productive way to get maximum outcome from educational institutes. It is concerned with unrevealing individual capabilities of the students and researchers, which can assist society in underlining and resolving many scientific and social problems and enables us to get more creative and critical thinkers. Innovation in education is thinking outside of the box, challenging the existing techniques and tools to acquire more valuable ways of learning. The chapter covers the essentials of innovation in education and aims to unveil the potential areas of innovation in existing education system; generally, it falls in the category of processes innovations, which include modern and meaningfully advanced techniques of classroom-based learning, assessment tools, and teaching techniques.

Social innovation and social entrepreneurship were rarely discussed till the 19th century. However, the topic has been in the limelight extensively since 1950. Moreover, the linkage between social innovation and social entrepreneurship still needs to be explored, especially in developing sides of the world where social entrepreneurship is required to optimize social and economic parameters. In fact, there is a severe increase in the level of opportunities for social entrepreneurship. The increase in the level of opportunities is massive, especially due to globalization. Therefore, this chapter has been written purposefully to reflect the role of social entrepreneurship with examples and opportunities for social entrepreneurship with reference to the developing sides of the world.

Chapter 11

Muhammad Faisal Sultan, Khadim Ali Shah Bukhari Institute of Technology, Pakistan
Aamir Hussain, Khadim Ali Shah Bukhari Institute of Technology, Pakistan
Shahid Khan, Khadim Ali Shah Bukhari Institute of Technology, Pakistan
Raza Ali Khan, NED University of Engineering and Technology, Pakistan

The role of higher education is to benefit society at large to generate sustainable socio-economic returns. Therefore, research and knowledge creation must be rendered to achieve anodyne to overcome social challenges and foster new and better practices. Hence, social innovation is the need of society, especially from higher education providers. Especially after the outbreak of COVID-19, there is a need of social innovation by all stake holders in order to attain a sustainable economy. Although, to provide catalyst to the model of social change and innovation, there is a need of an entrepreneurial model for higher education. However, most of the prior studies with the reference of education are not related with the innovation but with societal impact and produce educational change. Thus, this chapter has been written purposely to describe social innovation by higher education providers. The chapter also includes various examples of social innovation with respect to the higher education sector in order to make readers understand the importance of social innovation in the pre-COVID-19 and post-COVID-19 worlds.

Chapter 12

Erum Shah, University of Sindh, Pakistan
Sultan Ali, University of Sindh, Pakistan
Naveeda Katper, University of Sindh, Pakistan

Women's empowerment has remained a key concern for the development of society. The information in the current study has been extracted from the doctoral thesis of the corresponding researcher. The study argues that in the 20th century, developing countries were observed to bring various policies and programs to empower women. However, in this study, the researcher has tried to capture a few of the prominent policies and programs brought in Pakistan to empower women since its independence. Concurrently, this study aims to evaluate those policies and programs in the key domains of women's empowerment with the lens of social justice. It is mainly done with a desk review of various published resources and the support of key informant interviews with politicians, human rights activists, and bureaucrats. Findings of the study suggest, having various policies and programs for women empowerment, the situation of women is not improved in Pakistan, and there are significant rifts in policy implementation that need proper consideration to meet the requirements of social justice.

Chapter 13

Muhammad Asif Qureshi, Mohammad Ali Jinnah University, Pakistan
Syed Mir Muhammed Shah, Sukkur IBA University, Pakistan
Syed Ali Raza, Iqra University, Pakistan
Hayfa Kazouz, Faculty of Economics and Management Sciences of Sousse, University of
*   Sousse, Tunisia*

Producing something from low or nothing through entrepreneurial bricolage is an increasing phenomenon in emerging and dynamic markets. Recently, there is a dire need in developing affordable products and services targeting new markets. Entrepreneurs in the limited resources environments often develop such products. As suggested by Baker and Nelson, firms engage in bricolage to overcome the limitations imposed by the limited resources situation. With respect to the current situation, resource limitations and sustainability issues are pushing firms to develop affordable, quality products and services.

Chapter 14

Kamran Jamshed, Bahria University, Pakistan
Syed Haider Ali Shah, Bahria University, Pakistan
Samrah Jamshaid, Northeast Normal University, Jilin, China

This chapter aimed to understand and foster innovative technology by addressing social needs and developing innovative ideas to solve environmental issues. Social innovation is a new means of identifying better answers to social concerns, and it entails social individuals and communities generating, testing, and disseminating ideas to meet critical social needs. It's a collaborative and participatory technique that focuses on the whole system rather than individual elements. This chapter is an overview of the hospitality industry of Europe as the hospitality industry is the largest industry and the European hospitality industry is covering almost 50% of the global hospitality industry. In this chapter, the overview of the social innovation with the hospitality industry is associated with social causes like the leftovers can be distributed to needy people and hotels can offer discounts for those guests who are willing to participate in social causes.

Chapter 15

Karambir Singh Dhayal, Birla Institute of Technology and Science, Pilani, India
Mohsen Brahmi, University of Sfax, Tunisia
Shruti Agrawal, Malaviya National Institute of Technology, Jaipur, India
Luigi Aldieri, University of Salerno, Italy
Concetto Paolo Vinci, University of Salerno, Italy

The pandemic of COVID-19 has caused a serious effect on health, economic, social, political, demographic, and all other various aspects of the economy. It has given a huge impact on the education system in a worldwide manner that leads to the closure of universities, colleges, and schools. This study aims to assess the impact of the worldwide COVID-19 pandemic on the education sector in special reference to India. The loss of learning was majorly pronounced among students from a disadvantaged prospectus. The authors conducted a qualitative document analysis of all the published articles that explained the impact of COVID-19 pandemic on the education system from 2019-2021. The study provides an insight on the barriers in education due to the COVID-19 pandemic. The result shows the evolution of technology-enabled education in the learning sector. Finally, the challenges articulated by the learners during online learning include external as well as internal factors and causes.

The rise of digitalization has brought new challenges to the business world. E-commerce operations are growing as a result of digitalization, which is transforming traditional business processes, methods, and products into new ones. To address the global challenges posed by e-commerce and changes in markets, firms rely heavily on business innovation. Firms must be able to function under societal and operational challenges, as well as have the ability to integrate local knowledge with other types of expertise. Frugal innovation focuses on societal and operational issues and challenges as beginning points for innovative ideas that could ultimately drive for sustainable development. This chapter is about a mapping of the literature by focusing on certain research areas: the structure and identifying patterns of how the frugal innovation, social transition, and business sustainability are related in the digital era.

The chapter is written purposively in order to highlight the development of social innovation as the idea of discipline and work process. The chapter highlights not only the academic evolution of social innovation but also highlights the role of universities in the development of social innovation in developing sides of the world. Therefore, the chapter is much different from the other chapters that are written to highlight the birth, introduction, and growth of social innovation and the social innovation process. In fact, the purpose of this chapter is not only to emphasize the introduction of social innovation as the term and idea, but the chapter also defined factors that assist in the growth of social innovation in the developing world.

Foreword

Frugal innovations are greatly focused and paid high interest by the scholars in the better interest of the society in last decade, in this interest scholars have discussed the origins of the concept, definition, scope and theoretical ancients. Its evolution depicts the notion in the developing world where limited resources and unserved potential consumers live together. Resultantly, frugal products and services were observed as low-tech, low-price solutions. Latent studies have highlighted that frugal innovation are no more confined to the world of underserved consumers in the emerging and developing countries. World is looking for the highly affordable and high-quality solutions in both cases B2B as well as B2C.

This book *Frugal Innovation and Social Transitions in the Digital Era* focuses on the different topics under the umbrella of the frugal innovation in which it is observed that different scholars have contributed from the different universities, countries, and discipline. Such diversity of the book ensures the success of the editors who have invested their efforts, time, and energy to invite the interesting, relevant topics and publish them in the form of the book for the benefit of the emerging and developing countries.

In this regard, it shows the worth of the book titled *Frugal Innovation and Social Transitions in the Digital Era* edited by the emerging scholars Dr. Muhammad Nawaz Tunio and Dr. Atia Bano Memon, I would like to appreciate them for focusing on such interesting topic and congratulate them for successfully completing the project.

Best wishes,

Le Thanh Tiep
Faculty of Economics, Ho Chi Minh City International University, Vietnam

Preface

The concept of the frugal innovation originated in the context of the emerging markets and main idea behind it was to develop products and services that can satisfy the needs and wants of the customers. FIs try to show sustainability more than the mainstream innovations. There are different types of FIs in procedures, process, and practices. Some prominent examples of FIs include cars, medical devices, health services, solar energy, refrigerators, and water purifiers. Frugal innovation (FI) demonstrates a new entrepreneurial landscape where small firms with limited resources develop innovations for under-served customers in low-income countries. FIs also create new markets and contribute to sustainability. The studies so far have highlighted various frugal products introduced by large and small firms around the world. This study aims to explore the process of how individuals at the grassroots level successfully conceptualize, develop, and diffuse their FIs to achieve commercial success.

Effective and innovative solutions are mandatory to solve complex problems of these days, and FI is a way to accomplish this goal. There are three criteria to define frugal innovation: substantial cost reduction, concentration on core functionalities, and optimized performance level. Furthermore, frugality is a formative construct that encompasses four dimensions: basic quality, cost of consumption, simplicity, and sustainability. The low cost and sustainability need to be considered together when creating frugal products. Policymakers largely ignore the consumers within sustainable innovation. To address poverty at the grassroots level, the market-based approach has proven challenges when serving low-income customers, whereas a sustainable business model approach. Frugality is also an important issue for developing as well as developed countries.

In the spirit of the frugal innovation, this book, *Frugal Innovation and Social Transitions in the Digital Era,* expresses relevance and contribution in the literature in which different topics are invited for the publication in the book. In this book, around 73 authors are contributed their intellectual work from the different national and international universities. Large number for chapters were submitted, but the out of big number, only 17 chapters are selected and considered to include in the book for the publication based on the relevance with the aim and scope of the call.

In this regard, the summaries of each chapter are mentioned here below for the information of the reader. Each chapter is much valuable and very important because every chapter focuses on the new perspective of the frugal innovation, and it shows the transition in the digital era.

THE IMPACT OF FRUGAL INNOVATION ON SOCIAL SUSTAINABILITY AND THE GUIDING ROLE OF SUSTAINABLE DEVELOPMENT GOALS (SDGs) IN THE DIGITAL ERA

Understanding how frugal innovation supports social sustainability is necessary. Frugal innovation has strived to creatively address urgent societal issues while also creating income, it has had a tremendous influence on society. This essay's objective is to identify linkages between the ideas of social sustainability and cost-effective innovation. The objective of this book chapter is to identify linkages between the ideas of social sustainability and frugal innovation by reviewing the literature that is currently available in the field. This book will contribute by developing a link between these two concepts and will further expand our understanding of frugal innovation and social sustainability advancement while taking guidance from the Sustainable Development Goals (SDGs), particularly those pertaining to social sustainability.

IS FRUGAL INNOVATION A GLOBAL PHENOMENON? MULTIPLE PERSPECTIVES ON FRUGAL INNOVATION AND DIGITALIZATION

The purpose of this book chapter is to highlight and to explore the frugal innovation phenomenon whether it is global phenomena or local. Most importantly the frugal innovation different perspectives around the globe. Moreover, the role of digitalization is also crucial in the frugal innovation. How does digitalization impact the frugal innovation? The impact is boosting the frugal innovation or hindering the process of frugal innovation. The role of digitalization and globalization is impacting various business models and pave the way for the new products and services. It will be interesting to see the role of frugal innovation, the patterns of frugal innovation, the different trends of frugal innovation and the impact on the society level. Some studies suggested that frugal innovation lead to better competition and provide the environment for better products and services for consumers. This book chapter will explain the multiple perspective, trends of frugal innovation and its relation to the digitalization.

DOES IT MATTER? THE IMPACT OF FRUGAL INNOVATION ON SOCIETY AND UPLIFTING THE SOCIAL STANDARD IN THE DIGITAL ERA

The purpose of this book chapter is to highlight the different issues related to frugal innovation advancement and how the advancement of the frugal innovation change and affect the social life particularly the role in uplifting the standard of the living. Literature shows that there are some factors which need to be considered for frugal innovation. This area received a less attention from the researchers. The contribution of the book chapter will be elaborating different mechanisms which are affecting the growth and functions of organizations who are involve in the frugal innovation. The various definitions and multiple perspective regarding the frugal innovation will highlight the important elements for academia and practitioners to consider and conduct future research. This book chapter will highlight different components which will be helpful to the organization to involve in frugal innovation and make it a successful process by reviewing the literature.

A SYSTEMATIC REVIEW USING A FACTORS IN PESTLE FRAMEWORK: COVID-19 PANDEMIC AND EXPANSION OF ECONOMIC ENVIRONMENTS

The only aim of this study paper was to evaluate if the PESTLE analysis can be reformed to include healthcare as a new component. As per the thorough analysis of the data presented above, we can conclusively provide an ultimatum on the statement that the healthcare entity can indeed be classified as a separate dimension under a PESTLE analysis, simply because of the very significant direct impact this has had and continues to have on the macroeconomy as seen by the fruits of the COVID-19 pandemic.

ROLE OF FRUGAL INNOVATION, SOCIAL SUSTAINABILITY, CHALLENGES, AND OPERATIONAL CONSTRAINTS: INSIGHTS TO UNDERSTAND THE INTERLINKAGES BETWEEN THEM FROM PERSPECTIVE OF FRUGALITY

The chapter is about the role of frugal innovation and social sustainability in emerging nations and how it facilities the lives of people in developing countries. The development of any state depends upon the level of advanced technology, but all states are not in a sound conditions to use expensive technology to enhance quality of life. Therefore, such economies go towards the idea of frugal innovation where it offers 'low price' solutions that provide quality products and improves standard of living. This chapter focuses on how frugal innovation can provide latest technologies to people with limited resources. This chapter suggests the need of scientists and researchers and their leading role in order to enhance frugal innovation.

FRUGAL INNOVATIONS OF HRM PRACTICES IN SMEs

The chapter provides a comprehensive review of the extant literature dealing with the innovative HR practices in SME sector. The review encompasses studies associated with the innovative HR including workplace innovation, behavioral or developmental innovation and technological innovation driving innovative performance in SMEs. Findings highlight the pivotal role of innovative HRM practices in fostering innovation in SMEs. The workplace or behavioral innovation depict Human Resource Foundation's (HRF's) positioning, innovative HRM Practices including recruitment, selection, training, reward and compensation, employees` supporting attitude, knowledge management capacity, Customized performance measurement and collaborative performance management, Employers` support, time, information, knowledge, advice to employees in a form of gifts, and high performance work systems (HPWS) to be the catalysts for SMEs innovation.

HOW FRUGAL INNOVATION IS TRANSITIONING HUMAN LIFE AND IMPROVING THEIR QUALITY OF LIFE: FRUGAL INNOVATION AND QUALITY OF LIFE IN THE DIGITAL ERA

This book chapter explains how social sustainability and cost-effective innovation are enhancing the lives of individuals. This study can help scientists, researchers, academics, students, and policymakers embrace and implement cutting-edge frugal innovation strategies to raise social standards in developing countries. It is advised that future studies use an applicable research methodology to examine the relationship between social sustainability and frugal innovation. Both quantitative and qualitative methods can be used in scientific investigations. By developing a clear vision of frugal innovation, researchers and scientists should take the environmental protection component into consideration.

YOUNG LEADERSHIP SKILLS REQUIRED IN FRUGAL INNOVATION PROCESS AND ITS DEVELOPMENTS

This article examines the nature of demands on Army officers in the contemporary operating environment and their implications for leadership development. This is aroused from concerns about both the current operational environment and a closely related development, the Army's ongoing transformation of its structure, technologies, and operating techniques. How will the Army prepare its future leaders for the new demands that will inevitably be placed on them? The report describes analysis and findings on three major topics: the general attributes and intellectual qualities required by leaders in the modern environment; specific operational skills and depth the new environment requires; and the extent to which career paths can provide a foundation of operational experience while still meeting other demands on the officer corps.

INNOVATION IN EDUCATION

Innovation in education is pursuing knowledge that will support novel and distinctive ideas. We can describe the term Innovation in education as finding the most appropriate and productive way to get maximum outcome from educational institutes. It is concerned with unrevealing individual capabilities of the students and researchers, which can assist society in underlining as well as resolving many scientific and social problems and enables us to get more creative and critical thinkers. Innovation in education is thinking outside of the box, challenging the existing techniques and tools to acquire more valuable ways of learning. The chapter covers the essentials of innovation in Education and aims to unveil the potential areas of innovation in existing education system, generally it falls in the category of processes innovations which includes modern and meaningfully advanced techniques of classroom-based learning, assessment tools, and teaching techniques.

SOCIAL INNOVATION AND SOCIAL ENTREPRENEURSHIP AT THE WAKE OF COVID-19: A PERSPECTIVE FROM THE DEVELOPING SIDE OF THE WORLD

Companies always found difficult to accomplish their social responsibilities due to the contradiction between approach used to optimize business and social mission. Hence companies are often found to be struggling towards attainment of agenda of social responsibility. However, the established and well-known firms try to follow philosophy of Triple Bottom Line for creating social value and social impact without compromising on profitability or sustainability. Similar has been mentioned through literature that in order to generate sustainable value, companies need to formulate strategies and practices that may not only resulted in the increase of shareholders value but will also contributed progressively to sustainable world. Thus strive for social value resulted in social entrepreneurship and to do this there is a need of out of the box innovation in products, services and organizations, etc.

SOCIAL INNOVATION IN HIGHER EDUCATION: BUSINESS AND SOCIAL IMPACTS AND IMPLICATIONS

The role of higher education is to benefit society at large to generate sustainable socio-economic returns. Therefore, research and knowledge creation must be rendered to achieve anodyne to overcome social challenges & foster new and better practices. Hence social innovation are the need of society, especially from higher education providers. Especially after the outbreak of COVID-19 there is a need of social innovation by all stake holders in order to attain sustainable economy. Although to provide catalyst to the model of social change & innovation there is a need of entrepreneurial model for higher education. However, most of the prior studies with the reference of education is not related with the innovation but with societal impact & produce educational change. Thus, this chapter has been written purposely to describe social innovation by higher education providers. Chapter also includes various examples of social innovation with respect to higher education sector in order to make readers understand the importance of social innovation in pre-COVID-19 and post COVID-19 world.

AN OVERVIEW OF WOMEN EMPOWERMENT POLICY WITH SOCIAL JUSTICE LENS AND FRUGAL INNOVATION

This study began by setting its foot in the historical context of policy making for women empowerment. Literature reveals increased political consciousness and identification of patriarchy and capitalism as the barriers to women development were proved foundation for formal mobilization of women rights. Similarly, literature highlighted with the support of key informant interviews the complexities of Pakistani society that how it is shaped in the veil of culture with tag of religion. Women in this study conceptualize empowerment as having education, essential skills to participate in economic opportunities. Findings indicates having education and awareness about rights is a source of feeling independent.

FRUGAL INNOVATION AND DIFFERENT DYNAMICS

Efficient and effective innovative ways and solutions are mandatory to solve existing complex issues, and Frugal Innovation is a way to accomplish the goal. The following three criteria to define frugal innovation: substantial cost reduction, concentration on core functionalities, and optimized performance level.

SOCIAL INNOVATION AND ENVIRONMENT: AN OVERVIEW OF THE TOURISM AND HOSPITALITY INDUSTRY OF EUROPE

Social innovation is the term used to describe novel concepts that advance social objectives. Social innovation solutions in tourism play a crucial role in the transformation of the "consumer centric" viewpoint into the "community oriented" viewpoint, which takes into account the social capital of the community. A significant regional and national competitive challenge is the topic. Instead of the procedure, all parties should concentrate on improving the working environment and the game rules in order to create the conditions that allow the establishment of profitable businesses and start-up companies. Social innovation now includes technological advancement as an implication of fresh service options. Social innovations encompass both organizational and technical advances, as seen in theory and practice. Depending on the socioeconomic development of the destination, social innovation has different values. In more rural areas, they are more focused on social issues and missions. It might be said that social solutions in tourism entail sharing innovative information and offering solutions, goods, and services that are catered to the need of customers and local stakeholders.

A PARADIGM SHIFT IN EDUCATION SYSTEMS DUE TO COVID-19: ITS SOCIAL AND DEMOGRAPHIC CONSEQUENCES

The COVID-19 came along with many unprecedented challenges and one of them was that regular classroom teaching had to be abandoned with the immediate effect because social distancing norms had to be followed strictly. In the effort to provide continued education, institutions and governments realized the need to support online learning. As a result of this virtual classroom learning had to be adopted worldwide no matter whether a nation is developed or still on the development trajectory. Some countries were fast to adopt this change while others had to struggle. One particular example was that of India, where Internet penetration and availability of smartphones still remains a bottleneck. India happens to be one of the few nations which is continuously making significant advancements in terms of developing the technology for the spread of quality universal education. The availability of literature with respect to the role of learning is mainly about classroom based learning. Hence there is a need to look at the education after the Covid-19 pandemic.

HOW FRUGAL INNOVATION, SOCIAL TRANSITION, AND BUSINESS SUSTAINABILITY ARE RELATED: INSIGHTS ON THE CONTEMPORARY TRANSITION TOWARDS SUSTAINABILITY IN THE DIGITAL ERA

The rise of digitalisation has brought new challenges to the business world. E-commerce operations are growing as a result of digitalization, which is transforming traditional business processes, methods, and products into new ones. To address the global challenges posed by e-commerce and changes in markets and firms rely heavily on business innovation. Firms must be able to function under societal and operational challenges, as well as have the ability to integrate local knowledge with other types of expertise. Frugal innovation focuses at societal and operational issues and challenges as beginning points for innovative ideas that could ultimately drive for sustainable development. This chapter is about a mapping of the literature by focusing on certain research areas, structure and identifying patterns of how the Frugal Innovation, social transition and Business Sustainability is related in the digital era.

SOCIAL INNOVATION: CONCEPT AND IMPLICATIONS IN THE DEVELOPING WORLD

The chapter is written purposively in order to highlight the development of social innovation as the idea discipline and work process. The chapter highlights not only the academic evolution of social innovation but also highlights the role of universities in the development of social innovation in developing sides of the world. Therefore, the chapter is much different from the other chapters that are written to highlight the birth, introduction, and growth of social innovation and the social innovation process. In fact, the purpose of this chapter is not only to emphasize the introduction of social innovation as the term and idea, but the chapter also defined factors that assist in the growth of social innovation in developing sides of the world.

Muhammad Nawaz Tunio
Mohammad Ali Jinnah University, Karachi, Pakistan

Atia Bano Memon
University of Sindh, Badin, Pakistan

Chapter 1

The Impact of Frugal Innovation on Social Sustainability and the Guiding Role of the Sustainable Development Goals (SDGs) in the Digital Era

Syed Haider Ali Shah
Bahria University, Pakistan

Muhammad Jaffer
Bahria University, Pakistan

Eman Zameer Rahman
https://orcid.org/0000-0003-2420-625X
Bahria University, Pakistan

Arslan Asif
Bahria University, Pakistan

ABSTRACT

Understanding how frugal innovation supports social sustainability is necessary. Frugal innovation has strived to creatively address urgent societal issues while also creating income; it has had a tremendous influence on society. This essay's objective is to identify linkages between the ideas of social sustainability and cost-effective innovation. The objective of this book chapter is to identify linkages between the ideas of social sustainability and frugal innovation by reviewing the literature that is currently available in the field. This book will contribute by developing a link between these two concepts and will further expand our understanding of frugal innovation and social sustainability advancement while taking guidance from the sustainable development goals (SDGs), particularly those pertaining to social sustainability.

DOI: 10.4018/978-1-6684-5417-6.ch001

INTRODUCTION

The founding principle of frugal innovation is to reduce a product or service's complexity and cost (Tiwari and Herstatt 2013). Innovations are considered frugal if they concurrently satisfy the three following requirements: significant cost cut, focus on essential functions, and improved performance level (Weyrauch & Herstatt, 2016). The idea of sustainability, which emphasizes resource management that is affordable and appropriate and has a positive influence on the environment and society, is inextricably tied to frugal innovations for example, saving energy and limited material resources while fostering grassroots entrepreneurship shown in Figure 1. The notion that frugal innovation helps to aims and goals for sustainable development, such as the Sustainable Development Goals (SDGs) of the UN, is consistent with this viewpoint. Even though, it is further argued that sustainable development does not necessarily result from frugal innovation (Leliveld and Knorringa; 2018). It is argued that frugal innovation has the potential to simultaneously advance the SDGs and worsen capitalism's exploitation and inequalities, especially in developing countries (Schwittay 2011; Dolan, 2012). Leliveld and Knorringa (p. 2, 2018) advocated: "many of the frugal innovations for really short-term solutions (like cheap batteries or solar cells produced in Asia and sold in rural Africa) may qualify as frugal innovation on some indicators – low cost, affordable, functional – and may help to address short-term issues, but it is an open question to what extent these also contribute to longer-term developmental solutions for poor communities." Moreover, it is argued that while economical innovations may have a chance of being sustainable at the product level, a wider, more comprehensive perspective is required at the level of community stakeholders to reduce business risks and accomplish the wider societal impact of innovations (Hyvärinen et al. 2016). Dressler & Bucher (2018, p. 276) narrated as: "Achieving sustainability means rethinking economic growth completely. That is where the concept of frugal innovations comes to mind."

Various studies from the perspective of the organization highlights the need for a deeper comprehension of how frugal innovation and social sustainability innovation are related (Simoes et al. 2018; Khan 2016). Moreover, the way that frugal innovations are developed, controlled, and reported on in various contexts, such as top-down versus bottom-up, may help reveal how internal accountability and management systems can be used to reap the benefits and social implications of such innovations. This chapter highlights the role of frugal innovation on social sustainability and the guiding role of Sustainable Development Goals (SDGs) in the digital era. This chapter aim is to draw linkages between the ideas of social sustainability and frugal innovation while having the impact of SDGs by examining the literature that has already been written in both domains. Moreover, this link will deepen our understanding of how frugal innovation contributes to the advancement of the Sustainable Development Goals (SDGs) shown in figure 2, particularly those related to social sustainability.

BACKGROUND

There is no agreed definition of "frugal innovation," and the concept's origin is unclear (Hossain, 2020). While the other researchers defined by Melkas et., al (2019, p. 25) "frugal innovation will likely play a central part in the future of innovation management" due to its "ability to do more with less by creating more business and social value while minimizing the use of resources such as energy, capital and time". Further, Albert (2019, p. 13) highlighted that "frugal innovation is inherently socially and economically sustainable and has a significant potential to address ecological sustainability". In addition

Figure 1.
Source: https://www.google.com/search?q=frugal+innovation+products&tbm=isch&bih=560&biw=1366&hl=en&sa=X&v
ed=2ahUKEwiaxpOGvrr6AhWhgXMKHeg3DbMQrNwCKAB6BQgBEKYC#imgrc=rIbLHhiLR_E54M

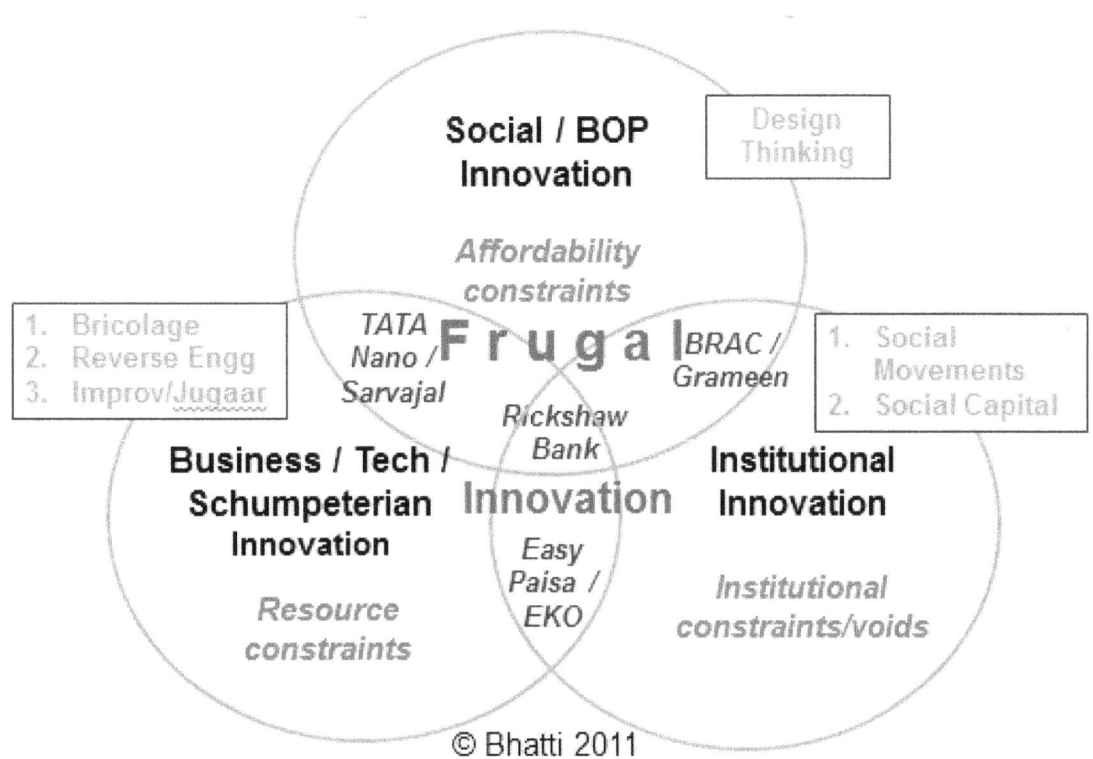

to it, there are several concepts like jugaad innovation, reverse innovation, disruptive innovation, green innovation, and open innovation are just a few that are related to and overlap with frugal innovation. Although these notions are related, they are not the same, and frugal innovation should be addressed separately in literature and implementation (Kroll & Gabriel, 2020). This book chapter take the concept of frugal innovation from a study by Hossain et al. (2016, p. 133), who explain it as "Frugal innovation is a resource scarce solution (i.e., product, service, process, or business model) that is designed and implemented despite financial, technological, material or other resource constraints, whereby the final outcome is significantly cheaper than competitive offerings (if available) and is good enough to meet the basic needs of customers who would otherwise remain un(der)served". Moreover, Agarwal et al., 2017, p.4 define the frugal innovation as *"Subset of disruptive innovations with high emphasis on social change, scalability and sustainability. Brem & Wolfram, 2014, p.19 Gandhian innovation "An approach that takes advantage from the adaption of existing technologies by integrating them into local context or/and establishing local expertise by spillovers through collaborations in order to increase social wealth of people from the BoP."

While Radjou et al., 2012, p.4 define the Jugaad s"a unique way of thinking and acting in response to challenges; it is the gutsy art of spotting opportunities in the most adverse circumstances and resource-fully improvising solutions using simple means."

Figure 2. Sustainable Development Goals
Source: https://www.google.com/search?q=sustainable+development&tbm=isch&bih=560&biw=1366&hl=en&sa=X&ved
=2ahUKEwiaxpOGvrr6AhWhgXMKHeg3DbMQrNwCKAB6BQgBEKQC#imgrc=ZUszBwpNscHswM

A key component of social sustainability is the creation of initiatives and procedures that support interactions and cultural amplification. It highlights safeguarding the poor while upholding social variety and is linked to more fundamental wants like fulfilment, security, autonomy, respect, and compassion (Vavik & Keitsch, 2020), shown in figure.3 Specifically, the biggest problems are found in the intersections and trade-offs between sustainable development and the multiple components (Lehtonen, 2004). Therefore, there is need to develop the idea of social sustainability through the use of the sustainable development framework (Partridge, 2005). The social pillar of sustainable development is integrated with its environmental and economic components, for instance, neither happiness nor a healthy community are feasible in an economically underprivileged society or in an area where air quality is inadequate (Khan, 2016).

Economically deprived communities have been able to improve their level of living by using frugal innovation to address a variety of wellness, literacy, and energy-related issues (Khan, 2016). Because it has direct relation to creatively address urgent societal issues while also creating income, frugal innovation has had a tremendous influence on society. Businesses have been asserted to have a crucial function in the direction of sustainable development (DeSimone & Popoff, 2000, Porritt, 2005), perform countless great actions for society (Ahlstrom, 2010). Additionally, frugal innovation may enhance a business' sustainability performance (Levänen et al., 2016). However, there has not been much discussion of the social benefits that frugal innovation can provide to society. An integrated comprehension of the literature on frugal innovation is provided by this article. In order to achieve this goal, we conduct a multidisciplinary systematic literature review that includes thematic and keyword assessments. The

Figure 3.
Source: https://www.google.com/search?q=frugal+innovation+products&tbm=isch&bih=560&biw=1366&hl=en&sa=X&v ed=2ahUKEwiaxpOGvrr6AhWhgXMKHeg3DbMQrNwCKAB6BQgBEKYC#imgrc=XWFkINHRFUP8ZM

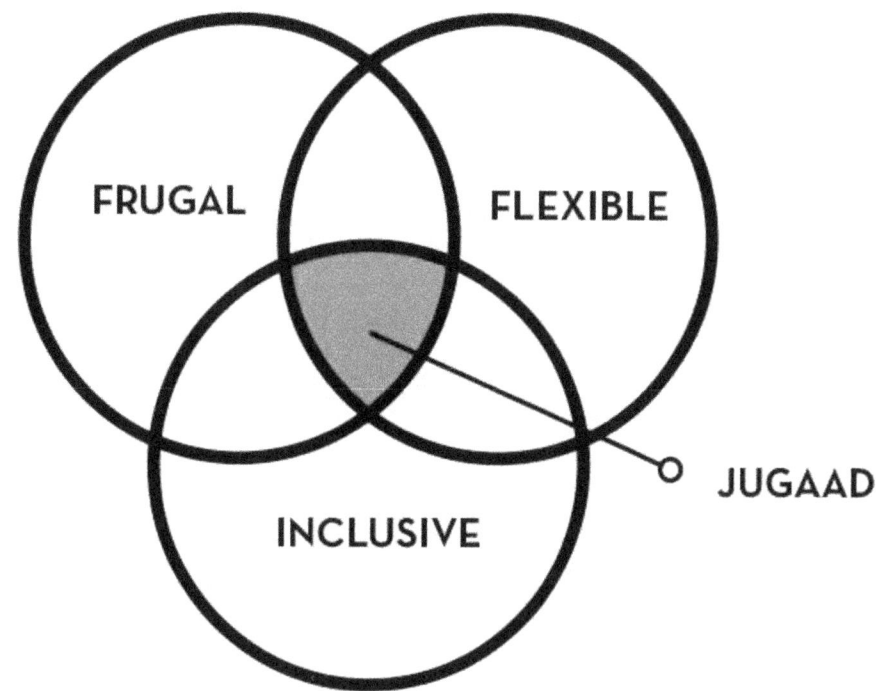

aim is to describe the conceptual framework of the frugal innovation area (Paul & Rialp-Criado, 2020). This book chapter contributes to the body of knowledge on frugal innovation and its relation to social sustainability.

MAIN FOCUS OF THE CHAPTER

This study's primary objective is to perform a literature review to comprehend the phenomenon of frugal innovation and its relation to the social sustainability an how that promotes the different Sustainable Development Goals (SDGs). There are several Sustainable Development Goals (SDGs) like number four is the education. To uplift the education. As above discussed that the frugal innovation is the creative approach towards the product development or offering services in a unique way (Hoassain et al., 2016), and for that the technical knowledge or theoretical knowledge both contribute, so the organizations involve in the frugal innovation are promoting the education level (technical or theoretical) for their benefits but it has direct implications on the society and sustainability. It can be comprehend that actually the frugal innovation leads to the uplifting the standard of society and also promote the Sustainable Development Goals (SDGs). Similarly the Sustainable Development Goals (SDGs) goal for poverty eradication, with the same notion the frugal innovation is mostly carried out in the developing countries by small organizations in majority. These small organizations provide the opportunity to the employees with less education and technical knowledge to create and innovate the product with freedom which actually lead to the product development with less cost and which turns out to be successful product and have indirect effect on the poverty elevation of employees as well as end user which are the consumers.

Additionally, the frugal innovation also serve another important goal of the Sustainable Development Goals (SDGs) which is pro environmental steps and actions. Since the frugal innovation takes place with less utilization of the resources with minimum cost which ultimately translate into the environmental sustainability concepts (Hossain, 2018).

Anecdotally, sustainable development has been linked to frugal innovation driven by resource limitations and consumer affordability. This chapter offers a conceptual framework for analyzing how frugal innovation and social sustainability mechanisms are aligned with Sustainable Development Goals (SDGs).

RECOMMENDATIONS AND FUTURE RESEARCH

This study proposes future study areas and opportunities after considering how frugal innovation and social sustainability mechanisms used and aligned with Sustainable Development Goals (SDGs) that can affect sustainable development. This research can assist academics, students, policymakers, and others in incorporating and putting into practice cutting-edge frugal innovation initiatives to influence the frugal innovation process in a way that elevate the social standards and social sustainability in emerging economies. It is recommended that future research investigate the connection between social standards and frugal innovation using an appropriate research methodology. This research is based on the literature review, it is recommended for future studies to employ both quantitative and qualitative techniques in order to obtain the in-depth understanding of the phenomena of frugal innovation and its impact on social sustainability. Researchers and scientists should consider the Sustainable Development Goals (SDGs) and its components by developing a clear vision of frugal innovation as the concept has disperse definition and operationalization depending upon the locality and geographic location. Moreover, to replace their current offerings, businesses should innovate their current products and services more economically. This will ultimately increase product value, reduce product costs, and benefit the social sustainability and will help to achieve the Sustainable Development Goals (SDGs) as well. This chapter presented the argument that products and services created using the concept of frugal innovation ought to be less expensive than comparable ones created without. Organizations should use renewable energy sources, such as switching to solar or hydropower for their electric needs, to become self-sufficient and produce products with less cost, through these ways the social sustainability will be served and SDGs goals as well. Future research also need to consider the impact of business model on frugal innovation and its relations to the social sustainability and how it serve the Sustainable Development Goals (SDGs).

REFERENCES

Agarwal, N., & Brem, A. (2017). Frugal innovation-past, present, and future. *IEEE Engineering Management Review*, *45*(3), 37–41. doi:10.1109/EMR.2017.2734320

Ahlstrom, D. (2010). Innovation and Growth: How Business Contributes to Society. *The Academy of Management Perspectives*, *24*, 11–24.

Albert, M. (2019). Sustainable frugal innovation-The connection between frugal innovation and sustainability. *Journal of Cleaner Production, 237*, 117747. doi:10.1016/j.jclepro.2019.117747

Brem, A., & Wolfram, P. (2014). Research and development from the bottom up - introduction of terminologies for new product development in emerging markets. *Journal of Innovation and Entrepreneurship, 3*(9), 9. doi:10.1186/2192-5372-3-9

DeSimone, L. D., & Popoff, F. (2000). *Eco-Efficiency: The Business Link to Sustainable Development*. MIT Press.

Dolan, C. (2012). The new face of development: The 'bottom of the pyramid' entrepreneurs. *Anthropology Today, 28*(4), 3–7. doi:10.1111/j.1467-8322.2012.00883.x

Dressler, A., & Bucher, J. (2018). Introducing a Sustainability Evaluation Framework based on the Sustainable Development Goals applied to Four Cases of South African Frugal Innovation. *Business Strategy & Development, 1*(4), p. 276-285. https://doi org.miman.bib.bth.se/10.1002/bsd2.37

HossainM. (2016). Frugal innovation: a systematic literature review. SSRN 2768254.

Hossain, M. (2018). Frugal innovation: A review and research agenda. *Journal of Cleaner Production, 182*, 926–936. doi:10.1016/j.jclepro.2018.02.091

Hossain, M. (2020). Frugal innovation: Conception, development, diffusion, and outcome. *Journal of Cleaner Production, 262*, 121456. doi:10.1016/j.jclepro.2020.121456

Hossain, M., Lev¨anen, J., & Wierenga, M. (2021). Pursuing frugal innovation for sustainability at the grassroots level. *Management and Organization Review, 17*(2), 374–381. doi:10.1017/mor.2020.53

Hyvärinen, A., Keskinen, M., & Varis, O. (2016). Potential and pitfalls of frugal innovation in the water sector: Insights from Tanzania to global value chains. *Sustainability, 8*(9), 888. doi:10.3390u8090888

Khan, R. (2016). How frugal innovation promotes social sustainability. *Sustainability, 8*(10), 1034. doi:10.3390u8101034

Kroll, H., & Gabriel, M. (2020). Frugal innovation in, by and for Europe. *International Journal of Lehtonen, M. The environmental-social interface of sustainable development: Capabilities, social capital, institutions. *Ecological Economics, 2004*(49), 199–214.

Leliveld, A., & Knorringa, P. (2018). Frugal innovation and development research. *European Journal of Development Research, 30*(1), 1–16. doi:10.105741287-017-0121-4

Leliveld, A., & Knorringa, P. (2018). Frugal innovation and development research. *European Journal of Development Research, 30*(1), 1–16. doi:10.105741287-017-0121-4

Levänen, J., Hossain, M., Lyytinen, T., Hyvärinen, A., Numminen, S., & Halme, M. (2016). Implications of Frugal Innovations on Sustainable Development: Evaluating Water and Energy Innovations. *Sustainability, 8*(1), 4. doi:10.3390u8010004

Melkas, H., Oikarinen, T., & Pekkarinen, S. (2019). Understanding frugal innovation: A case study of university professionals in developed countries. *Innovation and Development, 9*(1), 25–40. doi:10.1080/2157930X.2018.1437687

Partridge, E. (2005). Social sustainability: A useful theoretical framework? In *Proceedings of the Australasian Political Science Association Annual Conference*, Dunedin, New Zealand.

Paul, J., & Rialp-Criado, A. (2020). The Art of Writing Literature review: What do we know and What do we need to know? *International Business Review, 29*(4), 101717. doi:10.1016/j.ibusrev.2020.101717

Porritt, J. (2005). *Capitalism as if the World Matters; Earthscan*. Sterling.

Radjou, N., Prabhu, J., & Ahuja, S. (2012). Jugaad innovation: Think frugal, be flexible, generate breakthrough growth. Jossey-Bass (first ed.). San Francisco, California, USA, Whiley.

Schwittay, A. F. (2011). The financial inclusion assemblage: Subjects, technics, rationalities. *Critique of Anthropology, 31*(4), 381–401. doi:10.1177/0308275X11420117

Simoes, L., Garrido, S. R. and Carvalho, A. (2018) Assessing the Social Sustainability of Frugal Products. *Social LCA*, 86. *Technology Management, 83*(1/2/3), p. 34–54.

Tiwari, R., & Herstatt, C. (2013). *Open Global Innovation Networks as Enablers of Frugal Innovation: Propositions Based on Evidence from India*. The Hamburg University of Technology, Technology and Innovation Management. Working Paper No. 72

Vavik, T., & Keitsch, M. (2010). Exploring relationships between Universal Design and Social Sustainable Development: Some Methodological Aspects to the Debate on the Sciences of Sustainability. *Sustainable Development (Bradford), 18*(5), 295–305. doi:10.1002d.480

Weyrauch, T., & Herstatt, C. (2016). What is frugal innovation? Three defining criteria. *Journal of Frugal Innovation, 2*(1), 1. doi:10.118640669-016-0005-y

Chapter 2
Is Frugal Innovation a Global Phenomenon?
Multiple Perspectives on Frugal Innovation and Digitalization

Syed Haider Ali Shah
Bahria Business School, Bahria University, Pakistan

Muhammad Jaffer
Bahria University, Pakistan

Eman Zameer Rahman
ⓘ https://orcid.org/0000-0003-2420-625X
Bahria University, Pakistan

Syed Zeeshan Haider
Bahria University, Pakistan

ABSTRACT

The purpose of this book chapter is to highlight and to explore the frugal innovation phenomenon, whether it is global phenomena or local. Most importantly, the frugal innovation has different perspectives around the globe. Moreover, the role of digitalization is also crucial in the frugal innovation. How does digitalization impact the frugal innovation? The impact is boosting the frugal innovation or hindering the process of frugal innovation. The role of digitalization and globalization is impacting various business models and paving the way for the new products and services. It will be interesting to see the role of frugal innovation, the patterns of frugal innovation, the different trends of frugal innovation, and the impact on the society level. Some studies suggested that frugal innovation led to better competition and provided an environment for better products and services for consumers. This book chapter will explain the multiple perspectives, trends of frugal innovation, and its relation to the digitalization

DOI: 10.4018/978-1-6684-5417-6.ch002

INTRODUCTION

Scholars have been very interested in the frugal innovation paradigm, which aims to provide more value with fewer resources (Ernst et al., 2015) and practitioners (Albert, 2019), in the last ten years. Despite the fact that the idea originated in environments with limited resources (Soni & Krishnan, 2014). Global multinational corporations are currently using it and putting it into effect by developed markets (Hossain, 2020). Recognizing that frugal innovation has attracted a sizable audience due to its capacity to lower complexity and production costs, as well as its applicability in addressing major concerns (Steinfield & Holt, 2019), the study on this phenomenon has to be evaluated, and a plan needs to be made to progress the topic. Frugal innovation, "a resource-scarce solution (i.e., product, service, process, or business model) that is designed and implemented despite financial, technological, material or other resource constraints, whereby the outcome is significantly cheaper than competitive offerings (if available) and is good enough to meet the basic needs of customers who would otherwise remain un(der)served" (Hossain et al., 2016; p. 133). The term "frugal innovation," though its originator is uncertain, is believed to have been Carlos Ghosn, the former CEO of the Renault-Nissan Alliance, who also invented the phrase "frugal engineering" in 2006 (Dabic et al., 2022). Frugal innovation is differentiated based on the following three elements: cost reduction, focusing on core functions, and optimized performance levels. However, because of its broad applicability, scholarly literature on the subject is dispersed (Miesler et al., 2020). There is a need of an analysis that takes into account research from the engineering, medical, transportation, power, production, and other disciplines. The management of frugal innovation clearly needs to be thoroughly reviewed. This would connect the disparate lines of research within the field (Snyder, 2019). Moreover, through this way it is promoting a better comprehension of the theoretical and methodological underpinnings of the major research themes of this topic shown in figure.1 An integrated grasp of the literature on frugal innovation is provided by this book chapter. In order to achieve this goal, we conduct a multidisciplinary systematic literature review that includes topical and keyword assessments. The goal is to describe the conceptual framework of the frugal innovation area (Paul & Rialp-Criado, 2020). This work contributes to the body of knowledge on frugal innovation by expanding theoretical knowledge of frugal innovation; combining diverse literature on the topic to place it within the greater framework of innovation and general management literature, producing a unified map of the literature on this subject using topical and keyword assessments shown in Figure 2 and 3 In addition to that, this book chapter will highlight the main theoretical and procedural underpinnings of this literature.

Constrained-based innovation, grassroots innovation, Gandhian innovation, Jugaad innovation, catalytic innovation, and indigenous innovation are all metaphors for frugal innovation (Hossain 2018; Snyder, 2019). Despite being in its early stages, the frugal philosophy (Hossain, 2018). Due to the substantial advantages associated with greater resource production, reduced waste, and an indirect ecological focus, people moved from the east to the west. The terms "Jugaad" and "Gandhian" innovation are particular to India's geographic region while people who make less than $2.50 per day are referred to as being at the bottom of the pyramid (BoP). Despite being a more specific concept than frugal innovation, BoP has the strongest link (Dabic et al., 2022). Jugaad is a Hindi term that means an inventive improvement that depends on talent and imagination (Dabic et al., 2022; Radjou et al., 2012). Jugaad also describes improvisation and creative responses to problems encountered on a daily basis through fresh applications of resources already at hand. While the concept 'Constrained-based innovation' is even more inclusive than the phrase "frugal innovation" because it also includes the terms "reverse innovation," "blowback

Figure 1.
Source: https://www.google.com/imgres?imgurl=https%3A%2F%2Fwww.mdpi.com%2Fsustainability%2Fsustainability-14-01326%2Farticle_deploy%2Fhtml%2Fimages%2Fsustainability-14-01326-g001.png&imgrefurl=https%3A%2F%2Fwww.mdpi.com%2F2071-1050%2F14%2F3%2F1326%2Fhtm&tbnid=D3vgJhc7YfeYkM&vet=12ahUKEwiY3tDfxbr6AhXGnuAKHVTpAy4QMygJegUIARDNAQ..i&docid=iyCDYtfDzhUQlM&w=3172&h=1320&q=frugal%20innovation%20a%20global%20phenomenon&ved=2ahUKEwiY3tDfxbr6AhXGnuAKHVTpAy4QMygJegUIARDNAQ

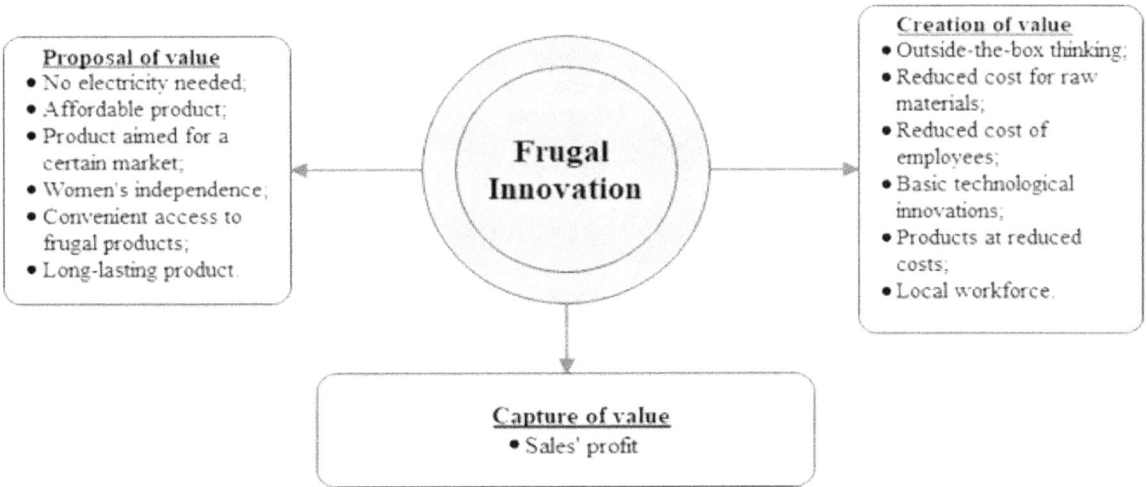

innovation," and "trickle-up innovation." (Agarwal et al., 2017). In light of this, the latter phrases are mostly used to refer to the transmission of knowledge from East to West (Hossain, 2018).

BACKGROUND

The nomenclature and the development of the idea of frugal innovation has been provided as the foundation for both differences and commonalities and are discussed below.

Hossain et al. (2016; p.133) described the frugal innovation as "a resource-scarce solution (i.e., product, service, process, or business model) that is designed and implemented despite financial, technological, material or other resource constraints, whereby the outcome is significantly cheaper than competitive offerings (if available) and is good enough to meet the basic needs of customers who would otherwise remain un(der)served." Moreover, Prabhu & Jain, (2015, p.847), explained the concept of Jugaad capability as "the art of overcoming harsh constraints by improving an effective solution using limited resources." Similarly the concept of Jugaad is described by Radjou et al., (2012, p.4) as "a unique way of thinking and acting in response to challenges; it is the gutsy art of spotting opportunities in the most adverse circumstances and resourcefully improvising solutions using simple means." In the same notion another definition of Indigenous innovation is provided by the von Zedtwitz et al., (2015, p.14), "A process of making use of technologies transferred from the advanced economies to develop superior technologies at home." And the Gandhian innovation is defined by Brem & Wolfram, (2014, p.19) as "An approach that takes advantage from the adaption of existing technologies by integrating them into local context or/and establishing local expertise by spillovers through collaborations in order to increase social wealth of people from the BoP." Moreover, another definition provided by Brem and Wolfram,

Figure 2.

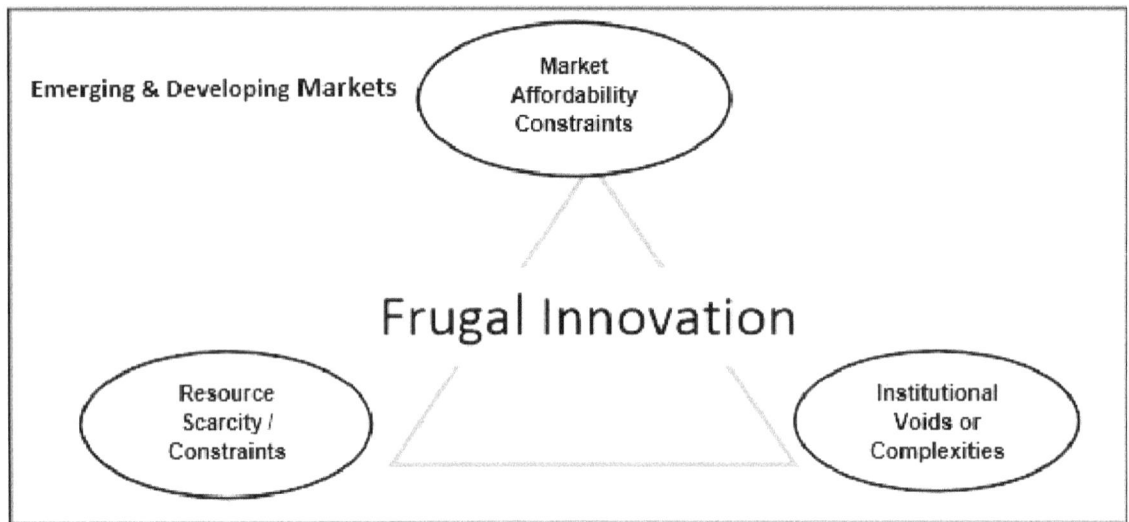

(2014) is that "Frugal innovation has low to medium sophistication, medium sustainability, and medium emerging market orientation."

Cunha et al. (2014), "Frugal innovation to be product innovation when there is a scarcity of affluent customers and distinguish it from bricolage, which is when material resources are scarce, and from improvisation, when time is scarce." Moreover, Gupta (2012)," FI is a new management philosophy, which integrates the needs of the base of the pyramid (BoP) market as a starting point to develop solutions that are expected to be very different from the alternative solutions." Numerous research have identified and distinguished various ideas that overlap with the FI notion, which is one of many that exist (Ahuja and Chan, 2014b; Grover et al., 2014; Christensen et al., 2006; Brem and Wolfram, 2014). Some, such as BoP innovation, catalytic innovation, cost innovation, good-enough innovation, inclusive innovation, indigenous innovation, resource restricted innovation, and value innovation, are prevalent in developing nations (Rosca et al., 2017). Some notions, including as disruptive innovation, grassroots innovation, blowback innovation, reverse innovation, and trickle-up innovation, are used to relate emerging and developed nations in terms of FI (Hossain et al., 2016). The latter three of these ideas focus on the transfer of innovation from developing to industrialized nations. The majority of these overlapping notions have grown independently, which prevents FI from developing into a recognized research area (Hossain, 2018). The sustainability component is absent from the majority of concepts. Among the concepts that overlap, FI and BoP innovation may have the closest ties. Despite the fact that BoP innovation exclusively targets individuals with annual earnings of less than $1500 (Hart and Christensen, 2002). FI, on the other hand, concentrates on underdeveloped nations that have both low-income people and a newly expanding middle-income section (Hossain et al., 2016). Therefore, it is evident that FI has a wider scope than BoP innovation. However, FI does incorporate the majority of the traits of the other overlapping concepts.

Figure 3.
Source: (Hossain, 2020)

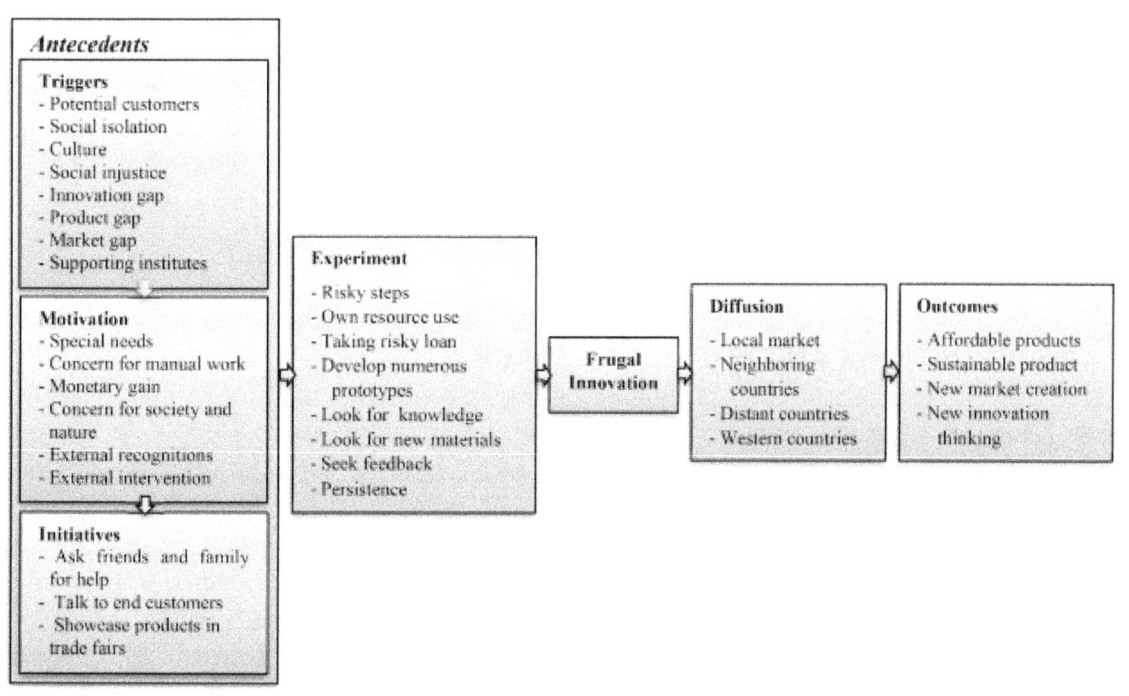

Various sources of frugal innovation, all start happening on various level at Individual, community, and societal (Hossain, 2018). Many FI cases have been reported in research, along with information about their sources and features (Hossain, 2017). To serve their low-income consumers, certain western multinational corporations (MNCs) have embraced FIs. With FI, emerging multinational firms (EMNCs) have improved chances of success (Prabhu and Jain, 2015). They can create FIs due to their vast resources and local expertise. Well-known EMNCs that have had great success with FIs include Tata, Godrej, Haier, Vodafone, Lenovo, EasyPaisa, and Galanz (Hoassain, 2017). Worldwide, small businesses are growing owing to their cost-effective ideas. Western startups created Embrace, LifeStraw, Shakerscope, and Solvatten (Hossain, 2017). State institutions should support FIs despite the fact that they were not created to foster innovation. Local startups are primarily engaged in grassroots activities, and people without formal professional training have created FIs like the Mitticool refrigerator (Hossain, 2018). FIs have therefore emerged from a wide range of sources.

MAIN FOCUS OF THE CHAPTER

The main focus of this research is to conduct the literature review to understand the phenomena of the frugal innovation. From where the concept of FI started right from its inception and then how the different developed, developing and under developing nations see the phenomena of FI. What are the different perspective exists reading the frugal innovation. What kind of literature exists? Moreover, interestingly the FI concept itself vary from place to place, region to region and we discussed in the background how the concept of the FI describe by various researchers (Hossain et al., 2016; Albert, 2019). This book identified the various perspective of the FI and related concepts which includes within the scope of the FI. Surprisingly, it was identified in the literature that FI phenomena is not only restricted to the developing nations but also moved to west (developed nations) and even some organizations are involved in FI for their low income consumer and trying to produce the product and services for them in developed nation economy (). The evolution process of the frugal innovation has been discussed and various perspective of the FI also identified. Hence, it can be said that the frugal innovation is the global phenomena and in order to benefit the low income consumers the organizations can adopt the FI which are profitable for them as well.

RECOMMENDATIONS AND FUTURE RESEARCH

Several theoretical viewpoints can be used to evaluate the frugal innovation phenomena. Multiple concepts that might be utilized to investigate FI have been mentioned in several studies. None of these theoretical stances have been carefully utilized in a study to investigate FI. Instead, the majority of studies are exploratory and qualitative in nature, and there are very few conceptual or analytical investigations that present hypotheses for further investigation. Furthermore, there are limited studies on quantitative investigations. Since FI calls for novel business models, linkages, affiliations, and partnerships, the current theories need to be extended to understand in more better and bigger perspective the FI. Moreover, lack of resources, inefficient institutions, and poor infrastructure both are the opportunity and challenge which can hinder or help FI phenomena. It can be difficult to categories different forms of FI into a standard framework since, unlike mainstream inventions, FIs come from a range of sources and have variable levels of sophistication. Therefore, firms that want to succeed with FI must take care this vital challenge. Further, it is essential to comprehend the causes of frugal innovation.

In addition to that, organizations must establishment the suitable distribution and infrastructure as it is required for frugal innovations. Although a unique business plan could lower customers' price sensitivity, the success of FI depends primarily on the pricing of services. Understanding the various aspects of frugal innovation requires extensive research, especially when the concept is still in its infancy in both academic and administrative circles. Future research may take into consideration the concepts mentioned in this study and others. Various theories could be used to investigate how resources can be used to promote or impede FI. Workers can be uneducated or highly educated, and businesses can be smaller, bigger, MNCs, or EMNCs. Hence, it is recommended to investigate the role of employees and problems these organizations face are challenging in achieving FI. Since the FI has societal impact, it is important to understand whether a FI has a greater social impact than alternative innovations because it is crucial to have in-depth understanding of these. The role of government is also crucial as government legislation and policy can support or impede attempts to promote frugal innovation since FI arises from new sources and in novel situations. So above all the highlighted points and factors need to be considered for FI as the frugal innovation is the global phenomena and it requires due consideration in academia and practitioners.

REFERENCES

Agarwal, N., & Brem, A. (2017). Frugal innovation-past, present, and future. *IEEE Engineering Management Review*, *45*(3), 37–41. doi:10.1109/EMR.2017.2734320

Ahuja, S., & Chan, Y. 2014b. The Enabling Role of IT in Frugal Innovation. https://aisel. aisnet.org/cgi/ viewcontent.cgi?article1/41374&context1/4icis2014

Albert, M. (2019). Sustainable frugal innovation-The connection between frugal innovation and sustainability. *Journal of Cleaner Production*, *237*, 117747. doi:10.1016/j.jclepro.2019.117747

Brem, A., & Wolfram, P. (2014). Research and development from the bottom up - introduction of terminologies for new product development in emerging markets. *Journal of Innovation and Entrepreneurship*, *3*(9), 9. doi:10.1186/2192-5372-3-9

Cunha, M.P., Rego, A., Oliveira, P., Rosado, P., Habib, N., 2014. Product innovation in resource-poor environments: three research streams. J. *Prod. Innovat. Manag. 31*(2).

Dabić, M., Obradović, T., Vlačić, B., Sahasranamam, S., & Paul, J. (2022). Frugal innovations: A multidisciplinary review & agenda for future research. *Journal of Business Research*, *142*, 914–929. doi:10.1016/j.jbusres.2022.01.032

Grover, A., Caulfield, P., & Roehrich, K. J. 2014. Frugal Innovation in Healthcare and its Applicability to Developed Markets.

Gupta, A.K., 2012. Innovations for the poor by the poor. *Int. J. Technol Learn. Innovat. Dev. 5*(1e2), 28e39

Hart, S.L., Christensen, C.M., 2002. The great leap: driving innovation from the base of the pyramid. *MIT Sloan Manag. Rev. 44*(1), 51e56.

HossainM. (2016). Frugal innovation: a systematic literature review. SSRN.

Hossain, M. (2018). Frugal innovation: A review and research agenda. *Journal of Cleaner Production*, *182*, 926–936. doi:10.1016/j.jclepro.2018.02.091

Hossain, M. (2020). Frugal innovation: Conception, development, diffusion, and outcome. *Journal of Cleaner Production*, *262*, 121456. doi:10.1016/j.jclepro.2020.121456

Hossain, M., Lev¨anen, J., & Wierenga, M. (2021). Pursuing frugal innovation for sustainability at the grassroots level. *Management and Organization Review*, *17*(2), 374–381. doi:10.1017/mor.2020.53

Miesler, T., Wimschneider, C., Brem, A., & Meinel, L. (2020). Frugal innovation for point- of-care diagnostics controlling outbreaks and epidemics. *ACS Biomaterials Science & Engineering*, *6*(5), 2709–2725. doi:10.1021/acsbiomaterials.9b01712 PMID:33463254

Paul, J., & Rialp-Criado, A. (2020). The Art of Writing Literature review: What do we know and What do we need to know? *International Business Review*, *29*(4), 101717. doi:10.1016/j.ibusrev.2020.101717

Prabhu, J., & Jain, S. (2015). Innovation and entrepreneurship in India: Understanding Jugaad. *Asia Pacific Journal of Management*, *32*(4), 843–868. doi:10.100710490-015-9445-9

Radjou, N., Prabhu, J., & Ahuja, S. (2012). Jugaad innovation: Think frugal, be flexible, generate breakthrough growth. Jossey-Bass (first ed.). San Francisco, California, USA. Whiley.

Rosca, E., Arnold, M., Bendul, J.C., 2017. Business models for sustainable innovationean empirical analysis of frugal products and services. *J. Clean. Prod. 162*.

Snyder, H. (2019). Literature review as a research methodology: An overview and guidelines. *Journal of Business Research*, *104*, 333–339. doi:10.1016/j.jbusres.2019.07.039

Soni, P., & Krishnan, R. T. (2014). Frugal innovation: Aligning theory, practice, and public policy. *Journal of Indian Business Research*, *6*(1), 29–47. doi:10.1108/JIBR-03-2013-0025

Steinfield, L. A., & Holt, D. (2019). Towards A Theory on the Reproduction of Social Innovations in Subsistence Marketplaces. *Journal of Product Innovation Management*, *36*(6), 764–799. doi:10.1111/jpim.12510

von Zedtwitz, M., Corsi, S., Veng Søberg, P., & Frega, R. (2015). A Typology of Reverse Innovation. *Journal of Product Innovation Management*, *32*(1), 12–28. doi:10.1111/jpim.12181

Chapter 3
Does It Matter?
The Impact of Frugal Innovation on Society and Uplifting the Social Standard in the Digital Era

Syed Haider Ali Shah
Bahria Business School, Bahria University, Pakistan

Bushra Alvi
Bahria University, Pakistan

Zahir Ud Din
Bahria University, Pakistan

Bilal Arshad
Bahria University, Pakistan

Madiha Suhail
Bahria University, Pakistan

Saleh Ahmed Salem Alyafe
University of Malaya, Malaysia

ABSTRACT

The purpose of this book chapter is to highlight the different issues related to frugal innovation advancement, and how the advancement of the frugal innovation change and affect the social life, particularly the role in uplifting the standard of the living. Literature shows that there are some factors which need to be considered for frugal innovation. This area received a less attention from the researchers. The contribution of the book chapter will be elaborating different mechanisms which are affecting the growth and functions of organizations who are involve in the frugal innovation. The various definitions and multiple perspective regarding the frugal innovation will highlight the important elements for academia and practitioners to consider and conduct future research. This book chapter will highlight different components which will be helpful to the organization to involve in frugal innovation and make it a successful process by reviewing the literature.

INTRODUCTION

The importance of frugal innovation in promoting contemporary economic growth, social programs,

DOI: 10.4018/978-1-6684-5417-6.ch003

and strategic engagement has been growing. Multiple researchers have made significant contributions to the development of the field of frugal innovation studies, with both great successes and difficulties. Therefore, it is appropriate to review the key developments and potential impact on the society uplifting. In-depth research should be done to better understand their relationship and establish a strong connection between the two ideas. A novel solution that is drastically more resource-efficient than existing options while remaining available and user-friendly, especially for low-income customers, is known as frugal innovation (Hossain 2020; Von Janda et al., 2020). Moreover, Hossain et al. (2016; p. 133) define "frugal innovation as a resource scarce solution (i.e., product, service, process, or business model) that is designed and implemented despite financial, technological, material or other resource constraints, whereby the final outcome is significantly cheaper than competitive offerings (if available) and is good enough to meet the basic needs of customers who would otherwise remain un(der)served." Typically, the innovation process begins with social sustainability concerns and operational limits while creating frugal solutions (Hossain, 2016) shown in Figure 1. Understanding the connections between socioeconomic and operating concerns is made easier by looking at sustainability issues from a frugal perspective. In reality, frugal offerings are new goods or services that contribute to resolving persistent issues like poverty and injustice (Bhatti et al., 2018). Moreover, frugal innovations often result in increased local resilience and quick scaling in addition to resource efficiency (Corsini et al., 2020). Local actors frequently create and apply frugal innovations (Hossain 2020), who come from a low-income family and have little formal education yet possess a wealth of conventional knowledge and practical skills (Pansera and Sarkar, 2016; Wierenga, 2020). Empirically, it is well established that economical improvements may have favourable effects on sustainability s (Albert, 2019; Hossain, 2020). But we still need a theoretical understanding of how these insights might be enhanced methodically and repeated in various places (Ratten, 2019). The technological idea of frugal innovation has also come under fire for failing to address the underlying causes of the societal issues and raising their standards these inventions purport to solve (Pansera, 2018). There are several different kinds of frugal innovations (FIs) in use. For example, cars, medical equipment, health programs, renewable power, appliances, and water filtration are a few well-known examples of FIs. Budget-friendly devices like the MAC 400 ECG machine and Mitticool freezer provide a new approach to serving low-income consumers (Hossain, 2020). Many frugal technologies successfully serve low-income consumers (Hossain, 2016). There are few scholarly studies on FI (Hossain, 2020). Products from frugal innovation are typically sufficient to meet the needs of target markets in underdeveloped nations while being much less costly than comparable offerings (Rao, 2013). While many of these innovations are targeted at low-income consumers in underdeveloped countries, a few of them stimulate demand to advanced economies. The MAC 400 portable ECG machine from GE costs US$800. As a result, developing nations like India may now purchase an ECG scan for just $1, as opposed to around $20 in industrialized nations. Since most developing nations' transportation infrastructure is underdeveloped, this portable device can be brought to a patient's location, which may be some distance from a nearby hospital, rather than transporting them there (Hossain, 2018). In developed nations, the MAC 400 ECG equipment is also utilized in emergency departments and ambulances. From the bottom up, frugal innovations are being produced (Hossain, 2018; Levänen et al., 2020).

According to researchers, FIs want to upend current innovation paradigms by drastically reducing costs while still retaining customer value (Knorringa, et al., 2016, Hossain, 2020). Since FIs' characteristics differ from those of conventional breakthroughs, it is necessary to understand them from different approaches. FIs need various theories for a number of important reasons, including: (1) the geographical setting is different (Rao, 2013), they require a new company strategy (Zeschky et al., 2011). They

Figure 1.
Source: https://www.google.com/search?q=frugal+innovation+on+society&sxsrf=ALiCzsYmk6hwd5xxcgYSTcjVpQ9h-cLeY
A:1664510985724&source=lnms&tbm=isch&sa=X&ved=2ahUKEwiXjZ3Q0rv6AhXg7jgGHW7yAMgQ_AUoAXoECAEQA
w&biw=1366&bih=617&dpr=1#imgrc=9JVO97ryvBm9iM

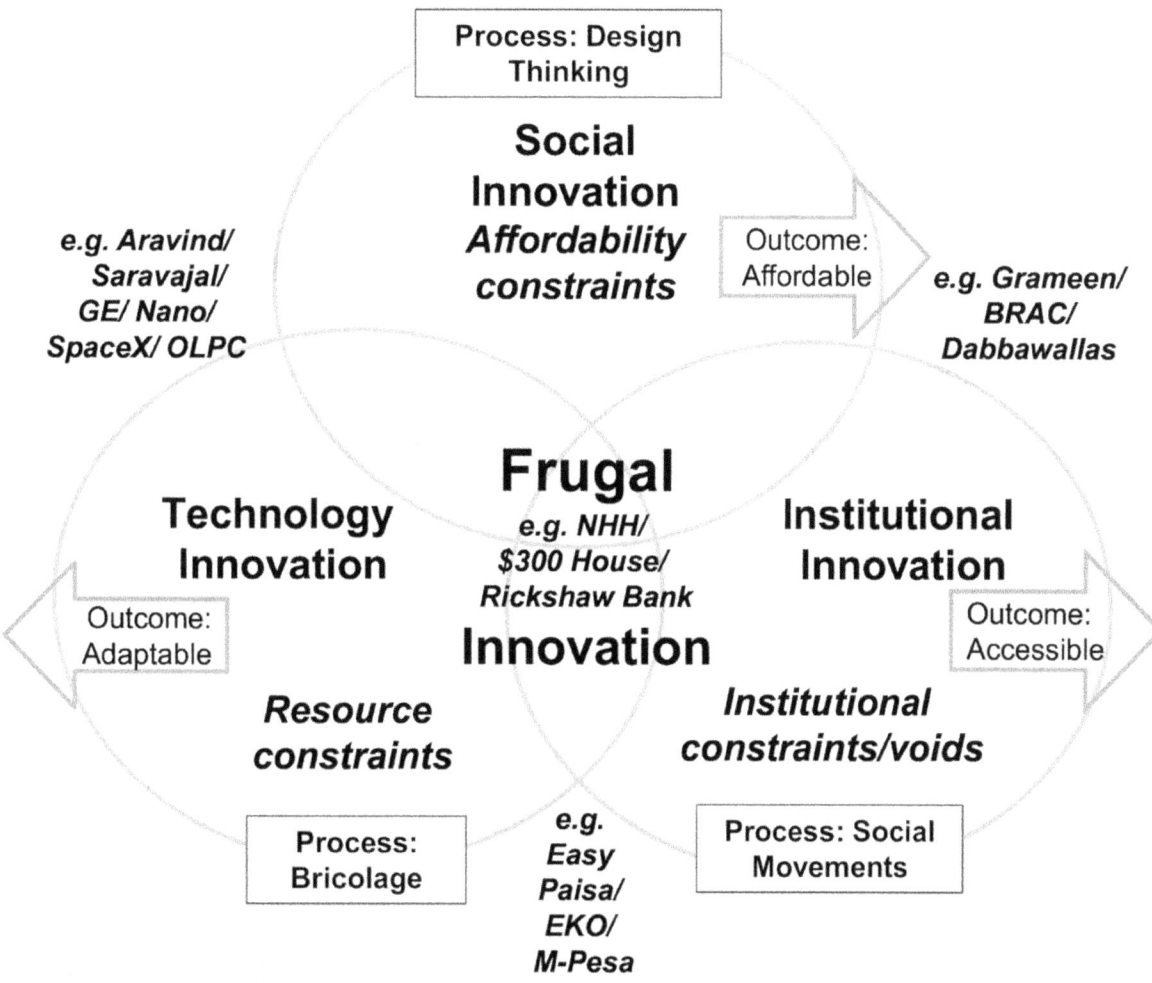

require a distinct channel of delivery (Simula et al., 2015). FI has emerged as a key innovation issue with a strong emphasis on underdeveloped nations (Hossain, 2020). Recent years have seen a substantial increase in FI studies, and there are many additional concepts that the FI concept is similar to (Agarwal et al., 2017; Hossain, 2020). The aims to examine the research on frugal innovation to understand how the concept is defined there.

BACKGROUND

The concept of frugal innovation's inception is unclear (Hossain, 2020). Furthermore, no study in the literature on frugal innovation explicitly revealed where the idea came from. The Web of Science database contains the earliest journal article on frugal innovation, which was authored by Zeschky et al.

(2011). The Economist first proposed the idea to the public in 2010 (economist.com/node/ 15879359) (as cited in the article of Hossain, 2018). But the "frugal engineering" idea, which Carlos Ghosn first used in 2006, is where the frugal innovation idea comes from (Hossain, 2020). There are various ways to describe frugal innovation (Hossain et al., 2016). Pisoni et al. (2017), revealed that there are three main ways in which the definition of frugal innovation has changed. First, product-oriented definition, market-oriented definition, and criteria-oriented definition. Gupta (2012) advocated that FI as a fresh approach to management that incorporates the requirements at the base of the pyramid, as a basis for creating solutions that significantly vary from those already in place as cited in Brem and Wolfram (2014, p. 36). The items produced by FIs are affordable but adequate, and the business practices for FIs were created in and for developing nations (George et al., 2012). Moreover, FI is the ability of an EMNC to copy, develop, and produce goods and services utilizing current technology while employing dynamic, small-scale operations, readily available raw resources, and other local resources (Rosca et al. (2017). Can be seen in figure 2.

Rosca et al. (2017), narrated that the following standards to be used for definition of frugal innovation. First, the state's industrial output relative to the level in the relevant economic area, secondly, where the primary procedures and an element of innovative production are located and third, how innovation is going. Moreover, it is evident and can be seen in figure 3. As advocated by Zeschky et al. (2014b) a "good enough" innovation, claim that frugal innovation requires a higher level of technical uniqueness and a bigger level of commercial novelty. Basu et al. (2013) conceive of frugal innovation as a creative approach to process design. Some researchers classify marketing strategies and organizational techniques as FI components (Hossain 2018), while FI has been characterized similarly by other academicians (Hossain, 2018; Soni & Krishnan, 2014).

Hossain et al. (2016) give a detailed and thorough definition that takes into account frugal innovation as a method, process, or operating model. Along the lines of this thorough definition, we also consider this as a proper definition of frugal innovation. In a nutshell, according to academic definitions of FI, sources of FI include local businesses, emerging multinationals, traditional multinationals (MNCs), and the community level. All of these descriptions refer to low-income consumers whose primary criterion for making a purchase is cost. Despite the potential for social change associated with the frugal innovation concept, the notion that this kind of innovation would inevitably help resolve societal emerging issues seems oversimplified given the profoundly complex reality in and for which frugal innovations are developed. Given the contentious character of frugal innovations, an examination of them should start from a multifaceted standpoint that simultaneously takes into account their sociological and practical repercussions (Leliveld and Knorringa, 2018), which the literature now in existence does not fully address. This is the contribution of this book chapter which address the FI impact of society and uplifting their living standard.

MAIN FOCUS OF THE CHAPTER

Frugal innovation phenomena is now everywhere and is currently affecting each and every industry. There is gap for innovative technology solutions globally to uplift the standard of living. Frugal innovation is a viable alternative that supports sustainability and offer the low cost product that they low income consumer can buy and utilize it. It can further be argued that the aim of frugal innovation is rebuilding and reorganizing products and services to uplift the living standards of consumers particularly those in the

Figure 2.
*Source: https://www.google.com/search?q=frugal+innovation+on+society&sxsrf=ALiCzsYmk6hwd5xxcgYSTcjVpQ9h-cLeY
A:1664510985724&source=lnms&tbm=isch&sa=X&ved=2ahUKEwiXjZ3Q0rv6AhXg7jgGHW7yAMgQ_AUoAXoECAEQA
w&biw=1366&bih=617&dpr=1#imgrc=9JVO97ryvBm9iM&imgdii=wZSG_LoJA0z_LM*

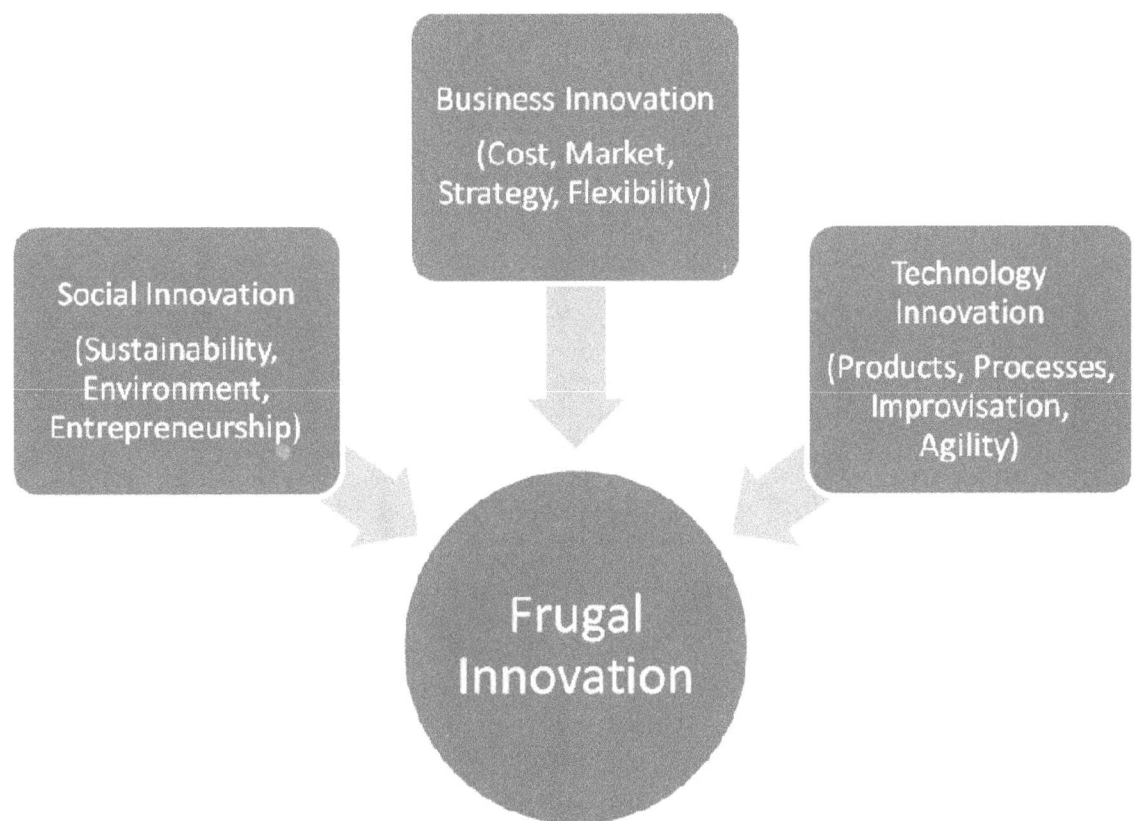

emerging markets. The link between the frugal innovation and society advancement is quite important and needs to be understood in order to improve and uplift the standard of consumers. The fundamental issue with frugal innovation is that researchers and academics give little attention to novel methods and tactics for fostering creativity in settings with limited resources. The role of the FI is very crucial as it provides lower-income consumers with greater value and gives businesses the possibility to increase their sales and profits (Hossain, 2020). It can also be referred as sustainable innovation promotes on three fronts, first is the societal, second is the economic and third is the environmental objectives (Albert, 2019; Levänen et al., 2020).

SOLUTIONS AND RECOMMENDATIONS

It places a strong emphasis on reorganizing products and services to get exceptional results while preserving key components, frequently exceeding expectations and even delivering ground-breaking advances improvements (Clausen & Fichter, 2019; Levänen et al., 2020). It's challenging to anticipate success, and it's very harder for FIs. Environments with limited resources in emerging nations are favor-

Figure 3. Frugal Education
Source: https://www.google.com/search?q=frugal+innovation+on+society&sxsrf=ALiCzsYmk6hwd5xxcgYSTcjVpQ9h-cLeY
A:1664510985724&source=lnms&tbm=isch&sa=X&ved=2ahUKEwiXjZ3Q0rv6AhXg7jgGHW7yAMgQ_AUoAXoECAEQA
w&biw=1366&bih=617&dpr=1#imgrc=iHDCTjLXQEY5rM

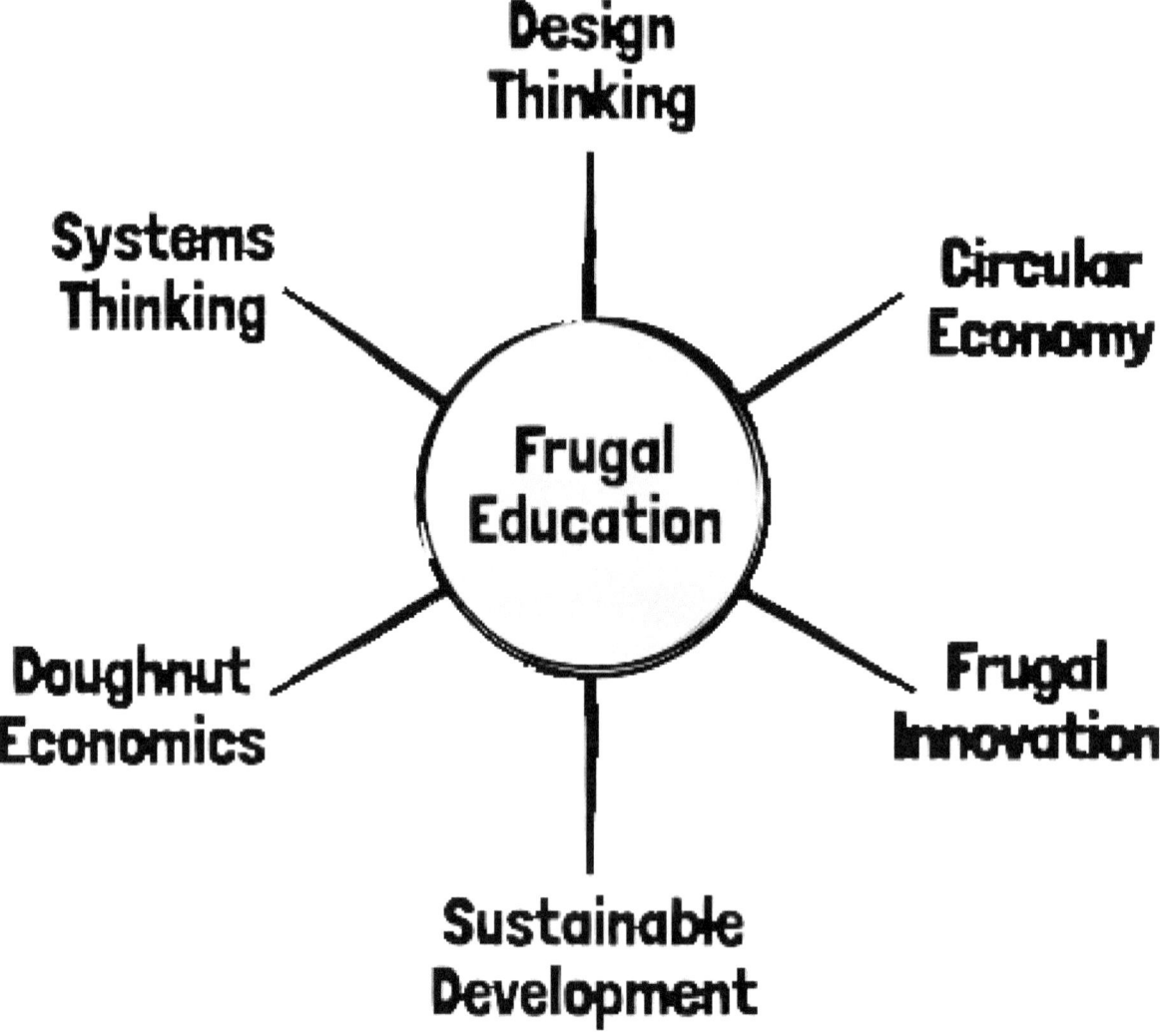

able for the expansion of FIs (Zeschky et al., 2011; Zeschky et al., 2014a). MNCs must comprehend FI and how they might affect the laws and policies in uncertain and volatile environments (Sako, 2009). Consequently, it contends that MNCs can build FI through effective cooperation with their subsidiaries and local businesses. To create effective FIs that target consumers who have strong price sensitivity, innovation teams must go unexplored territory (Tiwari and Herstatt, 2014). Jha and Krishnan (2013), emphasized the need for R&D centers to expand beyond their current technical skills and get a thorough awareness of the business world. For it, a significant mental and physical transformation is required, and a local FI frequently spreads to far-off geographic locations (Hossain et al., 2016). It's also necessary to incorporate novel features to satisfy regional requirements (Hossain, 2020). Another crucial element is the transmission of technical expertise and local market knowledge. In order to be successful with FIs, businesses must adopt a frugal mindset and adapt the company culture to influence consumers (Agnihotri, 2015). Moreover, Value evaluation, cost estimating, and the deployment of quality functions are crucial FI challenges (Zeschky et al., 2011). All the above highlighted factors are crucial for societal improvements particularly their living standards. The frugal innovation as mentioned earlier must occur and consider the above following elements in order to be successful and organizational success means that end user or consumer is taking advantages of the FIs which is the ultimate impact of the frugal innovation on their lives and their standard.

FUTURE RESEARCH DIRECTIONS

Several theoretical stances can be used to investigate the frugal innovation phenomena and many theories that could be employed to investigate have been mentioned in several research studies related to FIs. Moreover, FI calls for novel business models, partnerships, collaborations, and exchanges, the current theories are unable to comprehend FI. Lack of resources, shaky institutions, and inadequate infrastructure both hinder and help FI (Hossain, 2020). Framing numerous FI types into a common structure is difficult because FIs come in many different forms and range in sophistication (Hossain et al., 2016). Therefore, enterprises must take caution in order to succeed with FI. It is essential to comprehend the causes of frugal innovation. For instance, MNCs' frugal inventions are high-tech and sophisticated, but grassroots entrepreneurs' frugal ideas are low-tech and unsophisticated (Hossain, 2018; Levänen et al., 2020). Frugal inventions typically use less energies, recycled products, use substances that are readily available locally, offer the minimal amount of features at a cheap cost, and are simple to maintain. Consequently, the components of frugal inventions differ from those of traditional goods. They require various suppliers, distribution networks, and manpower. For businesses to encourage frugal innovation, a significant shift in perspective is required. For frugal innovation, both the business setting and workplace culture must be taken into account. The ability of the frugal innovation phenomena to spread to several geographical areas is what makes it successful.

REFERENCES

Agarwal, N., Grottke, M., Mishra, S., & Brem, A. (2017). A systematic literature review of constraint-based innovations: State of the art and future perspectives. *IEEE Transactions on Engineering Management, 64*(1), 3–15. doi:10.1109/TEM.2016.2620562

Agnihotri, A., 2015. *Low-cost innovation in emerging markets. J. Strat. Market. 23*(5), 399e411.

Albert, M. (2019). Sustainable frugal innovation-The connection between frugal innovation and sustainability. *Journal of Cleaner Production, 237*, 117747. doi:10.1016/j.jclepro.2019.117747

Baldo, R. A. (2020). Encyclopedia of Sustainable Management. Springer. .

Basu, R. R., Banerjee, P. M., & Sweeny, E. G. (2013). Frugal innovation: Core competencies to address global sustainability. *J. Manag. Glob. Sustain., 1*(2), 63–82. doi:10.13185/JM2013.01204

Bhatti, M. A., Mat, N., & Juhari, A. S. (2018). Effects of job resources factors on nurses job performance (mediating role of work engagement). *International Journal of Health Care Quality Assurance*, *1*(8), 254–274. doi:10.1108/IJHCQA-07-2017-0129 PMID:30415625

Brem, A., & Wolfram, P. (2014). Research and development from the bottom upintroduction of terminologies for new product development in emerging markets. *J. Innovat. Enterpren.*, *3*(1), 1–22.

Clausen, J., & Fichter, K. (2019). The diffusion of environmental product and service innovations: Driving and inhibiting factors. *Environmental Innovation and Societal Transitions*, *31*, 64–95.

Corsini, Dammicco, V., & Moultrie, J. (2020). 2020 L. Corsini, V. Dammicco, J. Moultrie Frugal innovation in a crisis: The digital fabrication maker response to COVID-19. *R & D Management*, *51*(2), 195–210. doi:10.1111/radm.12446

George, G., McGahan, A.M., Prabhu, J., 2012. Innovation for inclusive growth: towards a theoretical framework and a research agenda. J. *Manag. Stud.* 49(4), 661e683.

Gupta, A.K., 2012. Innovations for the poor by the poor. *Int. J. Technol Learn. Innovat. Dev.* 5(1e2), 28-39.

Hossain, Simula, H., & Halme, M. (2016). 2016 M. Hossain, H. Simula, M. Halme Can frugal go global? Diffusion patterns of frugal innovations. *Technology in Society*, *46*, 132–139. doi:10.1016/j.techsoc.2016.04.005

Hossain, M. (2018). Frugal innovation: A review and research agenda. *Journal of Cleaner Production*, *182*, 926–936. doi:10.1016/j.jclepro.2018.02.091

Hossain, M. (2020). Frugal innovation: Conception, development, diffusion, and outcome. *Journal of Cleaner Production*, *262*, 121456. doi:10.1016/j.jclepro.2020.121456

Hossain, M., Levänen, J., & Wierenga, M. (2021). Pursuing frugal innovation for sustainability at the grassroots level. *Management and Organization Review*, *17*(2), 374–381. doi:10.1017/mor.2020.53

Hossain, M. (2020). Frugal innovation: Conception, development, diffusion, and outcome. *Journal of Cleaner Production*, *262*, 121456.

Jha, S. K., & Krishnan, R. T. (2013). Local innovation: The key to globalisation. *IIMB Management Review*, *25*(4), 249–256. doi:10.1016/j.iimb.2013.07.002

Knorringa, P., Leliveld, A., & Van Beers, C., 2016. Frugal innovation and development: aides or adversaries? *Eur. J. Dev. Res.* 28(2), 143e153.

Leliveld, A., & Knorringa, P. (2018). Introduction: Frugal innovation and development research. *European Journal of Development Research*, *30*(1), 1–16. doi:10.1057/s41287-017-0121-4

Levänen, J., Hossain, M., & Wierenga, M. (2022). Frugal innovation in the midst of societal and operational pressures. *Journal of Cleaner Production*, *347*, 131308. doi:10.1016/j.jclepro.2022.131308

Pansera, M., & Sarkar, S. (2016). Crafting sustainable development solutions: Frugal innovations of grassroots entrepreneurs. *Sustainability*, *8*(1), 51–67. doi:10.3390u8010051

Pansera, M. (2018). Frugal or fair? The unfulfilled promises of frugal innovation Technol. *Innovation & Management Review*, 8(4), 6–13.

Pisoni, A., Michelini, L., Martignoni, G., 2017. Frugal approach to innovation: state of the art and future perspectives. *J. Clean. Prod. 171*, 107e126.

Rao, B.C., 2013. How disruptive is frugal? *Technol. Soc. 35*(1), 65e73.

Ratten, V. (2019). *Frugal innovation*. Routledge. doi:10.4324/9780429455803

Rosca, E., Arnold, M., Bendul, J.C., 2017. Business models for sustainable innovationean empirical analysis of frugal products and services. *J. Clean. Prod. 162*, S133eS145.

Sako, M., 2009. Technology strategy and management globalization of knowledge intensive professional services. *Commun. ACM 52*(7), 31e33.

Simula, H., Hossain, M., Halme, M., 2015. Frugal and reverse innovations-Quo Vadis? *Curr. Sci. 109*(9), 1e6.

Soni, P.T., Krishnan, R., 2014. Frugal innovation: aligning theory, practice, and public policy. *J. Indian Bus. Res. 6*(1), 29e47.

Tiwari, R., & Herstatt, C. (2014). Emergence of India as a Lead Market for Frugal Innovation. Opportunities for Participation and Avenues for Collaboration. *Consulate General of India, Hamburg, Germany*.

Von Janda, S., Kuester, S., Schuhmacher, M. C., & Shainesh, G. (2020). Kuester, M. Schuhmacher, G. Shainesh What frugal products are and why they matter: A cross-national multi-method study. *Journal of Cleaner Production*, 246, 118977. doi:10.1016/j.jclepro.2019.118977

Wierenga, M. (2020). Uncovering the scaling of innovations developed by entrepreneurs in low-income settings Enterpren. *Région et Développement*, 32(1–2), 63–90.

Zeschky, M., Widenmayer, B., & Gassmann, O. (2011). Frugal innovation in emerging markets. *Research Technology Management*, 54(4), 38–45. doi:10.5437/08956308X5404007

Zeschky, M., Widenmayer, B., & Gassmann, O. (2011). Frugal innovation in emerging markets. *Research Technology Management*, 54(4), 38–45. doi:10.5437/08956308X5404007

Zeschky, M., Widenmayer, B., Gassmann, O., 2014b. Organising for reverse innovation in Western MNCs: the role of frugal product innovation capabilities. *Int. J. Technol. Manag. 64*(2e4), 255-275.

Zeschky, M. B., Winterhalter, S., & Gassmann, O. (2014a). From cost to frugal and reverse innovation: Mapping the field and implications for global competitiveness. *Research Technology Management*, 57(4), 20–27.

Chapter 4

A Systematic Review Using a Factor in Pestle Framework:
COVID–19 Pandemic and Expansion of Economic Environments

Ramakrishnan Vivek
https://orcid.org/0000-0001-5691-6825
Faculty of Management, Technological Campus, Sri Lanka

Mohsen Brahmi
https://orcid.org/0000-0002-0995-0761
University of Sfax, Tunisia

Yogarajah Nanthagopan
https://orcid.org/0000-0003-1055-072X
Faculty of Business Studies, Sri Lanka

Luigi Aldieri
https://orcid.org/0000-0001-9300-6804
University of Salerno, Italy

ABSTRACT

The chapter mainly highlights the impact of the COVID-19 pandemic on the global economy, utilizing macroeconomic concepts and describing how organizations around the world can use the strategic management technique of drawing up a PESTLE analysis to provide focused attention to each factor and macroeconomic party. This ultimately comprises the entire economy, with special attention being focused on the expansion of the environmental factor. The key problem discussed in the following research chapter was whether healthcare should be considered as a separate dimension under the environmental category in a PESTLE analysis. The methodology used involved gathering data from online journals relating to the relevant ministries of healthcare, and an extended review was conducted based on existing sources. The scenarios that unfolded as the pandemic first broke out, the policies imposed by the governments, and their shortcomings as policymakers were discussed, and the current day policies utilized to make sure the brunt of the pandemic doesn't boomerang again were analyzed.

INTRODUCTION

Today's organisations confront difficult economic conditions, exacerbated by the recent global financial

DOI: 10.4018/978-1-6684-5417-6.ch004

crisis and mounting evidence of catastrophic climate change occurring at an unprecedented and fast rate. International and domestic companies are being forced to rethink their strategy. They must evaluate their organization's expenditures and realign their objectives in order to strategically choose the most cost-effective method of cost reduction. (2010) (Issa, Chang, & Issa). However, throughout time, individuals have broadened their framework to include demographic, intercultural, ethical, and ecological considerations, resulting in variations such as STEEPLED, DESTEP, and SLEPIT (Administrator, 2016).

PESTLE analysis is a term that is often used and is sometimes abbreviated as PEST analysis. It is a notion found in marketing concepts. Organizations utilise this idea to keep track of the external variables affecting them. This kind of study is then contrasted to the company's internal strengths and weaknesses using a SWOT analysis, which assists in defining the future scope of action and creating strategic management strategies. A PESTLE analysis is often used as a wide fact-finding exercise that assists an organisation in determining the external variables that may affect internal choices. By recognising the effect that these external variables may have on an organisation, businesses can align their goals with their resources, all while allowing sufficient planning time to account for possible roadblocks to such strategies. They may devise ways to mitigate risks and enhance their own chances (Pathak R., 2021). Similarly to what was stated before, this idea may be used in a macroeconomic context as well.

Macroeconomics is the field of economics that examines an economy's behaviour and performance. Macroeconomists are interested in aggregate economic developments such as unemployment, growth rate, Gross Domestic Product (GDP), and inflation. Macroeconomics examines the economy's aggregate indicators as well as the microeconomic variables that affect it. Governments and businesses rely on macroeconomic models to assist them in developing economic policies and strategies (The Economic Times, 2021).

A PESTLE analysis report is a valuable tool to have on hand before beginning the company planning process. This kind of document offers the senior management team with a wealth of contextual information about the firm, such as the business's strategy, brand positioning, growth goals, and areas of concern that may result in a decrease in growth and productivity. A PESTLE study enables companies to detect potentially disruptive changes to their business models that may have a significant effect on the future employment environment. Organizations are undergoing significant personnel transformations. Increased skill gaps, the development of employment positions that did not exist a decade ago, such as the IT department, and job cutbacks or displacements are just a few of the most noticeable changes that have occurred in sectors over the last few years. PESTLE research elicits a wealth of data about external variables and critical market insights. Spending time developing a PESTEL study may assist in prioritising company efforts in order to achieve particular marketing goals within a specified period. Additionally, PESTLE research provides critical market insights into how consumers react to a product or service. This enables companies to make informed decisions about whether to join or exit a market, how to alter an existing product, and when and what to launch as a new product. A PESTLE analysis is an effective technique for determining the context for change and concentrating efforts on the areas critical to the success of that change. PESTLE analysis works well in conjunction with a SWOT analysis in this instance. This enables a company to assess possible possibilities and risks associated with labour developments, such as talent shortages and workforce skills (Pathak R., 2021).

The epidemic poses grave risks to physical security, economic security, and institutional confidence. These risks may have an effect on cognitive, emotional, and behavioural consequences associated with financial decision-making, political conduct, and how others are treated. Perceived threats to one's health/ safety, economic well-being/status, and social group memberships such as identity, race/ethnic groups, and so forth can result in either a narrowing of concern for others (increased egocentric, self-protective thoughts and behaviours) or an expansion of concern for others (increased other-focus, altruistic and pro-social thoughts and behaviors). Additionally, these threats may foster hostility against people seen to be beyond one's circle of care (RSF, 2020).

Objective of the Study

The objective of this study is to identify whether pandemic included health as a new dimension in environmental factor along with PESTLE framework.

LITERATURE REVIEW

Components of PESTLE

The PESTEL framework is a "memonic used in strategic management to aggregate macro-environmental variables in order to assist strategists in identifying broad opportunities and dangers." The PESTEL framework examines the external business environment in order to get a better understanding of the 'big picture' in which the organisation works, allowing it to capitalise on opportunities and mitigate risks associated with the company's business operations (Issa, Chang, & Issa, 2010). PESTLE is a mnemonic that stands for Political, Economic, Social, Technological, Legal, and Environmental. This may be limited to PEST or other categories might be included, depending on the company (such as Ethical). The PESTLE analysis is a considerably more in-depth variant of the SWOT analysis (Pathak R., 2021).

Reviewing each Component of the PESTLE Factors

P - Political factors include government rules and legal requirements that organisations must follow. From a political standpoint, companies must regard their home country's laws and regulations. (Issa, Chang, & Issa, 2010). Tax policy, environmental laws, trade limitations and reform, tariffs, and political stability are all considered political issues. These variables affect the degree to which a government may exert influence on an industry or a business. For instance, the government may enact new tax changes that alter a business's whole revenue-generating structure. Customs policy and export subsidies are two examples of tariff trade barriers that may be a burden to the way a company is operated. Meanwhile, non-tariff trade obstacles include establishing minimum import prices and export prohibitions and limitations (Pathak R., 2021).

This includes government policy, political stability or insecurity, corruption, foreign trade policies, tax policies, labour laws, environmental laws, and trade restrictions. Additionally, the government may have a significant influence on a country's education system, infrastructure, and health laws. All of these variables must be considered when determining the market attractiveness of a prospective market (Administrator, 2016).

E – The economic element is linked with the organization's cost concerns (Issa, Chang, & Issa, 2010). Economic variables include economic growth/decline, interest rates, currency exchange rates, inflation and wage rates, minimum wage, working hours, local and national unemployment, credit availability, and cost of living. These variables are important drivers of an economy's success since they have a direct influence on a business and have long-term repercussions. For instance, an increase in any economy's inflation rate would have an effect on how businesses price their products and services. Such a hypothetical conduct would likewise impact a consumer's buying power and may result in a shift in the economy's demand/supply dynamics (Pathak R., 2021). Economic variables influence the performance of an economy.

S - The social element has an effect on how businesses evolve (Issa, Chang, & Issa, 2010). Cultural standards and expectations, health awareness, population growth rates, age distribution, career aspirations, and health and safety are all examples of social variables. This component of the general environment reflects the demographic, normative, and customs and values characteristics of the population in which the organisation works. This covers demographic factors such as population growth rate, age distribution, wealth distribution, career attitudes, a focus on safety, health awareness, lifestyle attitudes, and cultural obstacles. These characteristics are particularly critical for marketers when they are targeting specific consumers. Additionally, the'social' component paints a picture of the indigenous labour and their willingness to work under adverse circumstances (Administrator, 2016).

These variables enable businesses to more effectively design their marketing analytics and strategy. For instance, the Indian market often experiences a spike in car demand towards the end of the year owing to the holiday season. These characteristics are especially relevant for marketers who are attempting to target certain consumers. Additionally, they emphasise the indigenous labour and their willingness to operate under specific conditions (Pathak R., 2021).

T - This technology achieves exceptional performance at the lowest possible cost, and "a firm may always transfer its business to a competitor providing superior service or cheaper costs" (Issa, Chang, & Issa, 2010). Technological aspects are advancements and breakthroughs in technology. These variables have an effect on an organization's operations. Numerous new advancements in the technological sector, such as Artificial Intelligence (AI), Internet of Things (IoT), Machine Learning, and Deep Learning, are being created, and if a business does not keep up with the trend, they risk losing market share. The PESTLE study considers a variety of technical variables, including the pace of technological development, the evolution of infrastructure, and any government or institutional research (Pathak R., 2021).

Additionally, the 'technology' component encompasses technical incentives, the level of innovation, automation, research and development (R&D) activities, technological change, and the degree to which a market has technological awareness. These variables may affect choices to join or exit certain sectors, to launch or discontinue specific goods, and to outsource manufacturing operations to other countries. By staying current on technological developments, your business may be able to avoid spending a significant part of its budget creating a technology that will become outdated very quickly due to disruptive technical advancements elsewhere (Administrator, 2016).

L - Changes in law affecting employment, access to materials, quotas, resources, imports/exports, and taxes are all considered legal considerations. These variables have both external and internal components. Certain laws have an effect on a country's business climate. Apart from these laws/rules, businesses have their own set of internal rules and regulations that employees are required to follow. Thus, the legal analysis considers both of these perspectives and formulates solutions accordingly (Pathak R., 2021). While some of these variables overlap with political considerations, they include more particular legislation such as anti-discrimination laws, employment regulations, consumer protection laws, copyright and patent laws, and occupational health and safety laws. It is self-evident that businesses must understand what is and is not lawful in order to do business effectively and ethically. When a business operates on a worldwide scale, this gets much more complicated, since each nation has its own set of laws and regulations. Additionally, the firm should be informed of any possible changes in law and the effect they may have on future operations. Nowadays, the majority of companies maintain strong ties with their legal departments for just this reason.

E - With increased awareness of environmental problems, exacerbated by the escalating pressure exerted by climate change campaigners, businesses are increasingly expected to play a more active role in achieving sustainable development. However, defining this new position is a significant problem for businesses, as they are required to balance economic, environmental, and social performance. Managers must quantify the relationship between environmental activities and financial performance in order to incorporate sustainability concepts into their company plans and to assist in resource allocation choices (Issa, Chang, & Issa, 2010). These elements primarily address the effect of the surrounding environment and the impact of ecological factors. These include regulations governing trash disposal, environmental preservation, and energy usage, to mention a few.

This component of the PESTLE is critical for specific sectors, most notably tourism, agriculture, and farming. Global warming and the resulting increasing need for sustainable resources; ethical sourcing (both locally and nationally, including supply chain intelligence) have forced every business to address environmental issues. Corporate Social Responsibility (CSR) has been mandated for businesses (Pathak R., 2021)

Environmental issues have just lately gained prominence. They have grown in importance as a result of the growing scarcity of raw resources, government-set pollution goals, and carbon footprint objectives. These variables include ecological and environmental issues such as weather, climate, environmental offsets, and climate change, which may have a disproportionate impact on sectors such as tourism, agriculture, and insurance. Additionally, increasing knowledge of the possible consequences of climate change is having an effect on how businesses function and the goods they provide. This has resulted in an increasing number of businesses being engaged in CSR and environmental initiatives (Administrator, 2016).

THE IMPACT OF COVID-19 IN ENVIRONMENTAL FACTORS

Political

Alcohol, marijuana, and other controlled substances are only a handful of the heavily regulated markets in the United States. Changes in market circumstances result in more creative, entrepreneurial solutions in less regulated marketplaces. In these highly regulated markets, the rapid changes brought about by the pandemic and associated actions offer a window into the intertwined political interventions that occurred when governments altered a number of regulations influencing ease of entry. We demonstrate how a similar crisis, in this instance a pandemic, may result in the growth or reduction of highly regulated sectors' regulatory regimes depending on political concerns. A crisis may serve as a catalyst for the abolition or reduction of current policies, which can later cause major bottlenecks in the crisis recovery process (so long as a powerful opposition interest group is not in the way).

The epidemic brought to light flaws in the regulatory framework governing prescription and illegal medications. By increasing access to drug use disorder treatment, deregulation efforts mitigated the harmful consequences of increased substance use during the epidemic. However, as drug usage grows, more negative consequences emerge. Domestic violence, child abuse, and assault all decrease in response to an increase in the price of alcohol. The meta-analysis quantifies the statistically significant and eco-nomically significant impacts of alcohol pricing on injury outcomes, violence, traffic accidents, STDs, criminality, and other drug usage. Although violence-related injuries and damage increase when alcohol and other drug use increases, policymakers struggle to manage a complicated regulatory system beset by special interests and information gaps enmeshed in politics. Simplifying consumer access to high-quality goods by enabling entrepreneurs to supply customers with the items they want and simplifying access to treatment for individuals struggling with drug use disorders will almost certainly enhance a number of public health outcomes (Redford & Dills, 2021).

Although clerics in Iran have cooperated in advising communities to remain at home and adhere to the government's lockdown policies, as well as to perform religious obligations such as Friday prayers at home, the majority of people have heeded their advice, despite their vocal discontent with such a re-quest. The public did not engage in a suppression campaign, and the government did not prohibit visits to pilgrimage sites, which was the Irani administration's contradictory stance. This resulted in the fast spread of COVID-19 across Iran's regions as a result of the government's ineffective measures aimed at preventing disease transmission. The most notable feature is that this problem was first contained, then handled and controlled only after the bulk of the harm had been done. The second difficulty was diagnosing individuals with the illness; those with positive Polymerase Chain Reaction (PCR) tests were deemed halo, but those with symptoms were not reported on Computed Tomography (CT) scans for them, resulting in a disparity between official and reality data (Lebni et al., 2020)

COVID-19 has had a significant impact on national and international politics. Due to the emergence of the COVID-19 virus, certain governments/ruling parties seemed to be very concerned, while others exploited the epidemic as an opportunity for political advantage. Numerous industrialised and develop-ing nations swiftly proclaimed national health crises in response to the recommendation of competent medical experts. According to the United Nations Center for Civil and Political Rights' report, 84 nations have declared a state of emergency in response to the epidemic. Additionally, the study notes that certain nations' governing parties are abusing government machinery for political advantage by severely prohib-iting large protest movements. Certain nations' democratically elected leaders become authoritarian via the use of their powers. Reporters Without Borders notes that 38 nations worldwide have limited press freedom, that reporters face verbal assaults in the United States and Brazil, and that some journalists have been imprisoned in countries such as Algeria, Jordan, and Zimbabwe. COVID-19 also had an effect on the elections in a number of nations across the globe. According to the International Foundation for Electoral Systems (IFES), 61 nations and eight territories have postponed their elections, totaling 106 elections postponed due to COVID-19 (Reports of IFES, 17th June 2020). The eruption of Covid-19 also generated significant tensions in international politics. Numerous impediments have arisen in some nations' foreign ties as a result of the virus's propagation.

Tensions between the world's two largest economies, the United States and China, are at an all-time high following the American government's criticism of the Chinese government's disaster manage-ment procedures in the aftermath of the disease outbreak, which the Americans claimed originated in a laboratory in Wuhan, China. Additionally, Donald Trump, then-President of the United States of America, notoriously called the COVID-19 virus the 'Chinese Virus,' disregarding objections from social activists who felt the conduct was both pitiful and discriminatory. Donald Trump has vowed to sue the Chinese government for damages caused by the epidemic. The Chinese authorities vehemently denied ex-President Donald Trump's claim and instead blamed America for the emergence of this epidemic. China's Ministry of Foreign Affairs has said unequivocally that the American military is to blame for the COVID-19 outbreak (The Hindu, 9th May 2020). China has received criticism from a number of nations other than America as a result of the viral epidemic, including Brazil, Australia, and France. According to Brazilian politician Eduardo Bolsonaro, "the Chinese Communist Party is to responsible for the worldwide COVID-19 epidemic." (M. Pathak, 2020)

The revelation of the first case of COVID-19 in Sri Lanka in March 2020 prompted the government of Sri Lanka to immediately implement a cautious policy reaction and lockdown the whole nation, with the primary goal of limiting people's mobility in order to safeguard lives from the virus's potential effect on individuals with comorbidities. The strategy was effective in containing the epidemic, since the number of reported cases and fatalities was kept to a minimal. However, the programme had a detrimental effect on the economy. By examining monthly data in a univariate modelling framework, this research determined that the country's export and import commerce were significantly impacted by the pandemic in the months of March, April, and May of 2020. Extending the research to a second wave that may conclude in December 2020, the study predicts that the country's total exports and imports would decline by 67% and 45%, respectively, as the pandemic disrupts the behavioural patterns of the country's various export and import components. The government's passive reaction to the second wave of COVID-19 is aimed at sustaining economic activity during the epidemic. If, on the other hand, the strategy results in pandemic spread at the community level, a massive and prolonged negative impact on international commerce and the economy will be generated as the virus's life span becomes infinite, having a more lasting influence on the economy. (2021, Bandaranayake)

Economical

The Iranian government's financial incapacity to safeguard the country financially during quarantine was insufficient, which resulted in the loss of livelihoods for many individuals who normally earn their living and stay active in numerous busy areas and commercial hubs. Given Iran's present economic slump, spending a part of the budget to address the current COVID-19-induced problem risks luring the nation into another future crisis in the supply chain for essential commodities. Further depletion of foreign currency reserves, more unemployment, and ultimately greater inflation. Among the other important factors covered in this category is the health sector's credit limit for the delivery of medical equipment (Lebni, et al., 2020). Job losses accelerated to levels not seen since the Great Depression, with economic production expected to decline more than it did during the Great Recession of 2008/2009 in the first two quarters of 2020. Congress enacted substantial stimulus legislation, but it was inadequate in light of the fraying social safety net, which left millions of families struggling to make ends meet without paid sick/ family leave or health insurance. (Royal Society for the Prevention of Cruelty, 2020).

Additionally, a government-sponsored research assessing the economic effect of COVID-19 projected that this pandemic would have a negative impact on the lives and livelihoods of Assamese people. Around half of the state's population will fall below the poverty level as a result of this worldwide catastrophe. According to this study on Assam's economy, about 67,000,000 people would have difficulties earning a living. Additionally, this study said that Assam's unemployment rate would quickly rise as a result of the virus. Additionally, the economy's unemployment rate will rise to 27% from its current level of 8%. (Pathak M., 2020).

In terms of the economy and community well-being, the Sri Lankan government announced a stimulus package for SMEs, for which the government set aside a budget of LKR50 billion (approximately USD 270million). The stimulus package included a working capital loan of up to LKR 25 million (about USD

135,000), which was aimed at businesses with less than LKR 1 billion [approximately USD 5.4 million] in yearly revenue. When nearly 45,000 private sector companies applied for the loan, the government recognised that the LKR 50 billion allotment was insufficient to satisfy demand. As a consequence, the government increased the budget allocation to LKR 150 billion (approximately USD 810 million). However, a study of stimulus packages given in 18 other countries reveals that the GoSL's stimulus programme was insufficient when compared to an average of 3.5 percent of GDP allotted for stimulus packages in other nations (Amaratunga, Fernando, Haigh, & Jayasinghe, 2020).

Apart from that, SMEs' income tax arrears have been partly forgiven, payment conditions have been eased, and legal proceedings against non-payers have been halted. Similarly, the government enacted a loan repayment moratorium, which included a six-month moratorium on debt repayment for impacted industries such as tourism, textile, plantation, and information technology, as well as small and medium-sized enterprises. As stated before, the Government of Sri Lanka also offered a LKR5000 stipend to low-income families and economically vulnerable populations such as daily wage workers. Additionally, the government set a maximum retail price for some basic goods and a fund to stabilise gasoline prices. (Jayasinghe, Amaratunga, Fernando, Haigh, & Amaratunga, 2020)

The pandemic has significantly disrupted the usual temporal pattern of export value, with shipments falling 34% in March 2020 compared to the previous month and continuing to fall 57% in April. March and April export values decreased by about 71% as compared to February 2020 export values. The export volume index, which measures the country's overall exports, likewise showed a significant drop in March and April before gradually recovering.

Adopting a strong strategy to safeguard economic activity may be too risky, since it would amplify the pandemic's spreading impact. As shown by the second wave of the pandemic, the epidemic has spread across the population, resulting in daily reports of more cases and fatalities. Community spread will, of course, lengthen the virus's lifetime and also the duration of the shock, resulting in a lasting negative effect on the economy (Bandaranayake, 2021)

Social

Although the majority of individuals followed self-quarantine measures at home, empathy and closeness evolved on a greater scale among family members. However, these social variables undermined family ties, resulting in a rise in psychiatric disorders and violence through fostering interpersonal conflict and verbal and physical conflict. Additionally, prolonged confinement to one's house may result in melancholy, lethargy, and aggravation of pre-existing diseases such as hypertension, stress, and anxiety. The second social issue is an insufficient intake of antiseptics at home, which results in additional complications, such as respiratory system impairment. People have responded to this epidemic and developed an increased sensitivity to their interactions with other individuals in general (Lebni, et al., 2020)

To demonstrate the systemic nature of risk, the COVID-19 pandemic quickly evolved from a health catastrophe to a social and economic disaster, resulting in a slew of negative economic and social consequences across the nation. For example, Sri Lanka's GDP, which was anticipated to grow at a pace of 4.5–5% after the Easter Sunday assault in 2019, was forecast to grow at a rate of just 2.2 percent when the nation was struck by the epidemic. Additionally, the lockdown had a negative effect on the country's critical economic sectors, notably manufacturing and services. To elaborate, the tourism industry, which is a critical service sector in the nation, accounts for about 5% of GDP. However, as a result of the global travel restrictions implemented during the pandemic era, tourist arrivals in the nation dropped by 71%

in March 2020 and were non-existent in the following months of April, May, and June. Similarly, the manufacturing sector's Purchasing Manager's Index (PMI), which was at 54 in January 2020, fell to 24.2 in April 2020, due to a decrease in new orders, output, and employment. Additionally, industrial exports decreased by 74% year over year, while agricultural exports decreased by 32%, putting a damper on the country's export profits. (Jayasinghe, Amaratunga, Fernando, Haigh, & Amaratunga, 2020)

Additionally, private remittances sent to Sri Lanka by migrant workers contribute substantially to the country's foreign currency profits. For example, private remittances provided by migrant workers accounted for 63% of the country's overall export profits. However, remittances from employees dropped by 32% in April 2020, putting a damper on the country's foreign currency revenues. (Jayasinghe, Amaratunga, Fernando, Haigh, & Amaratunga, 2020)

Similarly, a recent labour market study of 2764 private sector businesses showed that throughout the pandemic period, 1465 establishments were completely closed, 1025 companies operated at or near maximum capacity, and just 94 establishments operated at full capacity. Of the entire number of businesses surveyed, 1084 were unable to pay their employees' wages throughout the country's epidemic period. Increased unemployment, job insecurity, and wage cutbacks all contributed to worry and economic stress among the working people in the economy. (Jayasinghe, Amaratunga, Fernando, Haigh, & Amaratunga, 2020)

The pandemic had a devastating effect on SMEs and the informal sector, especially daily wage workers. To illustrate this argument, the majority of SMEs in Sri Lanka have faced problems due to a lack of supplies required to continue manufacturing or service supply, a decrease in domestic and worldwide demand for their goods, and difficulty repaying loans (Amaratunga, Fernando, Haigh, & Jayasinghe, 2020).

One of the most urgent concerns about the pandemic's social consequences is the interruption of educational activities. Lockdown limitations imposed in response to social distancing demands led in the closure of elementary, secondary, and tertiary educational institutions such as schools, universities, and support courses. The GoSL responded by promoting the continuation of online educational offerings. While online education would have been the simplest solution, the pandemic exposed an issue in that it widened inequalities in access to education and fueled social unrest because certain population groups, particularly those living in rural areas, lacked access to the facilities and infrastructure required for online learning. (Jayasinghe, Amaratunga, Fernando, Haigh, & Amaratunga, 2020)

Another significant social consequence is the stigmatisation of demographic groups exposed to the public. Certain population groups, namely health sector workers and those who worked at supermarket counters, were stigmatised in their own communities since they provided essential services despite the country's pandemic situation and were therefore seen as potential disease carriers (Amaratunga, Fernando, Haigh, & Jayasinghe, 2020).

Legal

The absence of private sector involvement in the provision of semi-clinical services (laboratory and radiography) in outpatient units and inpatient wards for patients with COVID-19 in hospitals shows a lack of clear and defined regulations in this area. Additionally, the public's inappropriate and imprudent use of disinfectants in the city, along with the absence of adequate monitoring by authorised people, harms the environment and destroys public property such as machines and ATM cards (Lebni, et al., 2020)

METHODOLOGY

The study adopted the systematic review that uses specific techniques to locate, select and critically appraise relevant primary research on a clearly established topic and then uses those findings to extract and analyse data from the included studies (Aromataris, 2014). The systematic review presents previous work that describes and evaluates the research examined but does not provide a process for how the studies were discovered, chosen and evaluated. Instead, an overview, a discussion of previous studies, and a critique of the gaps in existing knowledge that researchers often use to explain the new findings to focus on interventions of various kinds (Denyer, 2009).

Researcher used qualitative method to explore the PESTEL framework. Qualitative research usually used to understand the human lives & social world through addressing questions to concern the experience and dimensions. Subjective meanings, actions & social contexts are the main ideas in qualitative research. To study the impacts of the environmental factors in the PESTEL framework before & after the pandemic, researchers selected existing literatures of PESTEL framework studies before and after the global pandemic. For a systematic review, many studies have to be retrieved. Even the articles which do not have abstracts cannot be neglected in such a scene. Taking the quantitative studies into the systematic review is time consuming although conducting a systematic review & meta-synthesis of qualitative research studies is a rewarding but demanding activity & adequate time & resources must be made available. Some recommendations are made which may facilitate such processes. Business, news websites & global business, project reports & data bases & journal articles published in English on Google Scholar, Research Gate & SAGE publication were taken for the review for the qualitative studies. Key words such as PESTEL, Environmental factors, Business impact, COVID-19 & business, and pandemic & health selection criteria to choose the data source was analyzed with the key words. Then, the researchers significantly analyzed only the environmental factor in the PESTEL framework to fulfill the objective of the study.

DISCUSSION

PESTLE Framework – External Environment Scanning & Impact of COVID-19 in the Environment

Social isolation, distant work, and the difference between "essential" and "non-essential" employees have had varying impacts on workers based on their gender, race/ethnic origin, education level, and profession.

The most vulnerable have faced higher dangers, including low-wage employees, the elderly, those with chronic health problems, and those living in close quarters, such as jails/prisons or immigration detention centres. Many low-wage service employees are more likely to lose their employment permanently or be called back to work more slowly than higher-wage workers in other sectors. The epidemic forced an abrupt halt to the normal patterns of social contact that drove economic and social activity. The majority of the population has suffered interruptions in their regular daily rhythms as a result of enforced social distance, with the possibility of more disruptions in job, school, social, and family connections. As a result, the infrastructures of education, health, social services, and faith-based organisations, as well as government, criminal justice, and the law, were obliged to quickly change their operations, bringing some online, delaying or postponing others, and closing down others entirely. Although the effects of these choices are unknown at the moment, they are likely to be long lasting, in part owing to disparate access to digital technologies (RSF, 2020).

COVID-19 factors connect directly with the mental health of ordinary people on one end of the illness, but there is a grave concern that thousands of fatalities occur on the other. The COVID-19 epidemic has had a detrimental effect on the economy, with many people losing employment and unable to earn a living wage. Fear of economic loss has heightened stress levels and contributed to mental health issues among individuals globally (Lebni, et al., 2020). Iran's government, for example, has implemented preventive measures and regulations aimed at reducing public concern in order to address mental health issues. Iran's government created dedicated health facilities to treat individuals infected with COVID-19 after they were discharged from major hospitals. This motivation aided in the separation of COVID-19 patients from their families until they recovered completely, thus preventing the fatal illness from spreading further. The government promised to postpone utility payments for three months, and paying in instalments aided in providing comfort to patients' families, thus alleviating mental stress (Lebni, et al., 2020).

The authorities made a concerted effort to alleviate worry, tension, and mental health problems via the implementation of essential measures. The government has established programmes to reward contributors who provide financial assistance to disadvantaged and low-income people. Through this government-sponsored programme, online and telephone psychological therapy services for patients infected with COVID-19 and other healthy individuals are beneficial. This has aided in the alleviation of the community's emotional tension. The government has begun offering low-interest loans to low-income individuals and has taken control of social media sites to detect and restrict the dissemination of sensational and misleading material regarding COVID-19 illness. This aided in the community's management of the fear generated by false information regarding COVID-19 (Lebni, et al., 2020).

Through mental health surveys, the government initiated social support programmes and psychological protocol services for survivors of COVID-19. To combat dread and terror in the society, plans were started to disperse places of public gathering and to educate the people via the media. The government established specific post moratorium services for those who died as a direct consequence of the illness, recognising that funerals are an important cultural component in every community. The government-started initiatives to educate the public about the disease's progress and to alleviate communal mental stress. The protective measures aided in the development of confidence in individuals, enabling them to overcome fear, anxiety, stress, and mental health issues (Lebni et al., 2020).

The health experts recommended solutions to slow, sustain, and overcome COVID-19 transmission problems, including prioritising investment in the health sector over other sectors such as military spending, allocating subsidies to all citizens with private businesses, and providing low-interest loans to relatively larger SMEs. They also recommended paying special attention to vu (Lebni et al., 2020).

The COVID-19 pandemic is a public health emergency that triggered an economic catastrophe, with employment losses exceeding job increases over the preceding decade within a few months and severe impacts on many aspects of American society. The disparate responses of institutions such as government, education, and industry aided in the virus's unequal transmission and impacts by location, race, ethnic origin, gender, and social status (RSF, 2020)

COVID-19

The pandemic of 19 had a significant effect on people's mental health. As with the rest of the globe, the people of Assam experienced sadness, frustration, anxiety, and lack of appetite during the time of national lockdown, which contributed to the state's fast rise in mental health-related cases. Dr. Sangeeta Datta, a psychiatrist based in Guwahati, said that the economic crisis is the primary reason for the rapid increase in such mental health-related cases in Assam (Pathak M., 2020).

Healthcare and Macroeconomics

The rise in healthcare costs is a sobering problem for developing economies. This is because an unchecked rise in healthcare costs has the potential to drive developing/underdeveloped countries into severe poverty. Increases in public healthcare costs could be attributed to an increase in deaths from diabetes, cardiovascular disease, and cancer, which could result in a crisis in emerging economies as a result of the growing demand for specialised equipment and training of experts to detect and treat the illnesses (Zhou et al., 2020). Additionally, the research indicates that labour force participation has an effect on public health expenditures.

A possible reason is that when a country's labour population is fully employed, some occupations such as mining and other sectors expose their employees and nearby communities to health risks that may result in illness and frequent trips to the health facility. When this occurs, it puts pressure on the government and relevant stakeholders to expand hospitals, which results in increased healthcare spending and vice versa, with the premise that all other variables remain constant (ceteris paribus). The findings of this research match those of a study conducted in the United States of America, which found that changes in the labour market and health workforce result in an increase in government healthcare expenditure (Zhou et al., 2020).

On the one hand, the findings suggest that inflation has a negative effect on healthcare expenses in developing economies. This implies that, although negative inflation is not a good thing for the economy in general, the impacts on healthcare may not result in a rise in healthcare expenses since the prices of health-related products and services are not rising. The negative connection between healthcare costs and inflation implies that the monetary value of healthcare expenses is constant or falling, since inflation does not increase prices but rather decreases them. On the other hand, the likelihood of inflation having a negative influence on overall economic development is apparent, and this may constrain revenue sources for the health system, eventually resulting in higher health expenses (Zhou et al., 2020).

The results of this research indicate that macroeconomic variables have a direct effect on healthcare costs, since a rise in a country's income levels enables governments to raise revenue via taxes. Inflation has an effect on public healthcare expenses because it influences the pricing of products and services, particularly the costs of health-related materials. While labour force participation may enhance the government's revenue base, some occupations expose employees and the broader population to health risks, resulting in higher healthcare costs. This implies that the cost of public healthcare in developing countries is directly or indirectly related to macroeconomic variables (Zhou et al., 2020). COVID-19 had a detrimental effect on the macroeconomy because to the rise in health care costs, which had a direct influence on a country's GDP.

How COVID-19 is Driving up Healthcare Costs

According to a recent Kaiser Family Foundation research, many insurers anticipate a rise in health expenditures this year as a result of pent-up demand after delayed care, direct costs associated with COVID-19 diagnosis and treatment, and vaccine costs. According to a second study from McKinsey & Company, although the direct impact of COVID-19 has already been significant, further layers of delayed or indirect impacts have the potential to dwarf the immediate effects, culminating in an extra yearly cost to the American healthcare system of $125-$200 billion. For example, the study estimates that the average cost of treating a patient with chronic obstructive pulmonary disease may rise by between 7% and 11%, from about $38,000 to nearly $41,000 per patient per year. This cost rise is mainly due to an anticipated increase in the intensity of a patient's symptoms as a result of delayed treatment (Carson, 2021).

The devastating effects of the COVID-19 epidemic and subsequent economic crisis on health care use, expenditure, and employment have been extensively studied by health sector specialists in the United States. A historic drop in health care expenditure and substantial job losses occurred mainly during the first two months of the pandemic, in part as a result of preventative measures taken by governments and health systems to halt in-person discretionary and elective treatment. As the USA remained quarantined to prevent the spread of COVID-19 and free up health care resources to treat new COVID-19 patients, health expenditure and employment fell by 24% and 10%, respectively, in April 2020, compared to only two months before. "Since that time, our team has been carefully monitoring the recovery of health care expenditure and employment, and we have seen that health employment has virtually returned in many settings/categories of care, and health spending growth rates seem to be returning to pre-pandemic levels" (Rhyan, 2021).

CONCLUSION

The only aim of this study paper was to evaluate if the PESTLE analysis can be reformed to include healthcare as a new component. As per the thorough analysis of the data presented above, we can conclusively provide an ultimatum on the statement that the healthcare entity can indeed be classified as a separate dimension under a PESTLE analysis, simply because of the very significant direct impact this has had and continues to have on the macroeconomy as seen by the fruits of the COVID-19 pandemic.

Hypothetically speaking, even if we were to ignore the contribution the pandemic has had on the healthcare industry, healthcare is one of the most vital industries in any given economy. One could even go as far to make a statement that in the absence of a smoothly functioning healthcare system, the entire functionality of an economy would come to a grinding halt as bottlenecks would be formed where consumer goods/services will be stagnant in the flow of production due to the absence of human labor, which is an essential part of the production process. Now, if we were to consider an act of God, such as a pandemic, the economy would plunge into chaos in a couple of days if not for a smoothly functioning healthcare system.

Although healthcare would be introduced as a sub-part of the already existing environmental factor, the PESTLE analysis would undergo a complete restructure as a new factor which impacts the macroeconomy is being introduced. The inclusion of this new dimension would have a very direct impact on other existing factors such as the political factor, social factor, technological factor, economical factor & most importantly, the legal factor as the impact this new introduction has on the macroeconomy should be accounted for in order to provide a more realistic & practical view of how entities such as corporations & even global governments tackle external shocks which affect the macroeconomy.

In conclusion, as per the findings of this research article, I am most definitely for the idea of including all healthcare associated costs in a PESTLE analysis under the environmental factor in the future. Economies tend to perform better when functioning healthcare systems exist, so, the introduction of this new dimension will only project the already underlying quantifiable impact the healthcare system has on the overall functionality of the macroeconomy.

REFERENCES

de Bruin, L. (2016). Scanning the Environment: PESTEL Analysis. *Business to You.* https://www.business-to-you.com/scanning-the-environment-pestel-analysis/

Amaratunga, D., Fernando, N., Haigh, R., & Jayasinghe, N. (2020, December 8). The COVID-19 outbreak in Sri Lanka: A synoptic analysis focusing on trends, impacts, risks and science-policy interaction processes. *Progress in Disaster Science.* doi:10.1016/j.pdisas.2020.100133

Aromataris, E., & Pearson, A. (2014). The systematic review: An overview. *AJN The American Journal of Nursing*, *114*(3), 53–58. doi:10.1097/01.NAJ.0000444496.24228.2c PMID:24572533

BandaranayakeS. (2021). The Impact of COVID-19 on Sri Lanka economy. doi:10.2139/ssrn.3911792

Carson, R. (2021, February 23). Why COVID-19 Is Driving Up The Cost Of Healthcare In Retirement And What You Can Do Now To Prepare. *Forbes.* https://www.forbes.com/sites/rcarson/2021/02/23/why-covid-19-is-driving-up-the-cost-of-healthcare-in-retirement-and-what-you-can-do-now-to-prepare/?sh=e85bd5c113bc

Denyer, D., & Tranfield, D. (2009). Producing a systematic review.

Fossey, E., Harvey, C., Mcdermott, F., & Davidson, L. (2002, December 1). Understanding and Evaluating Qualitative Research. *Australian & Newzland Journal of Psychiatry*, *36*(6), 717–732. doi:10.1046/j.1440-1614.2002.01100.x PMID:12406114

Issa, T., Chang, V., & Issa, T. (2010, August). Sustainable Business Strategies and PESTEL Framework. *GSTF International Journal on Computing*, *1*(1), 73–80. doi:10.5176/2010-2283_1.1.13

Jones, M. L. (2004, October 07). Application of systematic review methods to qualitative research: Practical issues. *Leading Global Nursing Research*, *48*(3), 271–278. doi:10.1111/j.1365-2648.2004.03196.x PMID:15488041

Lebni, J. Y., Abbas, J., Moradi, F., Salahshoor, M. R., Chaboksavar, F., Irandoost, S. F., & Ziapour, A. (2020, July). How the COVID-19 pandemic effected economic, social, political, and cultural factors: A lesson from Iran. *The International Journal of Social Psychiatry*, *67*(3), 298–300. doi:10.1177/0020764020939984 PMID:32615838

Pathak, M. (2020). Social, Political and Economic Impact of COVID-19 Pandemic on Assan: A Study. Jouranl if. *Critical Review*, *7*(16).

Pathak, R. (2021, February 15). What is PESTLE Analysis? Everything you need to know about it. *Business Analytics*. https://www.analyticssteps.com/blogs/what-pestle-analysis

Redford, A., & Dills, A. K. (2021, January). The Political Economy of Drug and Alcohol Regulation During the COVID-19 Pandemic. *Forthcoming Sourthern Economics Journal*. doi:10.2139/ssrn.3728996

Rhyan, C. (2021, April 16). Perspective: Are Rising Health Care Prices Another COVID-19 Side Effect? *Newroom*. https://altarum.org/news/are-rising-health-care-prices-another-covid-19-side-effect

RSF. (2020). Social, Political, Economic, and Psychological Consequences of the COVID-19 Pandemic. *Russel Sage Foundation*. https://www.russellsage.org/research/funding/covid-19-pandemic

The Economic Times. (2021, September). Definition of 'Macroeconomics. The Economic Times. https://economictimes.indiatimes.com/definition/macroeconomics

Zhou, L., Ampon-Wireko, S., Brobbey, E., Dauda, L., Owusu-Marfo, J., & Tetgoum, A. (2020). The Role of Macroeconomic Indicators on Healthcare Cost. *Health Care*, *8*(123), 123. doi:10.3390/healthcare8020123 PMID:32375346

Chapter 5
Role of Frugal Innovation Social Sustainability Challenges and Operational Constraints

Nosheen Rafiq
Bahria University, Pakistan

Syed Haider Ali Shah
Bahria Business School, Bahria University, Pakistan

Shahab Aziz
https://orcid.org/0000-0003-1275-3061
Bahria University, Pakistan

Afshan Sultana
University Malaya, Malaysia

Shams Ul Haq Khan
Bahria University, Pakistan

Zahir Ud Din
Bahria University, Pakistan

Muhammad Zeeshan Ahmed Sheikh
Bahria University, Pakistan

Ozair Ijaz Kiani
Bahria University, Pakistan

ABSTRACT

The chapter is about the role of frugal innovation and social sustainability in emerging nations and how it facilities the lives of people in developing countries. The development of any state depends upon the level of advanced technology, but all states are not in sound enough condition to use expensive technology to enhance quality of life. Therefore, such economies go towards the idea of frugal innovation where it offers 'low price' solutions that provide quality products and improves standard of living. This chapter focuses on how frugal innovation can provide latest technologies to people with limited resources. This chapter suggests the need of scientists and researchers and their leading role in order to enhance frugal innovation.

DOI: 10.4018/978-1-6684-5417-6.ch005

INTRODUCTION

The economic growth of emerging markets has significantly influenced the global business landscape (Winterhalter et al., 2017). With average growth rates far above Western markets, emerging economies and particularly the BRIICS countries (Brazil, Russia, India, Indonesia, China and South Africa) constitute strategic growth markets (Drummond, 2012; OECD, 2009). In order to compete successfully in these market segments, businesses need to provide customers with "resource-constrained" innovations and business models that create high value at very low cost (George et al., 2012). These innovations enable Western firms to access unexploited market segments, offering unparalleled growth opportunities (Baskaran and Mehta, 2016; Tunio, et al., (2021; Memon, et al., 2021; Afshan, et al., 2021).

According to Hossain et al., (2016), frugal innovation is a resource scarce solution (i.e., product, service, process, or business model) that is designed and implemented to deal with financial, technological, material or other resource constraints, whereby the final outcome is significantly cheaper than competitive offerings (if available) and is good enough to meet the basic needs of customers". There are many types of frugal innovation that include cars, medical devices, health services, solar energy, refrigerators, and water purifiers (Hossain, 2017). GE's handheld ECG machine MAC 400 costs US$800. It has reduced the cost of an ECG scan in the developing countries like India down to just US$1.0 compared to about US$20 in the developed countries. As transportation systems are not well developed in most of the developing countries, instead of bringing patients to a nearby hospital, this portable machine can be taken a patient's place which may be far away from a nearby hospital. The MAC 400 ECG machine is also used in developed countries in places, such as emergency rooms and ambulances. Frugal innovation offerings are generally good enough to fulfill the needs of local consumers in developing countries, yet they are significantly less expensive than alternative offerings (Ancarani et al., 2014; Rao, 2013). Even though such innovations are primarily aimed at low-income customers in developing countries, some of them trickle up to developed countries (Zedtwitz et al., 2015).

The role of frugal innovation is highly important in developing economies due to the rapid transition of business environment (Shafique et al., 2019). Therefore, recently, scientists and researchers are focusing on frugal innovation because they recognize the importance of frugal innovation during last three decades. Frugal innovation provides economical solutions to low-income consumers of developing economies (Hossain 2020; Iqbal et al. 2021). Numerous researchers used different terms for it such as 'Indovation' (Lamont, 2010), 'Jugaad' (Radjou et al., 2012b), or 'Gandhian Innovation' (Prahalad and Mashelkar, 2010). There are numerous types of frugal innovation such as technological, business, artistic and social innovations. However, the role of technological innovation is critical because it plays it part in facilitating human lives. Its major characteristics are affordability, sustainability, good performance and usability.

Frugal innovation requires major changes in the existing processes of business organizations (Niroumand et al., 2021). It focuses on the redesigns of products and services to achieve optimal performance while preserving core functionalities often exceeding expectations and even leading to breakthrough improvements (Bhatti et al. 2018). India is the epicenter of frugal innovation which is locally known as Jugaad (Shepherd et al., 2020). Recent studies suggested that low-end innovation may require different capabilities than regular innovation and that the capabilities that guide low-end innovation success may differ in relevance across different contexts (D'Angelo & Magnusson 2020). The idea of frugal innovation

Figure 1.
Source: https://www.researchgate.net/figure/Frugal-innovation framework_fig1_356565507

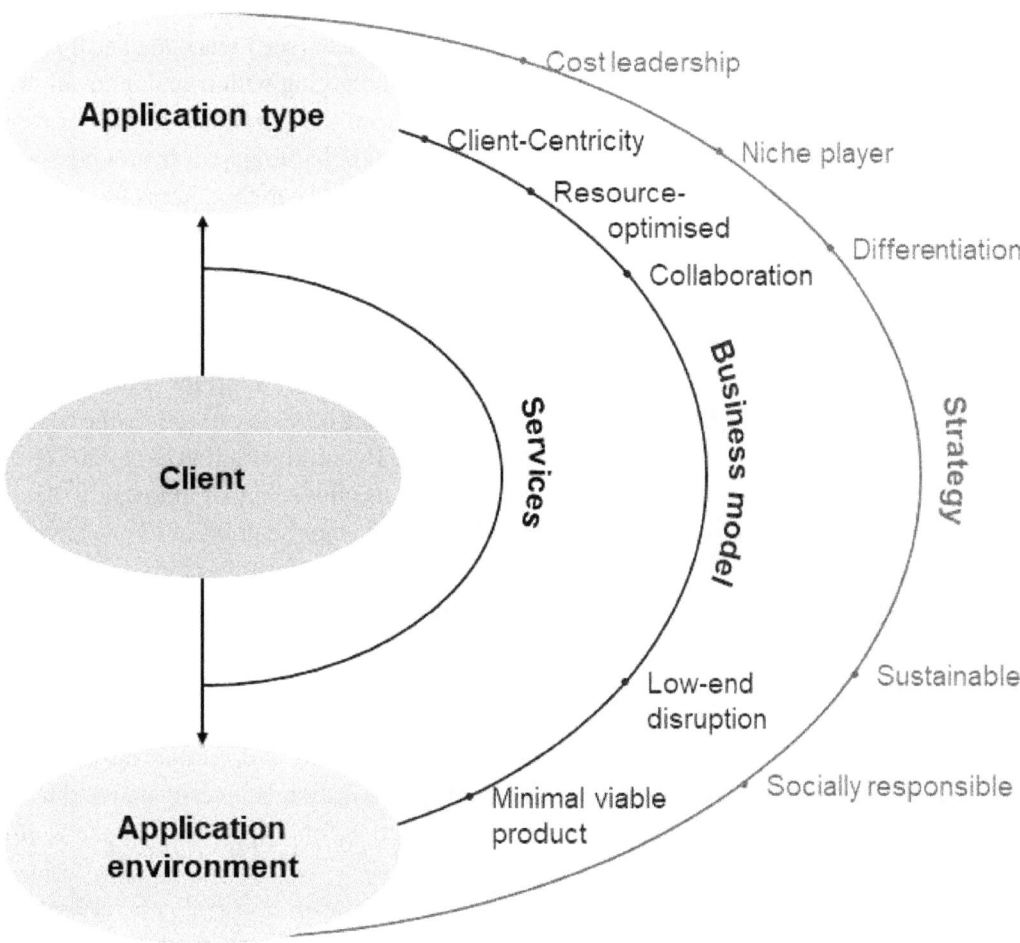

is not only limited to cost reduction (Weyrauch & Herstatt, 2017). Numerous researchers consider frugal innovation to be environmental friendly because it seeks to economize on the use of energy and material resources in the design of goods and services, production and marketing (Bocken 2020). However, empirical evidence on frugal innovation is still limited. The purpose of this book chapter is to reveal the current situation of frugal innovation at local, national and international levels, how it is playing its role in the world of technological advancements.

This is a review article in which already available data will be used from different databases such as Research Gate, Frontiers, Google Scholar, Emerald, and Springer, etc. along with scientific reports to analyze the impact of frugal innovation and the role of technologies for improving quality of life of people of developing economies.

BACKGROUND

Until recently, innovations mainly originated from developed countries like the USA and Japan (McCloskey, 2010). Some scholars criticize the western model of development (see Lizarralde and Tyl (2017)). Many businesses and individuals from developing countries are emerging with frugal innovations (FIs) (Rosca et al., 2017). Frugal innovations are being developed from the grassroots level. For example, a clay fridge Mitticool was invented by a school dropout Mansukhbhai Prajapati from Gujarat, India. The fridge costs less than US$100 and it does not need electricity and keep food items fresh for several days naturally. Frugal innovations like MAC 400 ECG machine and Mitticool fridge show a novel way to serve low-income customers. Numerous frugal innovations are successfully serving low-income customers (Hossain, 2017).

Frugal innovation is a concept developed in the context of emerging economies where a Hindi term 'jugaad' was used to describe a bottom-up innovation process able to develop low-cost and effective solutions (Radjou et al., 2012). Frugal innovation originates form the necessity to satisfy the basic needs of resource-constrained customers, the so-called 'Bottom of the Pyramid' (Radjou et al., 2012). Frugal innovation has gained a lot of attention in developed economies as philosophy of innovation that makes possible to develop sustainable and affordable solution from the economic point of view (Tiwari et al., 2016; Nesta, 2016).According to Radjou and Prabhu (2015) frugal innovation refers to the whole innovation process or product/ service characteristics and that can be applied to different typologies of innovation (Kwan et al., 2021). Frugal innovation is an alternative mindset to the new product development process (Radjou and Prabhu, 2015). They identified six kind of key principles for frugal innovation: shape customer behaviour, co- create value with prosumers, make innovative friends, flex your assets, engage and iterate. Complexity and particular significance are the aspects of economic development and sustainable growth (Dima et al., 2022). The concept of frugal innovation is investigated and treated as a new technological paradigm that can represent a possible solution for how to improve the well-being of individual (Dima et al., 2022).

The importance of new business models based on innovations in terms of frugality is receiving attention day-by-day (Dima et al., 2022). Frugal innovation processes with business models and sustainable development remains a major challenge (Dima et al., 2022). In advanced countries, frugal innovation should be examined as an incentive for accomplishing sustainable development (Albert, 2019). According to Dima et al., (2022), the word is facing a new paradigm nowadays in which business models and production processes need to adapt to reduce resource consumption while increasing recycling procedures at the same time. To provide a sustainable business opportunity (Brem & Ivens, 2013), frugal innovation and financial performance serve as a powerful driving factor for organizations (Dunk, 2011). Less attention has been given to how frugal innovation promotes social sustainability (Dima et al., 2022). Frugal innovation impacts society's environmental performance and significantly improves quality of life (Khan, 2016). The key goal of frugal innovation is to provide goods and services that met the specific demands and requirements of markets with affordable price (Dima et al., 2022). According to the Economist (2012), frugal innovation is also known as "reverse innovation" and it also made its ways in developed markets (Govindarajan & Ramamurti, 2011). Frugal innovation has three key characteristics: affordability, high performance and long-term viability (Angot & Plé, 2015). Hartley (2014) encourages academicians, policymakers and managers to take fresh look at innovative methods. A key goal of frugal

Figure 2.
Source: https://www.researchgate.net/figure/low---cost-philosophy-for-realizing-advanced-frugal-innovations_fig1_315695566

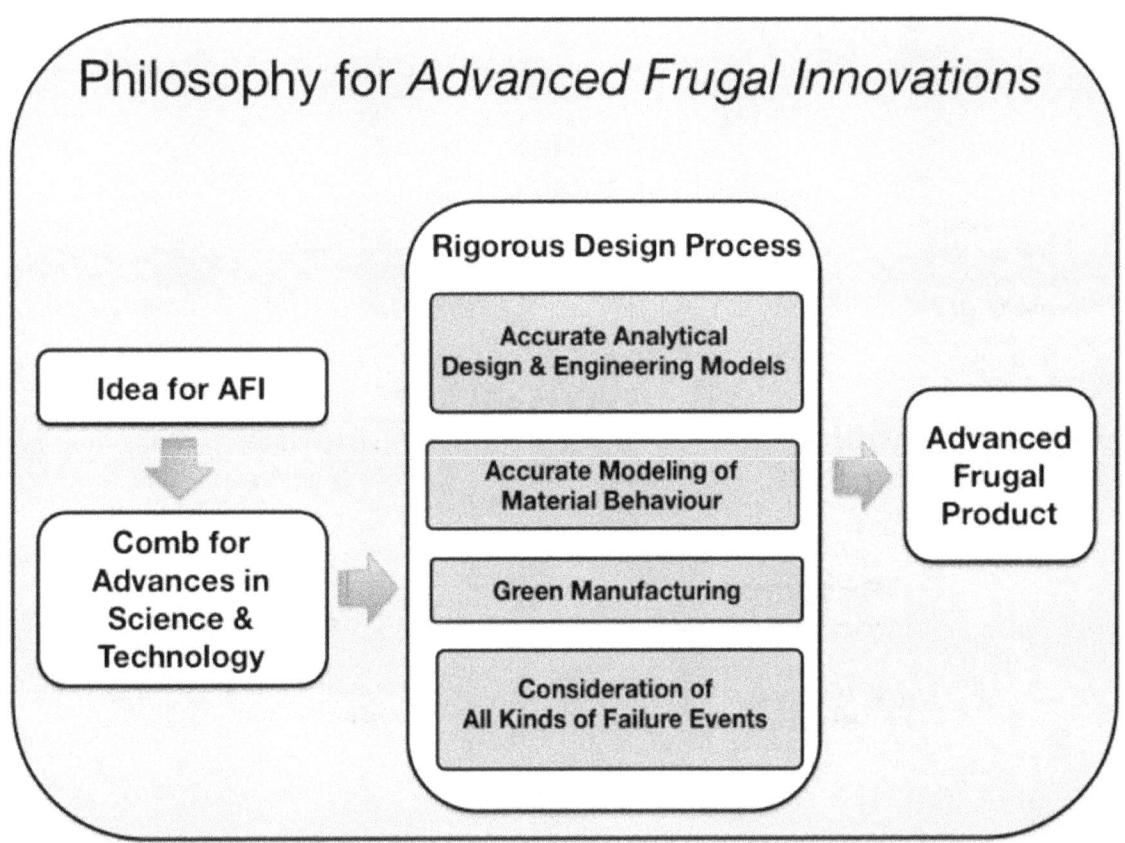

innovation is the capacity to solve issues without being hampered by financial resource or institutional restrictions (Dima et al., 2022). Fugal innovation differs from conventional innovation in four ways: the method, the driver, the location of the inventions and the fundamental capabilities (Dima et al., 2022).

All around the world, highly affordable and improved quality solutions are demanded. Frugal innovation is an optimal choice for businesses in emerging countries which are experiencing consumers demand for frugal products and services characterized by low-cost, focusing on core functionalities and optimized performance (Dost et al., 2019). It is a cost-effective solution that brings sustainable development in terms of social impacts, environmental benefits and business opportunities (Pansera, 2018). Clausen and Fichter (2019) also suggested that it influences economic sustainability because it provides a higher level of value to low-income consumers, there is an opportunity to increase firm's sales and profits. Numerous researchers consider frugal innovation to be environmental friendly because it seeks to economize on the use of energy and material resources in the design of goods and services, production and marketing (Hossain et al. 2021). However, empirical evidence on frugal innovation is still limited.

Frugal innovation is defined as "redesigning of products, services, business models and systems to decrease complexity and total lifecycle costs and improve functionality while providing high user value and affordable solutions for low-income consumers (Tiwari et al, 2016).

Figure 3.
Source: https://www.cambridge.org/core/books/abs/frugal-innovation/towards-a-theory-of-frugal-innovation/7934A9B91A8
BA57CA5A42E33668DB82E

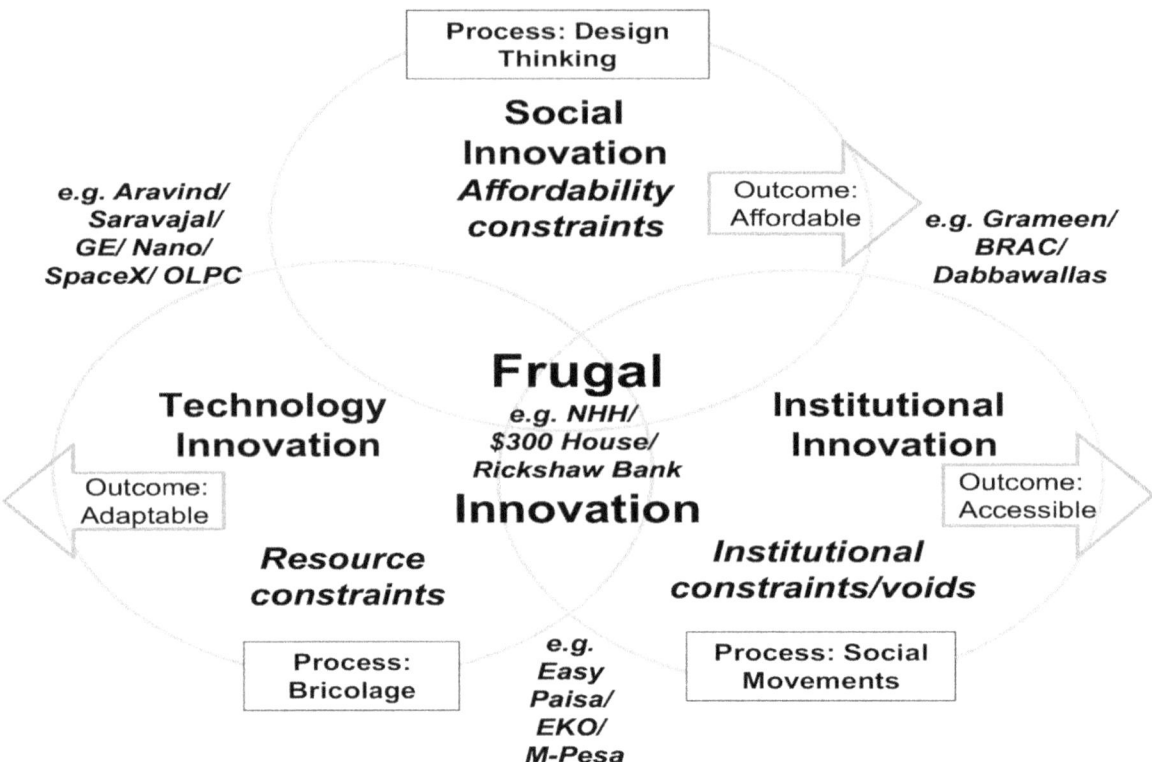

The characteristics of frugal innovation are low cost, optimized performance and multiple core functionalities (Kwan et al., 2021). In business perspectives, frugal innovation is referred as "the efforts made by businesses to improve their products and services through a low-cost process (Kwan et al., 2021). However, it lacks in high technology features; it can fulfill people's basic needs at a low-cost with comparably high value.

MAIN FOCUS OF THE CHAPTER

Frugal innovation influences almost all types of businesses all around the world. Worldwide, advanced technological solutions are demanded. Frugal products and services are 'low-cost solutions' for low-income consumers. Emerging nations innovate new technologies with time. According to Pansera (2018), frugal innovation is a cost-effective solution that brings sustainability. Frugal innovation focuses on the redesign and restructuring of the products and services to improve quality of life of developing economies. This chapter aims to focus on the how frugal innovation bring technological advancements and social sustainability in developing nations. The major issue of frugal innovation is the lack of attention of researchers and scholars on the new methods and techniques to bring innovation in limited resources.

Figure 4. Dimensions on which firms (frugally) innovate
Source: https://www.pinterest.com/pin/294985844315619672/

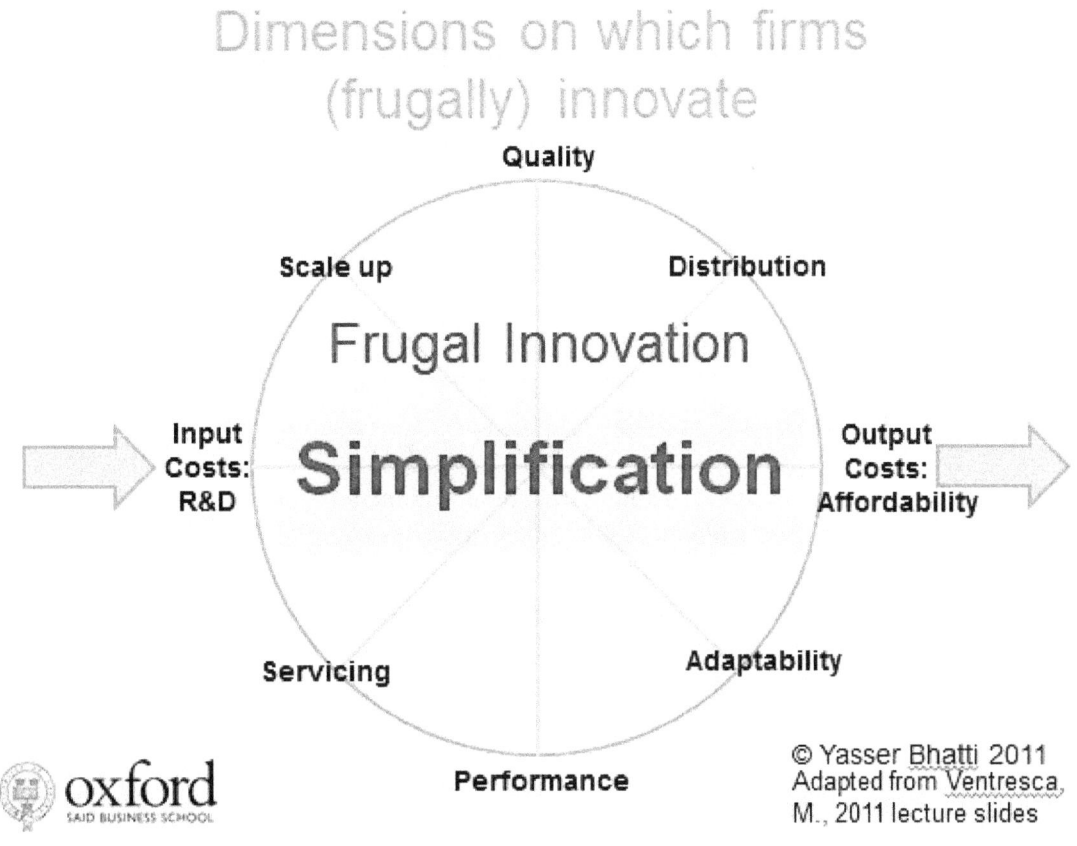

Worldwide, highly affordable technological solutions and improved quality solutions are provided to people through frugal innovation. It impacts the ways businesses operate moving from traditional ways to more innovative ways (Taghizadeh et al., 2016). For instance, in emerging economies, a frugal innovation is used cybercrime (Barclay, 2013). Frugal innovation is recognized an optimal choice for firms in emerging and developing countries which are experiencing consumers demand for frugal products and services characterized by low-cost, focusing on core functionalities and optimized performance (Weyrauch & Herstatt, 2017; Dost et al., 2019). Numerous researchers suggested that frugal innovation is a step for sustainable solutions (Hossain et al., 2021; Wigboldus & Jochemsen, 2021). Frugal innovation influences economic sustainability because it provides a higher level of value to low-income consumers, there is an opportunity to increase firm's sales and profits (Clausen & Fichter, 2019). Frugal innovation contributes towards environmental, economical, and societal development (Albert, 2019).

SOLUTIONS AND RECOMMENDATIONS

It focuses on the redesigns of products and services to achieve optimal performance while preserving core functionalities often exceeding expectations and even leading to breakthrough improvements (Bhatti et al. 2018). In emerging nations, people do not have enough resources to afford advanced technological solutions. Therefore, organizations have started to pay attention on the concept of 'doing more with less'. Worldwide, governments have become more lenient in their policies, and encourage frugal innovation to enhance quality life of common people. Frugal innovation provides cost-effective solutions. There is a need to increase the usage of more advanced processes with low-cost to promote frugal innovation. Organizations focus on customers' desired products and services to fulfill their needs with low-cost. Organizations have prioritized the implementation of sophisticated technologies (Phumbandit, 2021). Current chapter focuses on the role of frugal innovation in technological advancements and social sustainability that is connected with the idea of resource scarcity with quality solutions that are cheaper than the existing products (Hossain, 2020). Frugal innovation is a low-cost solution that is designed and implemented despite financial, technological, material or other resource constraints.

FUTURE RESEARCH DIRECTIONS

This book chapter help to understand that how frugal innovation and social sustainability are improving people's quality of life. This study is useful for scientists, researchers, academicians, students and policy makers to adopt and apply novel approaches of frugal innovation to improve standards of society for emerging nations. For future research, it is recommended to conduct applied research approach to investigate role of frugal innovation and social sustainability. Applied research can be quantitative and qualitative or both. Researchers and scientist should consider the environmental protection element by reviewing a clear vision of frugal innovation. Organizations should replace their products and service with frugal innovation of the existing products and services that will eventually enhance product value, reduce product cost and improve environmental impact. This chapter recommends that that products and services that are produced on the idea of frugal innovation must have reduced price than the product without frugal innovation. Frugal innovation helps to conserve energy, assist in recycling process and reduce pollution. The alternative tools and methods of frugal innovation are switching from electric to solar energy is an example of frugal innovation. It can be done by employing more methods and policies to reduce wastage. Organization should use renewable energy resources such as moving their electric use to solar or hydropower to become self-sufficient. Employees and management's personal involvement and their acts have favorable impacts on frugal innovation and employees will indulge in energy saving, recycling, low-cost technological solutions; therefore, the involvement of employees and management should be ensured.

REFERENCES

Albert, M. (2019). Sustainable frugal innovation-The connection between frugal innovation and sustainability. *Journal of Cleaner Production*, *237*, 117747. doi:10.1016/j.jclepro.2019.117747

Ancarani, F., Frels, J. K., Miller, J., Saibene, C., & Barberio, M. (2014). Winning in rural emerging markets: General electric's research study on MNCs. *California Management Review*, *56*(4), 31–52. doi:10.1525/cmr.2014.56.4.31

Angot, J., & Plé, L. (2015). Serving poor people in rich countries: The bottom-of-the-pyramid business model solution. *The Journal of Business Strategy*, *36*(2), 3–15. doi:10.1108/JBS-11-2013-0111

Barclay, A. E. (2013). Influence, Inspiration or Innovation? The importance of contexts in the Study of Iconography: the Case of the Mistress of Animals in 7th-Century Greece. *Regionalism and Globalism in Antiquity: Exploring Their Limits*, 143-176.

Baskaran, S., & Mehta, K. (2016). What is innovation anyway? Youth perspectives from resource-constrained environments. *Technovation*, *52*, 4–17. doi:10.1016/j.technovation.2016.01.005

Bhatti, M. A., Mat, N., & Juhari, A. S. (2018). Effects of job resources factors on nurses job performance (mediating role of work engagement). *International Journal of Health Care Quality Assurance*, *31*(8), 1000–1013. doi:10.1108/IJHCQA-07-2017-0129 PMID:30415625

Bocken, N. M., & Geradts, T. H. (2020). Barriers and drivers to sustainable business model innovation: Organization design and dynamic capabilities. *Long Range Planning*, *53*(4), 101950. doi:10.1016/j.lrp.2019.101950

Brem, A., & Ivens, B. (2013). Do frugal and reverse innovation foster sustainability? Introduction of a conceptual framework. *Journal of Technology Management for Growing Economies*, *4*(2), 31–50. doi:10.15415/jtmge.2013.42006

Clausen, J., & Fichter, K. (2019). The diffusion of environmental product and service innovations: Driving and inhibiting factors. *Environmental Innovation and Societal Transitions*, *31*, 64–95. doi:10.1016/j.eist.2019.01.003

D'Angelo, V., & Magnusson, M. (2020). A bibliometric map of intellectual communities in frugal innovation literature. *IEEE Transactions on Engineering Management*, *68*(3), 653–666. doi:10.1109/TEM.2020.2994043

Dima, A., Bugheanu, A. M., Dinulescu, R., Potcovaru, A. M., Stefanescu, C. A., & Marin, I. (2022). Exploring the Research Regarding Frugal Innovation and Business Sustainability through Bibliometric Analysis. *Sustainability*, *14*(3), 1326. doi:10.3390u14031326

Dost, M., Pahi, M. H., Magsi, H. B., & Umrani, W. A. (2019). Effects of sources of knowledge on frugal innovation: Moderating role of environmental turbulence. *Journal of Knowledge Management*, *23*(7), 1245–1259. doi:10.1108/JKM-01-2019-0035

Drummond, A. (2012). Research on emerging economies: Challenges are always opportunities. *Global Strategy Journal*, *2*(1), 48–50. doi:10.1002/gsj.1026

Dunk, A. S. (2011). Product innovation, budgetary control, and the financial performance of firms. *The British Accounting Review*, *43*(2), 102–111. doi:10.1016/j.bar.2011.02.004

Fraunhofer ISI & Nesta. (2016). Cheaper, better, more relevant: Is frugal innovation an opportunity for Europe? *Fraunhofer ISI*. http://www.isi.fraunhofer.de/isiwAssets/docs/p/de/projektberichte/FrugalInnovationSummary_ ISI_Nesta_mit-ISI.pdf.

George, G., McGahan, A. M., & Prabhu, J. (2012). Innovation for inclusive growth: Towards a theoretical framework and a research agenda. *Journal of Management Studies*, *49*(4), 661–683. doi:10.1111/j.1467-6486.2012.01048.x

Govindarajan, V., & Ramamurti, R. (2011). Reverse innovation, emerging markets, and global strategy. *Global Strategy Journal*, *1*(3-4), 191–205. doi:10.1002/gsj.23

Hartley, T. C. (2014). *The foundations of European Union law: an introduction to the constitutional and administrative law of the European Union.* Oxford University Press. doi:10.1093/he/9780199681457.001.0001

Hossain, M. (2017). Mapping the frugal innovation phenomenon. *Technology in Society*, *51*, 199–208. doi:10.1016/j.techsoc.2017.09.006

Hossain, M. (2020). Frugal innovation: Conception, development, diffusion, and outcome. *Journal of Cleaner Production*, *262*, 121456. doi:10.1016/j.jclepro.2020.121456

Hossain, M., Levänen, J., & Wierenga, M. (2021). Pursuing frugal innovation for sustainability at the grassroots level. *Management and Organization Review*, *17*(2), 374–381. doi:10.1017/mor.2020.53

Hossain, M., Simula, H., & Halme, M. (2016). Can frugal go global? Diffusion patterns of frugal innovations. *Technology in Society*, *46*, 132–139. doi:10.1016/j.techsoc.2016.04.005

Iqbal, Q., Ahmad, N. H., & Halim, H. A. (2021). Insights on entrepreneurial bricolage and frugal innovation for sustainable performance. *Business Strategy & Development*, *4*(3), 237–245. doi:10.1002/bsd2.147

Khan, R. (2016). How frugal innovation promotes social sustainability. *Sustainability*, *8*(10), 1034. doi:10.3390u8101034

Kwan, B. Y. M., Mbanwi, A., Cofie, N., Rogoza, C., Islam, O., Chung, A. D., Dalgarno, N., Dagnone, D., Wang, X., & Mussari, B. (2021). Creating a competency-based medical education curriculum for Canadian diagnostic radiology residency (Queen's fundamental innovations in residency education)—Part 1: Transition to discipline and foundation of discipline stages. *Canadian Association of Radiologists Journal*, *72*(3), 372–380. doi:10.1177/0846537119894723 PMID:32126802

Lamont, J. (2010). The age of 'Indovation' dawns. *The Financial Times*.

Lizarralde, I., & Tyl, B. (2018). A framework for the integration of the conviviality concept in the design process. *Journal of Cleaner Production*, *197*, 1766–1777. doi:10.1016/j.jclepro.2017.03.108

McCloskey, D. N. (2010). *The bourgeois virtues: Ethics for an age of commerce*. University of Chicago Press.

Niroumand, M., Shahin, A., Naghsh, A., & Peikari, H. R. (2021). Frugal innovation enablers, critical success factors and barriers: A systematic review. *Creativity and Innovation Management*, *30*(2), 348–367. doi:10.1111/caim.12436

OECD. (2009). *Globalisation and Emerging Economies*. OECD Publishing.

Pansera, M. (2018). Frugal or fair? The unfulfilled promises of frugal innovation. *Technology Innovation Management Review*, *8*(4), 6–13. doi:10.22215/timreview/1148

Prahalad, C. K., & Mashelkar, R. A. (2010). Innovation's holy grail. *Harvard Business Review*, *88*(7-8), 132–141.

Radjou, N., & Prabhu, J. (2015). *The frugal way to grow*. Frugal Innovation Hub.

Radjou, N., Prabhu, J., & Ahuja, S. (2012). *Jugaad innovation: Think frugal, be flexible, generate break-through growth*. John Wiley & Sons.

Rao, B. C. (2013). How disruptive is frugal? *Technology in Society*, *35*(1), 65–73. doi:10.1016/j.techsoc.2013.03.003

Rosca, E., Arnold, M., & Bendul, J. C. (2017). Business models for sustainable innovation–an empirical analysis of frugal products and services. *Journal of Cleaner Production*, *162*, S133–S145. doi:10.1016/j.jclepro.2016.02.050

Shafique, I., Ahmad, B., & Kalyar, M. N. (2019). How ethical leadership influences creativity and organizational innovation: Examining the underlying mechanisms. *European Journal of Innovation Management*, *23*(1), 114–133. doi:10.1108/EJIM-12-2018-0269

Shepherd, D. A., Parida, V., & Wincent, J. (2020). The surprising duality of jugaad: Low firm growth and high inclusive growth. *Journal of Management Studies*, *57*(1), 87–128. doi:10.1111/joms.12309

Taghizadeh, S. K., Jayaraman, K., Ismail, I., & Rahman, S. A. (2016). Scale development and validation for DART model of value co-creation process on innovation strategy. *Journal of Business and Industrial Marketing*, *31*(1), 24–35. doi:10.1108/JBIM-02-2014-0033

Tiwari, R., Kalogerakis, K., & Herstatt, C. (2016, July). Frugal innovations in the mirror of scholarly discourse: Tracing theoretical basis and antecedents. In *R&D Management Conference,* Cambridge, UK.

Von Zedtwitz, M., Corsi, S., Søberg, P. V., & Frega, R. (2015). A typology of reverse innovation. *Journal of Product Innovation Management*, *32*(1), 12–28. doi:10.1111/jpim.12181

Weyrauch, T., & Herstatt, C. (2017). What is frugal innovation? Three defining criteria. *Journal of frugal innovation, 2*(1), 1-17.

Wigboldus, S., & Jochemsen, H. (2021). Towards an integral perspective on leveraging sustainability transformations using the theory of modal aspects. *Sustainability Science*, *16*(3), 869–887. doi:10.100711625-020-00851-5

Winterhalter, S., Zeschky, M. B., Neumann, L., & Gassmann, O. (2017). Business models for frugal innovation in emerging markets: The case of the medical device and laboratory equipment industry. *Technovation*, *66*, 3–13. doi:10.1016/j.technovation.2017.07.002

Chapter 6
Frugal Innovations of HRM Practices in SMEs

Samreen Fazal
Greenwich University, Karachi, Pakistan

ABSTRACT

HRM is a significant element of management that positively shapes the performance of SMEs. A plethora of literature studying HRM innovative practices deals with the impact of innovative HR practices encompassing workplace, behavioral, technological, and innovative leadership roles on the firms` efficient and innovative performance. These studies exhibit a substantial and positive influence of the innovative HR practices on the innovative performance driving innovation in firms particularly in SMEs. However, hitherto no prominent effort has been done predominantly in Pakistan to review and synchronize the extant knowledge in a composed manner. Therefore, the proposed chapter aims to consolidate, compile, and review the current literature associated with the innovative trends of HR practices in SMEs. In addition, it also seeks to offer a comprehensive HRM model to promote innovations in HRM practices. To sum up, this chapter will significantly contribute to the existing body knowledge based on HRM innovative practices in SMEs.

INTRODUCTION

Organizational innovations deemed to be critical amid the current stiff competition among the firms (Tidd & Bessant, 2018). Organizational innovation being an umbrella term considers multiple facets (Armbruster *et al.*, 2008; Crossan & Apaydin, 2010) including the reception of novel thoughts or ways of behaving encompassing a system, policy, program, device, process, product or service (Damanpour, 1992). All in all, whatever is new to the firm can be named an advancement. To comprehend the idea of advancement and firms` innovativeness, scientists have recognized various aspects. One of these dimensions distinguishes among service and product developments from one perspective and innovation cycle and firms` advancement on another (Armbruster et al., 2008).

The prior type of innovativeness stresses the organizational outcomes and studied frequently (Pouwels & Koster, 2017). The said innovative approach mirrors the view that innovativeness alludes to the pro-

DOI: 10.4018/978-1-6684-5417-6.ch006

duction of novel outcomes in firms`, which has not been achieved by other organizations or which adds newness to the organizational performance. The second approach regarding organizational innovation emphasizes the enhancement of procedures, highlighting significant strategies for firms to design and manage the organizational processes (Maine *et al.*, 2012).

Considering both the said approaches, innovative HRM deals with both aspects of the developmental literature; On one hand it tries to identify creative and novel human resource (HR) policies and practices to address external pressures, while also inquiring and searching for suitable HR practices and strategies to improve the organizational innovations (as cited in Koster, F. and Benda, L. 2020).

Innovation in HRM Practices

HR (Human Resource) is one of the key principles of management, providing guidance in recruitment, hiring, and development of workforce in any organization. HR is also termed as HRM (Human Resource Management) dealing with managing employees and an organization's culture and environment. In other words, it is a comprehensive approach focusing on the recruitment, management, and general direction of the people who work in an organization. HRM encompasses many practices including, selection, recruitment, workforce planning, employee engagement, organizational design, performance management contract termination, placement, commitment, leadership, loyalty,, change and development, managing attendance and absence, career management, knowledge management, IT in HR, compensation, motivation, rewards, organizational/employee learning, information sharing, diversity management, benefits and services, discipline,, work time control, talent management, equality, ethics, labor relations, health and wellbeing, flexibility, corporate social responsibility, the work–life balance, downsizing, global HRM and communication (Dessler 2008., Truss et al. 2012; Torrington et al. 2011; Redman and Wilkinson 2009). All HR practices are not simultaneously adopted by SMEs and are employed as per the requirement and given situations (Bloom and Van Reenan 2007).

Various organizations utilize, connect, and emphasize HRM practices in a diverse manner. Keeping in view the said dimensions of HRM, the HR managers and relevant staff direly need to practice innovative techniques and methods in recruiting, managing, and developing the work force. In this endeavor, high expertise, skills and current knowledge about the modern trends need to be employed in HRM practices.

Additionally, the boom of a cutting-edge mechanization and the digital transformation made HR practitioners and policy maker to ponder over the frugal innovations in order to make the effective use of employees. Furthermore, the talent diversity caused by globalization has been accelerated, consequently rising a demand for having competent Human Resource Management in firms. HRM professionals need to play a key strategic role through embracing and enabling innovative HRM practices and revising the old processes to introduce innovation at its core. Moreover, they need to encourage work in teams jointly with line managers and other stakeholders in matters such as, planning, decision making, formulating and executing effective HRM policy and practices to achieve organizational strategic objectives (Bamber et al. 2017). Adhering to the involvement of HRM specialists, Koster, F; & Benda, L. (2020) opine that there is a strong propensity among creative scholars to follow specific criteria while measuring innovation, thereby enquiring about the development of novel products or services, exploration of new markets or introduction of innovative processes in enterprises from the informants. In addition, the field of HRM is focused on "best practice" instead of "best fit" measures of innovative HRM.

Alongside the HRM specialists, the human resource has a major influence within the enterprise and play a key role in attaining any sort of innovation. The innovational procedures and cycles are entirely void without the involvement of people. Considering both the radical or incremental innovation, wherever innovation happens, the capacities of the enterprise and people inside it should be saddled successfully to carry out change (as cited in Bamber et al. 2017). Moreover, HR practices at its core offer several methods for fostering employees` engagement, keeping in view the workforce diversity, their profile and specifications. It plays a significant part in devising strategies leading to innovation via working with relevant areas to make, create, and keep up with activities to help and recognize novel inputs and urge and motivate workforce to turn out to be effectively drawn in with the consideration of innovativeness in the routine day to day work (Azevedo et al. 2021).

In addition, effective HRM practices and knowledge management abilities are the paramount factors in fostering exploitative and exploratory innovations in the workplace. Lei, H., Khamkhoutlavong, M. and Le, P.B. (2021). Moreover, transformational leadership, HRM practices and collaborative culture proved to be the vital precursors to foster firm's innovation capability in term of product and process. (Lei., et al 2021).

Innovative HRM practices in SMEs

Resorting to the current context, the frugal innovations of HRM in SMEs refer to the innovative human resource practices employed in small and medium enterprises. HRM practices can be considered the paramount factors having a positive influence on the SMEs outcomes when estimated by the extension of activities and improvement in the productivity of workforce. HRM operations act as strategic asset for innovation and enlightened progress of SMEs experiencing economic turmoil. Hence, it has been evident that promoting and adopting HRM practices in SMEs is pivotal for boosting advancement and innovativeness (Nam, V, H; Luu·H, N, 2021).

Referring to the World Bank, SMEs have played a key role in the elevation of economic conditions among developing countries. In addition, SMEs represent majority of industries across the world acting as significant contributors for creating employment opportunities and economic development globally. To be sure, the Organization for Economic Cooperation and Development approximated that SMEs account for 90% of enterprises and 63% of labor force employed worldwide (Munro, 2013).

In the recently industrialized and developing nations, SMEs have shown to employ the biggest level of human resource and have a major role in creating prospects for generating income sources in global arena (Singh et al 2008). To be specific, these firms offer employment opportunities, maintain supply chain for goods and services on a larger scale to bigger organizations, foster cost-effectiveness and profitability (Rahman 2001), and accelerate the quality transformation progression (Bemonski, 1992). Moreover, they promote workers` morale, reducing the workforce untimely turnover (Shea and Gobeli, 1995).

Bringing innovativeness in SMEs can be a process of influencing employee behavior or a situation enabling innovation in HRM practices. Most of the SMEs tend to adopt the HRM operation models of bigger firms with larger workforce, plans, strict regulations, goals, budgets, remuneration models and compensation policies instead of devising the appropriate models and agile HRM practices considering the requirements of individual SME (Pia et al., 2020). In terms of workplace wellbeing, Pia et al. (2020) emphasized the presence of multiple opportunities through which SMEs can develop more applicable, novel or agile practices considering their specific needs.

SMEs must consider their own organizational needs and accordingly create novelty and develop specific models to promote advanced processes. As a matter of fact, the advanced and agile HRM practices depend on SMEs specific mores, cultural needs and are adopted by the sustainable and healthy organizations fostering innovations in a different way (Pia et al. 2020). Furthermore, small firms seldomly provide formal trainings to managers and they are not properly equipped with skills of executing HRM practices, these enterprises also don't be guaranteed to have any evolved HRM structures, standard HRM procedures, or projects (Heneman and Tansky 2002). SMEs transmit implicit HRM knowledge, hence, making it difficult for codification, understanding and transmission (Klaas et al. 2012). Informal HR practices includes, learning by doing, on-the-job training, observing, and exit interviews with the employees` leaving a job (Cameron et al. 2006). Whereas, agile HRM practices mostly consider recruitment, organizing, leadership, work wellbeing, interaction, flexible working hours, development, work equipment Innovation, work place, organizational cooperation, and work family balance.

Innovation is also enabled by knowledge management. Abubakar et al. (2017) opine that knowledge management is concerned with many aspects including, technology, culture and organizational structures, and human resources practices, making it systematic and standardized method for optimizing firm's innovativeness and knowledge economy. Knowledge-based HRM supports to develop and implement knowledge driven policies for encouraging attitudes and behaviors of workforce towards performance and innovation (Yousaf Al-tal & Emeagwali, 2019). Moreover, Knowledge-based HRM practices include knowledge-based recruitment, knowledge-based performance assessment, knowledge-based compensation, knowledge-based career management, and knowledge-based training and development. Knowledge-based HRM practices being meticulously planned help in fostering organizations` innovations and developing knowledge management processes (Yousaf Al-tal & Emeagwali, 2019).

In addition, Innovative practices and technology used in HR practices have also been under discussion in this chapter. As a matter of fact, still majority of SMEs operating in the developing nations haven`t implemented electronic Human Resource Management (e-HRM) in its true sense being oblivion of its` strong capacity in improving HRM practices regardless of its prominence in the advanced countries (Shah, N., Michael, F., & Chalu, H. 2020). The critical role of SMEs` in generating employment, leading to economic prosperity and their significance in raising GDP is globally recognized. Hence it is affirmative to implement the (e-HRM) in SMEs of developing countries.

Meacham et al., (2017) asserted that human resource management and innovation are interlinked, however, SME leaders and managers most often are incapable to apply or execute expensive HRM practices due to scarce resources (Adla, Gallego, & Calamel, 2020). Best case scenario, HRM is for the most part casual and in-built in SMEs, thus make it challenging for firms to enhance the innovation processes and yield effective and profitable outcomes owing to the betwixt interdependency of HR practices and innovation. (Pia et al., 2020).

Having discussed the innovation, innovation in HRM practices and specifically innovative HRM practices in SMEs fostering innovation, the research purpose will be explained.

PURPOSE OF THE STUDY

Ayoko (2021) suggested a need for the research agenda to explore the connection among SMEs, innovation and HRM and specifically the question of how SMEs could harness the HRM innovative practices for improving their efficiency and competitive advantage. Aligning with the agenda, this chapter tries to present a holistic picture of current innovative trends in HRM practices. The main purpose of this review is to shed some light on a topic that has not been in the mainstream discussion and research hitherto, regardless of being highlighted as a novel research agenda in HRM domain. Furthermore, it seeks to accumulate and thereby offer the diverse aspects of HRM innovations in SMEs in an absolute coherence and propose new research venues for future works. Therefore, the chapter aims to contribute to the existing body knowledge based on HRM innovative practices in SMEs. Hence, offers a substantial addition to the HRM theoretical models. After ascertaining purpose of the study, the key terms used in this chapters are explained and defined in the next paras.

Definitions of Key Terms

Organizational Innovation

Organizational innovation alludes to diverse facets including the adaptation of novel ideas or practices encompassing program, projects, policy, process, system, device, services or products (Armbruster et al., 2008; Crossan & Apaydin, 2010). To sum, the introduction of anything that is new to the firm is considered as an organizational innovation.

HRM Practices

Human resource management (HRM) is an inclusive approach focusing on the process of recruitment, management, and general direction of the people who work in an organization. HRM practices broadly includes: recruitment, selection, compensation, performance appraisal, training and development of the workforce.

Small and Medium Size Enterprises (SMEs)

SMEs account for most of the corporations across the globe. The definition of SMEs, or small and medium-sized enterprises varies world-wide. Its definition depends on the country where a firm is operating, considering the specified size of SME. The classification or sizing of an enterprise as an SME based on the country considers a variety of features. These elements encompass the number of assets owned by the company, number of employees, market capitalization, annual sales, or any merger of the said characteristics. To be more specific, SMEs are autonomous enterprises having fewer than 50 employees. Nevertheless, the maximum figure of th work force varies across different countries. In Pakistan`s perspective, SMEs refer to a company with up to 250 employees, having annual sales up to Rs.250 million and paid-up capital up to Rs.25 million (as cited in Waheed., et al 2020. P. 167). Despite the diverse range of definitions, there is a mutual consent among many countries in defining an SME in order to differentiate small and medium-sized corporations from large organizations (Ward, 2020).

Electronic Human Resource Management (E-HRM)

E-HRM can be termed as the integration of IT and the arena of HRM. It emphasizes all the HRM content that is shared through IT aiming to bring distinctiveness, efficiency, consistency, quality standard in HRM procedures and proposing long-standing prospects for targeted clienteles within and across corporations

(Bondarouk et al., 2017a). To add, it enables transmitting knowledge and information to employees via the Internet. Thus, E- HRM is a key enabler of executing the HR practices, policies and strategies using technological help.

Workplace Innovation

Innovation in the workplace refers to the process of introducing new ideas, services, products, business processes, or methodologies in a work environment. Dul and Ceylan (2011) elucidated twenty-one HR mechanisms improving innovation and novelty with a focus mainly on the key ones namely, job challenges, creative objectives supervisor mentoring, recognition of creative ideas, job rotation, self-sufficiency in the job, incentives, time for thinking, and teamwork. Likewise, Jiang et al. (2012) asserted the significant influence of good HR practices on enhancing work force creativity and organizational innovation. Effective HR practices tend to have a positive impact on workplace creativity in recruitment process, work delegation, rewards, and cooperation etc. Workplace innovation comprised of behavioral, developmental and technological innovation in organizations for meeting the company`s objectives effectively and efficiently. Literature review encompassing innovation of HRM practices in SMEs will be uncovered in the succeeding para.

LITERATURE REVIEW

Considering the frugal innovation of HRM practices in SMEs, the business pages of popular journals are adding up with novel HR practices that have overturned existing ways of working and significantly reformed human experiences. Keeping in view the context of this topic, the literature review section covers the extant literature related to the innovative HR practices in SMEs. Wherein, studies dealing with the innovative HR practices in SMEs dealing with the workplace innovations, employees behavioral or developmental innovations in SMEs and technological innovations of HR in SMEs are discussed.

Buisson et al. (2021) tracked down that the direction of inventive SMEs comprises of systematic arrangements to make the employees` competent and develop HRM practices during a specific duration. Moreover, the HRM practices find it hard to assist an enterprise undergoing innovation and advancement, rather making it challenging for firms to introduce creativity. The authors, therefore, identified a critical role of the Human Resources Foundation's (HRF's) standing and support in endorsing diversified SMEs' innovation trajectories in a very contingent dynamic perspective.

Regarding the innovative HR practices in SMEs, Gede Riana (2020) emphasized the importance of implementing HRM practices encompassing recruitment, participation, training, performance assessment, and reward management fostering firms` improved performance through enabling innovations. However, organizational proficiencies in terms of introducing innovation do not essentially create a competitive edge, nonetheless, the firms` efforts in effectively deploying the innovative abilities to mold or improve the effective HRM system for favorable outcomes considered to be critical. Moreover, Adla et al (2020) linked HRM and innovate processes by proposing a dynamic and contextualized model consisting of three steps: freeing up gifts, mobilizing them and rethinking them. A gift can take the following forms: support, time, information, knowledge, advice, etc. Through a case study of French SME, they have found that intense social ties, uniting the manager with some of his or her employees, remained at the heart of the link between HRM and innovation in SMEs. Placing gift/counter-gift in the relationship between HRM and innovation highlights the prominent place of employees in SMEs. Moreover, the technological know-how of the gift/counter-gift software has also been resulted in the upgradation and development of employees.

Considering an effective and innovative HR practices, Sardi et al (2021) further endorsed that HRM is a key driving force in the formation of organizational performance measurement and management systems. The authors propose a few key features need to be developed for ensuring robust HRM processes in the target organizations. Firstly, the adaptation of several characteristics when creating a balanced PMMS, i.e., democratic, and participative in performance measurement and management. Secondly, PMMS being based on real-time and visual measurement leading to democratic and participative performance management. Moreover, they indicate that easily accessible and customized performance measurement enhances self-performance management and continuous knowledge sharing, while collaborative performance management encourages high maturity performance measurement thus fostering innovation in HR practices.

Similarly, in a study regarding High-performance work systems, Shahzad et al. (2019) describes how HPWS impacts innovation performance in SMEs through providing a lucid knowledge regarding the fundamental mechanism driving novelty in firms. Results established the importance of employees' innovation-specific abilities, motivation and voice opportunities for innovative outcomes. Moreover, it was suggested that SMEs need to equip the work force with requisite capabilities, motivation and freedom of speech through the implementation of a bunch of HRM practices called HPWS.

In addition, Pia, H et al. (2020) made a significant contribution to the discussion of HRM practices in SMEs by elaborating and analyzing the key role of agility in organizational effectiveness. The authors proposed eleven HRM dimensions including some form of agility processes. Each HRM function cannot implement or utilize the agile practices to the same extent. The most highlighted agile HRM practices covered recruitment, organizing, workplace, work wellbeing, work equipment, development, organizational cooperation, interaction, work family balance, flexible working hours,

and leadership. Furthermore, they provided the following meaningful and viable solutions to tackle the challenges faced by the above mentioned agile HRM practices. Hence, authors advocate the agile HRM practices need to consider cultural needs of each SMEs', also the execution of these practices require audacity, informed decision making and a readiness of a firm to perform activities in a best suited manner. Accepting new challenges and trying novel and viable ideas and HRM practices proved to improve innovations, encourage cooperation and participation acting as the critical drivers for making the developing enterprises agile and resilient.

Another key effort done by (Nam, & Luu, 2021) focused on the HRM practices determining different categories of innovation such as, human and physical capital assets considering a transition economy in Veitnam with a focus on SMEs. Findings asserted significant improvement in standards of working human and physical capital assets after adjusting the endogenous difficulties faced by SMEs. These problems were managed through modifying the instrumental variables of HRM practices, while focusing on benefits and rewards to employees. Furthermore, HRM practices found to be crucial in positively influencing a few aspects of innovation in SMEs. They concluded that SMEs adopting more HRM practices are more likely to introduce innovations and bring advancement in the existing products.

Considering the employees behavioral and developmental paradigm, Yousaf Al-tal & Emeagwali (2019) confirmed that knowledge-based HRM practices positively effect knowledge management capacity of SMEs. Researchers recommend that the drive of SMEs to grow their knowledge management capabilities depends on the quality of their human resource. They further advise managers to implement knowledge based HRM strategies to foster a work climate that will maximize the advantages of KMS. Additionally, when knowledge based HRM processes are strengthened with appropriate knowledge management capacity and intellectual capital, process and product innovation are attained. Hence, managers need to promote teamwork among their employees so that knowledge can be explored, developed, and shared. Practically, the top management of organization can gain insights of knowledge based HRM practices in order to transforming their human capital into organizational success. Similarly, Abubakar et al. (2017) also studied the element of knowledge management consisting of knowledge acquisition, knowledge distribution and responsiveness to knowledge. Despite current resource and financial constraints, the study found that knowledge management adoption stimulated innovation in Balochistan's SMEs. The researchers argued that because more SMEs are uninformed of this process and the companies are also unable to leverage internal resources, the benefits associated with the notion of knowledge management are not completely grasped by SMEs. Hence, this study proposed the sound knowledge management for SMEs to use internal resources efficiently in order to develop competitive advantage.

Extending the literature on knowledge management and HR innovations, Asada, A. et al. (2020) examined the impact of external knowledge (EK), internal innovation (II) and knowledge management (KM) on firm's open innovation OI performance in

Bahawalpur district, Pakistan. Results revealed the key contribution of both external as well as internal knowledge in enhancing OI open innovation. Authors suggest that efficient KM is most important for maximizing the benefits of EK and II. KM plays a significant role in organizing various ideas and putting them into practice within the confines of the company. Therefore, KM is crucial in getting benefit as much as possible from EK and II. Likewise, Iqbal, S. et al. (2021) examined the relationship of knowledge-oriented leadership (KOL), knowledge management (KM) behavior and innovation performance in 32 small project-based software firms in Pakistan. Result displayed the positive interrelation of knowledge-oriented leadership with knowledge management behavior and innovation performance. Furthermore, knowledge management strengthens the association between KOL and innovation performance.

Regarding the technological innovations in HRM, Abdullah et al. (2020) asserted that because the amount of company data is growing rapidly, SMEs have significant issues in terms of flexibility, scalability, cost, and efficiency. Additionally, the dispersed locations of HRs provide a communication gap, which slows down decision-making, wastes data processing time, and prevents quick responses to environmental difficulties. The researchers investigated the idea of using cloud computing services to handle the vast data to improve HRM where the data stored at a central location to address the afore-mentioned concerns. The authors concluded that SMEs systems are undergoing a radical transformation. Due to the advantages it provides, such as the ability for SMEs to grow, the cloud technology is increasingly being used by SMEs to manage HR procedures successfully owing to the benefits it offers including the ability for SMEs to grow, flexible HR management, simple decision-making for managers, and an improvement in business efficiency. The report also revealed that for SMEs, cost savings is one of the biggest benefits of cloud adoption, with security serving as the main roadblock. The study also showed that reduced cost is one of the most important advantages of cloud adoption for SMEs while security being the most crucial barrier. The majority of contemporary and cutting-edge HRM solutions focus on resolving HRM issues in various life sectors and evaluate the advantages and disadvantages of adopting cloud technology from the viewpoint of the business. New technology approaches were also put up by Pia, H. et al. (2020), including mobile devices, cellphones, and software applications enabling work processes in a better way.

The adoption of EHRM procedures paved way to the efficient personnel management. In this context, Alkhodary (2021) reveals insight into the idea of Recruitment E performance management and E-learning and found the association of EHRM and Corporate Sustainability and determined the driving forces of E-Recruitment E performance management and E-learning in fostering CS Jordan`s SMEs. The author emphasized the positive influence of EHRM on SMEs CS in the context of Jordan. Since it offers benefits of cost savings, flexible services, and employee participation to attain competitive advantage, EHRM plays a crucial role in enhancing corporate sustainability.

Moreover, Waheed et al. (2020) discussed the predictors of E-HRM implementation and adoption in Pakistan`s SMEs of manufacturing industries. Researchers identified the attitudes of employees` towards E-HRM to be strongly influential in E-HRM execution phase. They further asserted that enterprise can maximize the capability of enhancing existing HRM practices through the integration of advanced technologies and knowledge. Moreover, constantly employing E-HRM competencies and knowledge tend to augment the HR performance positively. In addition, Waheed et al. (2020) brought forward some meaningful suggestions to the authoritative bodies, like initiating different coordinated projects with technical institutes may benefit SMEs to secure E-HRM implementation processes. Additionally, the government might also offer SMEs some incentives and subsidies to help them implement E-HRM. Organizations can establish training programs to increase the effectiveness of E-HRM. To transmit HR expertise and provide training for the successful implementation of EHRM, the government could conduct a conference and invite worldwide HR experts. Most importantly, E-HRM should be taught as a subject at universities to adequately prepare recent graduates and must be considered as a need of the hour.

To sum up the debate of EHRM practices, as per Bhosale, G. A., & Bagul, D. B. (2021), E-HRM is a technique for implementing HR plans, policies, and practices in businesses with a cognizant and coordinated assistance of and/or full exploitation of web technology-based networks. Researchers reviewed literature related to EHRM and examined the concept from various angles and deemed it to be quite beneficial as compared to the conventional HRM. They further added that some researchers have pointed out that organizations are in the process of migrating to EHRM and it would take some time for them to completely digitalize there HR management. The changes in the environment, for example, globalization, mechanical developments, and information-based economy, and the rapid pace of these changes are driving the endeavors to make more creative methods of working together and business measures. This rapid transformation has additionally influenced and adjusted human resources divisions' method of business. The author therefore suggested that it is in the interest of the organizations to adopt EHRM practices to reap various advantages that it has over conventional HRM.

RESEARCH METHODOLOGY

The research method employed in this chapter is qualitative and inductive in nature, while adopting interpretivism by analyzing the extant literature related to the topic under study. In this endeavor, the current area of study is cleaved into sub domains in order to ascertain the emerging trends in innovative HRM capabilities and most importantly, the significant impacts of avant-garde HRM on SMES.

The studies are selected through purposive sampling technique, and the reason being picking up the most appropriate, latest and relevant literature. The online search encompasses journal articles, book chapters and proceedings. The advance search is limited to workplace innovation, behavioral innovation, and technological innovation in combination with HRM and SMEs. In this regard, literature dealing with the forms or emerging trends of HRM innovations (workplace, digital) and their positive impacts on the employees` productivity and behavior is being considered.

However, the limitations from the article could be by the limited resources from the databases with specific keywords and the time frame of last five years. Moreover, the challenges faced by SMES in incorporating innovative HRM practices also served as the limitation of this chapter. In addition, literature review is taken from the developing countries but centered on Pakistan, hence, depicts a narrow picture about the current topic. Based on the end results of the search, themes are generated and are discussed in detail.

Theoretical Framework

The **seven-step model** Postulated by Williams (2018) has been adopted as a theoretical framework for a comprehensive analysis of literature. However, the data bases used in this chapter are different from the said framework data bases. This model indicates that the scholarly works needs to be reviewed following the seven steps:

1. First, the study motivation and topic of interest need to be identified.
2. Searching for initial list of relevant studies in a Web of Science, Scopus and bibliographic database.
3. Filtering and tallying articles from databases to remove overlaps.
4. Scrutinizing articles inline with themes and research purpose.
5. Arranging and organizing major themes from relevant studies.
6. Comprehensive analysis and synthesis of identified themes to develop conceptual framework.
7. Presentation of the results and findings in accordance with study objective.

LITERATURE REVIEW (CRUX)

The literature crux of this chapter is presented graphically. Graphical presentation provides a vivid picture and orients the reader in a suitable manner. Here, the themes and subthemes of innovative HR practices in SMEs dealing with the workplace innovations, employees behavioral or developmental innovations in SMEs and technological innovations of HR in SMEs are presented as a conceptual research framework and are discussed step wise.

ANALYSIS

The chapter provides a comprehensive review of the extant literature dealing with the innovative HR practices in SME sector. The review encompasses studies associated with the innovative HR including workplace innovation, behavioral or developmental innovation and technological innovation driving innovative performance in SMEs. Findings highlight the pivotal role of innovative HRM practices in fostering innovation in SMEs. The workplace or behavioral innovation depict Human Resource Foundation's (HRF's) positioning, innovative HRM Practices including recruitment, selection, training, reward and compensation, employees` supporting attitude, knowledge management capacity, Customized performance measurement and collaborative performance management, Employers` support, time, information, knowledge, advice to employees in a form of gifts, and high performance work systems (HPWS) to be the catalysts for SMEs innovation. Moreover, efficient treating and utilization of social capital including physical and human capital, knowledge-oriented leadership and agile HRM practices covering recruitment, organizing, workplace, work wellbeing, work equipment, development, organi-

Figure 1. Research Model for HRM Workplace and Behavioral Innovation

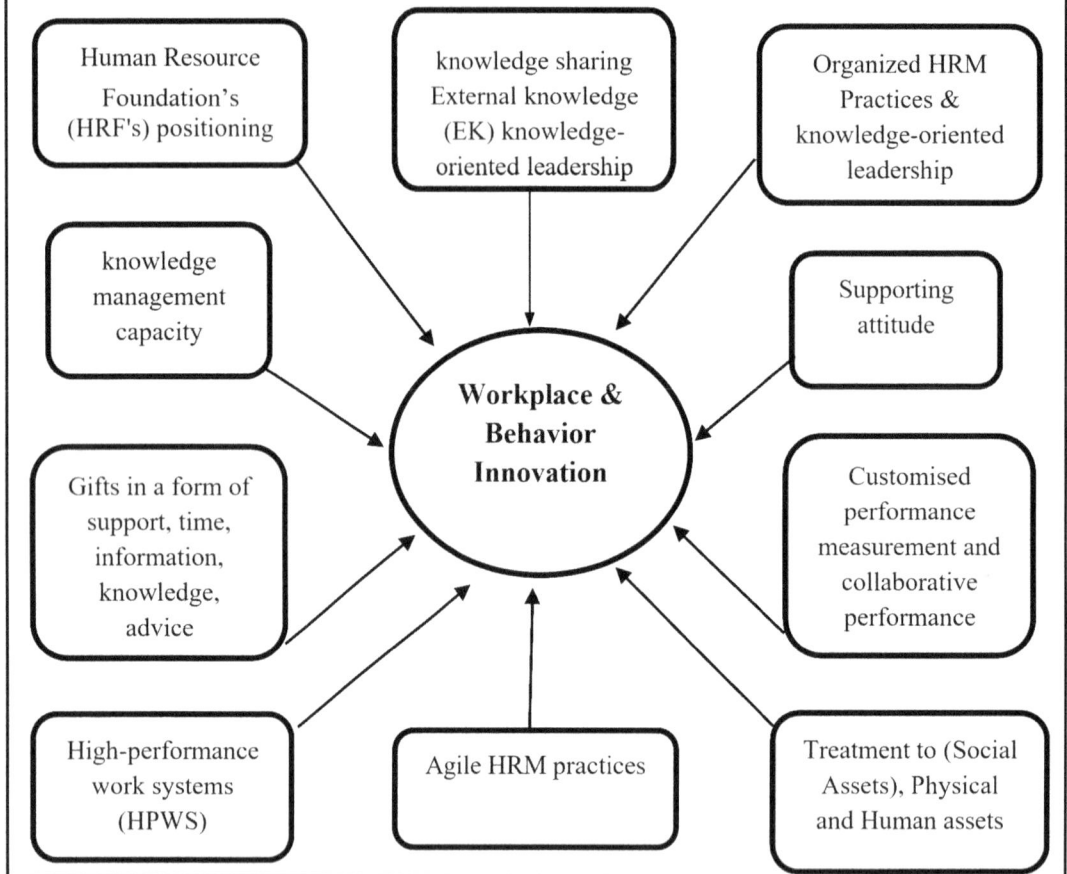

zational cooperation, interaction, work family balance, flexible working hours, and leadership proved to be the precursors for introducing innovation in SMEs.

The analysis drawn from the existing body knowledge pictured the nexus between HRM practices and Innovation in SMEs. Wherein, different studies examined the concept of HRM and innovation from different angles while studying the direct or indirect impacts or through employing mediators or moderators. The mediators or moderators deemed to be the critical elements and have been included in the prospect innovative model proposed in this chapter. A detailed discussion about the purpose of the study, its findings and future recommendations are highlighted in the discussion section.

DISCUSSION AND WAY FORWARD

It has been evident from this study that organized and innovative HR practices yield innovative capabilities in SMEs. As a matter of fact, the rapid globalization and technological advancement demand the state -of -the- art capabilities from the firms. In this pursuit, the top decision makers, managers and employees` need to harness the ever-changing dynamics of contemporary world through innovative HR

Figure 2. Research Model for HRM Technological Innovation

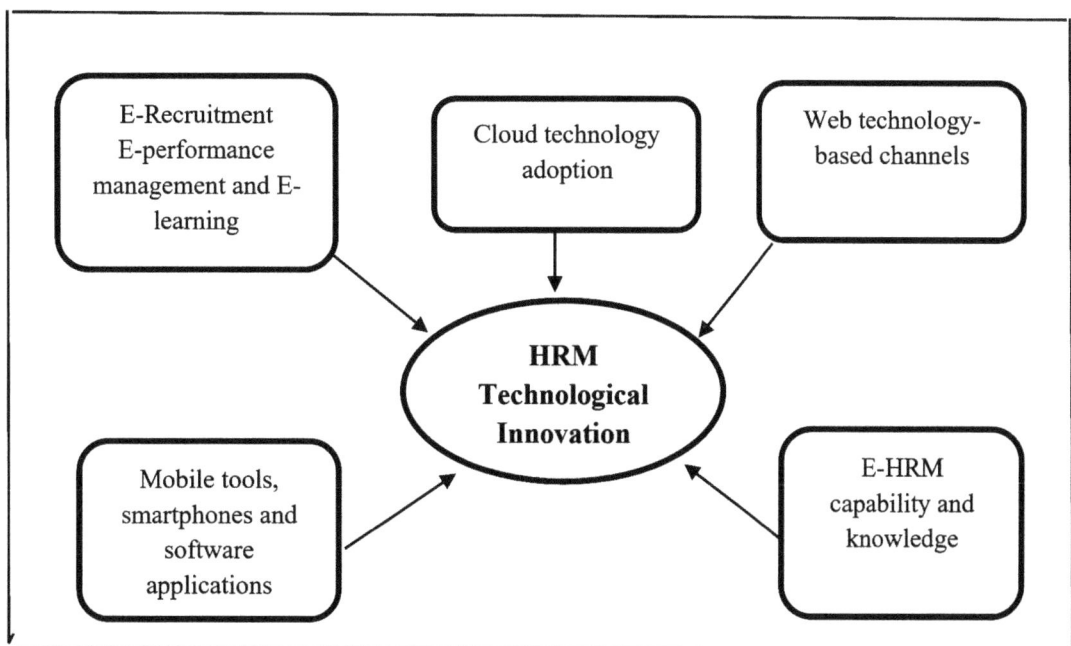

practices and healthy cooperation. Analysis highlights the key role of management in fostering performance and ultimately promoting innovation in SMEs. Hence, it can be said that systematic and organized HR practices have a positive impact on firms` innovation. Keeping in view the importance of leadership and management roles, it is therefore suggested to the policy makers, HR managers and consultants to promote novelty in the work experiences of employees and endorse favorable learning behavior and attitude in personnel. Furthermore, consistent training and developmental initiatives can be deemed as critical requisites for improving employees` knowledge capabilities and skills.

Considering the limitation of this chapter, prospect researchers may study the challenges in introducing and implementing innovative HR practices. Moreover, the region can be broadened by offering cross cultural dynamics of HR innovative practices. In addition, future topic may examine the transformation of HR innovative trends by extending the time frame to two decades.

In summary, it can be stated that this chapter has categorically added something significant to the existing literature associated with Innovation and Innovative HRM practices. To add, the theoretical model extracted from the data serve as a guideline for the prospect research scholars and management bodies.

REFERENCES

Abdullah, P., Zeebaree, S., Shukur, H., & Jacksi, K. (2020). HRM System using Cloud Computing for Small and Medium Enterprises (SMEs). *Technology Reports of Kansai University.*, *62*, 1977–1987.

Abubakar, A. M., Elrehail, H., Alatailat, M. A., & Elçi, A. (2017). Knowledge management, decision-making style and organizational performance. *Journal of Innovation & Knowledge*. doi:10.1016/j. jik.2017.07.003

Adla, L., Gallego-Roquelaure, V., & Calamel, L. (2020). Human resource management and innovation in SMEs. *Personnel Review*, *49*(8), 15191535. doi:10.1108/PR-09-2018-0328

Alkhodary, D. (2021). The Impact of E-HRM on Corporates Sustainability: A Study on the SMEs in Jordan. *International Journal of Entrepreneurship*, *25*(6), 1–15.

Armbruster, H., Bikfalvi, A., Kinkel, S., & Lay, G. (2008). Organizational innovation: The challenge of measuring non-technical innovation in large-scale surveys. *Technovation*, *28*(10), 644–657. doi:10.1016/j.technovation.2008.03.003

Ayoko, O. (2021). SMEs, innovation and human resource management. *Journal of Management & Organization*. *27*(1), 1-5. doi:10.1017/jmo.2021.8

Bamber, G., Bartram, T., & Stanton, P. (2017). HRM and workplace innovations: Formulating research questions. *Personnel Review*, *46*(7), 1216–1227. doi:10.1108/PR-10-2017-0292

Bhosale, G. A., & Bagul, D. B. (2021). Concept Of E-HRM: A Review of Literature. *International Interdisciplinary Research Journal.*, *11*(1), 313317.

Bondarouk, T., Harms, R., & Lepak, D. (2017a). Does e-HRM lead to better HRM service? *International Journal of Human Resource Management*, *28*(9), 1332–1362. doi:10.1080/09585192.2015.1118139

Buisson, M.-L., Gastaldi, L., Geffroy, B., Lonceint, R. and Krohmer, C. (2021). Innovative SMEs in search of ambidexterity: a challenge for HRM! *Employee Relations, 43*(2), 479-495. . doi:10.1108/ER-04-2020-0176

Cameron, A., Coetzer, A., Lewis, K., Claire, M., & Candice, H. (2006). *HR Management Practices: Home-Grown, But Effective*. Chartered Accountants Journal.

Crossan, M. M., & Apaydin, M. (2010). A multi-dimensional framework of organizational innovation: A systematic review of the literature. *Journal of Management Studies*, *47*(6), 1154–1191. doi:10.1111/j.1467-6486.2009.00880.x

Damanpour, F. (1992). Organizational size and innovation. *Organization Studies*, *13*(3), 375–402. doi:10.1177/017084069201300304

Dul, J., & Ceylan, C. (2011). Work environments for employee creativity. *Ergonomics*, *54*(1), 12–20. doi:10.1080/00140139.2010.542833 PMID:21181585

Rahman, S.-U. (2001, March). Evidence from small and medium enterprises in Western Australia. *Total Quality Management*, *12*(2), 201–210. doi:10.1080/09544120120011424

Heneman, R. L., & Tansky, J. W. (2002). Human resource management models for entrepreneurial opportunity: Existing knowledge and new directions. In Katz J. and Welbourne T. M. (eds.) Managing people in entrepreneurial organizations. 5, 55–82. JAI Press. doi:10.1016/S1074-7540(02)05004-3

Jiang, J., Wang, S., & Zhao, S. (2012). Does HRM facilitate employee creativity and organizational innovation? A study of Chinese firms. *International Journal of Human Resource Management*, *23*(19), 4025–4047. doi:10.1080/09585192.2012.690567

Jianwu, J; Shuo, W & Shuming, Z. (2012). Does HRM facilitate employee creativity and organizational innovation? A study of Chinese firms. *The International Journal*.

Klaas, B. S., Semadeni, M., Klimchak, M., & Ward, A.-K. (2012). High-performance work system implementation in small and medium enterprises: A knowledge creation perspective. *Human Resource Management, 51*(4), 487–510. doi:10.1002/hrm.21485

Koster, F. and Benda, L. (2020). Innovative human resource management: measurement, determinants and outcomes. *International Journal of Innovation Science, 12*(3), 287-302.

Maine, E., Lubik, S., & Garnsey, E. (2012). Process-based vs product-based innovation: Value creation nanotech ventures. *Technovation, 32*(3/4), 179–179. doi:10.1016/j.technovation.2011.10.003

Munro, D. (2013). *A guide to financing SMEs*. Palgrave Shaming. doi:10.1057/9781137373786

Nam, V. H., & Luu, H. N. (2021). How Do Human Resource Management Practices Affect Innovation of Small- and Medium-sized Enterprises in a Transition Economy? *Journal of Interdisciplinary Economics*. doi:10.1177/02601079211032119

Pia, H, Riitta. F, Astikainen, & Kultalahti, S. (2020). Agile HRM practices of SMEs. *Journal of Small Business Management, 58*(6), pp.1291-1306. Routledge. . doi:10.1111/jsbm.12483

Pouwels, I., & Koster, F. (2017). Inter-organizational cooperation and organizational innovativeness. A comparative study. *International Journal of Innovation Science, 9*(2), 184–204. doi:10.1108/IJIS-01-2017-0003

Gede Riana, I., Suparna, G., Gusti Made Suwandana, I., Kot, S., & Rajiani, I. (2020, February 12). Human resource management in promoting innovation and organizational performance. *Problems and Perspectives in Management, 18*(1), 107–118. doi:10.21511/ppm.18(1).2020.10

Rahman, S. U. (2001). Total quality management practices and business outcome: doi:10.1108/ER-03-2020-0101

Riana, I. G., Suparna, G., Suwandana, I. G. M., Kot, S., & Rajiani, I. (2020). Human resource management in promoting innovation and organizational performance.

Sardi, A., Sorano, E., Garengo, P., & Ferraris, A. (2021). The role of HRM in the innovation of performance measurement and management systems: A multiple case study in SMEs. *Employee Relations, 43*(2), 589–606. doi:10.1108/ER-03-2020-0101

Shah, N., Michael, F., & Chalu, H. (2020). Conceptualizing challenges to electronic human resource management (e-HRM) adoption: A case of Small and Medium Enterprises (SMEs) in Tanzania. *Asian Journal of Business and Management, 8*(4). doi:10.24203/ajbm.v8i4.6066

Shahzad, K., Arenius, P., Muller, A., Rasheed, M. A., & Bajwa, S. U. (2019). Unpacking the relationship between high-performance work systems and innovation performance in SMEs. *Personnel Review, 48*(4), 977–1000. doi:10.1108/PR-10-2016-0271

Singh, R. K., Garg, S. K., & Deshmukh, S. G. (2008). Strategy development by SMEs for competitiveness: A review. *Benchmarking: An International Journal, 15*(5), 525–547. doi:10.1108/14635770810903031

Tidd, J., & Bessant, J. R. (2018). *Managing Innovation: integrating Technological, Market and Organizational Change*. John Wiley and Sons.

Waheed, A., Xiaoming, M., Waheed, S., Ahmad, N., & Tian-tian, S. (2020). E-HRM implementation, adoption and its predictors: A case of small and medium enterprises of Pakistan. *International Journal of Information Technology and Management*, *19*(23), 162–180. doi:10.1504/IJITM.2020.106217

Ward, S. (2020). SMEs: What Are They? *The Balance Small Business*. https://www. The balance smb.com.

Williams, J. K. (2018). A Comprehensive Review of Seven Steps to a Comprehensive Literature Review. *Qualitative Report*, *23*(2). doi:10.46743/2160-3715/2018.3374

ADDITIONAL READING

Khan, S. (2021). Exploring the firm's influential determinants pertinent to workplace innovation. *Problems and Perspectives in Management*, *19*(1), 272–280. doi:10.21511/ppm.19(1).2021.23

Samma, M., Zhao, Y., Rasool, S. F., Han, X., & Ali, S. (2020). Exploring the Relationship between Innovative Work Behavior, Job Anxiety, Workplace Ostracism, and Workplace Incivility: Empirical Evidence from Small and Medium Sized Enterprises (SMEs). *Health Care*, *8*(4), 508. doi:10.3390/healthcare8040508 PMID:33238510

Zia, N. U. (2020). Knowledge-oriented leadership, knowledge management behaviour and innovation performance in project-based SMEs. The moderating role of goal orientations. *Journal of Knowledge Management*, *24*(8), 18191839. doi:10.1108/JKM-02-2020-0127

Chapter 7
How Frugal Innovation Is Transitioning Human Life and Improving Quality of Life in the Digital Era

Nosheen Rafiq
Bahria University, Pakistan

Syed Haider Ali Shah
Bahria University, Pakistan

Rafia Amjad
Bahria University, Pakistan

Ozair Ijaz Kiani
Bahria University, Pakistan

ABSTRACT

The chapter is about the role of frugal innovation and how it improves overall quality of life in digital era. The development of any state depends upon the level of advanced technology, but all states are not in a sound enough condition to use expensive technology to enhance quality of life. Therefore, such economies go towards the idea of frugal innovation where it offers 'low price' solutions that provide quality products and improve standard of living. It also focuses on the idea of environmental protection as well. This chapter focuses on how frugal innovation can reduce the emission of carbon dioxide, wastage, excess usage of water, and participate in environmental sustainability. This chapter suggests the need of scientists and researchers and their leading role in enhancing frugal innovation

DOI: 10.4018/978-1-6684-5417-6.ch007

INTRODUCTION

There is no signal agreed upon universally accepted definition of the frugal innovation (Hossain, 2020). However, the role of the frugal innovation has great impact on the utilization of resources in terms of environmental sustainability (Albert 2019; Shah et al., 2021; Ghazali et al., 2022). Various studies have investigated the relationship of frugal innovation and business sustainability and presented multiple results. Study conducted by the Hossain, (2020), advocated that frugal innovation idea is more successful when it provides the quality service or solution but that are cheaper than the existing product. Furthermore, it paves the way for first step towards sustainability initiatives (Van Mossel et al., 2018). Even though, the idea of frugal innovation is not revolve around the reducing cost only (Weyrauch & Herstatt, 2017). Frugal innovation also tends towards redesigning both, product and services to perform and offer the better services, functionalities, moreover, going beyond the expectations of satisfaction through improvement in the service or product (Bhatti et al., 2018). Further literature provides the evidences and studies have shown that due to frugal innovation, it has changed the dynamics of the organizational production and service as compare to the traditional production. Due to this the competition has also become stiff and challenging because of the low-income market segment shifted to high income market (Clausen and Fichter, 2019). It can further be argued that the ole of frugal innovation the is undeniable impact on the economic level, society level and environmentally friendly practices (Albert, 2019), by developing the cheap products that are affordable and valuable either in developed countries or in developing countries (Winkler et al., 2020) which provides the support for the trend of frugal innovation (Hossain, 2020). In literature, studies have argued that many authors linked and related the frugal innovation to be closely linked and suggested the significant impact on environment as the basic purpose of the frugal innovation is the to minimize the cost which translate into the economize the use of energy while taking care of the resources during production as well as in the designing phase (Hossain et al., 2021).

After the extensive literature, various studies suggested that due to process of frugal innovation the amount of carbon footprint is smaller or with fewer emissions (Albert, 2019). The major concern of the frugal innovation is the taking care of sustainability, economic and social impact. The social impact is in the form of raising the living standard of the low-income consumer by providing them the cost saving opportunities and to save money (Hossain, 2020). Furthermore, the saving cost of such consumers can be helpful for their personal development, to buy new products or to utilise that amount in the leisure activities which improves their quality of life (Khan, 2016). In terms of the economic impact, there is the opportunity for the organization to offer the product of high value to low-income consumers and to minimise their sales and expand business operations to the next level while also conserving the environmental factors (Bocken et al., 2014).

However, besides the multiple benefits of the frugal innovation, it is still less understanding and empirical evidence to show and prove the relationship of frugal innovation and sustainability (D'Angelo and Magnusson, 2020). Moreover, the frugal innovation is getting popularity not only in the developing countries but also in the developed countries. For example, in the United States, since 1970s, there is decline in the overall middle-income households and the gap of inequality is widening and there are variety of the factors but the experts are also not sure upon why this is expanding Hossain, 2020). Similarly, in Europe this phenomenon is occurring over the last two decades. This pattern has been declared as far-reaching impact on behavioural aspect of the western markets where consumers are facing the challenge of limited spending power. This reflects the notion that the concept of the low-income consumer is no

Figure 1.
Source: https://www.google.com/imgres?imgurl=https%3A%2F%2Fars.els-cdn.com%2Fcontent%2Fimage%2F1-s2.0-
S0160791X20313117-gr1.jpg&imgrefurl=https%3A%2F%2Fwww.sciencedirect.com%2Fscience%2Farticle%2Fpi-
i%2FS0160791X20313117&tbnid=KFdrv2KdFEE0NM&vet=12ahUKEwiLhN-Un7T6AhXBjtgFHdqCCtsQMygAegU
IARCgAQ..i&docid=BB3Z_3hTZLTABM&w=533&h=230&itg=1&q=different%20dimensions%20of%20frugal%20
innovation&hl=en&ved=2ahUKEwiLhN-Un7T6AhXBjtgFHdqCCtsQMygAegUIARCgAQ

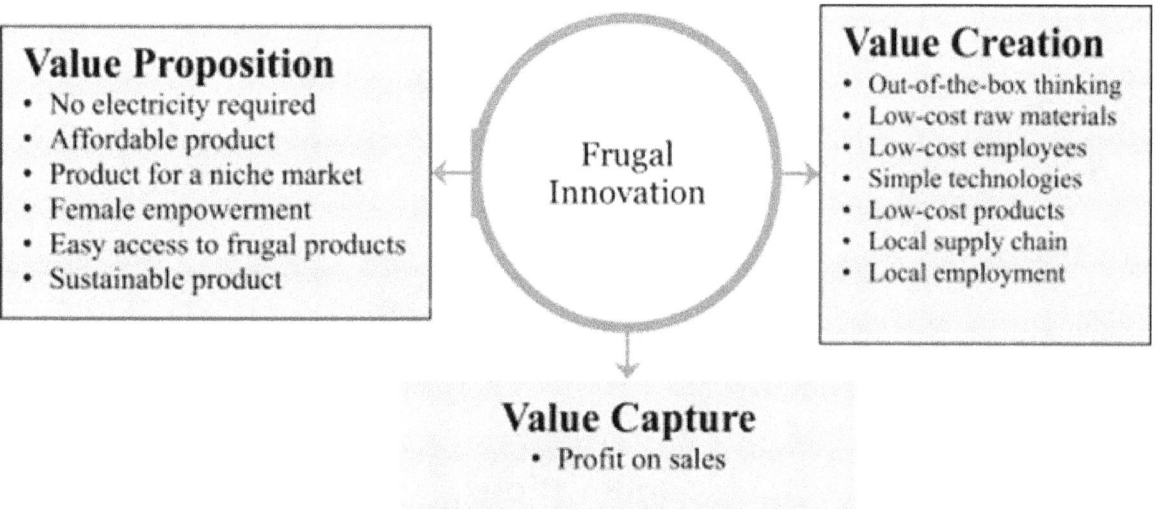

longer restricted to the developing countries but also occurred in the developed countries (Levänen et al., 2022). Furthermore, this phenomena is more accelerated by the covid-19 pandemic (IMF, 2020).

Despite of the fact that spending power of the low-income households has declined but this provides the opportunity to the business firms to attract these low income households though the sustainable products and services while considering for the frugal innovation which is offering the products with cheap rates and considering the environmental sustainability. Thus, frugal innovation can be utilised to capture that low end market and to be successful in that market. (Gordon & Hodgson, 2017).

Similarly, the challenges with the frugal innovation are developing and offering the product with resource efficient and user friendly while considering the novelty as well. In the frugal innovation the big challenges appear in the form of societal sustainability challenges, economic and operational level constraints (Hossain, 2020). The linkage between the societal and operational concerns have deep roots in the investigation of the environmental aspect of the frugality (This paper reference 1-s2.0). The frugal innovation opens avenue for the local products with resilience and which has the higher chance of getting scalability (Hossain et al., 2021). In order to grasp the idea of frugal innovation, often it comes from the grassroots players and they are the ones who develop and refine it for greater utilization for low income consumers (Hossain, 2016). Such idea providers are mostly with the background of low formal education but with sharp skills of developing innovation through their practical and traditional knowledge (Pansera and Sarker, 2016). Interestingly, the frugal innovation is considered as disruptive and can be utilised in multiple countries with same socio-economic conditions (Hossain, 2020).

Literature review provides the evidences that frugal innovation remained a positive and significant factor in promoting the sustainability implications (Albert, 2019). However, there are some studies which claim that due to the technical concept of the frugal innovation, it does not reflect the societal problems which these innovation are considered to provide (Pansera, 2018). There is a need to understand the

Figure 2.
Source: https://www.google.com/search?q=framework+frugal+innovation&tbm=isch&bih=560&biw=1366&hl=en&sa=X&
ved=2ahUKEwim7YDvnrT6AhVxyKACHYl2DmUQrNwCKAB6BQgBEO8B#imgrc=T-oRib7HSyKqhM

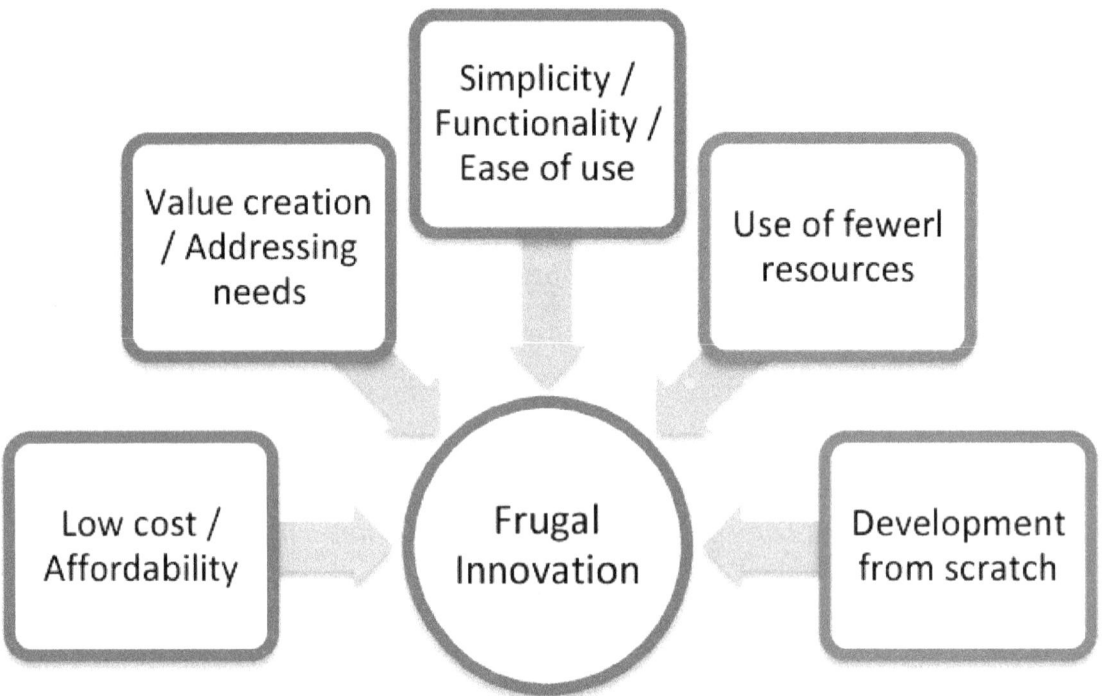

contested nature of frugal innovation and to consider this from multi-dimensional perspective that serve on both level of operational and societal level (Leliveld & Knorringa, 2018; Anser et al., 2021).

Furthermore, it is important for the organizations to consider the environmental and societal value in their business model to produce for consumer because of the economic value (Stubbs & Cocklin, 2008). This notion reflects the part of the business development which is shared value creation to offer the solution to the diverse societal concerns (Porter & Kramer, 2011). The conceptualization of business model with sustainable practices can trigger and initiate the better understanding of the societal pressure which can be integrated into the organizational processes and operations (Ludeke-Freund & Dembek, 2017). Moreover, in this era of digitalization frugal innovation can be a difficult task or series of tasks compare to developing a new product as it requires the suitable business model (Michaelis et al., 2020). Now a days the organizations face the biggest problems in terms of societal pressures.

BACKGROUND

The study of frugal innovation is still in its early stages Innovators in the twenty-first century are able to use available resources creatively by utilizing the collective intelligence of the grassroots community and creating solutions for those who have been under-resourced in light of advancements in digital technologies, changing economic and societal conditions, and a lack of resources (Lan & Liu, 2017;

Figure 3.
Source: https://www.researchgate.net/figure/Frugal-innovation framework_fig1_356565507

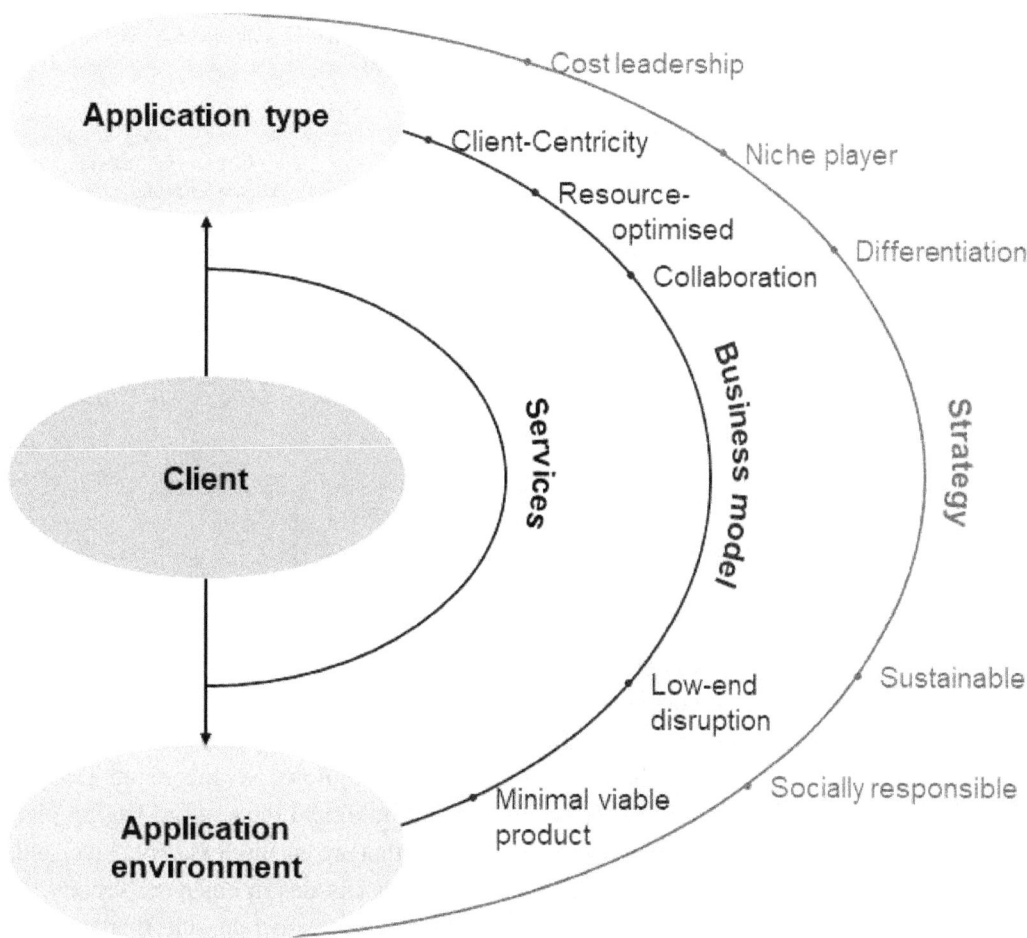

Zeschky et al., 2014). However, there is disagreement over what constitutes frugal innovation in the scholarly literature (Lan & Liu, 2017). One comprehensive definition by Wierenga (2015, p. 9), "frugal innovation includes product features, process and benefits of the output...a novelty product, thus is new to the market in terms of application, material used or business model...requires minimal resources, and the materials used are recycled or easily replaceable. The features of the product have a value-adding function, instead of a price-increasing or appearance purpose. Most importantly, the product has to have an affordable pricing, either low enough for a single payment or through credit schemes offer the possibility to pay in several instalments. The overall performance in relation to the price has to be in balance and indicate of high quality for the end user. Besides considering the environment and the economic background of the consumer, the product has to be inclusive, increase the quality of life of the customer and have obvious social benefits.

Moreover, precisely, the definition of frugal can be summed up in the three aspects of frugal innovation can be identified: business innovation, technology innovation, and social innovation (Hossain,

Figure 4.
Source: https://www.google.com/imgres?imgurl=https%3A%2F%2Fwww.mdpi.com%2Fsustainability%2Fsustainability-14-01326%2Farticle_deploy%2Fhtml%2Fimages%2Fsustainability-14-01326-g001.png&imgrefurl=https%3A%2F%2Fwww.mdpi.com%2F2071-1050%2F14%2F3%2F1326%2Fhtm&tbnid=D3vgJhc7YfeYkM&vet=12ahUKEwim7YDvnrT6AhVxyKACHYl2DmUQMygkegUIARCJAg..i&docid=iyCDYtfDzhUQlM&w=3172&h=1320&q=different%20dimensions%20of%20frugal%20innovation&ved=2ahUKEwim7YDvnrT6AhVxyKACHYl2DmUQMygkegUIARCJAg

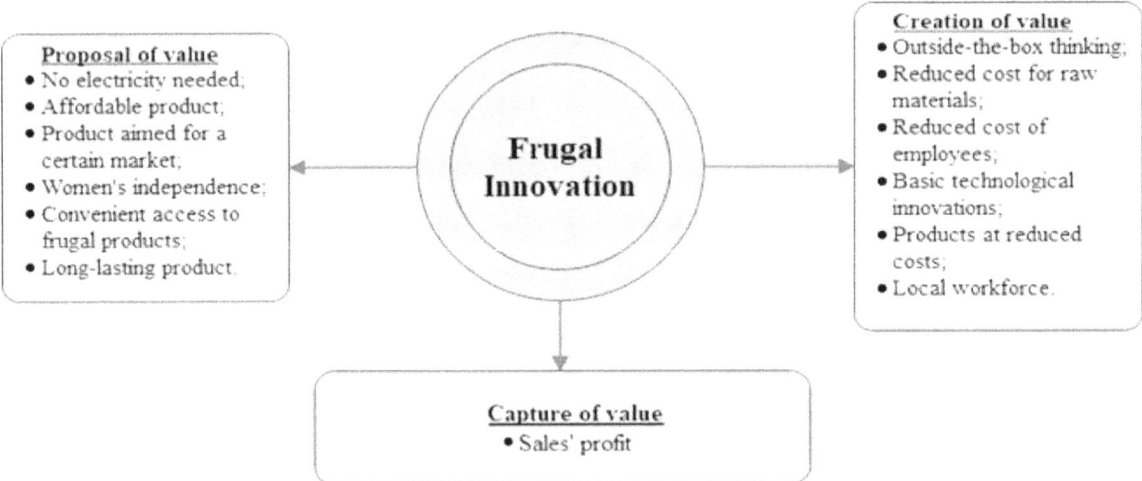

2020). Business innovation is the reconfiguration of a business model's foundational elements, such as its operations, profit formulations, product offerings, and resources, in order to increase, broaden, or create new sources of income (Winterhalter et al., 2017;). Technology advancements that improve the manufacturing of goods and services are referred to as technological innovation. Digital platforms and emerging technologies provide alternatives to current ones that are easier, less expensive, and more practical. These digital technologies are frequently used to address issues in business, society, and the environment. Social innovation is the development of new approaches to social issues that are more successful, efficient, and long-lasting than existing ones, and whose benefits largely benefit society as a whole instead of just specific people (Leong et al., 2016). Social innovation improves company relationships and capacities by making better use of resources and assets (Tiwari, 2016). Social innovation is necessary for social progress, inclusive growth, and prosperity at the bottom to be enabled in an affordable and sustainable way (Porter & Kramer, 2019) while focusing the problems (Khanna & Palepu, 2005;). The absence of regulatory contract regulatory oversight, transactional intermediary, or industry institutions of the type found in the West is referred to as an "institutional void" (Khanna & Palepu, 2005). It is well known that institutional gaps make it difficult to implement company strategy (Khanna & Palepu, 2005). Due to rising customer demands for investment opportunities, social innovation, particularly in environments where institutional shortages are seen, has attracted mainstream attention (Heeks & Arun, 2010).

MAIN FOCUS OF THE CHAPTER

Almost all industries and economic sectors around the world are impacted by frugal innovation. In today's world, global demand exists for cutting-edge technology solutions. For consumers with modest incomes, frugal goods and services are "low-cost alternatives." With time, developing countries introduce new technologies. A cost-effective option that promotes sustainability is frugal innovation. The goal of frugal innovation is to rebuild and restructure goods and services to raise living standards in emerging markets. How frugal innovation, social transition and business sustainability is related: Insights on the contemporary transition towards sustainability in digital era. The main problem with frugal innovation is that academics and researchers pay little attention to new approaches and strategies for bringing creativity in contexts of restricted resources. Frugal innovation affects financial sustainability since it offers low-income consumers a higher degree of value and presents a chance to boost a company's sales and profits (Clausen & Fichter, 2019). Frugal innovation helps to advance societal, economic, and environmental goals (Albert, 2019).

SOLUTIONS AND RECOMMENDATIONS

It emphasizes on restructuring goods and services to attain outstanding results while retaining essential features, frequently going above and beyond expectations and even producing ground-breaking advancements improvements (Clausen & Fichter, 2019). People in developing countries lack the money to pay for cutting-edge technology solutions. As a result, businesses are beginning to focus on the idea of "doing more with less." Governments all across the world are relaxing their regulations and promoting thrifty innovation to raise the standard of living for the general populace. Solutions with a low cost are provided by frugal innovation. In order to encourage frugal innovation, it is necessary to use more sophisticated methods that are inexpensively. In order to meet customers' needs at a reasonable cost, businesses concentrate on what they want to provide them. Organizations have made the use of complex technologies a priority (Bhatti et al. 2018). The chapter basically examines the importance of frugal innovation in social sustainability and technological improvements that are linked to the concept of resource scarcity with high-quality solutions that are less expensive than the competition (Albert, 2019; Bhatti et al. 2018).

FUTURE RESEARCH DIRECTIONS

This book chapter explains how social sustainability and cost-effective innovation are enhancing the lives of individuals. This study can help scientists, researchers, academics, students, and policymakers embrace and implement cutting-edge frugal innovation strategies to raise social standards in developing countries. It is advised that future studies use an applicable research methodology to examine the relationship between social sustainability and frugal innovation. Both quantitative and qualitative methods can be used in scientific investigations. By developing a clear vision of frugal innovation, researchers and scientists should take the environmental protection component into consideration. Companies should innovate their present products and services more economically to replace their current offerings, which will ultimately increase product value, lower product costs, and have a positive influence on the environment. This chapter suggests that services and goods built on the concept of frugal innovation should cost less than equivalent products that don't. To become self-sufficient, organizations should use renewable power sources, such as switching to solar or hydropower for their electric needs. Furthermore, it is important for the organizations to consider the environmental and societal value in their business model to produce for consumer because of the economic value.

REFERENCES

Al-Ghazali, B. M., Gelaidan, H. M., Shah, S. H. A., & Amjad, R. (2022). Green transformational leadership and green creativity? The mediating role of green thinking and green organizational identity in SMEs. *Frontiers in Psychology*, *13*, 977998. doi:10.3389/fpsyg.2022.977998 PMID:36211888

Albert, M. (2019). Sustainable frugal innovation-The connection between frugal innovation and sustainability. *Journal of Cleaner Production*, *237*, 117747. doi:10.1016/j.jclepro.2019.117747

Anser, M. K., Shabbir, M. S., Tabash, M. I., Shah, S. H. A., Ahmad, M., Peng, M. Y. P., & Lopez, L. B. (2021). Do renewable energy sources improve clean environmental-economic growth? Empirical investigation from South Asian economies. *Energy Exploration & Exploitation*, *39*(5), 1491–1514. doi:10.1177/01445987211002278

Bhatti, M. A., Mat, N., & Juhari, A. S. (2018). Effects of job resources factors on nurses job performance (mediating role of work engagement). *International Journal of Health Care Quality Assurance*, *1*(8), 254–274. doi:10.1108/IJHCQA-07-2017-0129 PMID:30415625

Clausen, J., & Fichter, K. (2019). The diffusion of environmental product and service innovations: Driving and inhibiting factors. *Environmental Innovation and Societal Transitions*, *31*, 64–95. doi:10.1016/j.eist.2019.01.003

D'Angelo, V., & Magnusson, M. (2020). A bibliometric map of intellectual communities in frugal innovation literature. *IEEE Transactions on Engineering Management*, *68*(3), 653–666. doi:10.1109/TEM.2020.2994043

Gordon, L., & Hodgson, A. (2017) Doing business at the bottom of the pyramid is not all about low-income countries. *Euromonitor International*. http:// bit. ly/2H6UO Hx

Heeks, R., & Arun, S. (2010). Social outsourcing as a development tool: The impact of outsourcing IT services to women's social enterprises in Kerala. Journal of International Development. *The Journal of the Development Studies Association*, *22*(4), 441–454.

Hossain, M. (2018). Frugal innovation: A review and research agenda. *Journal of Cleaner Production*, *182*, 926–936. doi:10.1016/j.jclepro.2018.02.091

Hossain, M. (2020). Frugal innovation: Conception, development, diffusion, and outcome. *Journal of Cleaner Production*, *262*, 121456. doi:10.1016/j.jclepro.2020.121456

Hossain, M., Levanen, J., & Wierenga, M. (2021). Pursuing frugal innovation for sustainability at the grassroots level. *Management and Organization Review*, *17*(2), 374–381. doi:10.1017/mor.2020.53

International Monetary Fund (IMF). (2022) IMF Annual Report. A year like no other. https:// www. imf. org/ exter nal/ pubs/ ft/ ar/ 2022/ eng

Khanna, T., & Palepu, K. G. (2005). Spotting Institutional Voids in Emerging Markets. https://www. hbs.edu/faculty/Pages/item.aspx?num=32645

Lan, F., & Liu, X. (2017). Business model transformation in digital enablement context through frugal innovation: Learning from Chinese experience. Int. J. Technology. *Policy and Management*, *17*(4), 15. doi:10.1504/IJTPM.2017.087272

Leliveld, A., & Knorringa, P. (2018). Introduction: Frugal innovation and development research. *European Journal of Development Research*, *30*(1), 1–16. doi:10.105741287-017-0121-4

Leong, C., Pan, S. L., Newell, S., & Cui, L. (2016). The Emergence of Self-Organizing E- commerce Ecosystems in Remote Villages of China: A Tale of Digital Empowerment for Rural Development. *Management Information Systems Quarterly*, *40*(2), 475–484. doi:10.25300/MISQ/2016/40.2.11

Levänen, J., Hossain, M., & Wierenga, M. (2022). Frugal innovation in the midst of societal and operational pressures. *Journal of Cleaner Production*, *347*, 131308. doi:10.1016/j.jclepro.2022.131308

Lüdeke-Freund, F., & Dembek, K. (2017). Sustainable business model research and practice: Emerging field or passing fancy? *Journal of Cleaner Production*, *168*, 1668–1678. doi:10.1016/j.jclepro.2017.08.093

Michaelis, T. L., Carr, J. C., Scheaf, D. C., & Pollack, J. M. (2020). The frugal entrepreneur: A self regulatory perspective of resourceful entrepreneurial behavior. *Journal of Business Venturing*, *35*(4), 105969. doi:10.1016/j.jbusvent.2019.105969

Pansera, M. (2018). Frugal or fair? The unfulfilled promises of frugal innovation. *Technology Innovation Management Review*, *8*(4), 6–13. doi:10.22215/timreview/1148

Pansera, M., & Sarkar, S. (2016). Crafting sustainable development solutions: Frugal innovations of grassroots entrepreneurs. *Sustainability*, *8*(1), 51. doi:10.3390u8010051

Porter, M. R., & Kramer, M. R. (2011). Creating shared value. *Harvard Business Review*, *89*(1–2), 1–17.

Shah, S. H. A., Cheema, S., Al-Ghazali, B. M., Ali, M., & Rafiq, N. (2021). Perceived corporate social responsibility and pro-environmental behaviors: The role of organizational identification and coworker pro-environmental advocacy. *Corporate Social Responsibility and Environmental Management*, *28*(1), 366–377. doi:10.1002/csr.2054

Stubbs, W., & Cocklin, C. (2008). Conceptualizing a "sustainable business model. *Organization & Environment*, *21*(2), 103–127. doi:10.1177/1086026608318042

Tiwari, R. (2016). Frugal Innovation in Scholarly and Social Discourse. *An Assessment of Trends and Potential Societal Implications.*, *28*, 1–25.

Van Mossel, A., van Rijnsoever, F. J., & Hekkert, M. P. (2018). Navigators through the storm: A review of organization theories and the behavior of incumbent firms during transitions. *Environmental Innovation and Societal Transitions*, *26*, 44–63. doi:10.1016/j.eist.2017.07.001

Weyrauch, T., & Herstatt, C. (2017). What is frugal innovation? Three defining criteria. *J Frugal Innov*, *2*(1), 1–17. doi:10.118640669-016-0005-y

Wierenga, M. (2015). Local frugal innovations: How do resource-scarce innovations emerge in India? https://aaltodoc.aalto.fi:443/handle/123456789/18429

Winkler, T., Ulz, A., Knöbl, W., & Lercher, H. (2020). Frugal innovation in developed markets—Adaption of a criteria-based evaluation model. *J Innov Knowl, 5*(4), 251–259. doi:10.1016/j.jik.2019.11.004

Winterhalter, S., Zeschky, M. B., Neumann, L., & Gassmann, O. (2017). Business Models for Frugal Innovation in Emerging Markets: The Case of the Medical Device and Laboratory Equipment Industry. *Technovation, 66–67*, 3–13. doi:10.1016/j.technovation.2017.07.002

Zeschky, M. B., Winterhalter, S., & Gassmann, O. (2014). From Cost to Frugal and Reverse Innovation: Mapping the Field and Implications for Global Competitiveness. *Research Technology Management, 57*(4), 20–27. doi:10.5437/08956308X5704235

Chapter 8
Young Leadership Skills Required in the Frugal Innovation Process and Its Developments

Shah Imran Ahmed
Shah Abdul Latif University, Pakistan

Shah Mohammad Farooq
Shah Abdul Latif University, Pakistan

Shakeel Ahmed
Greenwich University, Karachi, Pakistan

Muhammad Asif Qureshi
Mohammad Ali Jinnah University, Pakistan

ABSTRACT

Leadership measures the ability to accomplish the set goal(s) due to the act of inspiring and motivating a group of your peers. Former United States president Dwight D. Eisenhower stated famously that "Leadership consists of nothing but taking responsibility for everything that goes wrong and giving your subordinates credit for everything that goes well." The Army's definition of leadership is "the process of influencing people by providing purpose, direction, and motivation while operating to accomplish the mission and improving the organization."

INTRODUCTION

Leadership is defined as the ability to accomplish a set goal(s) due to the act of inspiring and motivating a group of your peers. Former United States president Dwight D. Eisenhower made famous a quote

DOI: 10.4018/978-1-6684-5417-6.ch008

that stated, "Leadership consists of nothing but taking responsibility for everything that goes wrong and giving your subordinates credit for everything that goes well."

The Army's definition of leadership is "the process of influencing people by providing purpose, direction and motivation while operating to accomplish the mission and improving the organization." An army leader is anyone who inspires and influences people to accomplish their goals (Alshareef et al., 2022, Shaikh et al., 2022; Tunio et al., 20201). Leaders motivate people both inside and outside the army to help them pursue their goals, focus thinking, and shape decisions for the better of the army. Leadership can be acquired by anyone as long as they have the self-determination to do so. The main principles of leadership in the army are broken down in to the acronym LDRSHIP (loyalty, duty, respect, selfless service, honor, integrity, personal courage), characteristics the army aims at instilling in each solider (Tunio et al., 2021; Memon et al., 2021; Afshan et al., 2021). Leadership skills are vitally needed for the development of young soldiers to cope up with the changes in the world over the past two decades, which have created a dynamic situation — volatile, unpredictable, and novel in many respects — making the conduct of military operations more complex and varied than in the past (Chaudhry et al., (2021; Tunio et al., 2021; Mushtaq et al., 2021). This article examines the nature of demands on Army officers in the contemporary operating environment and their implications for leadership development. This is aroused from concerns about both the current operational environment and a closely related development, the Army's ongoing transformation of its structure, technologies, and operating techniques (Tunio et al., 2021; Gul et al., 2021; Shaikh et al., 2021). How will the Army prepare its future leaders for the new demands that will inevitably be placed on them? The report describes analysis and findings on three major topics: the general attributes and intellectual qualities required by leaders in the modern environment; specific operational skills and depth the new environment requires; and the extent to which career paths can provide a foundation of operational experience while still meeting other demands on the officer corps (Aurangzeb et al., 2021; Tunio and Shaikh, 2020; Shaikh, and Tunio, 2020). Although the report concentrates on changes in leader skills needed to keep pace with the evolving operating environment, it also re-emphasizes that the Army should continue to acquire and develop leaders with the character traits and values that have always been the underpinning of effective leadership. Beyond that essential base of leadership, the findings imply that considerably more needs to be done to prepare leaders to meet the challenges of the contemporary environment and to continually learn and adapt to new circumstances (Tunio et al., 2021; Gilal et al., 2021). There have been different theories relating to leadership skills, some of them are defined as under:

Early Western History

The search for the characteristics or traits of leaders has continued for centuries. Philosophical writings from *Plato's Republic* to *Plutarch's Lives* have explored the question "What qualities distinguish an individual as a leader?" Underlying this search was the early recognition of the importance of leadership and the assumption that leadership is rooted in the characteristics that certain individuals possess. This idea that leadership is based on individual attributes is known as the "trait theory of leadership" (Abdullah et al., 2020; Tunio, 2020).

A number of works in the 19th century – when the traditional authority of monarchs, lords and bishops had begun to wane – explored the trait theory at length: note especially the writings of Thomas Carlyle and of Francis Galton, whose works have prompted decades of research. In Heroes and Hero Worship (1841), Carlyle identified the talents, skills, and physical characteristics of men who rose to power.

Galton's Hereditary Genius (1869) examined leadership qualities in the families of powerful men. After showing that the numbers of eminent relatives dropped off when his focus moved from first-degree to second-degree relatives, Galton concluded that leadership was inherited. In other words, leaders were born, not developed. Both of these notable works lent great initial support for the notion that leadership is rooted in characteristics of a leader (Katper et al., 2017; Tunio et al., (2017).

Cecil Rhodes (1853–1902) believed that public-spirited leadership could be nurtured by identifying young people with "moral force of character and instincts to lead", and educating them in contexts (such as the collegiate environment of the University of Oxford) which further developed such characteristics. International networks of such leaders could help to promote international understanding and help "render war impossible". This vision of leadership underlay the creation of the Rhodes Scholarships, which have helped to shape notions of leadership since their creation in 1903 (Gilal et al., 2020; Tunio, 2020).

Rise of Alternative Theories

In the late 1940s and early 1950s, a series of qualitative reviews of these studies prompted researchers to take a drastically different view of the driving forces behind leadership. In reviewing the extant literature, Stogdill and Mann found that while some traits were common across a number of studies, the overall evidence suggested that people who are leaders in one situation may not necessarily be leaders in other situations. Subsequently, leadership was no longer characterized as an enduring individual trait, as situational approaches (see alternative leadership theories below) posited that individuals can be effective in certain situations, but not others. The focus then shifted away from traits of leaders to an investigation of the leader behaviors that were effective. This approach dominated much of the leadership theory and research for the next few decades (Katpar et al., 2020; Tunio et al., 2021).

REEMERGENCE OF TRAIT THEORY

New methods and measurements were developed after these influential reviews that would ultimately reestablish trait theory as a viable approach to the study of leadership. For example, improvements in researchers' use of the round robin research design methodology allowed researchers to see that individuals can and do emerge as leaders across a variety of situations and tasks. Additionally, during the 1980s statistical advances allowed researchers to conduct meta-analyses, in which they could quantitatively analyze and summarize the findings from a wide array of studies. This advent allowed trait theorists to create a comprehensive picture of previous leadership research rather than rely on the qualitative reviews of the past. Equipped with new methods, leadership researchers revealed the following:

- Individuals can and do emerge as leaders across a variety of situations and tasks
- Significant relationships exist between leadership emergence and such individual traits as:
    ○ Intelligence
    ○ Adjustment
    ○ Extraversion
    ○ Conscientiousness
    ○ Openness to experience
    ○ General self-efficacy

While the trait theory of leadership has certainly regained popularity, its reemergence has not been accompanied by a corresponding increase in sophisticated conceptual frameworks.

Specifically, Zaccaro (2007) noted that trait theories still:

- Focus on a small set of individual attributes such as "The Big Five" personality traits, to the neglect of cognitive abilities, motives, values, social skills, expertise, and problem-solving skills.
- Fail to consider patterns or integrations of multiple attributes.
- Do not distinguish between the leadership attributes that are generally not malleable over time and those that are shaped by, and bound to, situational influences.
- Do not consider how stable leader attributes account for the behavioral diversity necessary for effective leadership.

Traits

Most theories in the 20th century argued that great leaders were born, not made. Current studies have indicated that leadership is much more complex and cannot be boiled down to a few key traits of an individual. Years of observation and study have indicated that one such trait or a set of traits does not make an extraordinary leader. What scholars have been able to arrive at is that leadership traits of an individual do not change from situation to situation; such traits include intelligence, assertiveness, or physical attractiveness However, each key trait may be applied to situations differently, depending on the circumstances. The following summarizes the main leadership traits found in research by Jon P. Howell, business professor at New Mexico State University and author of the book Snapshots of Great Leadership.

Determination and drive include traits such as initiative, energy, assertiveness, perseverance and sometimes dominance. People with these traits often tend to wholeheartedly pursue their goals, work long hours, are ambitious, and often are very competitive with others. Cognitive capacity includes intelligence, analytical and verbal ability, behavioral flexibility, and good judgment. Individuals with these traits are able to formulate solutions to difficult problems, work well under stress or deadlines, adapt to changing situations, and create well-thought-out plans for the future. Howell provides examples of Steve Jobs and Abraham Lincoln as encompassing the traits of determination and drive as well as possessing cognitive capacity, demonstrated by their ability to adapt to their continuously changing environments (Shaikh et al., 2022; Tunio et al., 2021).

Self-confidence encompasses the traits of high self-esteem, assertiveness, emotional stability, and self-assurance. Individuals who are self-confident do not doubt themselves or their abilities and decisions; they also have the ability to project this self-confidence onto others, building their trust and commitment. Integrity is demonstrated in individuals who are truthful, trustworthy, principled, consistent, dependable, loyal, and not deceptive. Leaders with integrity often share these values with their followers, as this trait is mainly an ethics issue. It is often said that these leaders keep their word and are honest and open with their cohorts. Sociability describes individuals who are friendly, extroverted, tactful, flexible, and interpersonally competent. Such a trait enables leaders to be accepted well by the public, use diplomatic measures to solve issues, as well as hold the ability to adapt their social persona to the situation at hand. According to Howell, Mother Teresa is an exceptional example who embodies integrity, assertiveness, and social abilities in her diplomatic dealings with the leaders of the world (Shaikh et al., 2021; Afshan et al., 2021).

Few great leaders encompass all of the traits listed below, but many have the ability to apply a number of them to succeed as front-runners of their organization or situation.

Identify Objectives

Rule No. 1 in leadership is to settle on a worthy goal. Nothing is more disheartening than doing hard, dirty, dangerous work in support of fuzzy objectives that nobody can even articulate. In the military, leaders don't always get to choose their objectives, but they should advocate vehemently for objectives that are worth their soldiers' efforts and risks.

Gather Intelligence

Most military units have a person or a unit in charge of collecting and collating intelligence. In business, we might think of this as market research and competitive analysis; in athletics, we might think of scouting the competition. Regardless, a great leader works to find out what challenges his or her people will face before sending them into action.

Plan a Course of Action

Good planning starts with the objective and works backward to where you are now. It's easy to articulate but can be very difficult to do, which might be why so few would-be leaders actually do it. Instead, they pursue interesting or promising strategies without truly considering how or whether any particular action will lead to their ultimate goals.

Scrounge for Resources

If you have every necessary asset to accomplish a goal when you first set out, either you're incredibly fortunate or you haven't set your sights high enough. Truly great leaders know that pursuing worthy goals means pushing teams beyond their abilities and assets. It's why we say that true entrepreneurship is "the pursuit of opportunity without regard to resources currently controlled."

Step to the Front

Your team needs to know that you're even more committed to the objective than it is. That means standing up for it and being visible--literally in front of team members at times. Optics can be most important. You're the leader. Act like it.

Encourage your Team

Optimism is a force multiplier. A team won't believe it succeed unless its leader believes it. So, acknowledge challenges and setbacks, but keep them in perspective. Unless you're convinced that your goal is now unattainable, don't let discouragement reign. (If you do become convinced that your goal is no longer attainable or worthwhile, go back to Rule No. 1!)

Correct When Wrong

Leadership isn't about being liked. It's about acting in a way that engenders respect, which also means holding your team accountable. When individual team members fall short, it's up to you as a great leader to correct them. Doing so in a constructive manner sends the message that you care about both your mission and your people.

Build Esprit De Corps

You want your people to feel that their team is more than the sum of its parts. (That's part of why most soldiers I know like the Army's current recruiting slogan, "Army Strong," more than the previous one, "An Army of One.") People also want to know that you'll have their backs even if they fall short, simply because they are part of the team.

Mentor Your People

Being a true leader means thinking long term and committing to your people even after they're no longer part of your effort. That means offering mentorship and opportunities for them to grow.

Exercise Body and Mind

If you haven't served in the military, you've at least seen the Hollywood version--soldiers working out together, running in formation, calling out cadences. Routine military workouts aren't going to turn people into superstar athletes, but they do set the tone. It's hard to be a great leader if you don't take care of your mind and body.

Communicate Effectively

As a leader, your words are among your most important tools, so if you're not communicating, you're failing. If your team doesn't know its ultimate goal, or if it doesn't have a good understanding of the plan to get there, or if it doesn't appreciate how its personal contributions are vital, you're probably doing something wrong as a leader.

Sacrifice as Necessary

When it's cold or wet or dangerous, soldiers want to know that their leader isn't asking them to do anything he or she won't do himself or herself. This is a universal leadership principle. If you're telling your team members that they have to work weekends or tightening your department's budget, you'd better be willing to share the pain.

Review and Adapt

As a leader, you don't just set a goal, devise a plan, give an order, and sit back. Instead, it's up to you to check progress continually. If things aren't working, figure out why, and make a change. You've probably heard the Albert Einstein quote: Insanity is "doing the same thing over and over again and expecting different results." So don't do that!

Admit Mistakes

If your team makes a mistake, as a leader it's your mistake. The buck stops with you. Take responsibility and embrace it.

Check Small Things

You can't possibly check everything, so instead, create a culture that suggests you could wind up checking just about anything. Your team members--whether they are soldiers or the staff of a marketing department--will take their cues from you. You need to be able to rely on them to follow up and to ensure that the things they can see are working correctly.

Find Reasons to Praise

It's remarkable how just a few good words from someone you respect can inspire you to work harder and achieve more. Great leaders know this, so they're always on the lookout for opportunities to offer words of praise and encouragement. The caveat is that these have to be sincere remarks, which in turn means you have to know your people well and care about them.

Take Time Away

This came home to me when I was in Iraq as a reporter, and I wanted to interview a high-ranking officer, only to be told that he had gone home on leave--basically the military word for vacation. I'm sorry, a general on vacation in the middle of a war? The theory was that if the top commanders didn't take leave, then nobody below them would, either. You need time away from your work and your team in order to see things clearly and lead better.

Thank and Appreciate

Thanking people is different from simply offering encouragement. It means pointing out the connection between their individual effort and how it affects the ultimate objective. It's a basic human need to want to do good work that means something. Show people that you see their work and value it.

Exercise Judgment

At a basic level, your good judgment is one of the only things you have to offer your team members. They need to know that you're weighing the cost of their efforts against the impact on the final objective--and whether the final objective remains worth it. If you're asking them to do something, you'd better believe it's worthwhile and will work.

Show Compassion

Your mission is important (otherwise it shouldn't be your mission). However, it's not the only thing going on in your people's lives. More than that, people screw up--and you will screw up, too (see Rule No. 14). So, although you want to hold people to high standards, you also want to embrace your humanity. People aren't machines; they need to be treated like people.

Recommit to the Life

Smart leaders know that external rewards are rare and often unsatisfactory. Medals and thanks are simply not enough to justify the horrors of war. Similarly, money alone is rarely enough to make people happy after working hard in business in entrepreneurship. Thus, if your work is not its own reward, you will probably never be truly happy. Ask yourself often whether you truly believe in what you're doing. If the answer is no, then find a way to change it.

Go to Sleep Content

Lack of sleep will ruin your life. Worse than that, it will make you a less effective leader. So, recognize that sometimes the secret to being a more effective leader isn't always to work harder; it can sometimes require you to get away, get some rest, and get recharged. If you're committed to what you're doing and fulfilled by it, you'll sleep better and be more effective.

By inculcating these traits in young officers we can develop them easily into the best leaders.

DEVELOPMENT OF LEADERSHIP SKILLS

For nurturing budding leaders we need to inculcate in them the following skills at junior level as to make them the inspiring leaders of tomorrow.

So these skills are divided into following groups:

Personal Skills

Self-Motivated

Motivated leaders desire to achieve above and beyond expectations.

This comes from their passion, pride and desire to become better and the motivation to do things better than everyone else.

To succeed as a leader, you need to be motivated, and no one else can do that for you except yourself.

"Nothing will work unless you do."

– Maya Angelou

Standards

Leaders hold themselves and the people around them to a higher standard than most, both on a personal and professional level.

Leaders understand that in order to achieve higher standards, they need to have strong values, hold themselves accountable for their words/actions and never make excuses.

Remember you're the average of the five people you spend the most time with.

Confidence

Unfortunately, confidence can be one of those things you either have or don't have, but I believe that it can be practiced and learned.

Confidence has to do with your inner perception of your ability to fulfill a particular role and is built through your experiences and dealings during your life.

To build your confidence you need to be open to new experiences and be willing to fail or you'll never grow and find the strength needed to push the limits of what you're capable of.

"You gain strength, courage and confidence by every experience in which you really stop to look fear in the face."

– Eleanor Roosevelt

Optimism and Positivity

Where others might think a project or task is too difficult, leaders face those challenges with energy and positivity.

Positivity is contagious, so be sure to focus on your attitude and understand you set the tone for your business and the people around you.

Accountable

Being accountable means that you accept responsibility for the outcomes expected of you, both good and bad.

You don't blame others. And you don't blame things that were out of your control.

Until you take responsibility, you are a victim. And being a victim is the exact opposite of being a leader.

Great leaders take initiative to influence the outcome and take responsibility for the results.

Courage

Aristotle called courage the first virtue, because it makes all of the other virtues possible.

Leadership sometimes involves making unpopular decisions which requires a certain level of bravery.

If you want to be more courageous you need to try new things, have more trust and confidence in others, as well as be able to raise difficult issues that others would leave unresolved.

"Keep your fears to yourself but share your courage with others."

– Robert Louis Stevenson

Engaged

Great leaders are able to focus their attention on the problem at hand without being distracted.

Even when your extremely busy, you need to make sure that you're participating in the process with team members and not giving orders from the sideline.

Character

Leaders are well defined and have unique personas that make them one-of-kind.

They are full of personality and are not afraid to stand lone and be different.

They understand that the things who make them different are the things that define their character.

Humor

Many leaders are perfectionists, which tends to make them critical of themselves and the people around them.

But let's face it, what can go wrong, usually will go wrong. That's life!

You should have a healthy sense of humor about life and not take yourself too seriously (which can be difficult when you want others to take you seriously).

However, leaders who take themselves too seriously risk alienating people.

Effective leaders have the ability to laugh at themselves and understand that they are only human and can make mistakes like everyone else.

Passion

Passionate leaders often have a strong, uncontrollable desire that pushes them forward.

The amount of passion you have directly affects your attitude, energy and that of your followers as well.

Use your excitement and to ignite the passion pf your followers!

"You have to be burning with an idea, or a problem, or a wrong that you want to right. If you're not passionate enough from the start, you'll never stick it out."

– Steve Jobs

Integrity

Having strong moral values is an important leadership trait because it will allow others to clearly identify with you.

Having sincerity and honesty in all your dealings assures your followers of your intentions.

Respectable

Enticing a deep sense of admiration and loyalty in your followers in key to successful leadership.

Being respected makes it easier to put your plans in action and have others quickly buy into your vision. Leaders garner respect by letting their actions speak louder than their words.

Likable

In some cases, leaders are respected for their negative qualities.

That's why it's important that you not only seek to be respected, but that you are likable as well.

It's very obvious, people want to work with and be around people they like and distance themselves from people they don't.

Ethical

When dealing with tough (sometime moral) decisions, great leaders should do so in accordance with their own values and ensure their actions are positive, not damaging.

Also, when you govern the moral principles of the people you are leading, you can establish an unspoken ethics code that helps better guide their decisions and behavior.

Loyal

When we are talking about loyalty and leadership it's usually about the followers, but loyalty is not a one-way street.

You need to give and show firm, constant support to your followers if you ever hope that they will give the same to you.

Charisma

Successful leaders are magnetizing and charming which inspires devotion in their followers.

This charisma can be difficult to learn, it usually requires most people to go outside of their comfort zone by speaking with more strangers as well as learning how to command the attention and speak to a group of any size.

Appreciation/Love for your Career

It might be cliché, but you really should be doing what you love and what you're passionate about.

If you aren't doing something you love, you'll never find the drive to push yourself to be better.

Self-Awareness

Emotional Intelligence

The ability to understand and manage your own emotions, and those of the people around you is crucial.

People with a high degree of emotional intelligence know what they're feeling, what their emotions mean, and how these emotions can affect other people.

For leaders, this is essential for success.

Emotional Control

Similar to emotional intelligence, once you can understand your emotions, you can learn to control them.

The ability to stay calm, assess your self, then make adjustments comes down to simple self-control.

If you can control your emotions and reactions to the world, you can better control the outcomes.

"Life is 10 percent what happens to me and 90 percent of how I react to it."

– Charles Swindoll

Understanding of Opportunity Cost

Leaders know that many situations and decisions in business involve risk and there is an opportunity cost associated with every decision you make.

An opportunity cost is the cost of a missed opportunity. This is usually defined in terms of money, but it may also be considered in terms of time, person-hours, or any other finite resource.

Great leaders understand the consequences of their decisions before making them.

Humility

Leaders should be humble by seeking out feedback and focusing on the needs of others.

You need to be open to people's feedback and criticisms and know how to admit that you're not perfect and when you've made a mistake.

"There is no respect for others without humility in one's self."

– Henri Frederic Amiel

Discipline

Discipline in leadership is less about punishing and rewarding others, but rather having self-control, inner calm and outer resolve.

A high level of determination and willpower play a significant part in your ability to be self-disciplined.

Perspective

Sometime the best solution is right in front of us, but we are too close to see it.

Leaders know how to remove themselves from a situation and observe it from multiple perspectives with a open mind.

"Unless you know the road you've come from, you cannot know where you are going."

– African proverb

Risk Management

You need to identify, evaluate and address risks so you can positively affect the outcome by handling that risk in the best-suited way.

They often say, "there is now reward, without risk."

But smart leaders know which risks to take and which to guard against.

Time Management

Great leaders know that time is their most valuable asset.

Leaders need to know how to effectively plans their time by knowing when and where to spend it; on your self, your business and family/friends.

Self-Assurance

Every road to success to filled with people who will find any reason to give you why it won't work.

You need a healthy level of self-assurance that gives you a practical (sometime impractical) sense of faith in your cause that drives you forward with no excuses, roadblocks or negativity holding you back.

Maturity

Contrary to popular belief, age is not a measure of maturity.

I've worked with young leaders who act like men and old men who act like teenagers.

Maturity comes from being courteous, knowing how to communicate like an adult and being the bigger person in difficult situations.

Also, your confidence in yourself and your ability to follow through without excuses are strong indicators of maturity.

Communication

Lead by example

Actions speak louder than words. The people around you will notice if you are dedicated and working hard to grow your business.

But if you're lazy and don't care, your team will note and follow suit.

Great leaders always lead by example.

"Example is not the main thing in influencing others. It is the only thing."

– Albert Schweitzer

Relationship Building

"It's all about who you know." Smart leaders know that there is a lot of truth to that saying.

Leaders understand the value of building long-lasting relationships with people in their industry and make a point to pursue partnerships whenever they can.

Building a network of valuable people is critical for your long-term success.

Social Skills

More often than not, leaders are charismatic, outgoing, friendly and approachable.

They have the ability to speak with anyone in a calm, respectful and engaging way.

Both employees and customers want to work for and purchase from people they like, you need to be one of those people if you want to succeed.

Public Speaking/Speaking Skills

Leaders should not have any issues with speaking in front of crowds.

Situations where public speaking is required can range from just speaking up at a meeting, to pitching a new idea in a room full of people.

Not only is this important for you to be able to get your message across clearly, but it improves your credibility as a leader.

Honesty and Transparency

There are no more secrets today, everything is out there on the worldwide web.

That's why honesty is the best policy.

People respect those who are able to honestly share and react calmly to good and bad news while being able to quickly put a plan in action to move forward.

We now live in a transparent world, embrace it.

Reasonable

One of the quickest ways to get people to dislike you is to be unreasonable.

That's why practical leaders are fair, sensible, never make unfound assumptions and have sound judgment when making decisions.

Boldness

Leaders do not hesitate or appear fearful (even if they are) in all aspects of their life.

They are willing to take the lead and show the way despite possible risks.

"The question isn't who is going to let me; it's who is going to stop me."

– Ayn Rand

Listening

In order to give your followers the feedback, support and attention they need to be successful, you need to make a true effort to listen when they speak.

Most people are waiting for their turn to speak, great leaders listen first, speak second.

Listening is more than being silent, you also need to ask the right questions.

Presence

True presence is just not about being the center of attention, it's about observation and seeking/giving meaningful feedback.

You need to be there for your people during important situations as well as help team members across your organization find solutions to roadblocks.

Authenticity

Leaders stay true to the things that make them unique and tirelessly move towards their goals despite outside pressures to change or conform.

Hard-word, dedication, and long-term focus are essential to authentic leadership.

Empathy and Compassion

When you are laser focused on your goals, it can be difficult to focus on the needs and feelings of others people.

You need to know not only how your actions effect people, but what you need to do in order to show understanding and sympathy for others.

Ability to Confront Others

Most people go out of their way to avoid confrontation for fear of an argument, leaders know how to approach others in a nice, honest way to address concerns.

Stopping a problem earlier on will save a huge amount of time (not to mention headaches) versus leaving it unresolved.

Empowerment

As a leader, you need to set others up for success by entrusting them to make good decisions.

Empowerment is not just about giving your followers the freedom to make their own choices, it's about giving them the tools and processes to make those choices effectively and productively.

Negotiation Skills

Leaders know how to get what they want and can be very convincing (which can be good and sometimes bad).

They do this by tapping the desires of others and building a sense of trust with people in order to come to a desirable outcome.

From settling differences to overseeing a large deal, leaders should be practical, fair and firm in their negotiations.

Social Savvy

Did you know that 71% of all online adults use Facebook? That's almost 1.2 billion people!

Smart leaders know that their followers' and potential followers' habits have changed. They are spending more time on social media than ever before.

When social media is used as a tool to engage, educate and connect with followers, it can have powerful results and attract countless new people to your cause.

Delegate

Clarity

When great leaders speak, they are able to clearly relay their thoughts in a way that's easy to understand.

Then they make sure there are no miscommunications and that their point(s) got across clearly.

This ensures projects and tasks that are delegated get done the right way and without mistakes.

Ability to Teach

Leaders need to be able to share the methodologies and processes that make their business run with the people they work with and hire.

If your managers are poorly trained, your staff will be poorly trained and it will reflect in your sales and operations.

Remember the best way to learn something your self is to teach it!

Interested in Feedback

In the same way great leaders are able to teach, they also value learning.

That involves being open to honest feedback and the ability to have a positive attitude about that feedback and use it make adjustments that benefit everyone.

Trust in Your Team

This can be difficult, but your trust in your team largely depends on the people you hire, your ability to train them and the work you delegate to them.

If you believe in their ability to do those things, you need to trust your team to get the results you want and not micro-manage every project.

Ability to Inspire

Let's face it, it's difficult to love every part of your work no matter what you do.

But great leaders have the ability to inspire their team and make sure they know what they are doing has a bigger impact than they realize.

Nike is about celebrating athletics not sneakers, Apple is about changing the world, not computers. What are you about?

"Leadership is the art of getting someone else to do something you want done because he wants to do it."

– Dwight D. Eisenhower

ID Team Strengths

When delegating work, leaders know their team and their strengths inside and out.

They use that knowledge to decide who gets assigned which projects/tasks so that everything gets completed the right way.

Sharing Your Vision

There are a lot of people out there who think they have the next great idea.

Sadly, as great as those ideas might be, they will never go anywhere if no one else knows about it.

Leaders have the ability to share their vision and get people to buy into their ideas.

Turning vision into reality

Not only can leaders share their vision, they have the ability to break that vision down into steps and a strategy that can be understood by others and executed over time.

Get the Best from Others

By understanding what people really want, you can help them better perform by properly incentivizing (not only with money) their work and progress towards larger goals.

To get the best from others a leader needs to understand their motivations, be positive, generous, open-minded and be able to control their attitude.

"If you want to build a ship, don't drum up the men to gather wood, divide the work, and give orders. Instead, teach them to yearn for the vast and endless sea."

– Antoine de Saint-Exupéry

Understand What Motivates Others

For better or worse, human beings tend to care mostly about themselves and are motivated by selfish altruism.

Simply put, you need to figure out what people want for them selves: Notoriety? Money? Recognition? Understand that to will be different for everyone.

Takes Responsibly

In the same way leaders are quick to give their team credit, they are also quick to take responsibility for negative outcomes.

Great leaders know that when they accept responsibility for their actions, they can postivey effect the outcomes.

"A good leader is a person who takes a little more than his share of the blame and a little less than his share of the credit."

– John Maxwell

Rewarding

People often seek recognition from people they follow, that's why it's important to reward your team members for their input, especially when they go above and beyond.

Monetary rewards are nice, but thoughtful, personal rewards can be more impactful.

Evaluative

Great leaders are able to carefully and quickly analyze a situation and/or person.

Being decisive doesn't mean making a decision quickly, it means making the right decisions in a practical, timely manner.

Don't allow your decisiveness to alienate team members from the decision making process.

Conduct Effective Meetings

Sadly, most meeting are never as productive as they could be.

After all, if your an entrepreneur, you usually get to work with people that you like which can be distracting.

Effective leadership is about using meeting time as effectively as possible.

Start by having an agenda, eliminate distractions, have a start/end time (no exceptions), encourage everyone to contribute, encourage note taking and follow up after the meeting.

Respect for Others

When you show respect towards other people, it is much easier to build meaningful, beneficial relationships.

You need to keep your promises, don't waste their time, stop gossiping, believe in other's ideas, stand up for them and truly care about their well-being.

Coaching Key People

It's one thing to identify your top performing employees, but you also need to nurture their success and help them grow within your organization.

In order for you to successfully lead a growing number of people, you need to enable your key people to lead as well and help push progress forward.

"Leaders must be close enough to relate to others, but far enough ahead to motivate them."

– John C. Maxwell

Enable others to Act

Unless there are strict guidelines/regulations or safety concerns, if you don't allow your followers to make their own decisions they likely will find reasons to disagree with yours.

You can enable others to act by giving them the tools and processes they need to succeed, trust them to handle the rest.

Set Expectations

People don't like to be surprised, that's why it's important to layout and agree to the expectations in place so everyone is one the same page from day one.

To make sure expectations are crystal clear, start by providing structure, clarifying roles, set motivating goals and continuously give/ask for feedback.

Fair

Some traits are more important than others.

When it comes to leadership, the ability to judge situations and people with fairness is essential because it shows them how you value them.

There's many examples in history of leaders who took advantage of the people they were leading, things hardly ever worked out in their favor.

The leaders who are fair to people, are the ones who are loved and remembered.

Agility and Adaptability

Urgency

The competition doesn't wait and there will always be someone out there trying to outwork you.

Leaders understand that in most situations it's about who gets there first which is why they value of both persistence and urgency.

Decisiveness

Being decisive is not just about making decisions quickly, it's about fostering a confident and effective way of thinking, deciding, and acting.

In order to make the best decisions possible, understand and assess each option carefully while approaching the right people and resources to help you make your decision.

Don't let indecision paralyze you.

Commitment to Vision

Every overnight success you've heard about likely has another side to the story: the long hours, bootstrapping and testing many iterations before finding the right combinations.

Leaders need to appreciate the process as much as the outcome and stay committed to their vision through thick and thin.

Consistency

Like professional quarterbacks, great leaders follow strict routines to keep their skills sharp and their delivery consistent.

Remember that practice makes perfect and the more consistent you can be, the more efficiently you and your organization will be.

Does not Fear Mistakes/Risk

Failure often provides us with some of life's biggest learning opportunities.

Leaders embrace this as well as the uncertainty and risk that are inherent parts of owning and running a business.

"I've missed more than 9000 shots in my career. I've lost almost 300 games. Twenty-six times I've been trusted to take the game winning shot and missed. I've failed over and over and over again in my life. And that is why I succeed."

– Michael Jordan

Ability to Pivot

The business world is changing quickly and will continue to do so.

Great leaders have the ability to recognize those changes and guide their organization and team accordingly.

Open Minded

It's fascinating how many business owners and managers refuse to change the simplest aspects of their business because they have the "if it ain't broke, don't fix it" mentality.

While that might work for a time, as years pass the business and their leaders who refuse to learn, adapt and grow will be left behind.

To be an effective leader you need to be open to learning about new things and exploring new experiences.

"To get something you never had, you have to do something you never did."

– Unknown

Tough-Minded

What can go wrong, usually does go wrong.

Leaders need to face life and business with strength and determination, especially when things get difficult.

When most people might give in, that's the exact moment you need to push through and overcome adversity.

Resourceful

When faced with a challenge, smart leaders are able to find creative solutions to problems.

Being resourceful involves understand all the resources at your disposal, adapting by applying other experiences, sometimes bending the rules and never being of afraid to ask for what you need.

Faces Obstacles with Grace

Life will always be full of obstacles, how you choose to deal with them is your decision.

Effective leaders approach roadblocks with a high level of positivity and creative problem solving that allows them to overcome situations that others might give up on.

"The ultimate measure of a man is not where he stands in moments of comfort, but where he stands at times of challenge and controversy."
– Martin Luther King, Jr.

Street Smart

It's hard to find a substitute for old-fashioned street smarts.

Knowing how to trust your gut, quickly analyzing situations as well as the people you're dealing with and knowing how-to spot a bad deal or scammer is an important aspect of leadership.

Make Good Decisions

When you make good, practical decisions, you build trust with your followers that gives you the power to make future decisions quicker, with less pushback.

Making good decisions involves generating good alternatives and analyzing each option diligently.

Once you've made your decision, evaluate then communicate plan and always learn from yours and others' mistakes.

Strategic Thinking

In order to think two steps ahead, you need to develop a long-term mindset, using research to make decisions and take time to reflect on your decisions.

When you plan for the long-term, you can layout, then take small, actionable steps towards a bigger picture.

"The only person you are destined to become is the person you decide to be."

– Ralph Waldo Emerson

Proactive

The opposite of proactive is reactive, which means you react to the world around you instead of taking steps to positive effect the outcomes.

Proactive leaders have a DIY mindset and approach new/difficult situations with enthusiasm and energy.

If you want to positively effect you life and the lives around you, start by learning to control (not manipulate) situations to cause something to happen, rather than waiting for it to happen.

Flexible

People in leadership positions are often gifted with flexible schedules.

Sure, we all work for someone, whether it's stakeholders, clients or someone else, we usually have the ability to make our own schedules.

Leaders need to use this flexibility the become more available and involved in organization initiatives as well as other people's lives.

Manage Setbacks/Uncertainty

After any failure, big or small, you usually have two options: give up or find a better way.

Leaders know when it's time to double down and when it's time to fold, they manage uncertainty by making thoughtful decisions on next steps.

Organized

You can't sail your ship if you don't know where the sail is, likewise, you can't run your business if you aren't organized.

Leaders know that value in keeping their personal and professional things (both physical and electronic) in order.

Creative

Contrary to popular belief, creativity is not something people are born with, like many leadership skills it can be learned and practiced.

Go out of your way to explore new experiences, learn new things and practice open mindedness by continually asking new questions.

Intuition

Intuition is to art as logic is to math.

Leadership is often about following your gut instinct.

It can be difficult to let go of logic in some situations, but uncertainty and risk are a natural in business.

Learn to trust yourself and not everyone else.

Cultivate Wisdom

Seeks Out Advice

Even though leader usually means "the person in charge" it's important that you seek out the experience and skill sets of trusted advisors, partners, customers and peers.

Outside perspectives are always helpful.

Pursue New Experiences

To stay prepared for any road bump in business, leaders actively pursue new experiences that allow them to learn and grow.

From starting a new venture, to coaching little league, challenge your self to be better by enjoying new experiences.

Read, Read, Read

Read everything related to business and your field that you can get your hands on, both print and digital.

Leaders understand that education does not stop after school, in order to stay relevant, you need to stay informed with both timeless and timely resources.

Curiosity

Leaders are often driven be an insatiable desire to learn, push the limits of what's possible and explore things other people have or will not explore themselves.

Expanding your mind can often be as simple as reading, asking "why?" more often and enjoying the journey your own.

Competence

Competence in most cases refers to someone being properly qualified and educated, but just people some people can learn something quicker than others doesn't necessarily mean they are more intelligent.

Willpower, determination, consistency and willingness to learn play important roles in your competence as a leader.

Focused

Life is full of distractions, great leaders know how to remain on track and block out distractions.

Remaining focused involves keeping your eye on the bigger picture, allocating your time deliberately and training your brain like a muscle to eliminate non-essential work.

'A man who wants to lead the orchestra must turn his back on the crowd."

– Max Lucado

Intentional Learner

Leaders go out of their way to stay educated and up-to date.

Intentional learning is a continuous process of acquiring, understanding information with the goal of making yourself more intelligent and prepared on a specific subject.

Enjoys The Ride

Smart leaders know that their journey is often more rewarding than their destination.

Which is why they take the time to enjoy life and what they have already achieved because they know nothing can last forever.

When you can enjoy the ride, you'll be amazed by what you can learn.

Effect Change

Improve Lives Around You

Leaders working toward a brighter future want to share that future and it's success with the people they care about.

Business partners and customers, family and friends, employees and their families, etc.

Leaders must act with generosity and gratitude by effecting positive change in the lives of the people around them.

Foster Potential

Improving the lives of people around you also means helping them become better individuals.

Help other people grow by encouraging and fostering their potential both professionally and personally and help them learn from your experiences.

"Don't judge each day by the harvest you reap but by the seeds that you plant."

– Robert Louis Stevenson

Belief that Success if Shared

Great leaders believe that success is something to be shared with everyone because there is no "I" in team.

When you share your success with others, you build loyalty, trust and admiration that enables you to push the success even further.

Help Other Succeed

Giving is always more satisfying than receiving. Leaders find great pride in helping other people succeed and become leaders themselves.

You need to be generous and make sure your team can share the organization's success as well as grow personally and professionally with your guidance.

Direction

Great leaders know where they are going and how they are going to get there.

They convey their mission clearly to followers and possess an unwavering drive that keeps them on track to their goals.

Challenge the Process

When leaders ignore the status quo, there can be incredible breakthroughs and innovations.

This is an essential part of achieving organizational growth.

Smart leaders know how to productively challenge the process, find bottlenecks and make improvements.

"If you really want the key to success, start by doing the opposite of what everyone else is doing."

– Brad Szollose

Performance Driven

Like a professional athlete, leaders strive to make improvements and become better every singe day.

They know that there is always room for improvements that can be made to make themselves and their team more effective.

Great leaders are driven by performance and the motivation to see how far they can take it.

Servant/Service

While it may seem counterintuitive, the best leaders often act more and servants by enabling their team to be great.

As a leader, you have more resources at your disposal than the average person, it's important you share those resources with people in your organization.

Assertive

It's important to make sure your voice is heard as a leader, but in a constructive, helpful way.

You need to get your point across clearly, and involve your self in the day-to-day operations of key team members.

Look out for opportunities to collaborate and trust your team to make important decisions.

Independent

This often refers to not depending on others, but a true leader knows how to collaborate with the right people while remaining resourceful when faced with a setback or roadblock on their own.

Conviction

A firm belief in a cause can often be a driving force in a leader's ability effect change in the world.

This deep faith often comes from being inspired and staying inspired throughout your journey.

Fill spare time with inspirational articles, stories, etc. to keep your spark and obsession going.

Patience

Smart leaders know not to expect results over night, whether it's a new marketing campaign or an entirely new business.

Leaders know that patience is not about waiting around for results, it's about following through and executing the plan, not giving up when you face hurdles, working hard and learning how to enjoy the journey as much as the destination.

High-Energy

It takes a lot to effect the status quo, leaders not only have high energy, but they know how to find and utilize their most productive time.

Remember, working long hours doesn't always equal success because time is a finite resource.

But energy can be fueled by staying healthy and active, passionate and positive about your work as well as establishing productive rituals.

REFERENCES

Abdullah, M., Katper, N. K., Chaudhry, N. I., and Tunio, M. N. (2020). An Impact of Workaholics on Creativity: the mediating role of Negative Mood and moderating role of Supervisor Support. *Sukkur IBA Journal of Management and Business*, 7(2).

Afshan, G., Ilyas, S., Tunio, M. N., & Kalhoro, M. (2021). CSR actions and post-COVID'19 consequences in hotel industry: A conceptual framework. *International Journal of Strategic Change Management*, 7(4), 1. doi:10.1504/IJSCM.2021.122845

Afshan, G., Ilyas, S., Tunio, M. N., & Kalhoro, M. (2021). CSR actions and post-COVID-19 consequences in the hotel industry: A conceptual framework. *International Journal of Strategic Change Management*, 7(4), 275–289. doi:10.1504/IJSCM.2021.122845

Alshareef, N., & Tunio, M. N. (2022). Role of Leadership in Adoption of Blockchain Technology in Small and Medium Enterprises in Saudi Arabia. *Frontiers in Psychology*, 13, 2284. doi:10.3389/fpsyg.2022.911432 PMID:35602740

Aurangzeb, M. T., Tunio, M. N., Rehman, Z., & Asif, M. (2021). Influence of administrative expertise on human resources practitioners on the job performance: Mediating role of achievement motivation. [IJM]. *International Journal of Management*, 12(4), 408–421.

Chaudhry, I. S., Paquibut, R. Y. & Tunio, M. N. (2021) Do workforce diversity, inclusion practices, & organizational characteristics contribute to organizational innovation? Evidence from the U.A.E. *Cogent Business & Management, 8*(1), 1947549, . doi:10.1080/23311975.2021.1947549

Gilal, F. G., Gilal, N. G., Channa, N. A., Gilal, R. A., Gilal, R. G., & Tunio, M. N. (2020). Towards an integrated model for the transference of environmental responsibility. *Business Strategy and the Environment*, 29(6), 1–10. doi:10.1002/bse.2524

Gilal, F. G., Gilal, N. G., Gilal, R. G., Gon, Z., Gilal, W. G., & Tunio, M. N. (2021). The Ties That Bind: Do Brand Attachment and Brand Passion Translate Into Consumer Purchase Intention? *Central European Management Journal*, 29(1), 14–38. doi:10.7206/cemj.2658-0845.39

Gul, A., Subhan, S., & Tunio, M. N. (2021). Learning experiences of women entrepreneurs amidst COVID-19. *International Journal of Gender and Entrepreneurship*, 13(2), 1756–6266. doi:10.1108/IJGE-09-2020-0153

Katpar., N. K., Chaudhry, N. I., Tunio, M. N. and Ali, M. A. (2020). Impact of Leadership Style and Organizational Culture on Organizational Commitment. *Sukkur IBA Journal of Management and Business –SIJMB 7*(1), 92-106.

Katper, N. K. Medan, A., Syed, K. B. S.., Tunio, M. N. (2017). Determinants of Debt Maturity Structure in Shariah and Non-Shariah Firms in Pakistan: A comparative Study. *Journal of Applied Economic Sciences 12*(4), p1210-1225. 16.

Memon, A.B., Meyer, K. and Tunio, M. N. (2021). Toward collaborative networking among innovation laboratories: a conceptual framework. *International Journal of Innovation Science*. doi:10.1108/IJIS-04-2021-0069

Mushtaq, T., Tunio, M. N., Akbar, Z., and Jariko, M. (2021). Green Organizational identity: Antecents and consequences: An Emprical Study. *Contemporary Issues in business and Government, 27*(3), p. 2056-2069.

Shaikh, E., Tunio, M. N. (2020). Customer satisfaction and Customer loyalty: An empirical case study on the impact of benefits generated through Smartphone applications. *International Journal of Public Sector Performance Management.*

Shaikh, E., Tunio, M. N., Khoso, W. M., Brahmi, M., & Rasool, S. (2022). The COVID-19 Pandemic Overlaps Entrepreneurial Activities and Triggered New Challenges: A Review Study. *Managing Human Resources in SMEs and Start-ups: International Challenges and Solutions*, 155-182.

Shaikh, E., Tunio, M. N., & Qureshi, F. (2021). Finance and women's entrepreneurship in DETEs: A literature review. *Entrepreneurial Finance, Innovation and Development*, 191-209.

Shaikh, E., Watto, W. A., & Tunio, M. N. (2022). Impact of Authentic Leadership on Organizational Citizenship Behavior by Using The Mediating Effect of Psychological Ownership. *ETIKONOMI, 21*(1), 89–102. doi:10.15408/etk.v21i1.18968

Shaikh, S., Sultan, M. F., Mushtaque, T., & Tunio, M. N. (2021). Impact of COVID-19 on GDP: A serial mediation effect on international tourism and hospitality. *International Journal of Management, 12*(84), 422–430.

Tunio, M. N. (2020). Role of ICT in Promoting Entrepreneurial Ecosystems in Pakistan. *Journal of Business Ecosystems, 1*(2), 1–21. doi:10.4018/JBE.2020070101

Tunio, M. N. (2020). Role of ICT in promoting entrepreneurial ecosystems in Pakistan. *Journal of Business Ecosystems, 1*(2), 1–21. doi:10.4018/JBE.2020070101

Tunio, M. N., Chaudhry, I. S., Shaikh, S., Jariko, M. A., & Brahmi, M. (2021). Determinants of the Sustainable Entrepreneurial Engagement of Youth in Developing Country—An Empirical Evidence from Pakistan. *Sustainability, 13*(14), 7764. doi:10.3390u13147764

Tunio, M. N., Jariko, M. A., Børsen, T., Shaikh, S., Mushtaque, T., & Brahmi, M. (2021). How Entrepreneurship Sustains Barriers in the Entrepreneurial Process—A Lesson from a Developing Nation. *Sustainability, 13*(20), 1–18. doi:10.3390u132011419

Tunio, M. N., & Shaikh, E. (2020). ((Forthcoming). Nascent entrepreneurs and challenges in digital market in developing countries. *International Journal of Public Sector Performance Management.*

Tunio, M. N., Shaikh, E., Niaz, S., & Katper, N. S. (2021). Multifaceted perils of the Covid-19 and implications: A Review. *Estudios de Economía Aplicada.* doi:10.25115/eea.v39i2.3957

Tunio, M. N., Soomro, A. A., & Bogenhold, D. (2017). The Study of Self-employment at SMEs Level with Reference to Poverty in Developing Countries. Business and Management Research, 6(2). doi:10.5430/bmr.v6n2p33

Tunio, M. N., Yusrini, L., Shah, Z. A., Katper, N., & Jariko, M. A. (2021). How Hotel Industry Cope up with the COVID-19: An SME Perspective. *Etikonomi, 20*(2), 213–224. doi:10.15408/etk.v20i2.19172

Tunio, M. N., Yusrini, L., & Shoukat, G. (2021). Corporate social responsibility (CSR) in Hotels in Austria, Pakistan, and Indonesia: small and medium Enterprise spillover of COVID-19. In Handbook of research on entrepreneurship, innovation, sustainability, and ICTs in the post-COVID-19 era, (pp. 263-280). IGI Global.

Zaccaro, S. J. (2007). Trait-based perspectives of leadership. *The American Psychologist*, *62*(1), 6–16.

Chapter 9
Innovation in Education

Kanwal Khaskheli
University of Sindh, Pakistan

ABSTRACT

Innovation in education is pursuing knowledge that will support novel and distinctive ideas. We can describe the term 'innovation' in education as finding the most appropriate and productive way to get maximum outcome from educational institutes. It is concerned with unrevealing individual capabilities of the students and researchers, which can assist society in underlining and resolving many scientific and social problems and enables us to get more creative and critical thinkers. Innovation in education is thinking outside of the box, challenging the existing techniques and tools to acquire more valuable ways of learning. The chapter covers the essentials of innovation in education and aims to unveil the potential areas of innovation in existing education system; generally, it falls in the category of processes innovations, which include modern and meaningfully advanced techniques of classroom-based learning, assessment tools, and teaching techniques.

INTRODUCTION

Innovation is very essential for the survival of the organizations as well as community to develop. it helps addressing new ideas and create more value added technologies and techniques, which could create easiness in life of individuals, help them in solving present day problems and improve standard of life. In similar way our education system also requires a continuous innovation process to get better outcomes although we cannot deny the fact that present day Education system is far more modernized and innovative then the traditional one, but the point of research is that "Does modern education system justifies the true purpose of Education? And to find out potential areas which needs to consider for further innovation and development.

Current Education system holds a quantifiable gap for exertion to make it more qualitative and sustainable. For the quality of education we assume to get maximum output from human resources residing across the world from the small town to the biggest cities, and it aims to increase standard of living and make earth a viable place for all living beings. Schumpeter in 1942, presented the standard definition of innovation as "creative destruction", which is "Abolishing an old combination and appreciating a novel

DOI: 10.4018/978-1-6684-5417-6.ch009

one". Education in true sense is learning the art of living without harming anyone else. Innovation in education has been a matter of considerable concern these days. Certainly, positive innovation depends upon the individual creativity, knowledge, skills and talents that are cherished and developed through education (Janet, 2009).

The purpose of education is stipulation of children, adults and young people in providing them with the knowledge, skills and understandings about the life and survival in sustainable manner, discovering and inventing possibilities for make life more equitable and easier on Earth.

PURPOSE OF EDUCATION AND NEED OF INNOVATION

It is essential to understand and convey the key purpose of education, which should be fundamental development of the person to live a healthy and peaceful life along with providing a positive contribution to the society. But unfortunately, it has been misinterpreted with the materialistic concepts of making money and attaining powers, due to upsurge of capitalist economy the people are succeeding toward getting maximum monetary benefits as well as crucial powers by compromising their physical and mental health, peace of mind and ultimately sustainability of our habitual environment. Although conferring to previous studies it has been observed that Innovation is being used interchangeably only with technology adoption in education.

Rendering to (Fuat and Dilek, 2016) varying needs of the society and global world encourages alignment of nature of education with the requirements of the viable needs of society and globalization. Existing education system mainly focuses on wealth maximization and a luxurious life, people have unconsciously become the part unnecessary competitions and somehow lost the true purpose of education.

CREATIVE LEARNING THROUGH EDUCATION

Innovation is entirely based on the concept of creative learning. Creative learning is deep understanding of concepts, which intends to initiate thinking process of the individual brain for generating more innovative ideas and discover possible solutions of the problems. The Global world needs more folks who can deploy creative thinking skills to solve problems as a team with the help of modern technology and the appropriate tactics of obtaining knowledge, addressed by (Fuat and Dilek, 2016).

Modern system of education is somehow indulged in career competitions, more focused on attainment of better job positions. Frequently applying and memorizing the existing theories, scenarios, technologies and ideas are perceived as standard of qualitative approach. Likewise (Zhao, 2015) explored that the global economy currently needs creative and innovative individuals; but the current educational system raising employment-oriented individuals and failed to nurture such kind of creative individuals. Due to rigidity of the system, it has been very complex and difficult process for the researchers to introduce and incubate the modernized ideas.

FINANCIAL BARRIERS IN EDUCATION

Modern world has made the education system a very complex and expensive process, however education aims to acquire profound knowledge and skills and utilizing it in a socially beneficial activities, due to business in education and unnecessary competitions it has mislaid its true meaning.

Due to business in education system like private schools, colleges and universities these exaggerated educational institutes has twisted the basic persistence of education and has divided them into class systems. Through the cleverish marketing techniques education has turned to be associated with status-quo of the person. Which is making the system more expensive and complex gradually. Educational systems glorify the individuals and their society. Societies always transform and they modify the internal dynamics of the country the person belong to (Pisanu and Menapace, 2014).

Especially in underdeveloped countries people are incapable of getting such education and eventually are unable to be part of such complex education system which is resisting them from utilizing their potentials and talents in social and scientific grounds. World is losing such skilful and compelling brains due to their unaffordability to reach the global competitions. The system has created a gap among the classes and made people unable to work on shared goals and interests those are equally favorable to mankind. In the similar manner (Hjeltnes and Hansson, 2005) also determined that educational institutes and educators must find more productive ways to make education more affordable and time efficient.

LITERATURE REVIEW

Innovation is ongoing process, the roots of innovation is proper education and research, therefore it also necessary to find out gaps in current education system. Many researchers have identified different parameters for innovation in education in different countries of world. Likewise (Cornali, 2012) elucidated innovation in education as dire need of world today. He further explained that social and economic well-being is depend on the degree on the quality education of their citizens. Current education system requires equally effective and efficient approaches, or we can say one should make best use of available resources, to achieve the goals. Tallying with importance of innovation in education, it can also be supposed that Absence of innovation can have intense economic and social consequences, believed by (Creating innovators, 2012).

(Hoffman and Holzhuter, 2012) compared the innovation with a biological process mutation, stated as the process in which species keep evolving themselves to adopt the surrounding environment, so they can better strive for survival. Therefore, Innovation is observed as an important mechanism for positive change. Individual activities like industrial, business, and education needs continuous innovation to remain sustainable. According to (Crichton, 2015), the process of innovation in Education is quite slow as compared to its importance. He further clarified that it is really disappointing for ignoring the fact that there is no any considerable difference between the approach we learn today and how we did so twenty years ago. Though (Peter, 2016) concluded the statement as for better and different results, the educational institutes must concentrate on increasing the value of quality education, exploiting the output of learning, improving educational affordability and time efficiency.

However, it is also essential to identify the true purpose of education. The Researchers (Fuat and Dilek, 2016) purposed in the context that varying needs of the society and global world encourages alignment of nature of education with the requirements of the viable needs of society and globalization.

Although Existing education system mainly focuses on wealth maximization and a luxurious life, people have unconsciously become the part unnecessary competitions and somehow lost the true purpose of education. The question arises whether, the educators can teach more effectively to make students learn more, creative, better and in limited time scale. Although it have deep social, economic and personal consequence as it can affect a learner's lifestyle and career, creates societal assertiveness toward education, and ultimately the country's well-being believed by (Barbera et al., 2015). To increase the efficiency and innovations it is mandatory to implement a culture of creative learning in our institutions.

"Creativity is thinking up new things. Innovation is doing new things" (Theodore Levitt).

Though, Anna Craft (2005) while researching on role of teaching techniques, has specified that it is expected that teaching creatively may lead to creative learning. She suggested that there is dire need to designate the notion of creative learning to evaluate its possible consequences. Even though it is also identified that Creativity cannot constantly be commenced on command. But due to these commands, creativity can actually be inhibited, causing someone to strictly adhere to such habits can make them feel susceptible by external pressure (Lene, 2014). Adding the important concern on creativity learning in education, Perception of creativity in schools is fairly hollow and need to find more developed arrangements for smoothing creativity and individual learning (Fasko, 2001). Similarly (Zhao, 2015) explored that the global economy currently needs creative and innovative individuals; but the current educational system raising employment-oriented individuals and failed to nurture such kind of creative individuals. Due to rigidity of the system, it has been very complex and difficult process for the researchers to introduce and incubate the modernized ideas. Hence Education is considered as most important function in this global world, but unfortunately it remained least understood till now (Peter, 2017).

On other side the cleverish marketing techniques education has turned to be associated with status-quo of the person. Which is making the system more expensive and complex gradually. (Hjeltnes and Hansson, 2005) also determined that educational institutes and educators must find more productive ways to make education more affordable and time efficient.

RESEARCH METHODOLOGY

To make the education system affordable and more efficient a thorough study is conducted to find the potential gaps in education system and addressed the specified needs to innovate them accordingly. Qualitative research approach is adopted for the purpose, secondary data is collected from different research papers, books and news articles. The data is analyzed prudently through varied content analysis techniques, Secondary method suggested by (Christen and Petra, 2017) is used for the purpose.

DATA ANALYSIS

Secondary data is collected from different Research articles, Books, news articles, data is analyzed with the content analysis method and method suggested by (Christen and Petra, 2017)

CONCLUSION

In this chapter current needs of innovation in education system is emphasized to education system more affective and affordable. Innovation is ongoing process which plays a vital role in survival and development of the organizations. Innovation is only possible through creative learnings and creative thinking. Education is considered as backbone for development of a nation, Therefore it is necessary to keep reviewing and improving educational strategies. Just like (Fuat and Dilek, 2016) examined that the education system modify the people and people modify the societies. And eventually societies have power to renovate the internal dynamics of their countries.

Alike others areas of growth, education system also needs to innovate, although we cannot deny the fact that today Education system is far more modernized and innovative then the traditional one, still current educations system holds certain gaps which need to be addressed and resolved. Financial barriers are realized as most upsetting obstacles in current education system, causing an ambiguity among the potential human resources in the world. Profit generation agendas from educational institutes specially in underdeveloped countries has transformed the true purpose of education and divided it into class system, which not only abstaining many underprivileged peoples from getting quality education but also responsible for killing creative skills by participating in useless competitions of getting better brands names and achieving high paid jobs, Employers are prioritizing brands of educational institutes over the creativity and talent.

Such capitalist approach encouraging people for more money making considerations in education, without concerning about sustainability, compromising their mental and physical health.

RECOMMENDATIONS

Few Recommendations on basis on above findings are…

- There is dire need to eliminate financial barriers from the education system, and education should be made affordable for everyone to ensure equal participations of individuals around the world. Government should steps to eradicate uncertainties in the educational institutes based on class system, And make sure education should not prioritized on the basis of status-quo but rely on creative skills a, knowledge and capabilities.
- Educational institutes should encourage creative thinking and incorporate the culture with modern techniques for enhancing creative learning skills, instead of focusing on attainment of job purpose only.
- Human resource management department should avoid prioritizing the candidates on basis of tags of educational institutes, every candidates should be assessed on individual talent, knowledge and capabilities
- Purpose of getting education should not be confused with money making approaches, improved Education should meant improve standard of life and sustainable development of the society

Table 1.

Meaning Unit	Condensed Meaning Units	Code	Categories	Themes
Innovation is considered as a mechanism of obligatory and positive change in the society. Any human activity (e.g. industrial, business, or educational) needs constant innovation to remain sustainable. (Peter, 2017)	Suitability and positive change through innovation	Innovation	Innovation for sustainability	Continuous Innovation plays a key role in sustainability of organizations in every field
Education is probably the most important function in our society today, yet it remains one of the least understood, despite incredible levels of investment from venture capitalists and governments." (Crichton, 2015).	Education is least understood and being ignored area.	Education	Lack of concern towards education	Education system need to pay proper attention for being an important pillar of developed society
Given the present situation of the world and global and knowledge economy today, the shortest possible ways of integrating educational systems into the knowledge economy are reconstructing the concept of knowledge, understanding what innovation really means and enriching human capital . (Sahlberg and Oldroyd, 2010) The purpose of education has evolved according to the needs of society. Today education needs to teach people about their shared rights and freedoms are, so that they may be respected, and to promote the will to protect those of others."(News article from Alison Academy)	Recreating the concept of knowledge and understanding can increase human capital and improvised economy. Purpose of education is varying from time to time, education today should teach people about their rights and freedom.	Educational Innovation Purpose of education	Educational innovation for improved Economy and human capital Purpose of education should vary With varying needs of society	For enriching human capital rebuilding a healthier economy world need to revise and innovate the current educational system by improving knowledge and understanding. Education should be focused according to the current needs of the society i-e concerning more about morals values. Giving equal rights and freedom to every individual.
The more educated people are, the better they will understand the world around them, and will be better able to improve their own quality of life and of others. This progress is particularly noticeable in vulnerable populations where education is the best solution for creating better perspectives and achieving success. (News article from Alison Academy)	Education is only the source which in true sense gives the understanding to people for improving their life standards.	Quality of life	Modified education system should be focused on improving quality of life.	The developed education system can make people understand true purpose of education that is intended to improve the quality of life of their own and others, which can ultimately lead to development of society
Individuals with low incomes are less likely to buy books, subscribe to newspapers, or to have jobs that require high levels of literacy practices. Compared with higher-income adults, these individuals are, therefore, limited in the extent of their learning and reading experiences (Holt & Smith, 2005).	Class difference, financial barriers are the main obstruction in making the educational system more affective	Financial Barriers in education	People are unable to get quality education due to poverty.	Due to poor financial conditions, and expensive educational institutes people are unable to afford the quality education, it resist many potential people to utilize their talent and capabilities in global Market
Educational system must help to restore and/or avoid killing among children. Human Creativity that may help make education more effective in relation to learning, and innovation. (Sawyer, 2012).	Human Creativity that may help make education more effective in relation to learning, and innovation.	Creative learning	Creative learning through education encourages innovation	Creative learning through education can help society to get more innovative ideas and understandings

111

REFRENCES

Barbera, E., Gros, B., & Kirschner, P. (2015). Paradox of time in research on educational technology. *Time & Society, 24*(1), pp. 96-108.http://tas.sagepub.com/ content/24/1/ 96.refs.

Cornali, F. (2012). Effectiveness and efficiency of educational measures. *Evaluation Practices, Indicators and Rhetoric, 2*(3), pp. 255-260. www.SciRP.org/journal/sm

Craft, A. (2005) Creativity in Schools: tensions and dilemmas. London: Routledge. . doi:10.4324/9780203357965

Creating Innovators. (2012). America's last competitive advantage. http:// creatinginnovators.com/ .

Crichton, D. (2015). Searching for the next wave of education innovation. *TechCrunch*. https://techcrunch. com/2015/06/27/education-next-wave/

Crichton, D. (2015). Searching for the next wave of education innovation. *TechCrunch*. https://techcrunch. com/2015/06/27/education-next-wave/.

Tanggaard, L. (2014). Faculty of Humanities, Department of Communication & Psychology, University of Aalborg, Denmark. *European Educational Research Journal, 13*(1), 2014. www.wwwords.eu/EERJ

Fasko, D. Jr. (2000-01). Education and Creativity. *Creativity Research Journal, 13*(3-4), 317–327. doi:10.1207/S15326934CRJ1334_09

Hoffman, A., & Holzhuter, J. (2012). The evolution of higher education: innovation as natural selection. In A. Hoffman & S. Spangehl (Eds.), *Innovation in Higher Education: Igniting the Spark for Success, American Council on Education*, (pp. 3–15). Rowman & Litttlefield Publishers Inc.

Ilhan, D., & Karatas, H. (2015). An analysis on motivational beliefs and attitudes of undergraduates regarding learning English. *International Journal of Educational Research, 6*(2).

Pisanu, F., & Menapace, P. (2014). Creativity and innovation: Four key issues from a literature review. *Creative Education, 5*(3), 145–154. doi:10.4236/ce.2014.53023

Sahlberg, P., & Oldroyd, D. (2010). Pedagogy for economic competitiveness and sustainable development. *European Journal of Education, 45*(2), 280–299. doi:10.1111/j.1465-3435.2010.01429.x

Sawyer, K. (2012). *Explaining Creativity: the science of human innovation*. Oxford University Press.

Serdyukov, P. (2016). Innovation in education: what works, what doesn't, and what to do about it? Journal of Research in Innovative Teaching & Learning, 10 (1).

Vieluf, S., Kaplan, D., Klieme, E., & Bayer, S. (2012). *Teaching Practices and Pedagogical Innovation: Evidence from TALIS*. OECD Publishing. www.oecd.org/edu/school/ TalisCeri%202012%20(tppi)–Ebook. pdf doi:10.1787/9789264123540-en

Zhao, Y. (2015). A world at risk: An imperative for paradigm shift to cultivate 21st century learners. *Society, 52*(2), 129–135. doi:10.100712115-015-9872-8

Chapter 10
Social Innovation and Social Entrepreneurship in the Wake of COVID-19:
A Perspective From the Developing Side of the World

Muhammad Faisal Sultan
Khadim Ali Shah Bukhari Institute of Technology, Pakistan

Muhammad Nawaz Tunio
iD https://orcid.org/0000-0003-1376-5371
Mohammad Ali Jinnah University, Karachi, Pakistan

Atif Aziz
Karachi Institute of Economics and Technology, Pakistan

Sadia Khurram Shaikh
Benazir Bhutto Shaheed University, Pakistan

ABSTRACT

Social innovation and social entrepreneurship were rarely discussed till the 19th century. However, the topic has been in the limelight extensively since 1950. Moreover, the linkage between social innovation and social entrepreneurship still needs to be explored, especially in developing sides of the world where social entrepreneurship is required to optimize social and economic parameters. In fact, there is a severe increase in the level of opportunities for social entrepreneurship. The increase in the level of opportunities is massive, especially due to globalization. Therefore, this chapter has been written purposefully to reflect the role of social entrepreneurship with examples and opportunities for social entrepreneurship with reference to the developing sides of the world.

DOI: 10.4018/978-1-6684-5417-6.ch010

INTRODUCTION

Companies always found difficult to accomplish their social responsibilities due to the contradiction between approach used to optimize business and social mission. Hence companies are oftenly found to be struggling towards attainment of agenda for social responsibility. However, the established & well-known firms try to follow philosophy of Triple Bottom Line for creating social value & social impact without compromising on profitability or sustainability. Similar has been mentioned through literature that in order to generate sustainable value, companies need to formulate strategies and practices that may not only resulted in the increase of shareholders value but will also contributed progressively to sustainable world (Tunio et al., 2021; Shaikh et al., 2021; Afshan et al., 2021). Thus strive for social value resulted in social entrepreneurship and to do this there is a need of out of the box innovation in products, services & organizations etc. Hence it is legitimate to declare that most unexplored area is social innovation. In fact, to deliver increase value from the corporate social responsibilities (CSR) organizations must try to learn how they must incorporate social innovations in their CSR. Therefore, social entrepreneurship came into the limelight, especially after the dawn of 20th century the term. However, the traces of social entrepreneurship might be found even before 100 years that is reflected through voluntary working by public and private organizations as well as by structuring and working of different communities (Phillips et al., 2015).

Zahra et al (2009) narrated social entrepreneurship as the hybrid of activities and process to focus more vividly on opportunities for new association or to optimize business of existing firms. The definition has major connection with the prospective association of social innovation with social entrepreneurship as Phills et al (2008) declared social innovation and social entrepreneurship are interrelated. In fact both the terms are about identification of social problems and its solution through capitalizing upon opportunity to overcome social need.

COMMON EXAMPLES OF SOCIAL ENTREPRENEURSHIP FROM DEVELOPING SIDES OF THE WORLD

Some of the most common examples of the social entrepreneurship that are conducted to benefit society and to leverage economies of developing sides of the world are as under:

Solar Skylights developed from plastic bottles containing simply water and bleach was one of the most creative social innovations which ultimately resulted in social entrepreneurship. The light generated from skylight was equivalent to 55 W bulbs and is sufficient to make one work effectively for longer working hours. Coupled with the fact that use of Skylight is also beneficial for decrease of electricity consumption and according to the estimate the use of skylight resulted in saving of $ US 10/ month (Sivathanu & Bhise, 2013; Tunio et al., 2021; Gilal et al., 2021; Abdullah et al., 2020; Tunio, 2020).

a) Amul founded as Anand Milk Union Limited is the company that creates white revolution in India and fostering development at societal and country level through white revolution of India. Through this revolution India became worlds' largest producer and exporter (Sivathanu & Bhise, 2013; Tunio et al., 2021; Gul et al., 2021; Shaikh et al., 2021).

b) Muhammad Younus stated Grameen Bank that removes the need of collateral for obtaining loans. Hence resulted in making banking operations creative, innovative, collaborative, accountable and trustworthy (Sivathanu & Bhise, 2013; Aurangzeb et al., 2021; Tunio and Shaikh, 2020; Shaikh, and Tunio, 2020).

c) Shri Mahila Griha Udyog Papad is a Mumbai based women organization. That was initially formulated through association of seven females of same residential building. The company started its business through general grocery items and penetrates allover India as its membership reaches 40,000 and sales raised up to 300 crores. Exports of the company also reaches 1 crores and thus able to resist against the hardships and strengthen the role of women in India (Sivathanu & Bhise, 2013).

d) In Pakistan emergence of innovation centers and incubation labs are also fostering social entrepreneurship; especially SMEDA & Social Innovation Lab-LUMS are the leading names that are providing facilities to young social entrepreneurs in Pakistan (Qamar et al., 2020).

SITUATION AT THE WAKE OF COVID-19 & NEED OF RESEARCH

Initially it has been assumed that pro social entrepreneur will work for social welfare and their pro social attitude makes them for social welfare. Although during COVID-19 it has been observed that several companies are also trying to resolve social problems caused by the outbreak of pandemic (Alshareef et al., 2022; Shaikh et al., 2022; Tunio et al., 20201). For e.g. manufacturing of plastic shields, ventilators and hand sanitizers and offering these to public at price lower than the cost all were in the interest of society and masses. However, the intent of the manufacturers is still unclear that whether these actions were taken to support and help others or not? Therefore, it has been assumed that the link between pro social motives and social outcomes is weak (Bacq & Lumpkin, 2021; Katpar. et al., 2020; Tunio et al., 2021; Shaikh et al., 2022).

Similar sort of indications was made by Defourny and Nyssens (2010), that there is need of proper understanding not only for social entrepreneurship but also about the linkage between social innovation and social entrepreneurship (Tunio et al., 2021; Memon et al., 2021; Afshan et al., 2021). On the other hand, it is also a fact that individuals as well as organizations are now keenly interested towards the betterment of the society especially for those who are at most vulnerable side of the society. The most common contributions of social entrepreneurship are women empowerment, poverty alleviation and management of institutional change (Qamar et al., 2020; Gilal. et al., 2020; Tunio, 2020). Therefore, there are several facets for Social Entrepreneurship i.e. Weerawardena and Mort (2006) posited non-profit facet while Yunus and Weber (2009) highlighted profit making and self-sustainability as the major feature of Social Entrepreneurship. However, as per the believe of masses Social Entrepreneurship is a delivery platform and basically used to create value for society through innovation (Dacin et al., 2011; Chaudhry et al., 2021; Tunio et al., 2021; Mushtaq et al., 2021).

NEED OF SOCIAL ENTREPRENEURSHIP IN THE CONTEXT OF PAKISTAN

Pakistan belongs to the developing side of the world and also faces severe issue of underutilization of human resources. Hence the country is far behind the other countries in terms of prosperity and economic growth. For attaining prosperity there are two possible solutions i.e. increase in employment ratio or development of new enterprises through giving opportunities to youth. Although poor economic growth is due to poor health conditions in the market, illiteracy, unemployment, and environmental degradation and to hamper the prevailing economic growth there is a need to improve social and economic indicators (Katper et al., 2017; Tunio et al., 2017).

Although it is a massive challenge to improve social and economic conditions especially in the absence of proper guidelines, opportunities and awareness regarding the improvement and optimization. Hence Social Entrepreneurship is the best element that may hamper the situation as its significance has been proved through authentic evidence across the globe (Qamar et al., 2020; Tunio et al., 2021; Gilal et al., 2021; Abdullah et al., 2020; Tunio, 2020).

REFERENCES

Abdullah, M., Katper, N. K., Chaudhry, N. I., and Tunio, M. N. (2020). An Impact of Workaholics on Creativity: the mediating role of Negative Mood and moderating role of Supervisor Support. *Sukkur IBA Journal of Management and Business, 7*(2).

Afshan, G., Ilyas, S., Tunio, M. N., & Kalhoro, M. (2021). CSR actions and post-COVID'19 consequences in hotel industry: A conceptual framework. *International Journal of Strategic Change Management, 7*(4), 1. doi:10.1504/IJSCM.2021.122845

Afshan, G., Ilyas, S., Tunio, M. N., & Kalhoro, M. (2021). CSR actions and post-COVID-19 consequences in the hotel industry: A conceptual framework. *International Journal of Strategic Change Management, 7*(4), 275–289. doi:10.1504/IJSCM.2021.122845

Alshareef, N., & Tunio, M. N. (2022). Role of Leadership in Adoption of Blockchain Technology in Small and Medium Enterprises in Saudi Arabia. *Frontiers in Psychology, 13*, 2284. doi:10.3389/fpsyg.2022.911432 PMID:35602740

Aurangzeb, M. T., Tunio, M. N., Rehman, Z., & Asif, M. (2021). Influence of administrative expertise on human resources practitioners on the job performance: Mediating role of achievement motivation. *International Journal of Management, 12*(4), 408–421.

Bacq, S., & Lumpkin, G. T. (2021). Social entrepreneurship and COVID-19. *Journal of Management Studies, 58*(1), 285–288. doi:10.1111/joms.12641

Chaudhry, I. S., Paquibut, R. Y. & Tunio, M. N. (2021) Do workforce diversity, inclusion practices, & organizational characteristics contribute to organizational innovation? Evidence from the U.A.E. *Cogent Business & Management, 8*(1), 1947549, . doi:10.1080/23311975.2021.1947549

Dacin, M. T., Dacin, P. A., & Tracey, P. (2011). Social entrepreneurship: A critique and future directions. *Organization Science, 22*(5), 1203–1213. doi:10.1287/orsc.1100.0620

Defourny, J., & Nyssens, M. (2010). Conceptions of social enterprise and social entrepreneurship in Europe and the United States: Convergences and divergences. *Journal of Social Entrepreneurship, 1*(1), 32–53. doi:10.1080/19420670903442053

Gilal, F. G., Gilal, N. G., Channa, N. A., Gilal, R. A., Gilal, R. G., & Tunio, M. N. (2020). Towards an integrated model for the transference of environmental responsibility. *Business Strategy and the Environment*, *29*(6), 1–10. doi:10.1002/bse.2524

Gilal, F. G., Gilal, N. G., Gilal, R. G., Gon, Z., Gilal, W. G., & Tunio, M. N. (2021). The Ties That Bind: Do Brand Attachment and Brand Passion Translate Into Consumer Purchase Intention? *Central European Management Journal*, *29*(1), 14–38. doi:10.7206/cemj.2658-0845.39

Gul, A., Subhan, S., & Tunio, M. N. (2021). Learning experiences of women entrepreneurs amidst COVID-19. *International Journal of Gender and Entrepreneurship*, *13*(2), 1756–6266. doi:10.1108/IJGE-09-2020-0153

Katpar., N. K., Chaudhry, N. I., Tunio, M. N. and Ali, M. A. (2020). Impact of Leadership Style and Organizational Culture on Organizational Commitment. *Sukkur IBA Journal of Management and Business –SIJMB 7*(1), 92-106.

Katper, N. K. Medan, A., Syed, K. B. S.., Tunio, M. N. (2017). Determinants of Debt Maturity Structure in Shariah and Non-Shariah Firms in Pakistan: A comparative Study. *Journal of Applied Economic Sciences 12*(4), p1210-1225.

Memon, A.B., Meyer, K. and Tunio, M. N. (2021). Toward collaborative networking among innovation laboratories: a conceptual framework. *International Journal of Innovation Science*. doi:10.1108/IJIS-04-2021-0069

Mushtaq, T., Tunio, M. N., Akbar, Z., and Jariko, M. (2021). Green Organizational identity: Antecents and consequences: An Emprical Study. *Contemporary Issues in business and Government, 27*(3), p. 2056-2069.

Phillips, W., Lee, H., Ghobadian, A., O'regan, N., & James, P. (2015). Social innovation and social entrepreneurship: A systematic review. *Group & Organization Management*, *40*(3), 428–461. doi:10.1177/1059601114560063

Phills, J. A., Deiglmeier, K., & Miller, D. T. (2008). Rediscovering social innovation. *Stanford Social Innovation Review*, *6*(4), 34–43.

Qamar, U., Ansari, N., Tanveer, F., & Qamar, N. (2020). Social Entrepreneurship in Pakistan: Challenges and Prospects. *Journal of Management Research*, *7*(2), 1–41.

Qamar, U., Ansari, N., Tanveer, F., & Qamar, N. (2020). Social Entrepreneurship in Pakistan: Challenges and Prospects. *Journal of Management Research*, *7*(2), 1–41.

Shaikh, E., Tunio, M. N. (2020). Customer satisfaction and Customer loyalty: An empirical case study on the impact of benefits generated through Smartphone applications. *International Journal of Public Sector Performance Management*.

Shaikh, E., Tunio, M. N., Khoso, W. M., Brahmi, M., & Rasool, S. (2022). The COVID-19 Pandemic Overlaps Entrepreneurial Activities and Triggered New Challenges: A Review Study. *Managing Human Resources in SMEs and Start-ups: International Challenges and Solutions,* 155-182.

Shaikh, E., Tunio, M. N., & Qureshi, F. (2021). Finance and women's entrepreneurship in DETEs: A literature review. *Entrepreneurial Finance, Innovation and Development*, 191-209.

Shaikh, E., Watto, W. A., & Tunio, M. N. (2022). Impact of Authentic Leadership on Organizational Citizenship Behavior by Using The Mediating Effect of Psychological Ownership. *ETIKONOMI, 21*(1), 89–102. doi:10.15408/etk.v21i1.18968

Shaikh, S., Sultan, M. F., Mushtaque, T., & Tunio, M. N. (2021). Impact of COVID-19 on GDP: A serial mediation effect on international tourism and hospitality. *International Journal of Management, 12*(84), 422–430.

Sivathanu, B., & Bhise, P. V. (2013). Challenges for social entrepreneurship. *International Journal of Application or Innovation in Engineering & Management (IJAIEM)*, 9-10

Tunio, M. N. (2020). Role of ICT in Promoting Entrepreneurial Ecosystems in Pakistan. *Journal of Business Ecosystems, 1*(2), 1–21. doi:10.4018/JBE.2020070101

Tunio, M. N., Chaudhry, I. S., Shaikh, S., Jariko, M. A., & Brahmi, M. (2021). Determinants of the Sustainable Entrepreneurial Engagement of Youth in Developing Country—An Empirical Evidence from Pakistan. *Sustainability, 13*(14), 7764. doi:10.3390u13147764

Tunio, M. N., Jariko, M. A., Børsen, T., Shaikh, S., Mushtaque, T., & Brahmi, M. (2021). How Entrepreneurship Sustains Barriers in the Entrepreneurial Process—A Lesson from a Developing Nation. *Sustainability, 13*(20), 1–18. doi:10.3390u132011419

Tunio, M. N., & Shaikh, E. (2020). ((Forthcoming). Nascent entrepreneurs and challenges in digital market in developing countries. *International Journal of Public Sector Performance Management.*

Tunio, M. N., Shaikh, E., Niaz, S., & Katper, N. S. (2021). Multifaceted perils of the Covid-19 and implications: A Review. *Estudios de Economía Aplicada.* doi:10.25115/eea.v39i2.3957

Tunio, M. N., Soomro, A. A., & Bogenhold, D. (2017). The Study of Self-employment at SMEs Level with Reference to Poverty in Developing Countries. Business and Management Research, 6(2). doi:10.5430/bmr.v6n2p33

Tunio, M. N., Yusrini, L., Shah, Z. A., Katper, N., & Jariko, M. A. (2021). How Hotel Industry Cope up with the COVID-19: An SME Perspective. *Etikonomi, 20*(2), 213–224. doi:10.15408/etk.v20i2.19172

Tunio, M. N., Yusrini, L., & Shoukat, G. (2021). Corporate social responsibility (CSR) in Hotels in Austria, Pakistan, and Indonesia: small and medium Enterprise spillover of COVID-19. In Handbook of research on entrepreneurship, innovation, sustainability, and ICTs in the post-COVID-19 era, (pp. 263-280). IGI Global.

Zahra, S. A., Gedajlovic, E., Neubaum, D. O., & Shulman, J. M. (2009). A typology of social entrepreneurs: Motives, search processes and ethical challenges. *Journal of Business Venturing, 24*(5), 519–532. doi:10.1016/j.jbusvent.2008.04.007

Chapter 11
Social Innovation in Higher Education:
Business and Social Impacts and Implications

Muhammad Faisal Sultan

Khadim Ali Shah Bukhari Institute of Technology, Pakistan

Aamir Hussain

Khadim Ali Shah Bukhari Institute of Technology, Pakistan

Shahid Khan

Khadim Ali Shah Bukhari Institute of Technology, Pakistan

Raza Ali Khan

NED University of Engineering and Technology, Pakistan

ABSTRACT

The role of higher education is to benefit society at large to generate sustainable socio-economic returns. Therefore, research and knowledge creation must be rendered to achieve anodyne to overcome social challenges and foster new and better practices. Hence, social innovation is the need of society, especially from higher education providers. Especially after the outbreak of COVID-19, there is a need of social innovation by all stake holders in order to attain a sustainable economy. Although, to provide catalyst to the model of social change and innovation, there is a need of an entrepreneurial model for higher education. However, most of the prior studies with the reference of education are not related with the innovation but with societal impact and produce educational change. Thus, this chapter has been written purposely to describe social innovation by higher education providers. The chapter also includes various examples of social innovation with respect to the higher education sector in order to make readers understand the importance of social innovation in the pre-COVID-19 and post-COVID-19 worlds.

DOI: 10.4018/978-1-6684-5417-6.ch011

INTRODUCTION

Higher Education is perceived as the tool to generate sustainable socio-economic returns through assisting society in marching towards creation of better employment opportunities & reduction of social inequality (McDonnell-Naughton & Păunescu, 2022). Thus, it is mandatory for universities and higher educational institutions to make their offerings and services distinctive as comparison to the competition. This may be achieved through research work but PhD Degrees awarded by the institutions might not make them sustain in longer versions of time. Similarly, innovation related with economic outcomes might also not be the part of innovation agenda of innovation practices at university level. Thus, research work and knowledge utilization must be in a novel manner to add value to industry and economy. This will resulted in attainment of "anodyne" that is the real purpose of innovation at higher education level. The most common example of these sort of innovations are Massive Open Online Courses (MOOC), that are available for anyone who wishes to study through internet. Although the attitude MOOC is also getting negative as these sort of courses does not encourages innovation and creativity (Blass & Hayward, 2014).

Thus, legitimate to quote Kapoor Weerakkody & Schroeder (2018) to mention in higher education segment novel solutions are required to overcome social challenges & foster new and better practices. Thus, it is better for higher educational institutions to strive for social innovation. Social innovations are important for entire set of organizational practices and forces several group of actors to initiate entrepreneurial action for social change. In fact, Stanford Business Center of Social Innovation (2018) provides definition of social innovation as "A process which utilizes effective solutions to challenging, complex, and systemic social issues." Thus, in light of this definition the purpose of social innovators is to figure out unmet social desire in a creative way to bridge the gap in service design and provision by applying unique work approaches, methods & means On the other side experience of COVID-19 make us understand the fact that society needs all of us to work together and therefore there is a legitimate need of social innovation by all stake holders. However, the catalyst of social change must beneficial for all the stakeholders and resulted in sustainability of economy. (McDonnell-Naughton & Păunescu, 2022).

Although to provide catalyst to the model of social change & innovation there is a need of entrepreneurial model for higher education therefore, higher education sector is going through massive change all over the globe. There are few other studies too that are demanding new model of governance for HEIs to incorporate social innovation in the system to fosters exchange of social innovation for optimization of education & its social impact (McDonnell-Naughton & Păunescu, 2022).

NEED OF RESEARCH STUDIES

Hunt (2011) indicated that higher education sector is facing multiple challenges and the sector is required to revamp its activities in order to improve to lure with the opportunity of serving diversified groups of students. However, most of the prior studies with the reference of education is not related with the innovation but with societal impact & produce educational change (McDonnell-Naughton & Păunescu, 2022). There is a high need of this form of research as prior studies related with innovation in education mostly related with curriculum design, pedagogical approaches, mechanism of support service & innovation. However, the need of entrepreneurial model in higher education is hanging on the shoulder of researchers (Carayannis et al., 2012 & Kolleck et al., 2017) and therefore indications of McDonnell-Naughton and Păunescu (2022), are legitimate to be considered. The relation of higher education providers with change is infancy at this moment. However, if universities can provide sustainability and leads to adoption of measurable change then higher education provider will be the advocates and driver of the change rather than only critics or victim (Blass & Hayward, 2014).

However, recently higher education is in transition phase not at any one country or continent but all over the globe. The reason of transition is common in the form of COVID-19 which is indicating the need of active engagement of active engagement of citizens but also a keen focus towards social innovation especially by public, private, and governmental actors (McDonnell-Naughton & Păunescu, 2022). However, higher education providers (Universities) are termed as major force behind social innovation as of the capability to solve those social problems that may address myriad but are beyond the control of public sector firms (Blass & Hayward, 2014). However due to the wide spectrum of social innovation the literature related with is not homogenous duherefore there is a systematic need of study to understand social innovation and its impact in more comprehensive manner (Morawska-Jancelewicz, 2021).

GROWING IMPORTANCE OF SOCIAL INNOVATION

Social Innovation is the solution of contemporary problems & has been explored from different forms of perspectives. Social Innovation are also known as "Innovation with in Human face" and encompasses various activities pertaining to diversified sectors. Although innovation is fruitful for the enhancement of personal experience through learning by doing and learning by interaction. This enhancement will positively related with enhancement of skills & qualification of personnel that would ultimately reflected upon increase in labor productivity & technological advancement. However, the major objective of social innovation is social change hence there are different classification of social innovation that are classified as (Morawska-Jancelewicz, 2021)

1.   On the bases of Nature (digital, technical, political, ethical, etc.)
2.   Focus on Intervention (medicine, health, education, urban transformation)
3.   Normative Approaches and Impacts (transformative, global, local), etc.

Past two decades resulted in evolution of several new concepts that are based on ongoing socio-economic changes related with the concept of innovation. Therefore, in recent time universities are subjected to public and scientific debate as these changes are consistent with mode 3 universities. Studies define Mode 3 University as a form of organization that encourages creativity and innovation in organizational context without compromising upon integrating of knowledge production and knowledge application (Morawska-Jancelewicz, 2021).

REFERENCES

Blass, E., & Hayward, P. (2014). Innovation in higher education; will there be a role for "the academe/university" in 2025? *European Journal of Futures Research*, 2(1), 1–9.

Hunt, C. (2011). *National Strategy for higher education to 2030 report of the strategy group*. Department of Education and Skills.

Kapoor, K., Weerakkody, V., & Schroeder, A. (2018). Social innovations for social cohesion in Western Europe: Success dimensions for lifelong learning and education. *Innovation (Abingdon)*, *31*(2), 189–203. doi:10.1080/13511610.2017.1419336

McDonnell-Naughton, M., & Păunescu, C. (2022). Facets of social innovation in higher education. *Social Innovation in Higher Education*, 9.

Morawska-Jancelewicz, J. (2021). The role of universities in social innovation within quadruple/quintuple helix model: Practical implications from polish experience. *Journal of the Knowledge Economy*, 1–42.

ADDITIONAL READING

Chow, J. C. C., Ren, C., Mathias, B., & Liu, J. (2019). InterBoxes: A social innovation in education in rural China. *Children and Youth Services Review*, *101*, 217–224. doi:10.1016/j.childyouth.2019.04.008

Elliott, G. (2013). Character and impact of social innovation in higher education. *International Journal of Continuing Education and Lifelong Learning*, *5*(2), 71–84.

Chapter 12
An Overview of Women Empowerment Policy With a Social Justice Lens and Frugal Innovation

Erum Shah
University of Sindh, Pakistan

Sultan Ali
University of Sindh, Pakistan

Naveeda Katper
University of Sindh, Pakistan

ABSTRACT

Women's empowerment has remained a key concern for the development of society. The information in the current study has been extracted from the doctoral thesis of the corresponding researcher. The study argues that in the 20th century, developing countries were observed to bring various policies and programs to empower women. However, in this study, the researcher has tried to capture a few of the prominent policies and programs brought in Pakistan to empower women since its independence. Concurrently, this study aims to evaluate those policies and programs in the key domains of women's empowerment with the lens of social justice. It is mainly done with a desk review of various published resources and the support of key informant interviews with politicians, human rights activists, and bureaucrats. Findings of the study suggest, having various policies and programs for women empowerment, the situation of women is not improved in Pakistan, and there are significant rifts in policy implementation that need proper consideration to meet the requirements of social justice.

DOI: 10.4018/978-1-6684-5417-6.ch012

INTRODUCTION

Power is the key word of the term empowerment, empower is the combination of prefix 'em' means to make, with noun 'power' from the French and Latin means having the capacity and the means to direct one's life towards desired social, political and economic goals or status; the combination of two 'Em' prefix with 'Power' makes it verbs 'empower' meaning to make or cause power. (Dominic & Jothi, 2012; Lincoln, Travers, Ackers, & Wilkinson, 2002; Tunio, 2020). Empowerment literally means to become powerful by improving status through education, economic opportunity, and health (Dominic & Jothi, 2012; Tunio, et al., 2021).

Empowerment traces its history from seventeenth century as the process to permit or enable. In the development discourse women empowerment entered in the domains of social, political, and economic rights movement. Academia discusses women empowerment in five main categories (political, economic, educational, social, and psychological) based on their attributes.

It has been a long time to listen the words women empowerment, policy for women empowerment and women rights in day-to-day life of Pakistan. However, lower education, fewer work opportunities, violence against women, acid attacks, honor killings and poor health status are notorious issues of Pakistan which are often rose by national and international organizations (United Nations Development Programme, 2016; Tunio, 2020; Memon, et al., 2021).

Social justice is widely defined as all people should have equal access and opportunity for social economic and political rights. Whereas the above literature confirms that empowerment is a given capacity or power to those who lacks it or denied before by creating an environment where they can enjoy their rights equally with others. Therefore, current study sets following objectives.

OBJECTIVES

1. To recognize key policies and programs for women empowerment in the history of Pakistan.
2. To evaluate women empowerment policy with the lens of social justice.

METHODOLOGY

This research is part of an exploratory study that uses qualitative method of data collection and analysis. The research has used two step of data collection i.e to meet the objective one mainly relied on desk review of documents that include national policy on women development and empowerment, national action plan, women empowerment policy (Sindh province), reports submitted to UN, GRASP and other published resources. Whereas to meet objective two findings arrived through fourteen key informant interviews (KII) of women politician, rights activists, and bureaucrats residing particularly in Sindh and Islamabad. Thematic analysis of data was carried out and finding are discussed in the research.

RESULTS AND DISCUSSION

Meaning of Empowerment

Findings of this study women conceptualize women empowerment as economic stability, social acceptability, educational achievement, and family harmony. Findings also discuss factors of empowerment and disempowerment. The enabling factor of empowerment includes working out of traditional roles and freedom of choice; while traditional influences, misinterpretation, patriarchy and feudal system are discussed as disabling factors of empowerment (Bustamante-Gavino, Rattani, & Khan, 2011; Tunio, 2017; Chaudhry, et al., 2021).

Key Policies/Programs and Institutional Mechanisms in Pakistan to Empower Women

To date, whatever has been done to empower women around the globe has deep roots in the history of struggle for the rights of women. To understand the policy process for women empowerment (government flexibility to bring reforms and the actors/advocates behind bringing the policy solutions) it is important to understand from the historical perspective. Literature gives a detailed account of several legislative and institutional arrangements which aim to empower women in Pakistan. Government of Pakistan talks about women empowerment as an equal opportunity to decent employment, education, health, political representation and creation of enabling environment without any discrimination. (Ministry of Planning, 2017; WDD-Sindh, 2011).

Struggle of Muslim women for their rights traces its history before the creation of Pakistan; after independence women continued their struggle to mobilize support for legal reforms and led to the Muslim personal law of sharia in 1948. In the 1950, in the decision to ratify the UN convention an important sociological reform was Muslim family law ordinance (MFLO). The state became the party of the 1953 convention on the political rights of women. Based on female suffrage, 1956 constitution reserved 5 percent special seats for women and a charter of women's rights was included in the 1956 constitution. The second major legislation affecting women's legal rights in Pakistan was 1973 constitution. The year 1979 saw the formation of the women's division. The 1956, 1962 and 1973 all provided for women reserved seats with 5 to 10 percent.

In the fourth world conference on women, it was accepted that patriarchal structure, rigid orthodox norms, stifling sociocultural norms and tradition are the oppressor of women in Pakistan. However, constitution of Pakistan discourages any discrimination against women by recognizing the equality for all citizen (Rasul, 2014).

However, there was apparent lack of attention on impacts of development projects and programs on women during the first three decades of development assistance 1950s through 1970s. Pakistan began to turn its attention back to women's rights in the 1990s, particularly after post Beijing women's conference (Ali & Akhtar, 2012; Weiss, 2001) In the consequences of recommendation in 1975 women's year conference at Mexico, governments started initiating institutional mechanisms. The fourth world conference identified Women Development Department (WDD) as the major policy coordinating unit inside the government, responsible for ensuring that nations signing the Beijing platform for action develop and implement a national plan of action on women and prepare country reports. The Pakistan women's division in mid 1980s became a fully-fledged federal ministry (MoWD); beside provincial level setup in the form of sections, wings and departments affixed with the social welfare departments.

In the wake of the 18th constitutional amendment the federal ministry of women dissolved, and portfolio of implementation of women development and gender mainstreaming handed over to the provincial WDD (NCSW, 2011; Zubeida, 2011). National Commission on Status of Women (NCSW) in 2000, cross party Women Parliamentarian Caucus (WPC) at national level in 2008 and later at provincial level and Provincial Commission on Status (PCSW) were setup (Mirza, 2011). Working women hostels, crises cells, trauma centers; legislation to secure women from honor killing and domestic violence are some of the main initiatives taken by the government.

There has been a wide shift towards decentralization from the years 2001; the devolution plan 2000 reserved 33 percent seats for women in legislative councils. In the year 2002, general Musharraf passed the act with allocating 17 percent seats for women at provincial and national assemblies and senate and 5 percent (now 10%) quota in government jobs. The establishment of national commission on status of women (NCSW) in 2002 sought national consensus on a national policy for women. Two laws, criminal law (amendment) act of 2004 popularly referred "honor killing law" followed by the protection of women act 2006 were step forward in providing relief to rape victims. Protection against harassment for women at the workplace act 2009, accompanied amendment to Pakistan's penal code-criminal law (amendment) act 2009, anti-women practices bill 2009 and the acid throwing legislation, elevation of NCSW with greater autonomy in 2012, domestic violence (prevention and protection) bill 2009 passed as 2012 act, were the major initiatives of the later phase (Riffat, 2010; Weiss, 2012; Tunio, et al., 2021). Child marriage restraint act and Hindu marriage registration act in Sindh province of Pakistan are the additions in the policies for social justice.

STATUS AGAINST EMPOWERMENT INDICATORS

Political Participation

For a gender fair government, it is highly essential to give women equal opportunity to participate in policy making. Findings of this study gives an impression that the role of women politicians is being tried to minimize by harassment and their involvement in certain maters especially related to women and jirga is highly threatened by religious groups or feudal. Key informants (KI) interviews in this study suggest crucial issues of political representation such as lack of education and ignorance of issues of women.

Despite various issues Pakistan has remained trend-setter in political empowerment of women for Muslim countries. There is no restriction on women's political participation in Pakistan; but it is observed that participation of women is scarce at all levels due to cultural and structural barriers. One of the reasons may be the political behavior of people is molded and shaped by the tradition of patriarchy as a political institution which gives more economic and political power to males. Although government show commitment to increase women's economic and political participation, but the dependency of females robs them of their basic human rights. women's wisdom, rationality and intellectual power are considered as inferior during politics. The prevailing mass illiteracy, lack of wisdom in women about politics and political administration, women's self-misperception that female does not like to take part in politics and women's restricted mobility are the main constraints in this regard. Similarly, the urban focused policy excluded rural and urban middle-class women.

To improve the indicators of political empowerment of women there is need for bottom-up approach for progressive socio-cultural change. To enhance women's political participation, it is essential to address the structural discriminations embodied socio-cultural practices within political parties (Ali & Akhtar, 2012; Awan, 2016; Naz & Chaudhry, 2011).

Social and Psychological Empowerment

Autonomy is an important attribute of social and psychological empowerment of women. In south Asia women's autonomy factors "control of their own lives, equal voice in matter affecting women and their families, control over material and other resources, access to knowledge and information, authority to make independent decisions, freedom from constraint to physical mobility and the ability to claim equitable power relationships" within families are determined by the regional and socio-cultural context. Due to the cultural context and specific operationalization all factors of women's autonomy are constrained in Pakistan. The conferring traditional factors suggest women's autonomy need to be expanded beyond education and employment options. It should be sought more comprehensive, direct and context specific (Jejeebhoy & Sathar, 2001; Sathar & Kazi, 2000).

Based on results from this study it is concluded violence against women is a dominant issue of women in Pakistan. There is need to do a lot to bring change in the life of women. Though laws are made, and institutions are established but the situation of women is not improving. Governance is missing throughout. Determination of government to improve the situation of women in country is highly required. Findings further pointed violence cases are treated as honor or family matter instead of act of crime.

Though, under international commitment states are responsible for a comprehensive legislation with enactment, implementation, and monitoring mechanisms to mitigate the issue of violence against women (United Nations, 2010). Nevertheless, in Pakistan the state's response to domestic violence is observed minimal and women encounter widespread bias against them in the violence cases (Niaz, 2003; Shaikh, et al., (2021). Poor health services for women particularly in rural and urban slums are one of the key issue of women discussed by the key informants of study referring to recent deaths in Tharparkar region of Sindh.

"State is responsible for our education and health. It is critical issue women die of giving birth (maternal mortality); child mortality is the issue of women health. There should be free health facilities and education for women. These should be the key part of policies for women".

Findings of this study suggest nutrition and maternal mortality is a significant issue of women particularly those living in disaster, flood and drought prone areas. Up to now development programs have considered family planning and contraceptive method to address the issue of women health. However, it is time to have a comprehensive way to define the health of women beyond family planning (Kumar, 2016). It is highly essential to mainstream equitable policies in the post MDGs scenario either the policies are addressing the drivers of disempowerment or other factors of patriarchy. Nevertheless, the resources for current health program should not be compromised instead additional investment should be mobilized for other health issues which are damaging the health (Hawkes & Buse, 2013). Influence of feudalist on the lives of women decision making was well expressed by the informants. Talking about land reform political informants not only shared about the efforts for land reform but also indicated how even a highly influential women politician could not change the mindset of feudal for relocation of land rights to women.

According to Cheema (2014) Pakistani society is living under a state of heightened fear where issues such as women's rights are considered controversial and can risk one being branded as western or liberal. Such picture verified from the sharing's of key informant interviews. Politicians are scared to talk about women issues. Although significant legislation has been carried out in the past. Issues regarding women's problem is that in some provinces, until now it is difficult to talk about women issues openly from house to assembly. Certain forces either religious groups or feudal consider it private matter they prefer to deal with sharia or jirga (tribal) system

Education

Education has the power to improve human development outcomes. Education not only gives awareness to women, but it has positive linkages with the economic growth. It boosts the earning of women which ultimately helps in controlling poverty. Whereas lower education has a negative impact on economic growth as it lowers the average level of human capital. In Pakistan girls' education is highly influenced by poverty; researches exhibit considerable gender inequality in education. Patriarchy is found as the source of suffering with all discriminations. (Chaudhry & Rahman, 2009).

Education has come as one of the main problems of Pakistani women. Almost all key informants mentioned this in their interviews irrespective of their occupation. They mentioned that lack of access to education has remained as a significant issue of women. They also mentioned that access to quality education is an essential way to achieve women empowerment.

"We have policies like article A-25 for free education. It is part of the constitution, but there is no implementation of the constitution. You must have heard of education ministers' statement that we haven't any resources to provide free education at all. But where they want to do corruption, they step ahead".

Findings of this study reveals educational indicators for women in Pakistan particularly in Sindh are not improving despite many initiatives. Dominant patriarchy and feudal system in rural areas impeding women's way to school and the remaining part is being performed by the policies of education department, which is unable to deliver quality education.

Economic Empowerment

Poverty is one of the major reasons for women's disempowerment. The ratio of women entrepreneur is very low in Pakistan. For poverty reduction and socio-economic development, women's participation in labor force has a key role. There are number of factors associated with lower labor force participation such factors include unavailability of jobs, education level and skills. In context of Pakistan level of education is highly associated with labor force participation. Generally, the women who belongs to upper class or with higher education reaches the upper positions and recognizes the entrepreneurship opportunities. There is need for policies on female employment and entrepreneurship, that should be carefully planned considering education, skills, and childcare facilities for women. Attention to non-economic issues is central for women empowerment with poverty alleviation programs (Hafeez & Amad, 2002; Khan, 2013; Rashid & Abdullah, 2013).

Job opportunities for women are the second prominent issue of majority of women shared by key informant. They shared various issues of exclusion of women. One of the key informants shared about the societal perception about the women by stating:

"So far, no spaces in employment sector for women. It is thought and taught that women would be mother and look after home. Lot of harassment and less opportunities for women".

Findings from this study suggest that job opportunities are understood as a central issue of Pakistani women by policy advocates. However, women empowerment idea is incomplete without equipping women with sufficient earning activities and making their contribution visible. But this idea has remained critical with scare job opportunities and with strong patriarchal control over choice of work. Another component highlighted in finding is missing planning about working environment for facilitating women to avail job opportunities with minimum barriers. However, the working environment for women is hostile. If out of economic need women are working, they face issues of unequal wages, unpleasant work conditions and a double burden of labor due to domestic responsibilities at home (Khan, 2007).

CONCLUSION

This study began by setting its foot in the historical context of policy making for women empowerment. Literature reveals increased political consciousness and identification of patriarchy and capitalism as the barriers to women development were proved foundation for formal mobilization of women rights. Similarly, literature highlighted with the support of key informant interviews the complexities of Pakistani society that how it is shaped in the veil of culture with tag of religion. Women in this study conceptualize empowerment as having education, essential skills to participate in economic opportunities. Findings indicates having education and awareness about rights is a source of feeling independent. Women feel such independence provide them opportunity to make decisions concerning them. Confidence, encouragement, freedom of making choices, opportunities and security were also found as key features of empowerment. Whereas this study also indicates limited funds and small projects with minimum authority to fulfill the international obligation for women empowerment. However, post 2000 era was quite appreciative in the context of Pakistan. Pakistan came up with many pro women legislations including political representation, job quotas, legislation for the protection of women rights particularly vulnerable groups and communities.

Regardless of all the above-mentioned measures for empowering women, it is fact that Pakistan has not proved himself effective in dealing with inequalities pertaining to women empowerment. The quantitative increase in policies and programs has no significant effect on the lives of the women. Lack of achievements in the basic dimensions of human development i.e. education, labor market and social empowerment require attention of researchers, policy makers and program implementers. There is significant gap between policy and actual practices.

The question of social justice still remains unresolved; women are refrained from claiming their legal and constitutional rights through forceful societal means. Economic dependency compels them to bargain on their rights. Women empowerment is highly essential for development of any nation and it is important to understand the needs and requirements of those for whom certain empowerment initiatives are designed.

REFERENCES

Ali, A. A., & Akhtar, M. J. (2012). Empowerment and political mobilization of women in Pakistan: A descriptive discourse of perspectives. *Pakistan Journal of Social Sciences*, *32*(1), 221–228.

Awan, M. A. (2016). *Political Participation of Women in Pakistan: Historical and Political Dynamics Shaping the Structure of Politics for Women*. Frankfurt Research Center on Global Islam. https://www.ffgi.net/files/dossier/polpart-pakistan-awan.pdf

Bustamante-Gavino, M. I., Rattani, S., & Khan, K. (2011). Women's Empowerment in Pakistan–Definitions and Enabling and Disenabling Factors: A Secondary Data Analysis. *Journal of Transcultural Nursing*, *22*(2), 174–181. doi:10.1177/1043659610395762 PMID:21467269

Chaudhry, I. S., Paquibut, R. Y., & Tunio, M. N. (2021). Do workforce diversity, inclusion practices, & organizational characteristics contribute to organizational innovation? Evidence from the UAE. *Cogent Business & Management*, *8*(1), 1947549. doi:10.1080/23311975.2021.1947549

Chaudhry, I. S., & Rahman, S. U. (2009). The impact of gender inequality in education on rural poverty in Pakistan: An empirical analysis. European Journal of Economics. *Finance and Administrative Sciences*, *15*, 174–188.

Cheema, M. (2014). Understanding the gender dynamics of curremt affairs talk shows in the Pakistani Television Industry. In M. Raicheva-Stover & E. Ibroscheva (Eds.), *Women in politics and media: perspectives from nations in transition*. Bloomsbury.

Dominic, B., & Jothi, C. A. (2012). Education-A tool of women empowerment: Historical study based on Kerala society. *International Journal of Scientific and Research Publications*, *2*(4), 1–4.

Hafeez, A., & Amad, E. (2002). Factors determining the labor force participation decision of educated married women in a district of Punjab. *Pakistan Economic and Social Review, 40*(1), 75-88.

Hawkes, S., & Buse, K. (2013). Gender and global health: Evidence, policy, and inconvenient truths. *Lancet*, *381*(9879), 1783–1787. doi:10.1016/S0140-6736(13)60253-6 PMID:23683645

Jejeebhoy, S. J., & Sathar, Z. A. (2001). Women's autonomy in India and Pakistan: The influence of religion and region. *Population and Development Review*, *27*(4), 687–712. doi:10.1111/j.1728-4457.2001.00687.x

Khan, A. (2007). *Women and Paid Work in Pakistan*. Retrieved from http://www.researchcollective.org/Documents/Women_Paid_Work.pdf

Khan, S. (2013). Women's empowerment through poverty alleviation: A socio- cultural and politico-economic assessment of conditions in Pakistan. *International Journal of Academic Research and Reflection, 1*(1), 16-40.

Kumar, A. (2016). Improvement of Women Health and Empowerment: A Study of the Self Help Group's (SHG's) Roles in the Patna District of Bihar. *Ind. J. of Applied & Clinical Sociology*, *11*(4), 68–71.

Lincoln, N. D., Travers, C., Ackers, P., & Wilkinson, A. (2002). The meaning of empowerment: The interdisciplinary etymology of a new management concept. *International Journal of Management Reviews*, *4*(3), 271–290. doi:10.1111/1468-2370.00087

Memon, A. B., Meyer, K., & Tunio, M. N. (2021). Toward collaborative networking among innovation laboratories: A conceptual framework. *International Journal of Innovation Science.*

Ministry of Planning. (2017). Annual Plan 2017-18. Ministry of Planning, Development & Reform.

Mirza, N. (2011). Seven pro-women laws in seven years. *Legislative Watch, 38.*

Naz, A., & Chaudhry, H. R. (2011). Developing gender equality: An analytical study of socio-political and economic constraints in women's empowerment in pakhtun society of Khyber Pakhtunkhwa province of Pakistan. *Indian Journal of Health and Wellbeing, 2*(1), 259–266.

NCSW. (2011). *Assesment of the capacities of women development departments.* Pakistan National Commission on Status of Women.

Niaz, U. (2003). Violence against women in South Asian countries. *Archives of Women's Mental Health, 6*(3), 173–184. doi:10.100700737-003-0171-9 PMID:12920615

Rashid, D. Y., & Abdullah, I. (2013). Women empowerment in the corporate sector of Pakistan. *Interdisciplinary Journal of Contemporary Research in Business, 5*(5), 518–523.

Rasul, S. (2014). Empowerment of Pakistani women: Perceptions and reality. *NDU Journal, 28,* 14.

Riffat, H. (2010). Gender and nexus of purdah culture in public policy. *South Asian Studies: A Research Journal of South Asian Studies, 25*(2), 303-310.

Sathar, Z. A., & Kazi, S. (2000). Women's autonoy in the context of rural Pakistan. *Pakistan Development Review, 39*(2), 89–110. doi:10.30541/v39i2pp.89-110

Shaikh, E., Tunio, M. N., & Qureshi, F. (2021). Finance and women's entrepreneurship in DETEs: A literature review. *Entrepreneurial Finance, Innovation and Development,* 191-209.

Tunio, M. N. (2020). [1]. Academic entrepreneurship in developing countries: Contextualizing recent debate. In *Research Handbook on Entrepreneurship in Emerging Economies.* Edward Elgar Publishing. doi:10.4337/9781788973717.00014

Tunio, M. N. (2020). Role of ICT in promoting entrepreneurial ecosystems in Pakistan. *Journal of Business Ecosystems, 1*(2), 1–21. doi:10.4018/JBE.2020070101

Tunio, M. N., Chaudhry, I. S., Shaikh, S., Jariko, M. A., & Brahmi, M. (2021). Determinants of the Sustainable Entrepreneurial Engagement of Youth in Developing Country—An Empirical Evidence from Pakistan. *Sustainability, 13*(14), 7764. doi:10.3390u13147764

Tunio, M. N., Soomro, A. A., & Bogenhold, D. (2017). The study of self-employment at SMEs level with reference to poverty in developing countries. *Business and Management Research, 6*(2), 33–39. doi:10.5430/bmr.v6n2p33

Tunio, M. N., Yusrini, L., & Shoukat, G. (2021). Corporate Social Responsibility (CSR) in Hotels in Austria, Pakistan, and Indonesia: Small and Medium Enterprise Spillover of COVID-19. In Handbook of Research on Entrepreneurship, Innovation, Sustainability, and ICTs in the Post-COVID-19 Era (pp. 263-280). IGI Global.

United Nations. (2010). Handbook for legislation on violence against women. United Nations Publications.

WDD-Sindh. (2011). *Provincial Policy for Women Empowerment*. Women Development Department.

Weiss, A. M. (2001). Social development, the empowerment of women and the expansion of civil society: Alternative ways out of the debt and poverty trap. *Pakistan Development Review*, *40*(4), 401–432. doi:10.30541/v40i4Ipp.401-432

Weiss, A. M. (2012). *Moving forward with the legal empowerment of women in pakistan*. United States Institute of Peace.

Zubeida, M. (2011). *Women and devolution, Dawn*. Retrieved from https://www.dawn.com/news/620470/women-and-devolution

Chapter 13
Frugal Innovation and Different Dynamics

Muhammad Asif Qureshi
Mohammad Ali Jinnah University, Pakistan

Syed Mir Muhammed Shah
Sukkur IBA University, Pakistan

Syed Ali Raza
Iqra University, Pakistan

Hayfa Kazouz
Faculty of Economics and Management Sciences of Sousse, University of Sousse, Tunisia

ABSTRACT

Producing something from low or nothing through entrepreneurial bricolage is an increasing phenomenon in emerging and dynamic markets. Recently, there is a dire need in developing affordable products and services targeting new markets. Entrepreneurs in the limited resources environments often develop such products. As suggested by Baker and Nelson, firms engage in bricolage to overcome the limitations imposed by the limited resources situation. With respect to the current situation, resource limitations and sustainability issues are pushing firms to develop affordable, quality products and services.

INTRODUCTION

Producing something from low or nothing through entrepreneurial bricolage is a increasing phenomenon in emerging and dynamic markets. Recently, there is a dire need in developing affordable products and services targeting new markets. Entrepreneurs in the limited resources environments often develop such products (Alshareef, et al., 2022). As suggested by Tunio, et al., (2021), firms engage in bricolage to overcome the limitations imposed by the limited resources situation. With respect to the current situation, resource limitations and sustainability issues are pushing firms to develop affordable, quality products and services.

DOI: 10.4018/978-1-6684-5417-6.ch013

Frugal innovation (FI) is is a translation of such offerings. The FI concept overlaps with several other concepts and new ideas (Agarwal and Brem, 2017; Hossain, 2018b), and generally, research scholars are not unified behind one definition of FI. However, FI can be broadly defined as developing limited resource but quality solutions that are affordable than the current products (Shaikh, et al., 2022).

Entrepreneurial activities are rapidly changing, and several entrepreneurs emerge from the grassroots level with limited education, poor technological knowledge, and no access to knowhow (Tunio, et al., 2021). They often dwell in impecunious environments and work under different resource challenges (Memon, et al., 2021), yet they propose frugal solutions to poor customers and make an impact on sustainability (Afshan, et al., 2021). People with a less education and limited access to expertise express novel ideas to solve regional and national issues (Chaudhry, et al., 2021). They go through innovative entrepreneurial paths and deal with different challenges. They contribute through cheap products, which have tangible contributions to the region and locality regarding sustainability. They therefore contribute to meeting sustainable development goals (SDGs) by offering sustainable products and services (Tunio, et al., 2021).

However, there is limited knowledge about how individuals with low resources survive an flourish with their frugal ingenuity. There is also lack knowledge about how FI contributes toward sustainability.

Frugal Innovation

Efficient and effective innovative ways and solutions are mandatory to solve existing complex issues (Mushtaq, et al., 2021), and Frugal Innovation is a way to accomplish this goal. Tunio, et al., (2021). suggest considering the following three criteria to define frugal innovation: substantial cost reduction, concentration on core functionalities, and optimized performance level. According to Gul, et al., (2021), frugality is a formative construct that encompasses four dimensions: basic quality, cost of consumption, simplicity, and sustainability. They argue that low cost and sustainability need to be considered together when creating frugal products. Policymakers largely ignore the consumers within sustainable innovation. To address poverty at the grassroots level, Shaikh, et al., (2021) argue that the market-based approach has proven challenging when serving low-income customers, whereas a sustainable business model approach has shown promising results. Frugality is also an important issue for western countries, however (Aurangzeb, et al., 2021).

It is widely accepted that innovation diffuses from the developed to the developing countries, from high-income customers to the low-income ones (Rogers & Greenhalgh, 2010). FIs, in contrast, diffuse in the opposite direction. Tunio and Shaikh, (2020) argue that the diffusion of FIs mainly shows four patterns. They label them as local, proximity, distance, and global diffusion. In general, FIs diffuse from low income customers to high-income ones, from developing countries to developed ones. However, before reaching the more developed countries, they diffuse through neighboring or distant countries with similar socioeconomic settings. When an innovation is successfully used in developing countries and then trickles up to developed countries, it is called reverse innovation. Diffusion is defined as the process through which an innovation spreads over time through markets, and it depends on several factors. Both individual and cultural factors are important for an innovation's diffusion. We know that advertising plays an important role in diffusing new products. Our extensive search and review of the extant literature reveal that studies into the diffusion of FIs and similar innovations in the context of developing countries are largely absent (Shaikh, and Tunio, 2020).

The academic community has recently exhibited an increasing interest into the investigation of how firms can create solutions for customers in resource-constraint segments in emerging markets. The fact that the dominant logic of the global economic landscape has been changed fundamentally, puts Western companies into a conundrum. The overall shift towards emerging markets is no longer only true for production sites and sourcing activities like we have seen in India and China but also for customers. A growing number of customers demand solutions that vary significantly from the Western ones. Consequently, leading firms have started to innovate tailored products/services and business models for these new customer segments. These innovations are summarised under the umbrella term 'resource-constrained innovations' (Tunio, et al., 2021). They differ significantly from traditional advanced innovations in developed markets, which are typically targeted at the affluent customers at the top of the economic pyramid. Advanced innovations are based on the latest technology and have high premium quality, while offering a wide range of functionalities. In contrast, resource-constrained innovations offer a completely different value proposition. They are typically low-cost and entail some sort of tailored functionality that creates unique value in resource-constrained environments in emerging markets (Gilal, et al., 2021). Coming from a capability perspective, the most challenging are so-called frugal innovation. The term 'frugal innovation' has been used to denote innovations specifically developed for resource-constrained customers in emerging markets. These innovations have been shown to have significant influence on the processes and the overall value chain that are being characterised by the market context (Abdullah, et al., 2020; Tunio, 2020). They require the most complex technical and organisational capabilities from firms. Other terms for frugal innovation are Ghandian innovation (Katper, et al., 2017; Tunio, et al., 2017), terms that emphasise the specific Indian context in which such innovations have often been created. In contrast to other resource-constraint innovations, frugal innovations are not reengineered solutions but originally developed products or services for very specific applications in resource-constrained environments.

The debate around frugal innovation has been growing for years, stimulating different discussions in management practice and academia. Still, the focus is on conceptualisations and definitions that are strongly characterised by markets and customers, which shape the challenges associates with frugal innovation heavily (Gilal. et al., 2020; Tunio 2020). Moreover, substantial parts of research focus on strategic aspects of the bottom of the pyramid (BoP), the emerging middle-class and their significance for Western firms (Katpar., et al., 2020). Additional areas of research are the role of sustainability (Tunio, et al., 2021), pattern-bases approaches to development (Shaikh, et al., 2022), relevance of business models (Tunio, et al., 2021) and rather anecdotal case evidence (Shaikh, et al., 2021). Few publications consider knowledge transferability in the context of frugal innovation (Afshan, et al., 2021). However, no publication focuses on the organisational processes and structures along the entire value chain that enable the appropriate transfer of technical and market knowledge, which is essential when organising for frugal innovation. Knowledge transfer in the context of frugal innovation has a particular relevance since firms have to deal with and learn about first time respectively non-customer. In this context knowledge flow is described as aggregate flow between organisations units (Sharif, et al., 2019) but can also happen outside of the firms boundaries. Often, first time customers in underserved areas are at the centre of these innovation efforts, requiring that firms learn to develop new solutions defined by entirely new parameters. The knowledge and insights that are gathered during the market research phase need to be relayed precisely to all relevant stakeholder along the value chain to guarantee a successful frugal innovation initiative that captures the requirements of the customers. In previous research knowledge transfer has been found to be a driver of performance whereas the adoption plays a big role (Qureshi, et al., 2019). Knowledge transfer being at the forefront of MNE research has been described as the attempt to close gaps between existing knowledge and what is readily available throughout the organisation (Raza, et al., 2018). However, knowledge transfer activities need to be managed and coordinated to yield successful results (Qureshi, et al., 2019). Firms need to strategically adapt their processes and structures to enable the successful transfer of newly acquired knowledge into their organisation. Besides enabling the transfer of knowledge at various steps along the value chain, processes and structures need to be organised in a way that allows them to overcome all challenges associated with frugal innovation.

INNOVATION IN EMERGING MARKETS

Previously the wealthy countries were considered focal markets for the world, but now the double edged phenomenon of economic growth in emerging markets combined with recession and slow growth in wealthy nations is forcing much attention to be redirected to populace markets in emerging markets. Compare the consistent 8-9% growth of BRIC nations with the slow 1-3% growth of developed nations. On 27 Dec 2011, as of writing this paper, the Brazilian economy overtook the UK to become the sixth largest economy in the world. Some among the business community are concerned that too much inequality is limiting the sustainability of long-term growth. The demand of high income groups is, in absolute terms, increasing at a much slower rate than that of lower income groups and this is especially true for the BRICS (Raza, et al., 2021).

Adil, et al. (2018) cited Singapore, Taiwan, South Korea, Israel, and Ireland as the new centers of innovative capacity outside of the OECD countries. Porter and Stern denied the innovative capacity of emerging nations. They claimed: "Conversely, several countries that have drawn much attention as potential economic powers — India, China and Malaysia — are not yet generating meaningful levels of world-class innovative output on an absolute or relative basis. These countries have developed neither a base for innovation nor clusters with a large innovative capacity." They further claim that although a location may be favorable for other reasons which are non-innovative capacity, such as offering low manufacturing costs or access to key markets, but would be unfavourable for innovation. Given the theoretical lens of the Diamond of Competitive Advantage Porter and Stern employed, their argument may be understandable. As such, it is often proclaimed that the developed nations maintain a distant edge in innovation capabilities as compared to the emerging nations.

We suggest this contrary to widely held belief of growth in innovation in emerging markets is better looked at from an alternative theoretical lens. It may be that emerging nations are approaching innovation in a different way that addresses contextual factors, constraints and local demands. So an alternate theoretical lens and accompanying evidence may prove to the contrary. Popular innovations that meet local emerging market demands include the TATA NANO car that costs less than 3000 dollars, GE's mini-handheld ECG machine in its Bangalore R&D centre that costs less than half of conventional bulky ECG machines, and Bahria Town's 5000 dollar homes in Pakistan. Tata stands at rank 17 on Business-Week's most innovative companies list while GE's local division in India ranked 9 (Qureshi, et al., 2018).

One side says not enough basic R&D is done in emerging markets which is relatively true as compared to the wealthier nations. But the flip side is that a different type of innovation is taking place, one that embodies 'frugal innovation' activity which attempts to serve large bottom and lower middle class population demands. And this is contrasted with the top-down sophisticated R&D led innovation to one that employs bottoms up, human centric, appropriate, local, and cost efficient approaches through processes such as design thinking, bricolage, creative improvisation, lean and reverse engineering. Although none of these concepts are independently new, but the shift in all working together through varied actors is what is solving the underserved needs and helping to build capacity for companies and nations (Ab Hamid, et al., 2014).

In the basic sense, frugal innovation has always occurred since the invention of Neanderthal hand tools from stones and bones to making do with what is on hand. Innovation in its most basic form is an old practice that has permeated our human make-up. However it is gaining renewed attention given economic, resource, and demographic shifts. Much of today's challenges in developing countries are chronic and may have historical precedence, indeed even in the West as it sought to grow and develop.

The Notion of Constraints in Emerging Markets

We believe that emerging markets offer a unique perspective on understanding how innovation itself evolves. These environments offer a unique context for innovating given the contextual constraints of functioning within. Three main challenges persist in emerging nations for innovation: First are resource constraints, second is the challenge and opportunity of dealing with institutional voids, and third is the need to address the needs of the bottom of the pyramid i.e. the largest and poorest socio-economic segment of the population. Despite institutional voids, emerging market entrepreneurs and firms are producing innovations which are resolving their local needs, and at the same time profiting to the extent that they can expand to neighboring developing nations and even beyond to developed markets (Shah, et al., 2016).

We call these environments extreme as ventures operating therein seek to mitigate or adapt often simultaneously to affordability, resource, and institutional constraints. An environment is resource constrained if it provides new challenges, whether opportunities or problems without providing additional or new resources (Shaikh, E., et al., (2021). Shaikh, et al., (2022) posits that all societies are resource-constrained and poor countries even more so. The procurement, control and combination of labor, skills, and material is crucial to the creation of new products and services (Shaikh, et al., (2021). Yet emerging and developing markets can be considered extreme environments given the penurious nature of basic facilities such as infrastructure, literacy, access to literacy, medical care, retail chains, communication networks, transportation, housing, and sanitation.

In moving beyond resource constraints, Memon, et al., (2019) suggests that on top of the general resource constraints faced by developing countries are the constraints on the capacity of government to deal with the number of issues it can pursue. That limitation to cope with issues poses both an institutional challenge and opportunity. Institutions can be defined as the humanly derived constraints that structure how humans interact. These constraints can be formal constraints as in the case of formal rules, laws, and constitutions, or they can be informal constraints as in the case of norms of behaviour, conventions, and codes of conduct (North, et al., 1997). Institutional concerns such as legal recourse and political structure are global concerns for anyone instituting change and innovation and perhaps more so in emerging markets given the institutionally complex contexts (Mair, Marti and Ventresca, 2012). Yet, perhaps for these challenges, these are the environments where social enterprises look to provide solutions for and operate in (Tunio, et al., (2022).

A third constraint or challenge and opportunity in emerging markets has to do with the social dynamics of vast number of populations living close to poverty. One billion people live in the least developed countries and four billion live in developing countries (Shaikh, et al., (2019). This large segment poses a challenge for multinational corporations, entrepreneurs and governments alike to provide affordable solutions that help mitigate poverty and its consequences. All three sectors need to and are in many ways joining hands to innovate for the global low-income population.

Although, the BOP has been a tacit market argument that projects consumers as waiting out there to be served, nevertheless we believe the BOP literature has provided an anchor to talk about frugal innovation. Rural markets and especially the BOP markets can be hotbeds of innovation (Tunio, et al., (2022). The BOP market can test a company's capabilities since it is comparatively difficult to market to the BOP than their rich counterparts not only in scale of operations but also in scope and sustainability (Shaikh, et al., 2022). Feedback from BoP users and from design developers upstream might result in reverse transfer of technology (from the South to the North), re-invigorating and motivating the research community in the highly developed world increasingly "in search of relevance" (Shaikh, et al., (2022). President of PATH, an international non-profit working for health solutions, writes in the Lancet: "We often assume that these frontiers of science will benefit only the richer nations of the world, …[But] in fact resource-poor settings can actually drive innovation, demanding ingenious product designs that are less expensive, and easier to use, and require less infrastructure. It is also easier to disrupt the technological status quo in the absence of entrenched commercial interests organised around existing products".

Intersection of Institutional and Social Innovation

Social enterprises may serve as the bridge between underserved communities and existing institutions. Yet as ventures act to mobilize resources they brush against existing political (lobbying), legal (business regulation), and technological (human development) institutional environments, or the lack thereof, and in the process may build upon the existing fragments to create new structures. Further, several needs or problems in extreme environments are not addressed or even recognized by existing public or private institutions which leads firms having to deal and operate within this basic institutional void. Bricolage often goes against the norm and occurs in the absence of institutional support (Shaikh, et al., 2022).

Institutions that achieve consistency, impartiality, and reliability in their enforcement allow entrepreneurs to form expectations about the future, such as whether to invest in innovation, by removing some of the uncertainty about whether they will be able to capture the value they create. Institutional entrepreneurship is one through which entrepreneurial actors change institutional structures or create new ones. Institutional entrepreneurs "lead efforts to identify political opportunities, frame issues and problems, and mobilize constituencies". An institutional entrepreneur actor develops new institutions or facilitates change in existing institutions, and secures resources to achieve this change (Raza, et al., 2022).

One stream of entrepreneurship literature looks at whether social entrepreneurship happens through or against existing institutions. While most ventures operate with the assumption their activities will be supported by formal institutions, other ventures may have to emerge despite a lack of institutional support (Sarasvathy, 2009). Research on institutional effects has shown that institutions can both support and preclude actors, entrepreneurs, and ventures. In such cases, institutional entrepreneurs emerge as a case of necessity.

Sarasvathy (2009) points out that social enterprises are sometimes forced to go against existing institutions and come up with creative mechanisms that incorporate the best of both market and non-market solutions. Dean and McMullen (2007) show how according to the entrepreneurship literature, entrepreneurs can seize opportunities that are inherent in environmentally relevant market failures. Environmental degradation can be as the result of a market failure caused by existing institutional arrangements (Peredo, & McLean, 2006). As in the development of the recycling industry in the USA (Saebi, et al., 2019), social movements together with entrepreneurs can layout proofs-of-concepts for the creation of sustainable businesses. As this proof develops, wider public perception is changed, and consequently the institutions governing those perceptions are reconfigured to accommodate the new market.

REFERENCES

Ab Hamid, K., Pahi, M. H., Qureshi, M. A., & Arshad, I. (2014). *The impact of leadership style on employee turnover and retention, and mediating job satisfaction and organization commitment.* Academic Press.

Abdullah, M., Katper, N. K., Chaudhry, N. I., & Tunio, M. N. (2020). An Impact of Workaholics on Creativity: the mediating role of Negative Mood and moderating role of Supervisor Support. *Sukkur IBA Journal of Management and Business, 7*(2).

Adil, M. S., Khan, M. N., Khan, I., & Qureshi, M. A. (2018). Impact of leader creativity expectations on employee creativity: Assessing the mediating and moderating role of creative self-efficacy. *International Journal of Management Practice, 11*(2), 171–189. doi:10.1504/IJMP.2018.090832

Afshan, G., Ilyas, S., Tunio, M. N., & Kalhoro, M. (2021). CSR actions and post-COVID-19 consequences in the hotel industry: A conceptual framework. *International Journal of Strategic Change Management, 7*(4), 275–289. doi:10.1504/IJSCM.2021.122845

Agarwal, N., & Brem, A. (2017). Frugal innovation-past, present, and future. *IEEE Engineering Management Review, 45*(3), 37–41. doi:10.1109/EMR.2017.2734320

Alshareef, N., & Tunio, M. N. (2022). Role of Leadership in Adoption of Blockchain Technology in Small and Medium Enterprises in Saudi Arabia. *Frontiers in Psychology, 13*, 2284. doi:10.3389/fpsyg.2022.911432 PMID:35602740

Aurangzeb, M. T., Tunio, M. N., Rehman, Z., & Asif, M. (2021). Influence of administrative expertise on human resources practitioners on the job performance: Mediating role of achievement motivation. *International Journal of Management, 12*(4), 408–421.

Baker, T., & Nelson, R. E. (2005). Creating something from nothing: Resource construction through entrepreneurial bricolage. *Administrative Science Quarterly, 50*(3), 329–366. doi:10.2189/asqu.2005.50.3.329

Chaudhry, I. S., Paquibut, R. Y. & Tunio, M. N. (2021) Do workforce diversity, inclusion practices, & organizational characteristics contribute to organizational innovation? Evidence from the U.A.E. *Cogent Business & Management, 8*(1), 1947549. . doi:10.1080/23311975.2021.1947549

Dean, T. J., & McMullen, J. S. (2007). Toward a theory of sustainable entrepreneurship: Reducing environmental degradation through entrepreneurial action. *Journal of Business Venturing, 22*(1), 50–76. doi:10.1016/j.jbusvent.2005.09.003

Gilal, F. G., Gilal, N. G., Channa, N. A., Gilal, R. A., Gilal, R. G., & Tunio, M. N. (2020). Towards an integrated model for the transference of environmental responsibility. *Business Strategy and the Environment, 29*(6), 1–10. doi:10.1002/bse.2524

Gilal, F. G., Gilal, N. G., Gilal, R. G., Gon, Z., Gilal, W. G., & Tunio, M. N. (2021). The Ties That Bind: Do Brand Attachment and Brand Passion Translate Into Consumer Purchase Intention? *Central European Management Journal*, *29*(1), 14–38. doi:10.7206/cemj.2658-0845.39

Govindarajo, N. S., Kumar, D., Shaikh, E., Kumar, M., & Kumar, P. (2021). Industry 4.0 and business policy development: Strategic imperatives for SME performance. *Etikonomi*, *20*(2), 239–258. doi:10.15408/etk.v20i2.20143

Gul, A., Subhan, S., & Tunio, M. N. (2021). Learning experiences of women entrepreneurs amidst COVID-19. *International Journal of Gender and Entrepreneurship*, *13*(2), 1756–6266. doi:10.1108/IJGE-09-2020-0153

Hossain, D. M. (2007). Social entrepreneurs in Bangladesh. Hossain, DM and Hossain, M.(2012), Social Entrepreneurs in Bangladesh, International Journal of Research in Commerce. *IT & Management*, *2*(9), 7–12.

Hossain, M. (2018). Frugal innovation: A review and research agenda. *Journal of Cleaner Production*, *182*, 926–936. doi:10.1016/j.jclepro.2018.02.091

Katpar., N. K., Chaudhry, N. I., Tunio, M. N., & Ali, M. A. (2020). Impact of Leadership Style and Organizational Culture on Organizational Commitment. *Sukkur IBA Journal of Management and Business, 7*(1), 92-106.

Katper, N. K. Medan, A., Syed, K. B. S., & Tunio, M. N. (2017). Determinants of Debt Maturity Structure in Shariah and Non-Shariah Firms in Pakistan: A comparative Study. *Journal of Applied Economic Sciences, 12*(4), 1210-1225.

Mair, J., Marti, I., & Ventresca, M. J. (2012). Building inclusive markets in rural Bangladesh: How intermediaries work institutional voids. *Academy of Management Journal*, *55*(4), 819–850. doi:10.5465/amj.2010.0627

Memon, A.B., Meyer, K., & Tunio, M. N. (2021). Toward collaborative networking among innovation laboratories: a conceptual framework. *International Journal of Innovation Science*. doi:10.1108/IJIS-04-2021-0069

Memon, A. R., Shaikh, E., & Khan, M. S. (2019). Determination of Customer Satisfaction of Hyderabad Restaurants. *Irish Interdisciplinary Journal of Science and Research*, *3*(3), 11–18.

Mushtaq, T., Tunio, M. N., Akbar, Z., & Jariko, M. (2021). Green Organizational identity: Antecedents and consequences: An Empirical Study. *Contemporary Issues in business and Government, 27*(3), 2056-2069.

North, A. C., Hargreaves, D. J., & McKendrick, J. (1997). In-store music affects product choice. *Nature*, *390*(6656), 132–132. doi:10.1038/36484

Peredo, A. M., & McLean, M. (2006). Social entrepreneurship: A critical review of the concept. *Journal of World Business*, *41*(1), 56–65. doi:10.1016/j.jwb.2005.10.007

Qureshi, J. A., Qureshi, M. S., & Qureshi, M. A. (2018). Mitigating risk of failure by expanding family entrepreneurship and learning from international franchising experiences of johnny rockets: A case stu¶#dy in Pakistan. *International Journal of Experiential Learning & Case Studies*, *3*(1), 110–127. doi:10.22555/ijelcs.v3i1.1972

Qureshi, M. A., Qureshi, J. A., Thebo, J. A., Shaikh, G. M., Brohi, N. A., & Qaiser, S. (2019). The nexus of employee's commitment, job satisfaction, and job performance: An analysis of FMCG industries of Pakistan. *Cogent Business & Management*, *6*(1), 1654189. doi:10.1080/23311975.2019.1654189

Ravishankar, M. N., & Gurca, A. (2015). A bricolage perspective on technological innovation in emerging markets. *IEEE Transactions on Engineering Management*, *63*(1), 53–66. doi:10.1109/TEM.2015.2494501

Raza, A., Shaikh, E., Tursoy, T., & Almashaqbeh, H. A. (2022). Economics and Business Perspectives of Sustainable HRM. In *Sustainable Development of Human Resources in a Globalization Period* (pp. 36–48). IGI Global. doi:10.4018/978-1-6684-4981-3.ch003

Raza, S. A., Abidi, M., Arsalan, G. M., Shairf, A., & Qureshi, M. A. (2018). The impact of student attitude, trust, subjective norms, motivation and rewards on knowledge sharing attitudes among university students. *International Journal of Knowledge and Learning*, *12*(4), 287–304. doi:10.1504/IJKL.2018.095955

Raza, S. A., Qureshi, M. A., Ahmed, M., Qaiser, S., Ali, R., & Ahmed, F. (2021). Non-linear relationship between tourism, economic growth, urbanization, and environmental degradation: Evidence from smooth transition models. *Environmental Science and Pollution Research International*, *28*(2), 1426–1442. doi:10.100711356-020-10179-3 PMID:32840747

Rogers, M., & Greenhalgh, C. (2010). *Innovation, intellectual property, and economic growth*. Princeton University Press.

Saebi, T., Foss, N. J., & Linder, S. (2019). Social entrepreneurship research: Past achievements and future promises. *Journal of Management*, *45*(1), 70–95. doi:10.1177/0149206318793196

Sarasvathy, S. D. (2009). *Effectuation: Elements of entrepreneurial expertise*. Edward Elgar Publishing.

Shah, S. M. M., Hamid, K. B. A., Malaysia, U. U., Shaikh, U. A., Malaysia, P. S. U. U., Qureshi, M. A., & Pahi, M. H. (2016). The Relationship between Leadership Styles and Job Performance: The Role of Work Engagement as a Mediator. *International Journal of Scientific Study*, *2*(10), 242–253.

Shaikh, E., Azhar, H., Brahmi, M., & Zehra, N. (2022). The impact of monetary and non-monetary motivation on employees' performance: A case study of Hyderabad Electric Supply Company. *International Journal of Technology Transfer and Commercialisation*, *19*(1), 127–141. doi:10.1504/IJTTC.2022.123088

Shaikh, E., Brahmi, M., Thang, P. C., Watto, W. A., Trang, T. T. N., & Loan, N. T. (2022). Should I Stay or Should I Go? Explaining the Turnover Intentions with Corporate Social Responsibility (CSR), Organizational Identification and Organizational Commitment. *Sustainability*, *14*(10), 6030. doi:10.3390u14106030

Shaikh, E., Khoso, I., & Chandio, F. (2019). Effects of Corporate Social Responsibility on Organizational Performance: A Conceptual and Literature Review. *Journal of Grassroot*, *53*(1).

Shaikh, E., Mishra, V., Ahmed, F., Krishnan, D., & Dagar, V. (2021). Exchange rate, stock price and trade volume in US-China trade war during COVID-19: An empirical study. *Estudios de Economía Aplicada, 39*(8). Advance online publication. doi:10.25115/eea.v39i8.5327

Shaikh, E., & Tunio, M. N. (2020). Customer satisfaction and Customer loyalty: An empirical case study on the impact of benefits generated through Smartphone applications. *International Journal of Public Sector Performance Management.*

Shaikh, E., Tunio, M. N., Khoso, W. M., Brahmi, M., & Rasool, S. (2022). The COVID-19 Pandemic Overlaps Entrepreneurial Activities and Triggered New Challenges: A Review Study. *Managing Human Resources in SMEs and Start-ups: International Challenges and Solutions,* 155-182.

Shaikh, E., Tunio, M. N., & Qureshi, F. (2021). Finance and women's entrepreneurship in DETEs: A literature review. *Entrepreneurial Finance, Innovation and Development,* 191-209.

Shaikh, E., Watto, W. A., & Tunio, M. N. (2022). Impact of Authentic Leadership on Organizational Citizenship Behavior by Using The Mediating Effect of Psychological Ownership. *ETIKONOMI, 21*(1), 89–102. doi:10.15408/etk.v21i1.18968

Shaikh, S., Sultan, M. F., Mushtaque, T., & Tunio, M. N. (2021). Impact of COVID-19 on GDP: A serial mediation effect on international tourism and hospitality. *International Journal of Management, 12*(84), 422–430.

Sharif, A., Afshan, S., & Qureshi, M. A. (2019). Acceptance of learning management system in university students: An integrating framework of modified UTAUT2 and TTF theories. *International Journal of Technology Enhanced Learning, 11*(2), 201–229. doi:10.1504/IJTEL.2019.098810

Simula, H., Töllmen, A., & Karjaluoto, H. (2015). Facilitating innovations and value co-creation in industrial B2B firms by combining digital marketing, social media and crowdsourcing. In *Marketing Dynamism & Sustainability: Things Change, Things Stay the Same...* (pp. 254–263). Springer. doi:10.1007/978-3-319-10912-1_84

Tunio, M. N. (2020). Role of ICT in Promoting Entrepreneurial Ecosystems in Pakistan. *Journal of Business Ecosystems, 1*(2), 1–21. doi:10.4018/JBE.2020070101

Tunio, M. N., Chaudhry, I. S., Mughal, F., & Shaikh, E. (2022). Marketing Mode and Survival of the Entrepreneurial Activities of Nascent Entrepreneurs. In Big Data Analytics (pp. 1-18). Auerbach Publications. doi:10.1201/9781003307761-1

Tunio, M. N., Chaudhry, I. S., Shaikh, S., Jariko, M. A., & Brahmi, M. (2021). Determinants of the Sustainable Entrepreneurial Engagement of Youth in Developing Country—An Empirical Evidence from Pakistan. *Sustainability, 13*(14), 7764. doi:10.3390u13147764

Tunio, M. N., Jariko, M. A., Børsen, T., Shaikh, S., Mushtaque, T., & Brahmi, M. (2021). How Entrepreneurship Sustains Barriers in the Entrepreneurial Process—A Lesson from a Developing Nation. *Sustainability, 13*(20), 1–18. doi:10.3390u132011419

Tunio, M. N., Shah, S. M. M., Qureshi, M. A., Tunio, A. N., & Shaikh, E. (2022). Career Predilections and Options to Opt Occupation for the Youth in Pakistan. In Developing Entrepreneurial Ecosystems in Academia (pp. 156-170). IGI Global. doi:10.4018/978-1-7998-8505-4.ch009

Tunio, M. N., & Shaikh, E. (2020). Nascent entrepreneurs and challenges in digital market in developing countries. *International Journal of Public Sector Performance Management*.

Tunio, M. N., Shaikh, E., Niaz, S., & Katper, N. S. (2021). Multifaceted perils of the Covid-19 and implications: A Review. *Estudios de Economía Aplicada*. Advance online publication. doi:10.25115/eea.v39i2.3957

Tunio, M. N., Soomro, A. A., & Bogenhold, D. (2017). The Study of Self-employment at SMEs Level with Reference to Poverty in Developing Countries. Business and Management Research, 6(2). doi:10.5430/bmr.v6n2p33

Tunio, M. N., Yusrini, L., Shah, Z. A., Katper, N., & Jariko, M. A. (2021). How Hotel Industry Cope up with the COVID-19: An SME Perspective. *Etikonomi*, *20*(2), 213–224. doi:10.15408/etk.v20i2.19172

Tunio, M. N., Yusrini, L., & Shoukat, G. (2021). Corporate social responsibility (CSR) in Hotels in Austria, Pakistan, and Indonesia: small and medium Enterprise spillover of COVID-19. In Handbook of research on entrepreneurship, innovation, sustainability, and ICTs in the post-COVID-19 era (pp. 263-280). IGI Global.

Tunio, M. N., Yusrni, L., Shah, Z. A., Katper, N. K., & Jariko, M. A. (2021). How hotel industry cope up with the COVID-19: An SME Perspective. *ETIKONOMI, 20*(2).

Chapter 14
Social Innovation and Environment:
An Overview of the Tourism and Hospitality Industry of Europe

Kamran Jamshed

https://orcid.org/0000-0001-8707-8625
Bahria University, Pakistan

Syed Haider Ali Shah
Bahria University, Pakistan

Samrah Jamshaid
Northeast Normal University, Jilin, China

ABSTRACT

This chapter aimed to understand and foster innovative technology by addressing social needs and developing innovative ideas to solve environmental issues. Social innovation is a new means of identifying better answers to social concerns, and it entails social individuals and communities generating, testing, and disseminating ideas to meet critical social needs. It's a collaborative and participatory technique that focuses on the whole system rather than individual elements. This chapter is an overview of the hospitality industry of Europe as the hospitality industry is the largest industry and the European hospitality industry is covering almost 50% of the global hospitality industry. In this chapter, the overview of the social innovation with the hospitality industry is associated with social causes like the leftovers can be distributed to needy people and hotels can offer discounts for those guests who are willing to participate in social causes.

INTRODUCTION

We are all familiar with the notion of "Where there is a will, there is a way" and this is the general

DOI: 10.4018/978-1-6684-5417-6.ch014

concept of frugal innovation to provide an ultimate solution with available resources. The main idea of frugal innovation is based on the temporary solutions with least investment or we can say that through available resources which was tossed by Sam Pitroda an Indian who worked in telecommunication sector in India. Now there have been several breakthroughs in the scientific field with frugal innovations which helped the world where we can see that in recent pandemic of COVID-19 there were a panic all over the world and most of the countries were not prepared to handle such kind of pandemics and there was a huge shortage of resources for everyone including the shortage of medical gadgets. Many countries promoted the solutions by common people through their frugal innovative ideas to prevent the spreading of the COVID-19 virus with their home made masks, sanitizers and other hygiene products. Governments of many countries have worked collaboratively with each other and promoted the social innovation which resulted in formulation of solutions for different items which were short in supply to handle the pandemic.

For example, in developing countries of south Asia there was shortage of ventilators and other respiratory tools which were very necessary for the COVID patients and the governments has taken the initiatives to promote the locally manufactured ventilators and other essential tools which had later on helped the entire nation and they also exported these products to the neighboring countries. This chapter is all about the social innovation and its importance and how as a community the issues can be resolved and how the social innovation is adapted by the hotels of Europe for revival of the hospitality industry. Social innovation can provide dynamic approaches to the environmental concerns in the hospitality industry with focus on innovative technologies or solutions which can prevent the environmental challenges. One effective way for bringing about change is social innovation, however the body of social innovation research on ecological issues is incomplete (Haskel et al, 2021). These pledges can be seen as a more reliable form of sustainability because they mix environmental principles with social and economic challenges (Battle et al., 2018). The preservation of the environment is essential to human survival, and human survival depends on the preservation of the environment. In contrast, social innovation is the application of fresh concepts that may be connected to already existing goods or services and that aim to address social problems. Frugal innovations are fresh responses to urgent societal problems that affect how people interact and aim to make people's lives better. By offering creative solutions to environmental problems, social innovation, on the other hand, aims to put often global environmental concerns in a local context. A more sustainable economy that depends on more sustainable supply chains, the circular economy in general, and consumer patterns and preferences is a major issue for social innovation for the environment (Schartinger et al., 2014). Frugal innovation was developed in emerging markets to meet the needs of low-income consumers by developing technologies that were high in quality and provided value but low in cost. Whether it will be replaced by fresh, similarly nebulous concepts, like the smart village approach, or whether it will endure as an organizing and capacity-building idea alongside more established principles, like community-led local development, which, while not quite social innovation, is very similar and is already deeply ingrained in policy guidance (Slee et al., 2022). A technological innovation that enabled the development of (social) practices in tourism and led to a change in the supply chain for tourist goods set off the third industry revolution. Online platforms have changed how people connect with tourism, giving visitors the chance to take control of their experiences and act as cultural brokers.

Figure 1. Four Dimensions of Social innovation

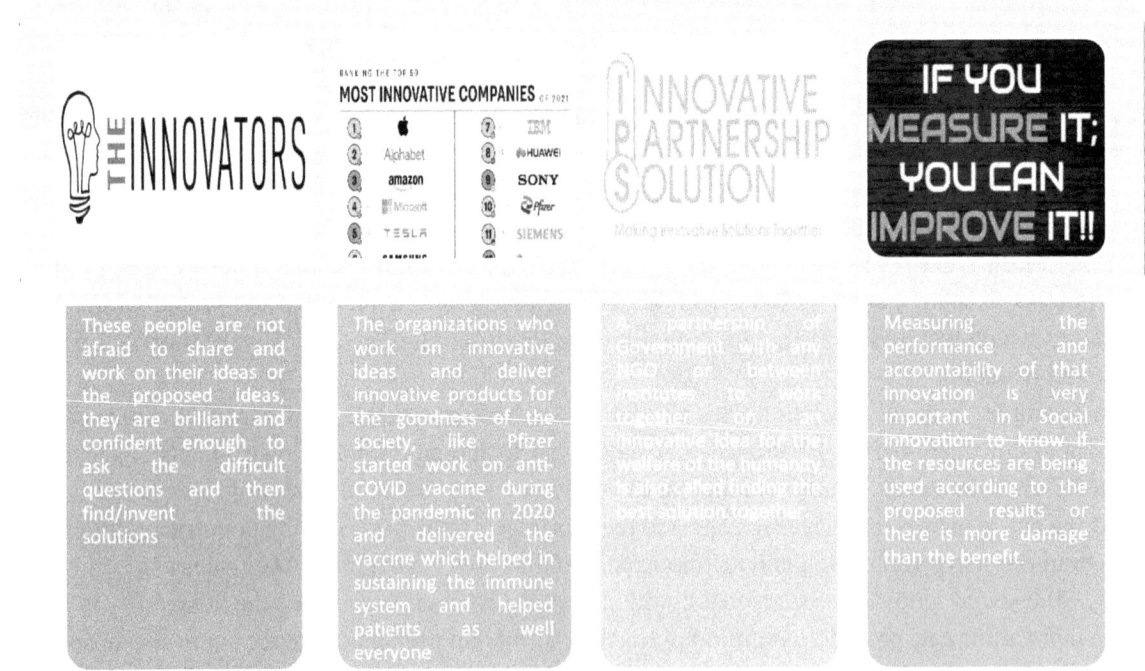

SOCIAL INNOVATION IS BEST DESCRIBED AS IT DEPENDS ON FOUR DIMENSIONS WHICH ARE:

Depending on the socioeconomic development of the destination, social innovation has different values. In more rural areas, they are more focused on social issues and missions. It is possible to draw the conclusion that social solutions in tourism entail the dissemination of innovation knowledge and the delivery of goods, services, and solutions that are suited to the requirements of visitors and stakeholders in the community (Alkier, et.al, 2017). Social innovation is being looked at as a potential solution because traditional governance methods are unable to respond rapidly enough to the plethora of issues brought on by systemic changes and modernization (Solov'eva et al.,2018). Social innovation, bottom-up initiatives, coproduction, and community-led local development are the conceptual instruments developed to address the current issues in socioecological systems. It is an integrated service system that satisfies numerous stakeholder criteria to promote sustainable tourism. It consists of multidisciplinary knowledge, multiple stakeholders, and local resources. Social innovation is concerned with the techniques used in service design to create innovative projects within the tourism industry and give both young people and senior residents access to work. The firm's success was largely attributed to its value proposition, appropriate market research, and stakeholder involvement, which supports earlier studies. Other elements that spur the development of social business models include social need pressures and managerial confidence in workers (Alegre, et al, 2016). Following the financial crisis of 2008–2009, the European Commission became very interested in social innovation. Even though it is less frequently used today, the term "social innovation" is still used at the European level in the EaSI Programme, which "provides financial support to achieve high employment levels, fair social protection, a skilled and resilient workforce ready for the future of work, as well as inclusive and cohesive societies aiming to eradicate poverty comfortably within the original Barroso narrative."

Figure 2. Social Innovation Framework
Source: Adapted from Social Enterprise UK, 2012 (https://www.researchgate.net/figure/A-collaborative-framework-for-social-innovation-adapted-from-Social-Enterprise-UK-2012_fig2_303024156)

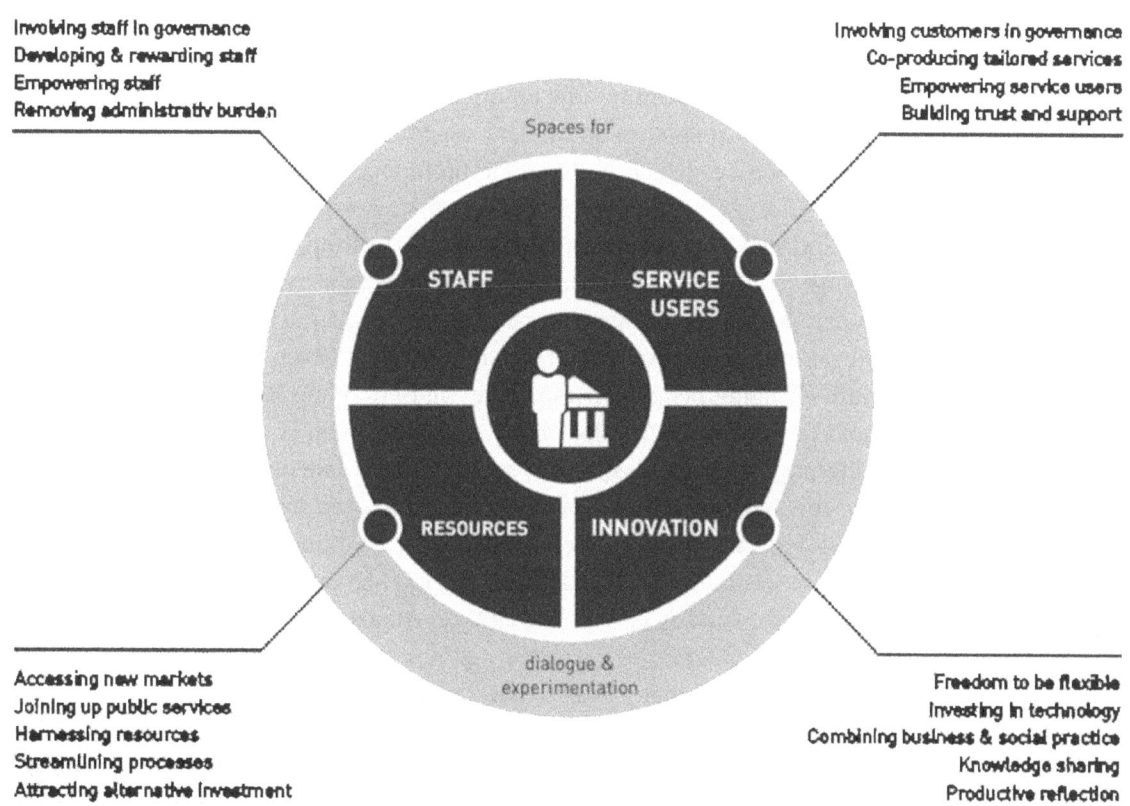

BACKGROUND

Social innovations are new concepts (i.e., goods, services, and models) that both address social needs (better than alternatives) and forge new social bonds or cooperative endeavors. These are the breakthroughs that advance society's capacity for action while simultaneously helping society. According to some academic's social innovation promotes environmental sustainability (Rosca et al., 2017), but, according to others it does not (Basu et al., 2013). Frugal innovation is a new management concept that begins with the particular demands of the bottom of the pyramid markets and works backward to generate suitable solutions that may be greatly different from current solutions created to serve the needs of higher market segments. Due to resource limitations, Frugal Innovation (FI) was created in order to concentrate on underrepresented demographic consumers. Given that there are people who earn less than the average income in every nation and that "frugal innovations can target customers in any segment of the economic pyramid who are price-sensitive by choice or looking for simple products that best meet their real needs," it is crucial to remember that those at the BOP are not only limited to markets in low-income countries (LICs), but also to markets in higher-income countries (HICs). Comparing a FI to an established alternative rather than a vague concept may be the most effective way to do so (Hindocha, & others, 2021). In times of low resources, frugal innovation can be a driving factor for growth and commercial success since it was a practical concept developed in developing nations (Mahr, J., & Imhof, M. 2017). Social innovation is growing in popularity in this area since it can assist in resolving environmental issues. Environmental forces like waste management challenges, traffic and pollution problems, biodiversity losses, and declining ecosystem services like wetlands' flood protection are already propelling social innovation. Although these factors are of an environmental nature, they have social repercussions. For example, air pollution causes health problems, inefficient waste disposal depletes resources, natural defenses are damaged during flooding, which worsens the problem of food insecurity, and poor soil quality or a lack of pollination affects agriculture and causes problems with food production. Or to put it another way, environmental and socioeconomic problems typically overlap, making collaborative solutions possible. Wood recycling social enterprises, organic gardening cooperatives, low-impact housing projects, farmers' markets, car-sharing programs, renewable energy cooperatives, and community composting systems are a few examples of environmental social innovation. Even while social innovations are still small-scale, they are changing people's perspectives and providing increasingly effective and pertinent answers all around the world. The notion that social innovation is about effecting systemic change as well as addressing pressing social issues like societal issues like climate change, aging, and poverty has gained support. It is thought to be a way of treating the roots of societal issues rather than just the symptoms. Institutions have an impact on social dimensions, enabling a transition from "simple" service innovation to "social" innovation, which is defined as the collaborative co-creation of practices that produce novel social practices, such as new value, culture, rituals, and symbols derived from the fusion of experiences (Polese, et al., 2018).

The methods being used to address climate change today are a reflection of our market-driven society's technological, commercial, and industrial superiority. People's behavior, in contrast, is perceived as distinct from these primarily technological solutions and is seen to be challenging to modify. To achieve smart, sustainable, and inclusive growth in Europe 2020, the European Union has established the Innovation Union policy, which aims to "create an innovation-friendly environment that makes it simpler for brilliant ideas to be translated into goods and services." Due to the significant number of fatalities and the uncertainty of employment, the outbreak caused people to feel fearful. Managers and business owners were suddenly forced to deal with their employees leaving the corporate headquarters, which served as a wake-up call to them about the drastic change to online meetings. The pandemic has also been difficult on working parents, who have had to come up with innovative ways to manage work at home. On the other side, lockdown and travel restrictions had a positive impact on the environment in terms of the purity of the air and water (Amankwah, et al., 2020). As an alternative, we highlight bottom-up social innovation in this article as a neglected but potentially important factor in the fight against climate change. In specialized locales like neighborhoods and workplaces, new low-carbon social practices are beginning to take shape. These innovations are less visible and supported because of the origins' separation from the dominant power structure. The problem is made worse by the fact that these breakthroughs typically aren't commoditized, which makes them incompatible with well-liked, market-based systems for distributing novelty throughout society. It is difficult for policymakers to overcome the various obstacles that can prevent the widespread adoption of policy measures to advance the

Figure 3.
Source: Polese, F., Botti, A., Grimaldi, M., Monda, A., & Vesci, M. (2018). Social innovation in smart tourism ecosystems: How technology and institutions shape sustainable value co-creation. Sustainability, 10(1), 140.

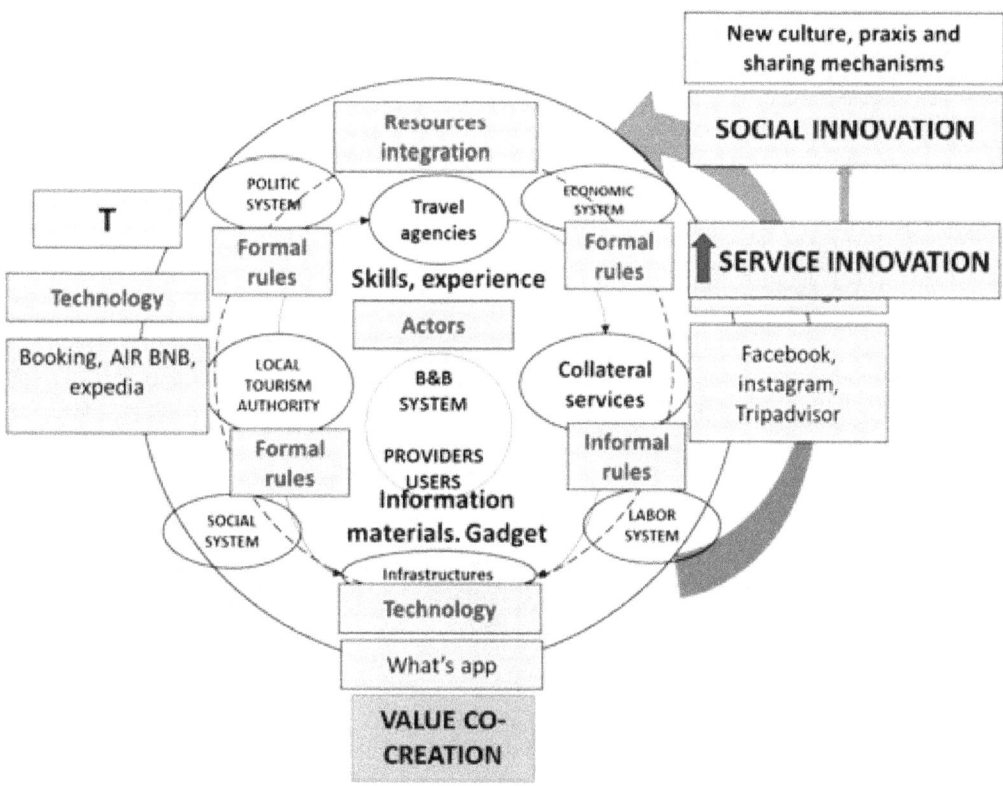

implementation of social innovation. The cultural foundation of social innovation can be thought of as a combination of exclusion, resentment, enthusiasm, and devotion. As the drivers of social innovation are anchored in discontent or an apparent need.

A growing number of mergers and acquisitions in the hotel sector are resulting in an amalgamation of legacy systems, loyalty programs, and websites, which is altering the hospitality industry in Europe. The use of technologies in the hospitality sector is currently undergoing a significant rethink as a result of significant events like the 2015 Marriott/Starwood merger that created the largest hotel chain in the world. Companies are evaluating which technologies are required to achieve their strategic goals. By encouraging a feeling of community, social innovation can aid in the fight against social exclusion and promote more sustainable forms of development at the local level. This has an impact on the types of governance systems that promote the scale-wide diffusion of social innovation. We start by delving into the idea of social innovation and examining the circumstances that might lead to its potential for transformation. Then, using a social, cultural, and ecological knowledge of place, we examine the connections between social innovation and ecologically sustainable placemaking. This demonstrates the way in which social innovation may promote both ecological and social resilience. We will wrap up our discussion of the connections between social innovation and governance practices with a focus on

Figure 4.

 Social innovation focuses on local needs and priorities.

 Ongoing community mobilization as part of social innovation projects can be rapidly adapted for COVID-19 responses.

 Digital social innovations (e.g., Chipatala Cha Pa Foni) can be used to enhance COVID-19 communications.

 Multi-sectoral collaboration developed through social innovation can address social determinants of health.

 The strong focus on equity and people-centeredness provides ways to strengthen COVID-19 responses for vulnerable groups.

creative ways that social, economic, and state actors could cooperate to promote social transformation. innovation. Social innovation can be seen as being closely tied to a number of ideas that have an impact on both innovation and rural development, despite the fact that it lacks a clear theoretical "home." It's crucial to consider any potential drawbacks of social innovation. Three case studies showcase social innovation strategies and outcomes across Europe. When committed individuals, regional enabling organizations, and general policy are in agreement, social innovations can have a substantial impact. Even when transformational successes are rare, social innovation has shown the ability to have positive socioeconomic and environmental consequences in more confined spatial contexts. Although not exactly social innovation, community-led local development is very similar and has already been deeply ingrained in policy guidance. It is unclear whether social innovation will continue to exist as an organizing and capacity-building concept alongside more established principles, such as the smart village approach, or if it will be replaced by new, equally hazy ideas. A new business effort for hospitality and tourism firms, the 2S approach (sustainable & social Innovation) in the hospitality management focuses on the construction of innovative models in the fields of sustainable and social management. The outcome of combining two distinct working tracks provides our students with a unique and specific know-how in new kinds of effective and accountable 2s administration.

The European sovereign debt crisis of 2010–2011 and the global financial crisis of 2007–2009 both provided evidence of how short-term profit mindsets among individuals, organizations, and politicians, as well as related strategies, policies, and actions, contributed to the economic crisis and recession (Dominici et al., 2016). The majority of businesses at the time were using unsustainable business models, which were not sustainable in terms of innovation, commercial performance, or economics (Boons et al, 2013). Social isolation, economic inequality, and pollution were caused by the economic crisis paired with the use of unsustainable business methods. A new product (assistive technologies for people with disabilities), a service (mobile banking), a method (peer-to-peer collaboration and crowdsourcing), a market development (fair trade or time banking), a platform (legal or regulatory frameworks, ways of providing assistance), an organizational form (community interest companies), a business model (social franchising), or a combination of the above can all be considered social innovations (Grice et al., 2012). According to the European Commission, "new ideas (products, services, and models) are developed and put into practice to meet social demands and foster new social connections or collaborations" (EUC, 2013). Prior research on the sustainably managed tourist and hospitality industries shown that sustainable development has the potential to provide underdeveloped rural communities with job opportunities, infrastructure, and financial incentives (Alkier et al., 2015). Social innovation as a concept can be connected to environmental care in order to offer a distinctive, novel approach to tourism environmental care. Beyond that, it can also contribute by bringing a fresh viewpoint that emphasizes learning and development as well as, ultimately, meaning and holistic action (Batle, et al., 2018). A wide range of stakeholders are impacted by the growth of tourism in a certain area, which can lead to both positive social and economic outcomes as well as negative social, environmental, and economic ones (Carlisle et al., 2012). The construction of an innovative environment that supports tourism entrepreneurial enterprises that provide value not only to tourists but to all local stakeholders reflects the fact that the tourism industry requires special attention in order to achieve long-term growth (Gabriel and Laeis, 2016). Social innovation solutions in tourism are a crucial aspect in the growth of the industry because they have an impact on the transformation of the "consumer centric" perspective into the "community oriented" perspective, which takes into account the social capital of the community (Petrou and Daskalopoulou, 2013). It concerns a significant regional and international competitive issue. Instead of focusing on the process, all parties should concentrate on better preserving the working environment and the game's rules in order to provide the framework for the development of successful businesses and start-up companies (Van Oort and Lambooy, 2014). Social innovations have become a part of organizational and/or technological advancements since the third industrial revolution began in 2008. As a result of technical advancements that permit the development of (social) activities in tourism, the supply chain for tourist goods has changed. Online platforms have altered tourism interactions, giving tourists the opportunity to use their agency and become cultural agents (Sigala, 2015). A sustainable sharing economy model has a big impact on starting social innovation in the travel industry when it's connected to digital technology. It seeks to create social platforms and mobile apps that enable knowledge, goods, and services to be shared between consumers, businesses, and other businesses (C2C, B2C, and B2B) (Roblek et al., 2016). All forms of social innovation must be utilized if Europe is to remain cohesive and united. On the other side, some emerging movements are concentrating institutional assistance on those connected to a flimsy solidarity. It is critical to stress the relevance of what the solidarity economy a powerful type of solidarity means in this setting.

SOLUTIONS AND RECOMMENDATIONS

Travelers now have a wide range of possibilities for exercising their agency and acting as cultural agents because to the potential of new (social) kinds of engagement made possible by technological advancements. Given that it upends established social norms and makes place (virtually) for novel human interactions, the sharing economy in particular can be considered as one of the causes behind new social innovations in tourism. Today's social innovations in tourism frequently use web-based tools like social platforms that enable one-on-one transactions akin to those seen in the sharing economy. These technological developments have led to new social practices as the hospitality and tourism industries develop and online social networks become physical social networks. Persuading customers to stay and consume with confidence, particularly in regards to the property's hygiene, safety, and cleanliness, is the most difficult aspect of getting the business back on track (Ardani, E. G., & Harianto, A., 2021). Social innovation can be expressed as a new service product, technology, or individual elements of its implementation for the arrangement of hotel operations, or as new approaches to hotel management or marketing that will target the effective satisfaction of consumer needs and increased competitiveness of services organizations. Innovative technologies in the hospitality industry are an obvious change in their delivery. A varied collection of stakeholders were brought together by the "SPREAD" Sustainable Lives 2050 project, a social platform in Europe, to create a vision for sustainable lives by the year 2050. It has identified several social changes that are occurring in Europe that have the potential to alleviate the unsustainable effects of current lifestyles. Many of them are social innovations in and of themselves, or they are behavioral patterns that might be. An increase in collaborative consumption, which is the sharing, trading, and exchanging of goods and services through programs like time banks, cohousing projects, and carpools. This would suggest that consumers value access to goods and services more than ownership of them. More environmentally responsible ways to use goods and services are becoming more and more evident. Examples of strategies to live more efficiently include efficient living (waste reduction), different living (focus on high-quality goods and services rather than a throwaway culture), and sufficient living (reducing consumption). Ecotowns, co-housing initiatives, and Transition Towns are participatory approaches to sustainable living and transportation options at the neighborhood and governmental levels. With growing investment in technology that reduces energy use and costs, there is evidence of behavior change at the household level. the improvement of health, equity, and well-being through a change in the way we eat, exercise, and live.

FUTURE RESEARCH DIRECTIONS

In the future, social innovation evaluation should incorporate concepts from social innovation, such as teamwork and participation. A thorough evaluation will require regular input from persons involved in social innovation and must be adaptable enough to capture the nuances of its effects. Although general guidelines and evaluation instruments, like the Reeder scorecard and fast assessment tool, can be employed, additional in-depth analysis in particular fields, like the environment, is necessary to bolster recommendations and assessment procedures. Green leadership and green training are found to be major predictors of green process innovation, which can further contribute to social innovation, and they also increase the green managerial innovation in the hotel business (Jamshed et al., 2022). The innovative use of technology may also open up new opportunities for travel partnerships. One illustration is the capacity of mobile apps to create transient, location-based social networks of previously unconnected individuals. It is projected that the use of augmented reality in the tourism industry would serve as another strong catalyst for social changes brought about by technological breakthroughs. Live web content will become more prevalent in a rising variety of everyday contexts as a result of augmented reality. imagines a change in traveler behavior based on wearable technology, including "tourists becoming explorers," a sharp rise in "first-person visual travel tales," and more social travel made possible by real-time networking. Significant investment does not usually occur on its own because of the unpredictability and risk involved with social innovation. Policymakers may aid in creating the enabling environments for social innovation to thrive by establishing legal and regulatory frameworks, providing financial assistance, commissioning research, and fostering markets (Davies et al., 2012).

CONCLUSION

Social innovation is the term used to describe novel concepts that advance social objectives. Social innovation solutions in tourism play a crucial role in the transformation of the "consumer centric" viewpoint into the "community oriented" viewpoint, which takes into account the social capital of the community (Petrou and Daskalopoulou, 2013). A significant regional and national competitive challenge is the topic. Instead of the procedure, all parties should concentrate on improving the working environment and the game rules in order to create the conditions that allow the establishment of profitable businesses and start-up companies (Van Oort and Lambooy, 2014). Social innovation now includes technological advancement as an implication of fresh service options. Social innovations encompass both organizational and technical advances, as seen in theory and practice. Depending on the socioeconomic development of the destination, social innovation has different values. In more rural areas, they are more focused on social issues and missions. It might be said that social solutions in tourism entail sharing innovative information and offering solutions, goods, and services that are catered to the need of customers and local stakeholders.

REFERENCES

Alegre, I., & Berbegal-Mirabent, J. (2016). Social innovation success factors: Hospitality and tourism social enterprises. *International Journal of Contemporary Hospitality Management*, *28*(6), 1155–1176. doi:10.1108/IJCHM-05-2014-0231

Alkier, R., Milojica, V., & Roblek, V. (2015). A holistic framework for the development of a sustainable touristic model. *International Journal of Markets and Business Systems*, *1*(4), 366387. doi:10.1504/IJMABS.2015.074213

Alkier, R., Milojica, V., & Roblek, V. (2017). Challenges of the social innovation in tourism. *Tourism in South East Europe.*, *4*, 1–13. doi:10.20867/tosee.04.24

Amankwah-Amoah, J. (2020). Stepping up and stepping out of COVID-19: New challenges for environmental sustainability policies in the global airline industry. *Journal of Cleaner Production*, *271*, 123000. doi:10.1016/j.jclepro.2020.123000 PMID:32834564

Ardani, E. G., & Harianto, A. (2021). Surviving strategy of hospitality sector in pandemic situation: Case hospitality business in Jakarta. *E-Journal of Tourism.*, *8*(1), 77–86. doi:10.24922/eot.v8i1.71449

Aurangzeb, M. T., Tunio, M. N., Rehman, Z., & Asif, M. (2021). Influence of administrative expertise on human resources practitioners on the job performance: Mediating role of achievement motivation. *International Journal of Management*, *12*(4), 408–421.

Barosso, M. (n.d.). *Employment, Social Affairs & Inclusion*. Available online: https://ec.europa.eu/social/main.jsp?langId=en&catId=89&newsId=445&furtherNews=yes

Basu, R. R., Banerjee, P. M., & Sweeny, E. G. (2013). Frugal innovation. *Journal of Management for Global Sustainability, 1*(2).

Batle, J., Orfila-Sintes, F., & Moon, C. J. (2018). Environmental management best practices: Towards social innovation. *International Journal of Hospitality Management, 69*, 14–20. doi:10.1016/j.ijhm.2017.10.013

Boons, F., Montalvo, C., Quist, J., & Wagner, M. (2013). Sustainable innovation business models and Economic performance: An overview. *Journal of Cleaner Production, 45*, 1–8. Advance online publication. doi:10.1016/j.jclepro.2012.08.013

Buch-Hansen, H. (2014). Capitalist diversity and de-growth trajectories to steady-state economies. *Ecological Economics, 106*, 167–173. doi:10.1016/j.ecolecon.2014.07.030

Bureau of European Policy Advisers. (2010). *Empowering People, Driving Change. Social Innovation in the European Union*. Publications Office of the European Union.

Caramizaru, A., & Uihlein, A. (2020). *Energy Communities: An Overview of Energy and Social Innovation. EUR 30083 EN*. Publications Office of the European Union.

Carlisle, S., Kunc, M., Jones, E., & Tiffin, S. (2013). Supporting innovation for tourism development through multi-stakeholder approaches: Experiences from Africa. *Tourism Management, 35*, 59–69. doi:10.1016/j.tourman.2012.05.010

Chaudhry, I. S., Paquibut, R. Y. & Tunio, M. N. (2021) Do workforce diversity, inclusion practices, & organizational characteristics contribute to organizational innovation? Evidence from the U.A.E. *Cogent Business & Management, 8*(1), 1947549. doi:10.1080/23311975.2021.1947549

Cressey, P., Totterdill, P., Exton, R., & Terstriep, J. (2015). *Stimulating, resourcing and sustaining social innovation: Towards a new mode of public policy production and implementation*. Academic Press.

Dominici, G., & Roblek, V. (2016). Complexity theory for a new managerial paradigm: a research framework. In I. Vrdoljak Raguž, N. Podrug, & L. Jelenc (Eds.), *Neostrategic Management* (pp. 223–241). Springer International Publishing., doi:10.1007/978-3-319-18185-1_14

European Commission. (2013). *Guide to Social Innovation*. https://ec.europa.eu/growth/industry/innovation/policy/social_en

European Commission. EaSI Call. (2021). Available online: https://ec.europa.eu/info/funding-tenders/opportunities/docs/2021 -2027/esf/wp-call/2021/call-fiche_esf-2021-ag-ncp_en.pdf

European Commission EU Programme for Employment and Social Innovation (EaSI). (n.d.). Available online: https://ec.europa.eu/ social/main.jsp?catId=1081

Grice, J. C., Davies, A., Robert, P., & Norman, W. (2012). *The Young Foundation social innovation overview. A deliverable of the project: the theoretical, empirical and policy foundations for building social innovation in Europe (TEPSIE). In European Commission-7th framework Programme*. European Commission, DG Research.

Gupta, V. (2011). Corporate response to global financial crisis: A knowledge-based model. *Glob Econ J, 11*(2), 1850224. doi:10.2202/1524-5861.1706

Hindocha, C. N., Antonacci, G., Barlow, J., & Harris, M. (2021). *Defining frugal innovation: A critical review*. Academic Press.

Jamshed, K., Shah, S. H. A., Majeed, Z., Al-Ghazali, B. M., & Jamshaid, S. (2022). Role of Green Leadership and Green Training on the Green Process Innovation: Mediation of Green Managerial Innovation. *Journal of Xidian University*, *16*(2), 66–72.

Koerich, G. V., & Cancellier, E. (2019). Frugal innovation: Origins, evolution and future perspectives. *Cadernos EBAPE.BR*, *17*(4), 1079–1093. doi:10.1590/1679-395174424x

Laeis Stefanie Lemke, G. C. M. (2016). Social entrepreneurship in tourism: Applying sustainable livelihoods approaches. *International Journal of Contemporary Hospitality Management*, *28*(6), 1076–1093. doi:10.1108/IJCHM-05-2014-0235

Mahr, J., & Imhof, M. (2017). *Applying Frugal Innovation to Serve the Bottom of the Pyramid in Germany*. Academic Press.

Pel, B., Haxeltine, A., Avelino, F., Dumitru, A., Kemp, R., Bauler, T., Kunze, I., Dorland, J., Wittmayer, J., & Jørgensen, M. S. (2020). Towards a theory of transformative social innovation: A relational framework and 12 propositions. *Research Policy*, *49*(8), 104080. doi:10.1016/j.respol.2020.104080

Petrou, A., & Daskalopoulou, I. (2013). Social capital and innovation in the services sector. *European Journal of Innovation Management*, *16*(1), 50–69. doi:10.1108/14601061311292850

Polese, F., Botti, A., Grimaldi, M., Monda, A., & Vesci, M. (2018). Social innovation in smart tourism ecosystems: How technology and institutions shape sustainable value co-creation. *Sustainability*, *10*(1), 140. doi:10.3390u10010140

Roblek, V., Mesko-Stok, Z., & Mesko, M. Complexity of a sharing economy for tourism and hospitality. In *Proceedings of 23rd International Congress "Tourism and Hospitality Industry 2016 – Trends and Challenges"* (pp. 374-387). Faculty of Tourism and Hospitality Management, University of Rijeka.

Rosca, E., Arnold, M., & Bendul, J. C. (2017). Business models for sustainable innovation–an empirical analysis of frugal products and services. *Journal of Cleaner Production*, *162*, S133–S145. doi:10.1016/j.jclepro.2016.02.050

Sigala, M. (2015). From demand elasticity to market plasticity: A market approach for developing revenue management strategies in tourism. *Journal of Travel & Tourism Marketing*, *32*(7), 812–834. doi:10.1080/10548408.2015.1063801

Slee, B., Lukesch, R., & Ravazzoli, E. (2022). Social Innovation: The Promise and the Reality in Marginalised Rural Areas in Europe. *WORLD (Oakland, Calif.)*, *3*(2), 237–259. doi:10.3390/world3020013

Solov'eva, T. Y. S., Popov, A. V., Caro-Gonzalez, A., & Hua, L. (2018). Social innovation in Spain, China and Russia: key aspects of development. *Economic and Social Changes: Facts, Trends, Forecast*, *11*(2), 52–68.

van Oort, F. G., & Lambooy, J. G. (2014). *Cities, knowledge, and innovation*. In M. M. Fischer & P. Nijkamp (Eds.), *Handbook of Regional Science* (pp. 475–488). Springer Berlin Heidelberg. doi:10.1007/978-3-642-23430-9_27

KEY TERMS AND DEFINITIONS

Frugal Innovation: The term "frugal innovation" (FI) is ill-defined and used to refer to many different types of innovation, including bricolage, disruptive, cost, and grass-roots innovation.

Social Innovation: The creation and application of novel approaches entailing conceptual, procedural, organizational, or product change with the ultimate objective of enhancing the welfare and well-being of people and communities. As a result of issues like working conditions, education, community development, or health, social innovations are creative social practices that strive to meet societal demands more effectively than existing options.

Chapter 15
A Paradigm Shift in Education Systems Due to COVID–19:
Its Social and Demographic Consequences

Karambir Singh Dhayal
Birla Institute of Technology and Science, Pilani, India

Mohsen Brahmi
https://orcid.org/0000-0002-0995-0761
University of Sfax, Tunisia

Shruti Agrawal
Malaviya National Institute of Technology, Jaipur, India

Luigi Aldieri
https://orcid.org/0000-0001-9300-6804
University of Salerno, Italy

Concetto Paolo Vinci
University of Salerno, Italy

ABSTRACT

The pandemic of COVID-19 has caused a serious effect on health, economic, social, political, demographic, and all other various aspects of the economy. It has given a huge impact on the education system in a worldwide manner that leads to the closure of universities, colleges, and schools. This study aims to assess the impact of the worldwide COVID-19 pandemic on the education sector in special reference to India. The loss of learning was majorly pronounced among students from a disadvantaged prospectus. The authors conducted a qualitative document analysis of all the published articles that explained the impact of COVID-19 pandemic on the education system from 2019-2021. The study provides an insight on the barriers in education due to the COVID-19 pandemic. The result shows the evolution of technology-enabled education in the learning sector. Finally, the challenges articulated by the learners during online learning include external as well as internal factors and causes.

DOI: 10.4018/978-1-6684-5417-6.ch015

INTRODUCTION

COVID-19 came along with many unprecedented challenges (Agrawal, Jamwal, et al., 2020). One of them was that regular classroom teaching had to be abandoned immediately because social distancing norms had to be followed strictly. In the effort to provide continued education, institutions and governments realized the need to support online learning (Soledad Ramírez-Montoya et al., 2021). As a result, virtual classroom learning had to be adopted worldwide whether a nation is developed or still on the development trajectory. Some countries were fast to embrace this change, while others had to struggle (González-Zamar et al., 2020). One particular example was that of India, where Internet penetration and availability of smartphones remain a bottleneck. India happens to be one of the few nations which are continuously making significant advancements in terms of developing the technology for the spread of quality universal education. The availability of literature concerning the role of learning is mainly about classroom-based learning (McCluskey et al., 2021; Ali et al., 2022; Celia et al., 2021). Hence there is a need to look at education after the Covid-19 pandemic.

Until now, the available literature examined the impact of summer vacations on learning, or disruptions from various events such as extreme weather conditions, loss of natural calamities, or strikes by teachers (Hayran & Anik, 2021). COVID-19 accumulates unique and unanticipated challenge that makes it vague how to apply earlier lessons. Simultaneous effects on the entire economy make parents limited equipped to provide resources and support. They struggle with poor economic conditions, uncertainty, loss of jobs, salary reduction from their working places, and working from home. It gives birth to the risk of health and mortality aspects of the pandemic to incur further psychological costs along with the impost of social isolation (Schelhorn et al., 2021; Wilson et al., 2021; Giardino et al., 2020; Schröpfer et al., 2021; Haesebaert et al., 2020). Family and domestic violence cases have also projected to rise, putting vulnerable students at more risk (Foley et al., 2021; Ragavan et al., 2020; Every-Palmer et al., 2020; Duby et al., 2022). At a similar time, the scope of a pandemic may drive educational institutes and governments to counter more intently than during other disruptive circumstances.

By that time, studies on the loss of learning on the part of learners during the lockdown period have started to emerge. In the education sector, teachers and students have struggled the most in adopting the new teaching-learning style, online-based solutions for instructions (Marcén-Román et al., 2021). Adopting an online-learning platform is the most challenging as educators and learners were not trained to follow up on this earlier. The channelizing of face-to-face learning is one of the most traditional ways of teaching (Bulut et al., 2021).

In face-to-face learning, work slackens whenever learners duel with the educators to facilitate understanding of concepts (Giusti et al., 2021). Whereas in online teaching, the role of a student is not just dependent upon educators; instead, they become self-regulate in their different activities and understand concepts alone or via available online resources. The Online learning process needs very detailed and attentive preparation by educators as it is the only way to ensure the maximum output of students. To achieve maximum and successful learning, students must gradually develop their self-regulation strength, maintain their schedule of study, and experiment (Brahmi et al., 1 C.E.).

However, during the first wave of the pandemic of COVID-19, continuous lockdown, social distancing, and abandoning face-to-face classes perceived that teaching had immediately to be adopted the concept of online methodologies for which neither the learners nor the educators were prepared to opt. This unprecedented situation might convey that ideas and knowledge were not grasped as well as in online classes as earlier it had been face-to-face classes, accompanying the inevitable statement that

Figure 1. Disruption in Education System

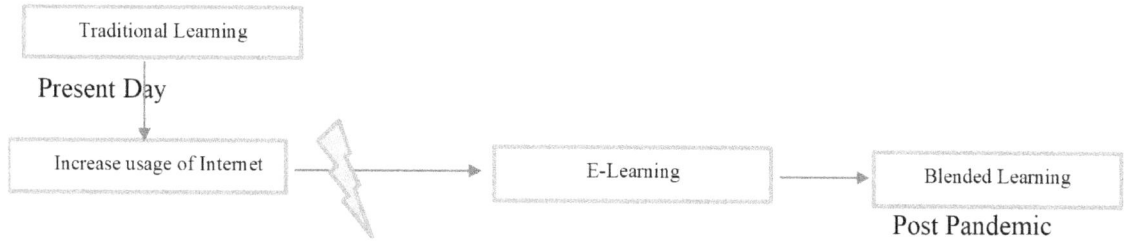

the quality of teaching was worse. If it is meant to persist, it may depict poorly trained learners with a negative outcome for society.

According to the United Nations Educational, Scientific and Cultural Organization (UNESCO), the adoption of online learning has had a significant impact on marginalized and vulnerable children and their families, including interrupted education, poor nutrition, confusion and stress, cost of technology that causes risk of dropouts and high economic price.

RESHAPING OF THE EDUCATION SECTOR IN THE WAKE OF THE COVID-19 PANDEMIC

In history education worldwide, 2020 can be called the year of change, adaptation, involvement, and evolvement. In unprecedented times, schools, colleges, and universities were hit majorly along with unsure about the re-opening of institutions (Agrawal, Sharma, et al., 2020). This caused a disorder in the academic schedule and disturbed students' learning graphs.

The lockdown during the pandemic has compelled the education sectors to come along with innovations in learning styles to sustain learning among students. As a response, education sectors have switched to online learning modes. Instead of adopting this new learning model in education, various factors have evolved (Agrawal & Sharma, 2022).

In India as promptly, a nationwide lockdown imposed by the federal government has closed each academic institution from primary to higher education. According to UNESCO, the pandemic of COVID 19 lead to affect around 290 million college students in 22 international locations around the globe. It is estimated that approximately 32 crore college students are involved in India.

Various factors have contributed to reshaping the education system, including digital technologies and machine applications.

Components of Online Learning

Digital technology has played a pivotal role in the education sector, and the sudden switch towards online learning during the pandemic has accelerated the digital transformation in the education sector (Hung, 2022). From remote learning to screen learning, it envisaged the evolution of the digital world (Loveys et al., 2021). The classes are conducted via the use of technologies and the internet, which has also encouraged digital literacy among educators and learners (Barzilay et al., 2020). Schools and uni-

Figure 2. Factors that contribute to reshaping the education system

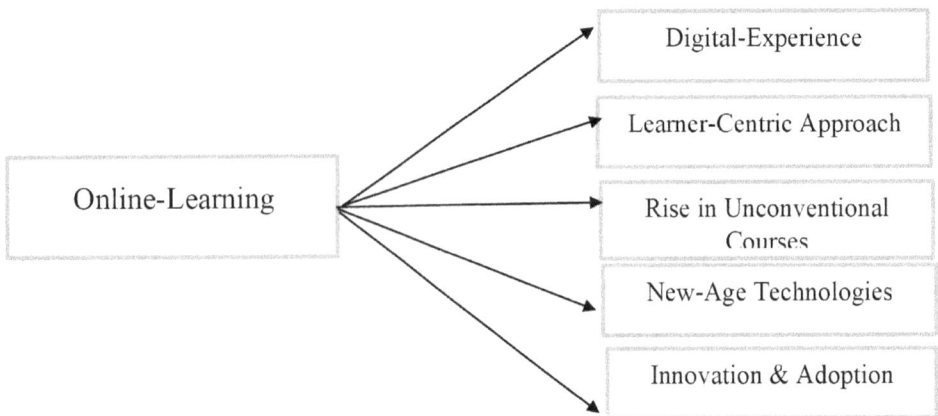

versities started providing access and opportunities to all. Though it was difficult to adopt such a new learning environment, students gradually accepted this new learning norm (Abdul Bujang et al., 2020).

The new era of online education is focused on the student-centric approach where students are expected to come along with solutions to a given problem. They can use the resources at their own pace and timing. Students are encouraged to finish the assigned task and assignments; the opportunity for self-evaluation is to be focused. The reflective learning approach emphasizes that students are skilled, reskilled and up-skilled by the given technologies and resources in decision-making and creative problem-solving (Craig et al., 2021; (Agrawal & Sharma, 2022b).

Online education will continue to become an integral part of the education sector. There is an increase in the usage of unconventional courses such as supply chain management, data analytics, and strategic management. There is an increased demand for new-age modules for which such courses are being focused in the higher education sector. The forthcoming fourth industrial revolution will target such technologies (Agrawal et al., 2021).

The adoption of new technologies such as Artificial Intelligence, Machine Learning, and Cyber-Physical Security has been adopted on a large scale in higher education institutions, and the education sector has realized its role in forming online learning more agile, innovative, creative, and responsive (Anand, 2020). These technologies must be adopted in order to the fourth industrial revolution and the fourth educational revolution. The pandemic of COVID-19 has diverted the shift from the traditional way of teaching and learning to a more advanced and technological-prone teaching-learning style (Chu et al., 2022)

Education institutes have turned the challenges into opportunities to ensure students' best and maximum learning outcomes; they have developed various innovative tools and techniques. They have reinvented the education system to provide an educational experience that can continue with the desired products and services (Bulut et al., 2021). Many of the lectures and tutorials have been updated by various organizations in a more innovative manner that is not just limited to textbook courses (Pauw et al., 2015).

METHODOLOGY

In this study, we have conducted a document analysis review methodology of online newspaper articles in the public domain (Mackieson et al., 2018). For that, we have focused on the published newspaper articles and research reports published by government organizations. These documents are a publicly available source of deviating data that constitute a publically traditional form of discourse (majorly discussed on the social platform, in person or broadcast media at large) (Bowen, 2009).

The research is based on the Qualitative document analysis approach and includes the critical discourse analysis that provides for implicit and explicit understandings within a discourse (Sankofa, 2022). This applied analytical research approach enables the researcher to explain both implicit and explicit sense-making narratives in place of the COVID-19 pandemic and its impact social and demographic impact on the education system with broader implications of such perspectives.

SOCIAL AND DEMOGRAPHIC CONSEQUENCES OF ONLINE EDUCATION

The education sector's curriculum may be considered a document of organized knowledge and experience through which learners are expected to learn and implement learning in life situations. The practice of education makes learners eligible to know and understand in accord with their intellectual and social experiences.

It harms college graduates' income and employment after completing their studies. In another section of society, women and young female students consider the impact of education on health and prosperity concerning online learning and society-specifically how the dimension of online learning programs enhances their potential in the social context. Social dimensions include belonging to rural areas, and students who follow different local languages can access and utilize online resources. The social consequences of the ongoing pandemic of coronavirus situation are several and varied.

Social Isolation: At the time of pandemic it is the foremost factor that affects the entire population, although any subsequent interchange to the process that was expected to connect is also relevant significantly because of social distancing commitment and prevention of family and friends gatherings at social events. These restrictions significantly impact the workplace, educational institutes, industries, supply chain, and healthcare passage, and restrictions on the usage of available spaces (Graupensperger et al., 2020). In addition to this complex situation, isolation from friends and family for a long period may result in stress, anxiety, and fear among students. To avoid this situation, education institutes should consider students' personal circumstances (Giardino et al., 2020).

Increase in dropout rate: According to UNESCO, it is estimated that 24 million children in 180 counties may not return to education in the coming years due to the pandemic. In India, The National Educational Policy 2020 has unveiled an appropriate mechanism for "tracking students" who are left out due to unforeseen circumstances. The National Sample Survey Organisation (NSSO) in 2017-18 reported a dropout of 3.22 crore of students from schools in India. According to the MNREGA scheme in India, it is projected to double this year. In January 2020, the school dropout rate was less than 3%.

Effect on Productivity: At the time of the pandemic, the situation has become alarming in the university education sector as it was challenging for both the teacher and students. Students from the final year in university soon finish their education and embark upon a career that may not capture the required knowledge due to the distribution of classes and move to online teaching, which will never be

Table 1. Barriers to Online Learning at the time of the COVID-19 pandemic

S.No.	Barriers
B1.	Adjusting Learning Style
B2.	Infrastructure Cost
B3.	Accessibility of Internet
B4.	Challenges for Marginalized Families
B5.	Impact on Well-being
B6.	Interaction and Communication
B7.	Anxiety, Stress and Depression
B8.	Financial Distress
B9.	Community Issues
B10.	Technological Issues

delivered to them. However, in some particular fields, such as medicine and psychiatry, the effects of the pandemic of COVID 19 have ratcheted up both productivity and pressure (Bonanomi et al., 2021).

Level of Competences: There is a difference in the level of competence among students who are perceived as having a high and low level that affects the self-regulation process, colossal motivation, and procrastination. Online learning, compared to face-to-face learning, is flexible, which makes the self-learning process easy and can be both negative and positive for the learners. The greater flexibility provided in online education requires high demands from learners' ability to continue their motivation, and thus it can pose passive procrastination as an increased risk.

BARRIERS TO HIGHER EDUCATION SYSTEM DURING COVID-19

In the available literature, we have also found the ten barriers to online education during the COVID-19 pandemic that has severely impacted students from primary to higher education level. The barriers are the factors that have a negative impact on the learners. The sudden shift from classroom communication to social distancing and the switch towards online learning were most challenging for young learners (Baticulon et al., 2021). It has changed their lifestyle as they were pursuing the pandemic earlier. Some students were unable to understand the lectures and lessons through online mode. The conduction learning to teaching to assigning notes and sheets, were challenging to adopt (Baticulon et al., 2021). From textbooks to the Portable Document Format, daily meeting via various virtual apps has shifted the entire pattern of learning and implementation. Online delivery of education requires a high intrauterine cost to adopt (Xiao et al., 2022). The internet service to smartphones, laptops and desktops was quite expensive for most families to adopt. Accessibility to various facilities also becomes a significant challenge in online learning—the disruption of connection, and issues of the poor network, especially in rural areas. Marginalized families are facing the problem of providing resources to their children (Rahiem et al., 2021). The families cannot cope with such a situation because of poor financial conditions and limited sources of earnings. The major problem being faced by students are psychological and mental issues (Vidourek et al., 2014). It significantly impacts their overall well-being, which may be caused by the isolation at home for an extended period. There is stress, anxiety, and fear among students. There is a lack of personal connection and physical appearance with friends and family (Agrawal & Sharma, 2022). The closure of schools and universities also leads to a lack of personal touch with teachers, positively affecting students' communication skills (Craig et al., 2021).

CONCLUSION

India can harness its vast demographic dividend by managing the COVID situation in a manner that our human capital grows, irrespective of the change in pedagogy adopted by the education sector. "Digital India" is vital in ensuring that technology adoption happens across the nation. The best aspect of this paradigm shift in education is that now it is universally accessible to all. Students can undertake and enrol on any MOOCs (Massive open online courses) without restrictions. This can help us achieve SDG Goal 4 of Quality Education, which emphasizes ensuring inclusive and equitable quality education and promoting lifelong learning opportunities for all. Education can play the role of a leveller in achieving economic and social mobility, inclusion, and equality if everything happens in the desired manner. The New Education Policy envisions transforming our nation sustainably into an equitable and vibrant knowledge society by providing high-quality education to all.

REFERENCES

Bujang, S. D. A., Selamat, A., Krejcar, O., Maresova, P., & Nguyen, N. T. (2020, April). Digital learning demand for future education 4.0—Case studies at Malaysia education institutions. In Informatics (Vol. 7, No. 2, p. 13). MDPI.

Agrawal, S., Jamwal, A., & Gupta, S. (2020). Effect of COVID-19 on the Indian economy and supply chain. doi:10.20944/preprints202005.0148.v1

Agrawal, S., & Sharma, N. (2022, January). Barriers and Role of Higher Educational Institutes in Students' Mental Well-being: A Critical Analysis. In *2nd International Conference on Sustainability and Equity (ICSE-2021)* (pp. 173-180). Atlantis Press. 10.2991/ahsseh.k.220105.021

Agrawal, S., Sharma, N., & Bhatnagar, S. (2021). Education 4.0 to Industry 4.0 Vision: Current Trends and Overview. In *Recent Advances in Smart Manufacturing and Materials* (pp. 475–485). Springer. doi:10.1007/978-981-16-3033-0_45

AgrawalS.SharmaN.SinghM. (2020). *Employing CBPR to understand the well-being of higher education students during COVID-19 lockdown in India.* doi:10.2139/ssrn.3628458

Kumar, A., Anand, A., & Kesri, V. (2020). Industry 4.0 to education 4.0: An Indian Student Perspective. *International Journal of Innovative Research in Technology*, 6(12), 417–423. https://www.researchgate.net/publication/341343880

Barzilay, R., Moore, T. M., Greenberg, D. M., DiDomenico, G. E., Brown, L. A., White, L. K., Gur, R. C., & Gur, R. E. (2020). Resilience, COVID-19-related stress, anxiety and depression during the pandemic in a large population enriched for healthcare providers. *Translational Psychiatry, 10*(1), 1–8. doi:10.103841398-020-00982-4 PMID:32820171

Baticulon, R. E., Sy, J. J., Alberto, N. R. I., Baron, M. B. C., Mabulay, R. E. C., Rizada, L. G. T., Tiu, C. J. S., Clarion, C. A., & Reyes, J. C. B. (2021). Barriers to online learning in the time of COVID-19: A national survey of medical students in the Philippines. *Medical Science Educator, 31*(2), 615–626. doi:10.100740670-021-01231-z PMID:33649712

Bonanomi, A., Facchin, F., Barello, S., & Villani, D. (2021). Prevalence and health correlates of Onine Fatigue: A cross-sectional study on the Italian academic community during the COVID-19 pandemic. *PLoS One, 16*(10), e0255181. doi:10.1371/journal.pone.0255181 PMID:34648507

Bowen, G. A. (2009). Document analysis as a qualitative research method. *Qualitative Research Journal, 9*(2), 27–40. Advance online publication. doi:10.3316/QRJ0902027

Brahmi, M., Aldieri, L., Dhayal, K. S., & Agrawal, S. (2022). Education 4.0: Can It Be a Component of the Sustainable Well-Being of Students? In Sustainable Development of Human Resources in a Globalization Period (pp. 215-230). doi:10.4018/978-1-6684-4981-3.ch014

Bulut, N. S., Yorguner, N., & Akvardar, Y. (2021). Impact of COVID-19 on the Life of Higher-Education Students in Istanbul: Relationship Between Social Support, Health-Risk Behaviors, and Mental/Academic Well-Being. *Alpha Psychiatry, 22*(6), 291-300. doi:10.5152/alphapsychiatry.2021.21319

Chu, A. M., Chan, T. W., & So, M. K. (2022). Learning from work-from-home issues during the COVID-19 pandemic: Balance speaks louder than words. *PLoS One, 17*(1), e0261969. doi:10.1371/journal.pone.0261969 PMID:35025893

Craig, S. L., Leung, V. W., Pascoe, R., Pang, N., Iacono, G., Austin, A., & Dillon, F. (2021). AFFIRM online: Utilising an affirmative cognitive–behavioural digital intervention to improve mental health, access, and engagement among LGBTQA+ youth and young adults. *International Journal of Environmental Research and Public Health, 18*(4), 1541. doi:10.3390/ijerph18041541 PMID:33562876

Duby, Z., Bunce, B., Fowler, C., Bergh, K., Jonas, K., Dietrich, J. J., Govindasamy, D., Kuo, C., & Mathews, C. (2022). Intersections between COVID-19 and socio-economic mental health stressors in the lives of South African adolescent girls and young women. *Child and Adolescent Psychiatry and Mental Health, 16*(1), 1–16. doi:10.118613034-022-00457-y PMID:35346316

Every-Palmer, S., Jenkins, M., Gendall, P., Hoek, J., Beaglehole, B., Bell, C., Williman, J., Rapsey, C., & Stanley, J. (2020). Psychological distress, anxiety, family violence, suicidality, and wellbeing in New Zealand during the COVID-19 lockdown: A cross-sectional study. *PLoS One, 15*(11), e0241658. doi:10.1371/journal.pone.0241658 PMID:33147259

Foley, S., Badinlou, F., Brocki, K. C., Frick, M. A., Ronchi, L., & Hughes, C. (2021). Family function and child adjustment difficulties in the COVID-19 pandemic: An international study. *International Journal of Environmental Research and Public Health, 18*(21), 11136. doi:10.3390/ijerph182111136 PMID:34769654

Giardino, D. L., Huck-Iriart, C., Riddick, M., & Garay, A. (2020). The endless quarantine: The impact of the COVID-19 outbreak on healthcare workers after three months of mandatory social isolation in Argentina. *Sleep Medicine*, *76*, 16–25. doi:10.1016/j.sleep.2020.09.022 PMID:33059247

Giusti, L., Mammarella, S., Salza, A., Del Vecchio, S., Ussorio, D., Casacchia, M., & Roncone, R. (2021). Predictors of academic performance during the covid-19 outbreak: Impact of distance education on mental health, social cognition and memory abilities in an Italian university student sample. *BMC Psychology*, *9*(1), 1–17. doi:10.118640359-021-00649-9 PMID:34526153

González-Zamar, M. D., Ortiz Jiménez, L., Sánchez Ayala, A., & Abad-Segura, E. (2020). The impact of the university classroom on managing the socio-educational well-being: A global study. *International Journal of Environmental Research and Public Health*, *17*(3), 931. doi:10.3390/ijerph17030931 PMID:32028598

Graupensperger, S., Benson, A. J., Kilmer, J. R., & Evans, M. B. (2020). Social (un)distancing: Teammate interactions, athletic identity, and mental health of student-athletes during the COVID-19 pandemic. *The Journal of Adolescent Health*, *67*(5), 662–670. doi:10.1016/j.jadohealth.2020.08.001 PMID:32943294

Hayran, C., & Anik, L. (2021). Well-being and fear of missing out (FOMO) on digital content in the time of COVID-19: A correlational analysis among university students. *International Journal of Environmental Research and Public Health*, *18*(4), 1974. doi:10.3390/ijerph18041974 PMID:33670639

Hung, J. (2022). Digitalisation, Parenting, and Children's Mental Health: What Are the Challenges and Policy Implications? *International Journal of Environmental Research and Public Health*, *19*(11), 6452. doi:10.3390/ijerph19116452 PMID:35682037

Loveys, K., Sagar, M., Pickering, I., & Broadbent, E. (2021). A digital human for delivering a remote loneliness and stress intervention to at-risk younger and older adults during the COVID-19 pandemic: Randomized pilot trial. *JMIR Mental Health*, *8*(11), e31586. doi:10.2196/31586 PMID:34596572

Mackieson, P., Shlonsky, A., & Connolly, M. (2019). Increasing rigor and reducing bias in qualitative research: A document analysis of parliamentary debates using applied thematic analysis. *Qualitative Social Work: Research and Practice*, *18*(6), 965–980. doi:10.1177/1473325018786996

Marcén-Román, Y., Gasch-Gallen, A., Vela Martín de la Mota, I. I., Calatayud, E., Gómez-Soria, I., & Rodríguez-Roca, B. (2021). Stress perceived by University Health Sciences Students, 1 year after COVID-19 pandemic. *International Journal of Environmental Research and Public Health*, *18*(10), 5233. doi:10.3390/ijerph18105233 PMID:34069066

McCluskey, G., Fry, D., Hamilton, S., King, A., Laurie, M., McAra, L., & Stewart, T. M. (2021). School closures, exam cancellations and isolation: The impact of Covid-19 on young people's mental health. *Emotional & Behavioural Difficulties*, *26*(1), 46–59. doi:10.1080/13632752.2021.1903182

Boeve-de Pauw, J., Gericke, N., Olsson, D., & Berglund, T. (2015). The effectiveness of education for sustainable development. *Sustainability*, *7*(11), 15693–15717. doi:10.3390u71115693

Ragavan, M. I., Culyba, A. J., Muhammad, F. L., & Miller, E. (2020). Supporting adolescents and young adults exposed to or experiencing violence during the COVID-19 pandemic. *The Journal of Adolescent Health*, *67*(1), 18–20. doi:10.1016/j.jadohealth.2020.04.011 PMID:32409152

Rahiem, M. D., Krauss, S. E., & Ersing, R. (2021). Perceived consequences of extended social isolation on mental well-being: Narratives from Indonesian university students during the COVID-19 pandemic. *International Journal of Environmental Research and Public Health*, *18*(19), 10489. doi:10.3390/ijerph181910489 PMID:34639788

Sankofa, N. (2022). Critical method of document analysis. *International Journal of Social Research Methodology*, 1–13. doi:10.1080/13645579.2022.2113664

Schelhorn, I., Ecker, A., Lüdtke, M. N., Rehm, S., Tran, T., Bereznai, J. L., Meyer, M. L., Sütterlin, S., Kinateder, M., Lugo, R. G., & Shiban, Y. (2021). Psychological Burden During the COVID-19 Pandemic in Germany. *Frontiers in Psychology*, *12*, 640518. Advance online publication. doi:10.3389/fpsyg.2021.640518 PMID:34557124

Ramírez-Montoya, M. S., Loaiza-Aguirre, M. I., Zúñiga-Ojeda, A., & Portuguez-Castro, M. (2021). Characterization of the Teaching Profile within the Framework of Education 4.0. *Future Internet*, *13*(4), 91. doi:10.3390/fi13040091

Vidourek, R. A., King, K. A., Nabors, L. A., & Merianos, A. L. (2014). Students' benefits and barriers to mental health help-seeking. *Health Psychology and Behavioral Medicine*, *2*(1), 1009–1022. doi:10.1080/21642850.2014.963586 PMID:25750831

Li, W., Zhao, Z., & Wang, D. (2022). Anxiety, depression and satisfaction with life among college students in China: Nine months after initiation of the outbreak of COVID-19. *Frontiers in Psychiatry*, *2427*, 777190. Advance online publication. doi:10.3389/fpsyt.2021.777190

Chapter 16
How Frugal Innovation, Social Transition, and Business Sustainability Are Related:
Insights on the Contemporary Transition Towards Sustainability

Syed Haider Ali Shah
Bahria Business School, Bahria University, Pakistan

Nida Aman
Bahria University, Pakistan

Sanaullah Al Azhari
Bahria University, Pakistan

Bushra Alvi
Bahria University, Pakistan

Rafia Amjad
Bahria University, Pakistan

Farhat Ishaque Ishaque
Bahria University, Pakistan

Ozair Ijaz Kiani
Bahria University, Pakistan

Muhammad Zeeshan Ahmed Sheikh
Bahria University, Pakistan

ABSTRACT

The rise of digitalization has brought new challenges to the business world. E-commerce operations are growing as a result of digitalization, which is transforming traditional business processes, methods, and products into new ones. To address the global challenges posed by e-commerce and changes in markets, firms rely heavily on business innovation. Firms must be able to function under societal and operational challenges, as well as have the ability to integrate local knowledge with other types of expertise. Frugal innovation focuses on societal and operational issues and challenges as beginning points for innovative ideas that could ultimately drive for sustainable development. This chapter is about a mapping of the literature by focusing on certain research areas: the structure and identifying patterns of how the frugal innovation, social transition, and business sustainability are related in the digital era.

DOI: 10.4018/978-1-6684-5417-6.ch016

INTRODUCTION

There is no signal agreed upon universally accepted definition of the frugal innovation (Hossain, 2020). However, the role of the frugal innovation has great impact on the utilization of resources in terms of environmental sustainability (Albert 2019; Shah et al., 2021; Ghazali et al., 2022). Various studies have investigated the relationship of frugal innovation and business sustainability and presented multiple results. Study conducted by the Hossain, (2020), advocated that frugal innovation idea is more successful when it provides the quality service or solution but that are cheaper than the existing product. Furthermore, it paves the way for first step towards sustainability initiatives (Van Mossel et al., 2018). Even though, the idea of frugal innovation is not revolve around the reducing cost only (Weyrauch & Herstatt, 2017). Frugal innovation also tends towards redesigning both, product and services to perform and offer the better services, functionalities, moreover, going beyond the expectations of satisfaction through improvement in the service or product (Bhatti et al., 2018). Further literature provides the evidences and studies have shown that due to frugal innovation, it has changed the dynamics of the organizational production and service as compare to the traditional production. Due to this the competition has also become stiff and challenging because of the low-income market segment shifted to high income market (Clausen and Fichter, 2019). It can further be argued that the ole of frugal innovation the is undeniable impact on the economic level, society level and environmentally friendly practices (Albert, 2019), by developing the cheap products that are affordable and valuable either in developed countries or in developing countries (Winkler et al., 2020) which provides the support for the trend of frugal innovation (Hossain, 2020). In literature, studies have argued that many authors linked and related the frugal innovation to be closely linked and suggested the significant impact on environment as the basic purpose of the frugal innovation is the to minimize the cost which translate into the economize the use of energy while taking care of the resources during production as well as in the designing phase (Hossain et al., 2021).

After the extensive literature, various studies suggested that due to process of frugal innovation the amount of carbon footprint is smaller or with fewer emissions (Albert, 2019). The major concern of the frugal innovation is the taking care of sustainability, economic and social impact. The social impact is in the form of raising the living standard of the low-income consumer by providing them the cost saving opportunities and to save money (Hossain, 2020). Furthermore, the saving cost of such consumers can be helpful for their personal development, to buy new products or to utilise that amount in the leisure activities which improves their quality of life (Khan, 2016). In terms of the economic impact, there is the opportunity for the organization to offer the product of high value to low-income consumers and to minimise their sales and expand business operations to the next level while also conserving the environmental factors (Bocken et al., 2014).

However, besides the multiple benefits of the frugal innovation, it is still less understanding and empirical evidences to show and prove the relationship of frugal innovation and sustainability (D'Angelo and Magnusson, 2020). Moreover, the frugal innovation is getting popularity not only in the developing countries but also in the developed countries. For example, in the United States, since 1970s, there is decline in the overall middle-income households and the gap of inequality is widening and there are variety of the factors but the experts are also not sure upon why this is expanding Hossain, 2020). Similarly, in Europe this phenomenon is occurring over the last two decades. This pattern has been declared as far-reaching impact on behavioural aspect of the western markets where consumers are facing the challenge of limited spending power. This reflects the notion that the concept of the low-income consumer is no

Figure 1.
Source: https://www.google.com/imgres?imgurl=https%3A%2F%2Fars.els-cdn.com%2Fcontent%2Fimage%2F1-s2.0-
S0160791X20313117-gr1.jpg&imgrefurl=https%3A%2F%2Fwww.sciencedirect.com%2Fscience%2Farticle%2Fpi-
i%2FS0160791X20313117&tbnid=KFdrv2KdFEE0NM&vet=12ahUKEwiLhN-Un7T6AhXBjtgFHdqCCtsQMygAegU
IARCgAQ..i&docid=BB3Z_3hTZLTABM&w=533&h=230&itg=1&q=different%20dimensions%20of%20frugal%20
innovation&hl=en&ved=2ahUKEwiLhN-Un7T6AhXBjtgFHdqCCtsQMygAegUIARCgAQ

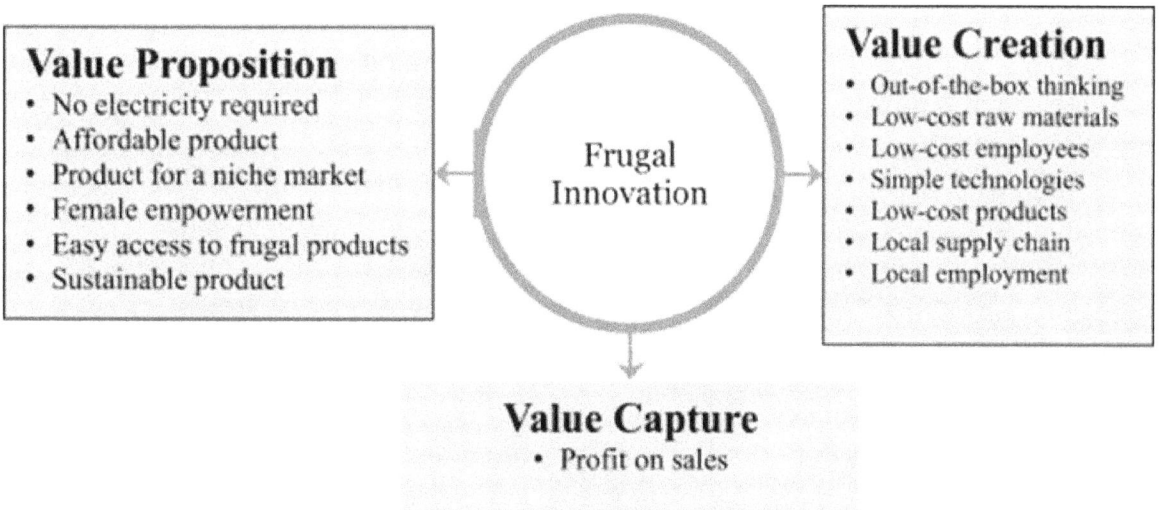

longer restricted to the developing countries but also occurred in the developed countries (Levänen et al., 2022). Furthermore, this phenomena is more accelerated by the covid-19 pandemic (IMF, 2020).

Despite of the fact that spending power of the low-income households has declined but this provides the opportunity to the business firms to attract these low income households though the sustainable products and services while considering for the frugal innovation which is offering the products with cheap rates and considering the environmental sustainability. Thus, frugal innovation can be utilised to capture that low end market and to be successful in that market. (Gordon & Hodgson, 2017).

Similarly, the challenges with the frugal innovation are developing and offering the product with resource efficient and user friendly while considering the novelty as well. In the frugal innovation the big challenges appear in the form of societal sustainability challenges, economic and operational level constraints (Hossain, 2020). The linkage between the societal and operational concerns have deep roots in the investigation of the environmental aspect of the frugality (This paper reference 1-s2.0). The frugal innovation opens avenue for the local products with resilience and which has the higher chance of getting scalability (Hossain et al., 2021). In order to grasp the idea of frugal innovation, often it comes from the grassroots players and they are the ones who develop and refine it for greater utilization for low income consumers (Hossain, 2016). Such idea providers are mostly with the background of low formal education but with sharp skills of developing innovation through their practical and traditional knowledge (Pansera and Sarker, 2016). Interestingly, the frugal innovation is considered as disruptive and can be utilised in multiple countries with same socio-economic conditions (Hossain, 2020).

Literature review provides the evidences that frugal innovation remained a positive and significant factor in promoting the sustainability implications (Albert, 2019). However, there are some studies which claim that due to the technical concept of the frugal innovation, it does not reflect the societal problems which these innovations are considered to provide (Pansera, 2018). There is a need to understand the

Figure 2.
Source: https://www.google.com/search?q=framework+frugal+innovation&tbm=isch&bih=560&biw=1366&hl=en&sa=X&
ved=2ahUKEwim7YDvnrT6AhVxyKACHYl2DmUQrNwCKAB6BQgBEO8B#imgrc=T-oRib7HSyKqhM

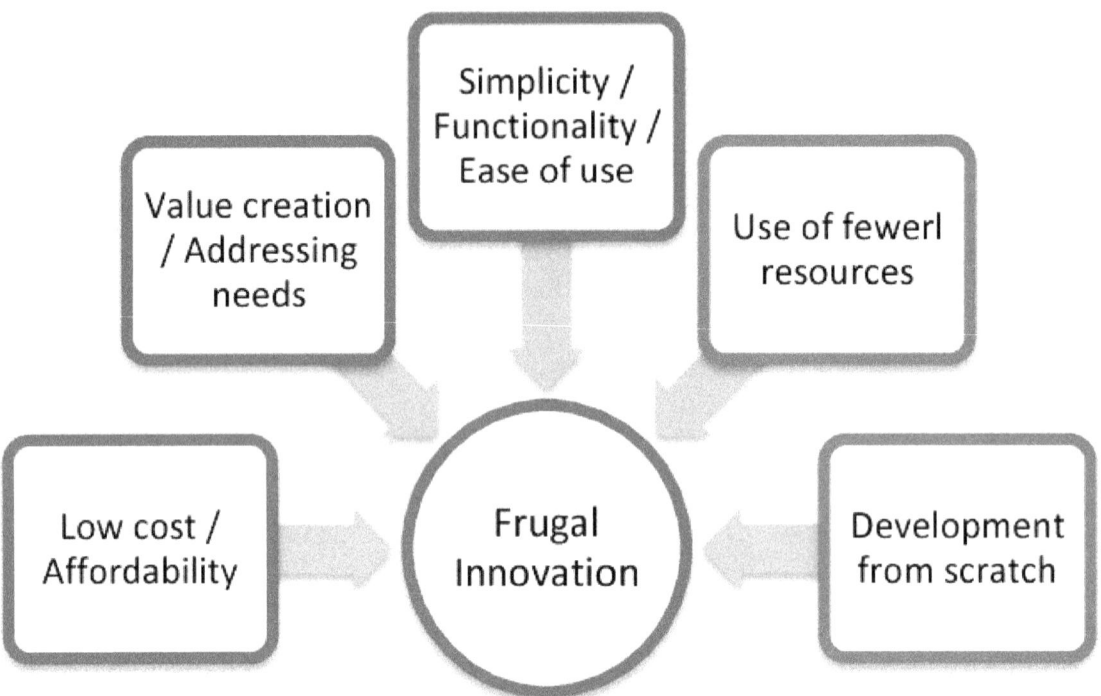

contested nature of frugal innovation and to consider this from multi-dimensional perspective that serve on both level of operational and societal level (Leliveld & Knorringa, 2018; Anser et al., 2021).

Furthermore, it is important for the organizations to consider the environmental and societal value in their business model to produce for consumer because of the economic value (Stubbs & Cocklin, 2008). This notion reflects the part of the business development which is shared value creation to offer the solution to the diverse societal concerns (Porter & Kramer, 2011). The conceptualization of business model with sustainable practices can trigger and initiate the better understanding of the societal pressure which can be integrated into the organizational processes and operations (Ludeke-Freund & Dembek, 2017). Moreover, in this era of digitalization frugal innovation can be a difficult task or series of tasks compare to developing a new product as it requires the suitable business model (Michaelis et al., 2020). Now a days the organizations face the biggest problems in terms of societal pressures.

BACKGROUND

The study of frugal innovation is still in its early stages Innovators in the twenty-first century are able to use available resources creatively by utilizing the collective intelligence of the grassroots community and creating solutions for those who have been under-resourced in light of advancements in digital

Figure 3.
Source: https://www.researchgate.net/figure/Frugal-innovation framework_fig1_356565507

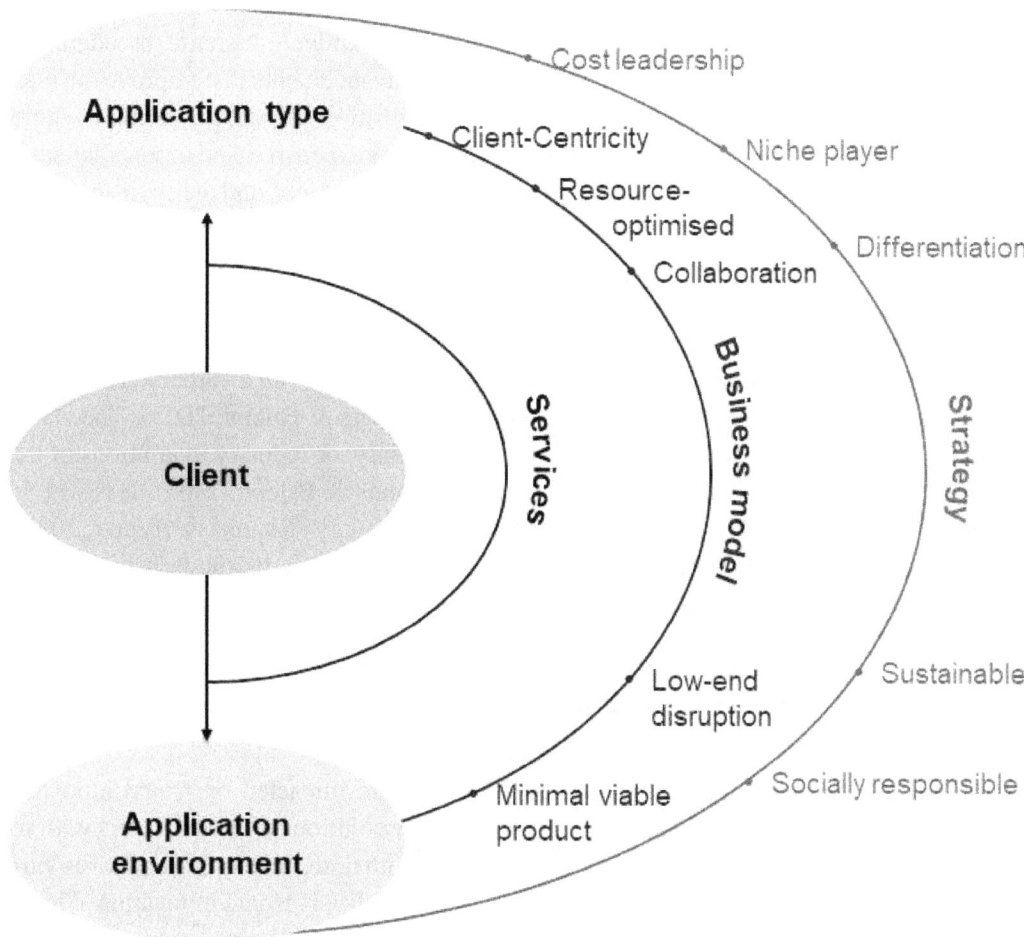

technologies, changing economic and societal conditions, and a lack of resources (Lan & Liu, 2017; Zeschky et al., 2014). However, there is disagreement over what constitutes frugal innovation in the scholarly literature (Lan & Liu, 2017). One comprehensive definition by Wierenga (2015, p. 9), "frugal innovation includes product features, process and benefits of the output...a novelty product, thus is new to the market in terms of application, material used or business model...requires minimal resources, and the materials used are recycled or easily replaceable. The features of the product have a value-adding function, instead of a price-increasing or appearance purpose. Most importantly, the product has to have an affordable pricing, either low enough for a single payment or through credit schemes offer the possibility to pay in several instalments. The overall performance in relation to the price has to be in balance and indicate of high quality for the end user. Besides considering the environment and the economic background of the consumer, the product has to be inclusive, increase the quality of life of the customer and have obvious social benefits."

Moreover, precisely, the definition of frugal can be summed up in the three aspects of frugal innovation can be identified: business innovation, technology innovation, and social innovation (Hossain, 2020). Business innovation is the reconfiguration of a business model's foundational elements, such as its operations, profit formulations, product offerings, and resources, in order to increase, broaden, or create new sources of income (Winterhalter et al., 2017). Technology advancements that improve the manufacturing of goods and services are referred to as technological innovation. Digital platforms and emerging technologies provide alternatives to current ones that are easier, less expensive, and more practical. These digital technologies are frequently used to address issues in business, society, and the environment. Social innovation is the development of new approaches to social issues that are more successful, efficient, and long-lasting than existing ones, and whose benefits largely benefit society as a whole instead of just specific people (Leong et al., 2016). Social innovation improves company relationships and capacities by making better use of resources and assets (Tiwari, 2016). Social innovation is necessary for social progress, inclusive growth, and prosperity at the bottom to be enabled in an affordable and sustainable way (Porter & Kramer, 2019) while focusing the problems (Khanna & Palepu, 2005). The absence of regulatory contract regulatory oversight, transactional intermediary, or industry institutions of the type found in the West is referred to as an "institutional void" (Khanna & Palepu, 2005). It is well known that institutional gaps make it difficult to implement company strategy (Khanna & Palepu, 2005). Due to rising customer demands for investment opportunities, social innovation, particularly in environments where institutional shortages are seen, has attracted mainstream attention (Heeks & Arun, 2010).

MAIN FOCUS OF THE CHAPTER

Almost all industries and economic sectors around the world are impacted by frugal innovation. In today's world, global demand exists for cutting-edge technology solutions. For consumers with modest incomes, frugal goods and services are "low-cost alternatives." With time, developing countries introduce new technologies. A cost-effective option that promotes sustainability is frugal innovation. The goal of frugal innovation is to rebuild and restructure goods and services to raise living standards in emerging markets. How frugal innovation, social transition and business sustainability is related: Insights on the contemporary transition towards sustainability in digital era. The main problem with frugal innovation is that academics and researchers pay little attention to new approaches and strategies for bringing creativity in contexts of restricted resources. Frugal innovation affects financial sustainability since it offers low-income consumers a higher degree of value and presents a chance to boost a company's sales and profits (Clausen & Fichter, 2019). Frugal innovation helps to advance societal, economic, and environmental goals (Albert, 2019).

SOLUTIONS AND RECOMMENDATIONS

It emphasizes on restructuring goods and services to attain outstanding results while retaining essential features, frequently going above and beyond expectations and even producing ground-breaking advancements improvements (Clausen & Fichter, 2019). People in developing countries lack the money to pay for cutting-edge technology solutions. As a result, businesses are beginning to focus on the idea of "doing more with less." Governments all across the world are relaxing their regulations and promoting thrifty

Figure 4.
Source: https://www.google.com/imgres?imgurl=https%3A%2F%2Fwww.mdpi.com%2Fsustainability%2Fsustainability-14-01326%2Farticle_deploy%2Fhtml%2Fimages%2Fsustainability-14-01326-g001.png&imgrefurl=https%3A%2F%2Fwww.mdpi.com%2F2071-1050%2F14%2F3%2F1326%2Fhtm&tbnid=D3vgJhc7YfeYkM&vet=12ahUKEwim7YDvnrT6AhVxyKACHYl2DmUQMygkegUIARCJAg..i&docid=iyCDYtfDzhUQlM&w=3172&h=1320&q=different%20dimensions%20of%20frugal%20innovation&ved=2ahUKEwim7YDvnrT6AhVxyKACHYl2DmUQMygkegUIARCJAg

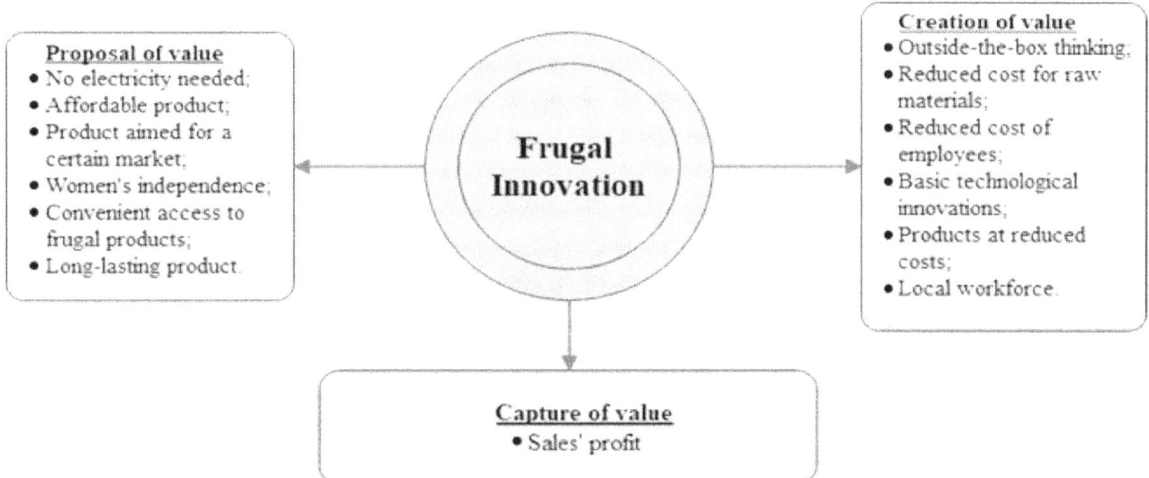

innovation to raise the standard of living for the general populace. Solutions with a low cost are provided by frugal innovation. In order to encourage frugal innovation, it is necessary to use more sophisticated methods that are inexpensively. In order to meet customers' needs at a reasonable cost, businesses concentrate on what they want to provide them. Organizations have made the use of complex technologies a priority (Bhatti et al. 2018). The chapter basically examines the importance of frugal innovation in social sustainability and technological improvements that are linked to the concept of resource scarcity with high-quality solutions that are less expensive than the competition (Albert, 2019; Bhatti et al. 2018).

FUTURE RESEARCH DIRECTIONS

This book chapter explains how social sustainability and cost-effective innovation are enhancing the lives of individuals. This study can help scientists, researchers, academics, students, and policymakers embrace and implement cutting-edge frugal innovation strategies to raise social standards in developing countries. It is advised that future studies use an applicable research methodology to examine the relationship between social sustainability and frugal innovation. Both quantitative and qualitative methods can be used in scientific investigations. By developing a clear vision of frugal innovation, researchers and scientists should take the environmental protection component into consideration. Companies should innovate their present products and services more economically to replace their current offerings, which will ultimately increase product value, lower product costs, and have a positive influence on the environment. This chapter suggests that services and goods built on the concept of frugal innovation should cost less than equivalent products that don't. To become self-sufficient, organizations should use renewable power sources, such as switching to solar or hydropower for their electric needs. Furthermore, it is important for the organizations to consider the environmental and societal value in their business model to produce for consumer because of the economic value.

REFERENCES

Al-Ghazali, B. M., Gelaidan, H. M., Shah, S. H. A., & Amjad, R. (2022). Green transformational leadership and green creativity? The mediating role of green thinking and green organizational identity in SMEs. *Frontiers in Psychology*, *13*, 977998. doi:10.3389/fpsyg.2022.977998 PMID:36211888

Albert, M. (2019). Sustainable frugal innovation-The connection between frugal innovation and sustainability. *Journal of Cleaner Production*, *237*, 117747. doi:10.1016/j.jclepro.2019.117747

Anser, M. K., Shabbir, M. S., Tabash, M. I., Shah, S. H. A., Ahmad, M., Peng, M. Y. P., & Lopez, L. B. (2021). Do renewable energy sources improve clean environmental-economic growth? Empirical investigation from South Asian economies. *Energy Exploration & Exploitation*, *39*(5), 1491–1514. doi:10.1177/01445987211002278

Bhatti, M. A., Mat, N., & Juhari, A. S. (2018). Effects of job resources factors on nurses job performance (mediating role of work engagement). *International Journal of Health Care Quality Assurance*, *1*(8), 254–274. doi:10.1108/IJHCQA-07-2017-0129 PMID:30415625

Clausen, J., & Fichter, K. (2019). The diffusion of environmental product and service innovations: Driving and inhibiting factors. *Environmental Innovation and Societal Transitions*, *31*, 64–95. doi:10.1016/j.eist.2019.01.003

D'Angelo, V., & Magnusson, M. (2020). A bibliometric map of intellectual communities in frugal innovation literature. *IEEE Transactions on Engineering Management*, *68*(3), 653–666. doi:10.1109/TEM.2020.2994043

Gordon, L., & Hodgson, A. (2017). Doing business at the bottom of the pyramid is not all about low-income countries. *Euromonitor International*. http:// bit. ly/2H6UO Hx

Heeks, R., & Arun, S. (2010). Social outsourcing as a development tool: The impact of outsourcing IT services to women's social enterprises in Kerala. Journal of International Development. *The Journal of the Development Studies Association*, *22*(4), 441–454.

Hossain, M. (2018). Frugal innovation: A review and research agenda. *Journal of Cleaner Production*, *182*, 926–936. doi:10.1016/j.jclepro.2018.02.091

Hossain, M. (2020). Frugal innovation: Conception, development, diffusion, and outcome. *Journal of Cleaner Production*, *262*, 121456. doi:10.1016/j.jclepro.2020.121456

Hossain, M., Lev̈anen, J., & Wierenga, M. (2021). Pursuing frugal innovation for sustainability at the grassroots level. *Management and Organization Review*, *17*(2), 374–381. doi:10.1017/mor.2020.53

International Monetary Fund (IMF). (2022). *IMF Annual Report. A year like no other.* https:// www. imf. org/ exter nal/ pubs/ ft/ ar/ 2022/ eng

Khanna, T., & Palepu, K. G. (2005). *Spotting Institutional Voids in Emerging Markets*. Retrieved from https://www.hbs.edu/faculty/Pages/item.aspx?num=32645

Lan, F., & Liu, X. (2017). Business model transformation in digital enablement context through frugal innovation: Learning from Chinese experience. *Int. J. Technology, Policy and Management, 17*(4), 15. doi:10.1504/IJTPM.2017.087272

Leliveld, A., & Knorringa, P. (2018). Introduction: Frugal innovation and development research. *European Journal of Development Research, 30*(1), 1–16. doi:10.105741287-017-0121-4

Leong, C., Pan, S. L., Newell, S., & Cui, L. (2016). The Emergence of Self-Organizing E- commerce Ecosystems in Remote Villages of China: A Tale of Digital Empowerment for Rural Development. *Management Information Systems Quarterly, 40*(2), 475–484. doi:10.25300/MISQ/2016/40.2.11

Levänen, J., Hossain, M., & Wierenga, M. (2022). Frugal innovation in the midst of societal and operational pressures. *Journal of Cleaner Production, 347*, 131308. doi:10.1016/j.jclepro.2022.131308

Lüdeke-Freund, F., & Dembek, K. (2017). Sustainable business model research and practice: Emerging field or passing fancy? *Journal of Cleaner Production, 168*, 1668–1678. doi:10.1016/j.jclepro.2017.08.093

Michaelis, T. L., Carr, J. C., Scheaf, D. C., & Pollack, J. M. (2020). The frugal entrepreneur: A self regulatory perspective of resourceful entrepreneurial behavior. *Journal of Business Venturing, 35*(4), 105969. doi:10.1016/j.jbusvent.2019.105969

Pansera, M. (2018). Frugal or fair? The unfulfilled promises of frugal innovation. *Technology Innovation Management Review, 8*(4), 6–13. doi:10.22215/timreview/1148

Pansera, M., & Sarkar, S. (2016). Crafting sustainable development solutions: Frugal innovations of grassroots entrepreneurs. *Sustainability, 8*(1), 51. doi:10.3390u8010051

Porter, M. R., & Kramer, M. R. (2011). Creating shared value. *Harvard Business Review, 89*(1–2), 1–17.

Shah, S. H. A., Cheema, S., Al-Ghazali, B. M., Ali, M., & Rafiq, N. (2021). Perceived corporate social responsibility and pro-environmental behaviors: The role of organizational identification and coworker pro-environmental advocacy. *Corporate Social Responsibility and Environmental Management, 28*(1), 366–377. doi:10.1002/csr.2054

Stubbs, W., & Cocklin, C. (2008). Conceptualizing a "sustainable business model". *Organization & Environment, 21*(2), 103–127. doi:10.1177/1086026608318042

Tiwari, R. (2016). Frugal Innovation in Scholarly and Social Discourse. *An Assessment of Trends and Potential Societal Implications., 28*, 1–25.

Van Mossel, A., van Rijnsoever, F. J., & Hekkert, M. P. (2018). Navigators through the storm: A review of organization theories and the behavior of incumbent firms during transitions. *Environmental Innovation and Societal Transitions, 26*, 44–63. doi:10.1016/j.eist.2017.07.001

Weyrauch, T., & Herstatt, C. (2017). What is frugal innovation? Three defining criteria. *J Frugal Innov, 2*(1), 1–17. doi:10.118640669-016-0005-y

Wierenga, M. (2015). *Local frugal innovations: How do resource-scarce innovations emerge in India?* Retrieved from https://aaltodoc.aalto.fi:443/handle/123456789/18429

Winkler, T., Ulz, A., Knöbl, W., & Lercher, H. (2020). Frugal innovation in developed markets—Adaption of a criteria-based evaluation model. *J Innov Knowl*, *5*(4), 251–259. doi:10.1016/j.jik.2019.11.004

Winterhalter, S., Zeschky, M. B., Neumann, L., & Gassmann, O. (2017). Business Models for Frugal Innovation in Emerging Markets: The Case of the Medical Device and Laboratory Equipment Industry. *Technovation*, *66–67*, 3–13. doi:10.1016/j.technovation.2017.07.002

Zeschky, M. B., Winterhalter, S., & Gassmann, O. (2014). From Cost to Frugal and Reverse Innovation: Mapping the Field and Implications for Global Competitiveness. *Research Technology Management*, *57*(4), 20–27. doi:10.5437/08956308X5704235

Chapter 17
Social Innovation:
Concept and Implications in the Developing World

Muhammad Faisal Sultan
Khadim Ali Shah Bukhari Institute of Technology, Pakistan

Muhammad Nawaz Tunio
ⓘD https://orcid.org/0000-0003-1376-5371
Muhammad Ali Jinnah University, Karachi, Pakistan

Harris Masood
Binazir Bhutto Shahid University, Pakistan

Mehwish Jabeen
K-Electric, Pakistan

ABSTRACT

The chapter is written purposively in order to highlight the development of social innovation as the idea of discipline and work process. The chapter highlights not only the academic evolution of social innovation but also highlights the role of universities in the development of social innovation in developing sides of the world. Therefore, the chapter is much different from the other chapters that are written to highlight the birth, introduction, and growth of social innovation and the social innovation process. In fact, the purpose of this chapter is not only to emphasize the introduction of social innovation as the term and idea, but the chapter also defined factors that assist in the growth of social innovation in the developing world.

INTRODUCTION

Social innovation is the process, method, technique, etc. that is developed or implemented to attain social objectives. The concept came into the limelight in early 2000 when governments, businesses, and civic

DOI: 10.4018/978-1-6684-5417-6.ch017

and philanthropic organizations started to use the concept for the betterment of social life by reducing social problems. The method has been developed by combining different unrelated techniques, actors, and ideas that are not related to serving humanity and resolving social problems. In fact, government, non-government, business, and academic communities treat social innovation as way to help, develop and improve the social economy through the co-production of outcomes (Milley et al., 2018). By definition, there is not a necessity to include words like intention or outcome in the definition of social innovation and it has vividly defined as any form of new ideas to attain unmet requirements (Arocena & Sutz, 2021). Thus, there are several public & private that are getting aware of their social responsibility and working for the solution of social problems. In fact, there is a significant increase in the number of firms that are purposively trying to solve social problems that were not been solved through traditional methods previously. Although, uncertainty is significantly high in the case of social innovation as social innovations tend to satisfy a larger set of stakeholders coupled with the fact that the science of sustainability is still evolving and needs to be fully accepted by scientific, political, and management communities. (Lettice & Parekh, 2010). Ayob et al (2016) mentioned Gallie (1955) to reflect five main components of the concept these are as under:

1. **Appraisive:** Through social innovation one aims to gain valued achievement.
2. **Internally Complex:** Regardless to the worth of the social innovation to society the internal element for the innovation are complex as these are described in a complex and different manner by different authors.
3. **Heterogeneous Explanation:** The entire concept can also be described differently by different actors.
4. **Open for Modification:** The concept is open for modification with the passage of time.
5. **Contested:** Each actor tends to define the concept in his own way by asserting their own authority and this may result in competition among the arguments.

One of the latest studies by Fougère and Meriläinen (2021) classified social innovation into two major categories i.e., Social innovation for vulnerable communities and Social innovation for societies.

Social Innovation for Vulnerable Communities

Vulnerable communities are defined as groups of people that have common geographical boundaries and are threatened by any severe external threat. Here threat does not only includes natural disasters like flood and earthquake etc. but here term threat also includes any threat like exposing young students to any risk like unemployment or addiction to cell phone applications etc.

Social Innovation for Society

This is termed as the most structural form of social innovation and through this social innovation is directed towards any specific community but towards the entire society as a whole. This may be related to the alteration of healthcare mechanisms for providing better healthcare services to the entire society. This type of social innovation may be observed more commonly in those areas or countries that are affected by natural disasters or suffering from severe economic or financial issues.

RELATIONSHIP BETWEEN SCHOLARLY RESEARCH AND SOCIAL INNOVATION

Ayob et al (2016) do not believe that the concept of social innovation is not a contested concept neither it has been used or researched widely. In fact, studies indicated that social innovation gained popularity in the twenty-first century. This lacking can be understood more comprehensively by examining numeric figures i.e., only academic articles based on social innovation were only 2,190 out of 44,100 till 1989 and the tally only reaches 4,150 in 1999.

SOCIAL INNOVATION, SCARCITY OF SOUTH & ROLE OF UNIVERSITIES

The side of the world that is largely industrialized is termed as North and the side that is weak in industrialization and development is termed as south. The southern countries are weak not only due to their technological constraints but also due to the subordination of central countries. Hence "Specificity of peripheral conditions" must be used to focus on social innovation, especially in the context of southern countries.

Although innovation in the South will never become up to the mark until or unless it is socially committed innovation in order to solve collective problems. Universities in the Southern part of the world are perceived as the major factor that may bring social innovation, especially during scarcity conditions. However, universities are required to foster relationships with other actors, tracing niches, protecting niches, transforming their conversations into interactive learning spaces & promoting connections between learning spaces to attain strong variants of innovation interstitially (Arocena & Sutz, 2021).

METHODS OF SOCIAL INNOVATION WITH REFERENCE TO THE DEVELOPING SIDES OF THE WORLD

et al (2020) indicated several methods which may result in the growth of social enterprises and also provided them with a way to understand and enhance business activities in developing sides of the world.

a) **Environment:** One of the most potent predictors of innovation in social enterprises. Therefore, in order to attain growth in business and social innovation. Studies indicated that doing conventional banking in northern areas was so difficult due to the lesser level of acceptance. Although with the launch of Islamic banking services people get inclined towards banking & that does not only increases the business of the firm but also increases the gross provincial product and provides a better shape to the economy. Moreover, a social enterprise must also consider factors like income, household structures as well as the overall population of the location in order to provide innovative as well as customized solutions to society. Hence, it is legitimate to conclude that culture and environment are potent predictors of opportunities associated with social innovation that may flourish the business activities of the firm and also provide significant support to the economic conditions of the society.

b) **Community** Members and Stake Holders: The study reflected that in order to gain acceptance and attain growth in society there is a need for acceptance from society. Similar is related to social enterprises as their mission, vision, as well as work practices, must be aligned with the values and norms of the community. Therefore social enterprises use committee that has a fair representation of community members to evaluate the acceptance and significance of any of the social task or activity that is planned. However, there is some decisions that cannot be disclosed or require a high level of secrecy hence social enterprises are required to deal with these matters directly. However, the study also indicated some of the major methods by virtue of which social enterprises may address the concerns of stakeholders. These methods include newsletters, sponsorship, case studies, after-sales report, meetings, discussions, and entrepreneurial awards, etc. A combination of these activities is used to collect data and to take entrepreneurial actions in order to meet the needs of different geographical locations on customized bases Although, these efforts cannot make project altered with respect to any one specific community and therefore there are some elements that must remain confidential and must have some privacy.

c) **Partnerships:** Partnerships with other social enterprises as well as stakeholders like the government may also provide an effective way to increase business as well as social activities through fostering social innovation. Working together with these partners also resulted in an increase in value for all forms of stakeholders. Although the objectives of different forms of partners may also differ from each other and therefore there are also some chances of conflict and hence some of the social enterprises may not agree with the partnership as well as its significance. On the other hand, it is also recommended that social enterprises must only select those partners that may have the same objectives and goals as differences in goals and objectives may result in the failure of the projects.

d) **Beneficiaries' Feedback:** Beneficiaries' Feedback is also a famous method for innovation within social enterprises as well as in products, services, and policies of social enterprises. These adaptations as well as enhancements are actually made by the users after the consumption of services or products etc.

Hence the beneficiaries are in a much better position to indicate gaps and areas for betterment in the services provided by social enterprises hence it is also a better way to enhance social innovation and the social innovation process.

e) **Knowledge of Employees:** Social enterprises have the leverage of employees from different backgrounds, cultures, and work areas. Therefore, the use of employee knowledge is also included in the set of activities that are used by social enterprises for the enhancement of operations as well as for the enhancement of social innovation practices for the community. The combination of experienced, as well as new employees, provides the firm experience of dealing as well as ways to foster innovation in a new and emphatic manner. Hence, companies must also try to invest in the capacity development of their employees in order to foster innovation through new as well as existing employees.

f) **Regional Differences:** For the success of social enterprise the knowledge of regional differences is also termed one of the most important factors. In fact, for the enhancement of social innovation, a regionally expanded firm must try to focus on opportunities that may rise from the integration of the firm but must also avoid threats that may rise from cultural differences. In recent times social enterprises are required to expand not only in different regions within the country but also to outside the country. Therefore, enterprises must take advantage of innovative people from diverse locations in order to float ideas properly from one location to the other. In fact, similar is the need of globalization and hence social enterprises must connect with each other in order to serve humanity and enhance social innovation across the globe.

g) **Social Media:** Social media has massive importance for social enterprises as well as for social innovation. Through capitalizing on social media firms may be able to persuade their users and beneficiaries and may also launch innovative campaigns and conduct interactive sessions. One may also question about the presence of technology and the use of social media by the users and beneficiaries of social enterprises in developing sides of the world.

However, the study reflected that social media is one of the most preferred media by the inhabitants and media aids firms in dealing with challenges more effectively. Social media also prove to be an effective marketing tool by virtue of which social enterprises may create awareness, reduce cost and create better knowledge and impact of their work and process of social innovation.

h) **Youth:** Use of youth in social innovation projects may also assist the company in its development and may also optimize its operations. The statement is effective as youth have updated knowledge related to relevant issues of the community and regions and therefore involving youth may become helpful in transforming ideas into reality. Social enterprises may use open forums, discussions, meetings, workshops, etc. in order to get youth involved in social innovation projects hence youth may take an active part in social innovation projects by attaining required empowerment.

i) **Technology:** The inclusion of technology in the work process is not only beneficial for research and operational effectiveness. Through the inclusion of technology, social enterprises may be able to reduce the use of energy and induce digitization in every aspect of the work. Moreover, through the inclusion of technology in the work process social enterprises become able to optimize the process of learning and also extend their reach to local and international markets.

THREE-CYCLE MODEL FOR SOCIAL INNOVATION

Social innovation is a multi-level and argentic process that is used to provide a novel solution to those problems that are hampering the growth and development of society. Although the term has been discussed over-extensively which makes people believe that term is over-determined? Therefore, it is better to relate it with three cycle model as social innovation does not only based upon the will of the actor but also upon the internal condition of the institution that is initiating the innovation. Other than these two elements prevailing conditions are also a potent predictor of social innovation. Hence it is better to use the three-cycle model for a better understanding of the concept of social innovation. (Van Wijk et al., 2019; Alshareef, et al., 2022; Tunio, et al., 20201).

The model uses three cycles i.e. micro, meso, and macro-cycles that are interconnected firmly. The initial cycle is termed as micro0-cycle embedded individual actors. These actors are proposed to become more agentic when they interact with others. In fact, interactions with others will boost their emotions and increase their ability to hear and understand the viewpoints of others. On the other hand, this will also diminish their taken-for-granted perspective and creates room for new innovation by disembedding these actors from their primary institutions.

The second environment is termed a meso environment and has the purpose to increase interactions among diverse members in order to increase cohesiveness. Meso environment also elaborated on how interactions and framing among diverse actors create resistance and hindrance to social innovation. However, the environment is also effective to understand and renegotiate the structures beliefs, methods, and structures that are major components of the social world.

The third cycle is used to elaborate the impact of institutional practices that are different from other institutions to influence the actions of various actors at micro and meso levels. Hence macro environment has special importance in reflecting institutional context upon the energy levels that are initiated from micro and meso levels.

CONCLUSION

The chapter provides a detailed overview of the development of the concept of social innovation with respect to social and research perspectives. Moreover, also provide the base for differentiating in major forms of social innovation along with the role of universities and method to pursue social innovation in developing sides of the world. At last, chapter also uses a three-cycle model for elaborating social innovation in a more emphatic and desired manner in order to provide detailed knowledge regarding the process in a contemporary manner

REFERENCES

Arocena, R., & Sutz, J. (2021). Universities and social innovation for global sustainable development as seen from the south. *Technological Forecasting and Social Change, 162*, 120399. doi:10.1016/j.techfore.2020.120399 PMID:33071365

Ayob, N., Teasdale, S., & Fagan, K. (2016). How social innovation 'came to be': Tracing the evolution of a contested concept. *Journal of Social Policy, 45*(4), 635–653. doi:10.1017/S004727941600009X

Fougère, M., & Meriläinen, E. (2021). Exposing three dark sides of social innovation through critical perspectives on resilience. *Industry and Innovation, 28*(1), 1–1844. doi:10.1080/13662716.2019.1709420

Gallie, W. B. (1955). Essentially contested concepts. *Proceedings of the Aristotelian Society, 56*, 167-198.

Lettice, F., & Parekh, M. (2010). The social innovation process: Themes, challenges and implications for practice. *International Journal of Technology Management, 51*(1), 139–158. doi:10.1504/IJTM.2010.033133

Mahmood, M. A., Irfan, S., Jabeen, N., & Moazzam, A. (2020). Sources of Innovation in Social Enterprises Working in Pakistan. *Journal of the Research Society of Pakistan, 57*(3), 1.

Milley, P., Szijarto, B., Svensson, K., & Cousins, J. B. (2018). The evaluation of social innovation: A review and integration of the current empirical knowledge base. *Evaluation, 24*(2), 237–258. doi:10.1177/1356389018763242

Van Wijk, J., Zietsma, C., Dorado, S., De Bakker, F. G., & Marti, I. (2019). Social innovation: Integrating micro, meso, and macro level insights from institutional theory. *Business & Society, 58*(5), 887–918. doi:10.1177/0007650318789104

Compilation of References

Ab Hamid, K., Pahi, M. H., Qureshi, M. A., & Arshad, I. (2014). *The impact of leadership style on employee turnover and retention, and mediating job satisfaction and organization commitment.* Academic Press.

Abdullah, M., Katper, N. K., Chaudhry, N. I., & Tunio, M. N. (2020). An Impact of Workaholics on Creativity: the mediating role of Negative Mood and moderating role of Supervisor Support. *Sukkur IBA Journal of Management and Business, 7*(2).

Abdullah, M., Katper, N. K., Chaudhry, N. I., and Tunio, M. N. (2020). An Impact of Workaholics on Creativity: the mediating role of Negative Mood and moderating role of Supervisor Support. *Sukkur IBA Journal of Management and Business*, 7(2).

Abdullah, P., Zeebaree, S., Shukur, H., & Jacksi, K. (2020). HRM System using Cloud Computing for Small and Medium Enterprises (SMEs). *Technology Reports of Kansai University.*, *62*, 1977–1987.

Abubakar, A. M., Elrehail, H., Alatailat, M. A., & Elçi, A. (2017). Knowledge management, decision-making style and organizational performance. *Journal of Innovation & Knowledge.* doi:10.1016/j.jik.2017.07.003

Adil, M. S., Khan, M. N., Khan, I., & Qureshi, M. A. (2018). Impact of leader creativity expectations on employee creativity: Assessing the mediating and moderating role of creative self-efficacy. *International Journal of Management Practice*, *11*(2), 171–189. doi:10.1504/IJMP.2018.090832

Adla, L., Gallego-Roquelaure, V., & Calamel, L. (2020). Human resource management and innovation in SMEs. *Personnel Review*, *49*(8), 15191535. doi:10.1108/PR-09-2018-0328

Afshan, G., Ilyas, S., Tunio, M. N., & Kalhoro, M. (2021). CSR actions and post-COVID'19 consequences in hotel industry: A conceptual framework. *International Journal of Strategic Change Management*, *7*(4), 1. doi:10.1504/IJSCM.2021.122845

Agarwal, N., & Brem, A. (2017). Frugal innovation-past, present, and future. *IEEE Engineering Management Review*, *45*(3), 37–41. doi:10.1109/EMR.2017.2734320

Agrawal, S., Jamwal, A., & Gupta, S. (2020). Effect of COVID-19 on the Indian economy and supply chain. doi:10.20944/preprints202005.0148.v1

Agrawal, S., & Sharma, N. (2022, January). Barriers and Role of Higher Educational Institutes in Students' Mental Wellbeing: A Critical Analysis. In *2nd International Conference on Sustainability and Equity (ICSE-2021)* (pp. 173-180). Atlantis Press. 10.2991/ahsseh.k.220105.021

Agrawal, S., Sharma, N., & Bhatnagar, S. (2021). Education 4.0 to Industry 4.0 Vision: Current Trends and Overview. In *Recent Advances in Smart Manufacturing and Materials* (pp. 475–485). Springer. doi:10.1007/978-981-16-3033-0_45

AgrawalS.SharmaN.SinghM. (2020). *Employing CBPR to understand the well-being of higher education students during COVID-19 lockdown in India.* doi:10.2139/ssrn.3628458

Ahlstrom, D. (2010). Innovation and Growth: How Business Contributes to Society. *The Academy of Management Perspectives, 24,* 11–24.

Ahuja, S., & Chan, Y. 2014b. The Enabling Role of IT in Frugal Innovation. https://aisel. aisnet.org/cgi/viewcontent.cg i?article1/41374&context1/4icis2014

Albert, M. (2019). Sustainable frugal innovation-The connection between frugal innovation and sustainability. *Journal of Cleaner Production, 237,* 117747. doi:10.1016/j.jclepro.2019.117747

Alegre, I., & Berbegal-Mirabent, J. (2016). Social innovation success factors: Hospitality and tourism social enterprises. *International Journal of Contemporary Hospitality Management, 28*(6), 1155–1176. doi:10.1108/IJCHM-05-2014-0231

Al-Ghazali, B. M., Gelaidan, H. M., Shah, S. H. A., & Amjad, R. (2022). Green transformational leadership and green creativity? The mediating role of green thinking and green organizational identity in SMEs. *Frontiers in Psychology, 13,* 977998. doi:10.3389/fpsyg.2022.977998 PMID:36211888

Ali, A. A., & Akhtar, M. J. (2012). Empowerment and political mobilization of women in Pakistan: A descriptive discourse of perspectives. *Pakistan Journal of Social Sciences, 32*(1), 221–228.

Alkhodary, D. (2021). The Impact of E-HRM on Corporates Sustainability: A Study on the SMEs in Jordan. *International Journal of Entrepreneurship, 25*(6), 1–15.

Alkier, R., Milojica, V., & Roblek, V. (2015). A holistic framework for the development of a sustainable touristic model. *International Journal of Markets and Business Systems, 1*(4), 366387. doi:10.1504/IJMABS.2015.074213

Alkier, R., Milojica, V., & Roblek, V. (2017). Challenges of the social innovation in tourism. *Tourism in South East Europe., 4,* 1–13. doi:10.20867/tosee.04.24

Alshareef, N., & Tunio, M. N. (2022). Role of Leadership in Adoption of Blockchain Technology in Small and Medium Enterprises in Saudi Arabia. *Frontiers in Psychology, 13,* 2284. doi:10.3389/fpsyg.2022.911432 PMID:35602740

Amankwah-Amoah, J. (2020). Stepping up and stepping out of COVID-19: New challenges for environmental sustainability policies in the global airline industry. *Journal of Cleaner Production, 271,* 123000. doi:10.1016/j.jclepro.2020.123000 PMID:32834564

Amaratunga, D., Fernando, N., Haigh, R., & Jayasinghe, N. (2020, December 8). The COVID-19 outbreak in Sri Lanka: A synoptic analysis focusing on trends, impacts, risks and science-policy interaction processes. *Progress in Disaster Science.* doi:10.1016/j.pdisas.2020.100133

Ancarani, F., Frels, J. K., Miller, J., Saibene, C., & Barberio, M. (2014). Winning in rural emerging markets: General electric's research study on MNCs. *California Management Review, 56*(4), 31–52. doi:10.1525/cmr.2014.56.4.31

Angot, J., & Plé, L. (2015). Serving poor people in rich countries: The bottom-of-the-pyramid business model solution. *The Journal of Business Strategy, 36*(2), 3–15. doi:10.1108/JBS-11-2013-0111

Anser, M. K., Shabbir, M. S., Tabash, M. I., Shah, S. H. A., Ahmad, M., Peng, M. Y. P., & Lopez, L. B. (2021). Do renewable energy sources improve clean environmental-economic growth? Empirical investigation from South Asian economies. *Energy Exploration & Exploitation, 39*(5), 1491–1514. doi:10.1177/01445987211002278

Ardani, E. G., & Harianto, A. (2021). Surviving strategy of hospitality sector in pandemic situation: Case hospitality business in Jakarta. *E-Journal of Tourism., 8*(1), 77–86. doi:10.24922/eot.v8i1.71449

Armbruster, H., Bikfalvi, A., Kinkel, S., & Lay, G. (2008). Organizational innovation: The challenge of measuring non-technical innovation in large-scale surveys. *Technovation*, *28*(10), 644–657. doi:10.1016/j.technovation.2008.03.003

Arocena, R., & Sutz, J. (2021). Universities and social innovation for global sustainable development as seen from the south. *Technological Forecasting and Social Change*, *162*, 120399. doi:10.1016/j.techfore.2020.120399 PMID:33071365

Aromataris, E., & Pearson, A. (2014). The systematic review: An overview. *AJN The American Journal of Nursing*, *114*(3), 53–58. doi:10.1097/01.NAJ.0000444496.24228.2c PMID:24572533

Aurangzeb, M. T., Tunio, M. N., Rehman, Z., & Asif, M. (2021). Influence of administrative expertise on human resources practitioners on the job performance: Mediating role of achievement motivation. [IJM]. *International Journal of Management*, *12*(4), 408–421.

Awan, M. A. (2016). *Political Participation of Women in Pakistan: Historical and Political Dynamics Shaping the Structure of Politics for Women*. Frankfurt Research Center on Global Islam. https://www.ffgi.net/files/dossier/polpart-pakistan-awan.pdf

Ayob, N., Teasdale, S., & Fagan, K. (2016). How social innovation 'came to be': Tracing the evolution of a contested concept. *Journal of Social Policy*, *45*(4), 635–653. doi:10.1017/S004727941600009X

Ayoko, O. (2021). SMEs, innovation and human resource management. *Journal of Management & Organization*. *27*(1), 1-5. doi:10.1017/jmo.2021.8

Bacq, S., & Lumpkin, G. T. (2021). Social entrepreneurship and COVID-19. *Journal of Management Studies*, *58*(1), 285–288. doi:10.1111/joms.12641

Baker, T., & Nelson, R. E. (2005). Creating something from nothing: Resource construction through entrepreneurial bricolage. *Administrative Science Quarterly*, *50*(3), 329–366. doi:10.2189/asqu.2005.50.3.329

Bamber, G., Bartram, T., & Stanton, P. (2017). HRM and workplace innovations: Formulating research questions. *Personnel Review*, *46*(7), 1216–1227. doi:10.1108/PR-10-2017-0292

BandaranayakeS. (2021). The Impact of COVID-19 on Sri Lanka economy. doi:10.2139/ssrn.3911792

Barbera, E., Gros, B., & Kirschner, P. (2015). Paradox of time in research on educational technology. *Time & Society*, *24*(1), pp. 96-108.http://tas.sagepub.com/ content/24/1/ 96.refs.

Barclay, A. E. (2013). Influence, Inspiration or Innovation? The importance of contexts in the Study of Iconography: the Case of the Mistress of Animals in 7th-Century Greece. *Regionalism and Globalism in Antiquity: Exploring Their Limits*, 143-176.

Barosso, M. (n.d.). *Employment, Social Affairs & Inclusion*. Available online: https://ec.europa.eu/social/main.jsp?langId=en&catId=89&newsId=445&furtherNews=yes

Barzilay, R., Moore, T. M., Greenberg, D. M., DiDomenico, G. E., Brown, L. A., White, L. K., Gur, R. C., & Gur, R. E. (2020). Resilience, COVID-19-related stress, anxiety and depression during the pandemic in a large population enriched for healthcare providers. *Translational Psychiatry*, *10*(1), 1–8. doi:10.103841398-020-00982-4 PMID:32820171

Baskaran, S., & Mehta, K. (2016). What is innovation anyway? Youth perspectives from resource-constrained environments. *Technovation*, *52*, 4–17. doi:10.1016/j.technovation.2016.01.005

Basu, R. R., Banerjee, P. M., & Sweeny, E. G. (2013). Frugal innovation. *Journal of Management for Global Sustainability*, *1*(2).

Baticulon, R. E., Sy, J. J., Alberto, N. R. I., Baron, M. B. C., Mabulay, R. E. C., Rizada, L. G. T., Tiu, C. J. S., Clarion, C. A., & Reyes, J. C. B. (2021). Barriers to online learning in the time of COVID-19: A national survey of medical students in the Philippines. *Medical Science Educator, 31*(2), 615–626. doi:10.100740670-021-01231-z PMID:33649712

Batle, J., Orfila-Sintes, F., & Moon, C. J. (2018). Environmental management best practices: Towards social innovation. *International Journal of Hospitality Management, 69*, 14–20. doi:10.1016/j.ijhm.2017.10.013

Bhatti, M. A., Mat, N., & Juhari, A. S. (2018). Effects of job resources factors on nurses job performance (mediating role of work engagement). *International Journal of Health Care Quality Assurance, 31*(8), 1000–1013. doi:10.1108/IJHCQA-07-2017-0129 PMID:30415625

Bhosale, G. A., & Bagul, D. B. (2021). Concept Of E-HRM: A Review of Literature. *International Interdisciplinary Research Journal., 11*(1), 313317.

Blass, E., & Hayward, P. (2014). Innovation in higher education; will there be a role for "the academe/university" in 2025? *European Journal of Futures Research, 2*(1), 1–9.

Bocken, N. M., & Geradts, T. H. (2020). Barriers and drivers to sustainable business model innovation: Organization design and dynamic capabilities. *Long Range Planning, 53*(4), 101950. doi:10.1016/j.lrp.2019.101950

Boeve-de Pauw, J., Gericke, N., Olsson, D., & Berglund, T. (2015). The effectiveness of education for sustainable development. *Sustainability, 7*(11), 15693–15717. doi:10.3390u71115693

Bonanomi, A., Facchin, F., Barello, S., & Villani, D. (2021). Prevalence and health correlates of Onine Fatigue: A cross-sectional study on the Italian academic community during the COVID-19 pandemic. *PLoS One, 16*(10), e0255181. doi:10.1371/journal.pone.0255181 PMID:34648507

Bondarouk, T., Harms, R., & Lepak, D. (2017a). Does e-HRM lead to better HRM service? *International Journal of Human Resource Management, 28*(9), 1332–1362. doi:10.1080/09585192.2015.1118139

Boons, F., Montalvo, C., Quist, J., & Wagner, M. (2013). Sustainable innovation business models and Economic performance: An overview. *Journal of Cleaner Production, 45*, 1–8. Advance online publication. doi:10.1016/j.jclepro.2012.08.013

Bowen, G. A. (2009). Document analysis as a qualitative research method. *Qualitative Research Journal, 9*(2), 27–40. Advance online publication. doi:10.3316/QRJ0902027

Brahmi, M., Aldieri, L., Dhayal, K. S., & Agrawal, S. (2022). Education 4.0: Can It Be a Component of the Sustainable Well-Being of Students? In Sustainable Development of Human Resources in a Globalization Period (pp. 215-230). doi:10.4018/978-1-6684-4981-3.ch014

Brem, A., & Ivens, B. (2013). Do frugal and reverse innovation foster sustainability? Introduction of a conceptual framework. *Journal of Technology Management for Growing Economies, 4*(2), 31–50. doi:10.15415/jtmge.2013.42006

Brem, A., & Wolfram, P. (2014). Research and development from the bottom up - introduction of terminologies for new product development in emerging markets. *Journal of Innovation and Entrepreneurship, 3*(9), 9. doi:10.1186/2192-5372-3-9

Buch-Hansen, H. (2014). Capitalist diversity and de-growth trajectories to steady-state economies. *Ecological Economics, 106*, 167–173. doi:10.1016/j.ecolecon.2014.07.030

Buisson, M.-L., Gastaldi, L., Geffroy, B., Lonceint, R. and Krohmer, C. (2021). Innovative SMEs in search of ambidexterity: a challenge for HRM! *Employee Relations, 43*(2), 479-495. . doi:10.1108/ER-04-2020-0176

Bujang, S. D. A., Selamat, A., Krejcar, O., Maresova, P., & Nguyen, N. T. (2020, April). Digital learning demand for future education 4.0—Case studies at Malaysia education institutions. In Informatics (Vol. 7, No. 2, p. 13). MDPI.

Bulut, N. S., Yorguner, N., & Akvardar, Y. (2021). Impact of COVID-19 on the Life of Higher-Education Students in Istanbul: Relationship Between Social Support, Health-Risk Behaviors, and Mental/Academic Well-Being. *Alpha Psychiatry, 22*(6), 291-300. doi:10.5152/alphapsychiatry.2021.21319

Bureau of European Policy Advisers. (2010). *Empowering People, Driving Change. Social Innovation in the European Union.* Publications Office of the European Union.

Bustamante-Gavino, M. I., Rattani, S., & Khan, K. (2011). Women's Empowerment in Pakistan–Definitions and Enabling and Disenabling Factors: A Secondary Data Analysis. *Journal of Transcultural Nursing, 22*(2), 174–181. doi:10.1177/1043659610395762 PMID:21467269

Cameron, A., Coetzer, A., Lewis, K., Claire, M., & Candice, H. (2006). *HR Management Practices: Home-Grown, But Effective.* Chartered Accountants Journal.

Caramizaru, A., & Uihlein, A. (2020). *Energy Communities: An Overview of Energy and Social Innovation. EUR 30083 EN.* Publications Office of the European Union.

Carlisle, S., Kunc, M., Jones, E., & Tiffin, S. (2013). Supporting innovation for tourism development through multi-stakeholder approaches: Experiences from Africa. *Tourism Management, 35*, 59–69. doi:10.1016/j.tourman.2012.05.010

Carson, R. (2021, February 23). Why COVID-19 Is Driving Up The Cost Of Healthcare In Retirement And What You Can Do Now To Prepare. *Forbes.* https://www.forbes.com/sites/rcarson/2021/02/23/why-covid-19-is-driving-up-the-cost-of-healthcare-in-retirement-and-what-you-can-do-now-to-prepare/?sh=e85bd5c113bc

Chaudhry, I. S., Paquibut, R. Y. & Tunio, M. N. (2021) Do workforce diversity, inclusion practices, & organizational characteristics contribute to organizational innovation? Evidence from the U.A.E. *Cogent Business & Management, 8*(1), 1947549, . doi:10.1080/23311975.2021.1947549

Chaudhry, I. S., & Rahman, S. U. (2009). The impact of gender inequality in education on rural poverty in Pakistan: An empirical analysis. European Journal of Economics. *Finance and Administrative Sciences, 15*, 174–188.

Cheema, M. (2014). Understanding the gender dynamics of curremt affairs talk shows in the Pakistani Television Industry. In M. Raicheva-Stover & E. Ibroscheva (Eds.), *Women in politics and media: perspectives from nations in transition.* Bloomsbury.

Chu, A. M., Chan, T. W., & So, M. K. (2022). Learning from work-from-home issues during the COVID-19 pandemic: Balance speaks louder than words. *PLoS One, 17*(1), e0261969. doi:10.1371/journal.pone.0261969 PMID:35025893

Clausen, J., & Fichter, K. (2019). The diffusion of environmental product and service innovations: Driving and inhibiting factors. *Environmental Innovation and Societal Transitions, 31*, 64–95. doi:10.1016/j.eist.2019.01.003

Cornali, F. (2012). Effectiveness and efficiency of educational measures. *Evaluation Practices, Indicators and Rhetoric, 2*(3), pp. 255-260. www.SciRP.org/journal/sm

Craft, A. (2005) Creativity in Schools: tensions and dilemmas. London: Routledge. . doi:10.4324/9780203357965

Craig, S. L., Leung, V. W., Pascoe, R., Pang, N., Iacono, G., Austin, A., & Dillon, F. (2021). AFFIRM online: Utilising an affirmative cognitive–behavioural digital intervention to improve mental health, access, and engagement among LGBTQA+ youth and young adults. *International Journal of Environmental Research and Public Health, 18*(4), 1541. doi:10.3390/ijerph18041541 PMID:33562876

Creating Innovators. (2012). America's last competitive advantage. http:// creatinginnovators.com/ .

Cressey, P., Totterdill, P., Exton, R., & Terstriep, J. (2015). *Stimulating, resourcing and sustaining social innovation: Towards a new mode of public policy production and implementation.* Academic Press.

Crichton, D. (2015). Searching for the next wave of education innovation. *TechCrunch.* https://techcrunch.com/2015/06/27/education-next-wave/

Crichton, D. (2015). Searching for the next wave of education innovation. *TechCrunch.* https://techcrunch.com/2015/06/27/education-next-wave/.

Crossan, M. M., & Apaydin, M. (2010). A multi-dimensional framework of organizational innovation: A systematic review of the literature. *Journal of Management Studies, 47*(6), 1154–1191. doi:10.1111/j.1467-6486.2009.00880.x

Cunha, M.P., Rego, A., Oliveira, P., Rosado, P., Habib, N., 2014. Product innovation in resource-poor environments: three research streams. J. *Prod. Innovat. Manag. 31*(2).

D'Angelo, V., & Magnusson, M. (2020). A bibliometric map of intellectual communities in frugal innovation literature. *IEEE Transactions on Engineering Management, 68*(3), 653–666. doi:10.1109/TEM.2020.2994043

Dabić, M., Obradović, T., Vlačić, B., Sahasranamam, S., & Paul, J. (2022). Frugal innovations: A multidisciplinary review & agenda for future research. *Journal of Business Research, 142*, 914–929. doi:10.1016/j.jbusres.2022.01.032

Dacin, M. T., Dacin, P. A., & Tracey, P. (2011). Social entrepreneurship: A critique and future directions. *Organization Science, 22*(5), 1203–1213. doi:10.1287/orsc.1100.0620

Damanpour, F. (1992). Organizational size and innovation. *Organization Studies, 13*(3), 375–402. doi:10.1177/017084069201300304

de Bruin, L. (2016). Scanning the Environment: PESTEL Analysis. *Business to You.* https://www.business-to-you.com/scanning-the-environment-pestel-analysis/

Dean, T. J., & McMullen, J. S. (2007). Toward a theory of sustainable entrepreneurship: Reducing environmental degradation through entrepreneurial action. *Journal of Business Venturing, 22*(1), 50–76. doi:10.1016/j.jbusvent.2005.09.003

Defourny, J., & Nyssens, M. (2010). Conceptions of social enterprise and social entrepreneurship in Europe and the United States: Convergences and divergences. *Journal of Social Entrepreneurship, 1*(1), 32–53. doi:10.1080/19420670903442053

Denyer, D., & Tranfield, D. (2009). Producing a systematic review.

DeSimone, L. D., & Popoff, F. (2000). *Eco-Efficiency: The Business Link to Sustainable Development.* MIT Press.

Dima, A., Bugheanu, A. M., Dinulescu, R., Potcovaru, A. M., Stefanescu, C. A., & Marin, I. (2022). Exploring the Research Regarding Frugal Innovation and Business Sustainability through Bibliometric Analysis. *Sustainability, 14*(3), 1326. doi:10.3390u14031326

Dolan, C. (2012). The new face of development: The 'bottom of the pyramid' entrepreneurs. *Anthropology Today, 28*(4), 3–7. doi:10.1111/j.1467-8322.2012.00883.x

Dominic, B., & Jothi, C. A. (2012). Education-A tool of women empowerment: Historical study based on Kerala society. *International Journal of Scientific and Research Publications, 2*(4), 1–4.

Dominici, G., & Roblek, V. (2016). Complexity theory for a new managerial paradigm: a research framework. In I. Vrdoljak Raguž, N. Podrug, & L. Jelenc (Eds.), *Neostrategic Management* (pp. 223–241). Springer International Publishing., doi:10.1007/978-3-319-18185-1_14

Dost, M., Pahi, M. H., Magsi, H. B., & Umrani, W. A. (2019). Effects of sources of knowledge on frugal innovation: Moderating role of environmental turbulence. *Journal of Knowledge Management, 23*(7), 1245–1259. doi:10.1108/JKM-01-2019-0035

Dressler, A., & Bucher, J. (2018). Introducing a Sustainability Evaluation Framework based on the Sustainable Development Goals applied to Four Cases of South African Frugal Innovation. *Business Strategy & Development, 1*(4), p. 276-285. https://doi org.miman.bib.bth.se/10.1002/bsd2.37

Drummond, A. (2012). Research on emerging economies: Challenges are always opportunities. *Global Strategy Journal, 2*(1), 48–50. doi:10.1002/gsj.1026

Duby, Z., Bunce, B., Fowler, C., Bergh, K., Jonas, K., Dietrich, J. J., Govindasamy, D., Kuo, C., & Mathews, C. (2022). Intersections between COVID-19 and socio-economic mental health stressors in the lives of South African adolescent girls and young women. *Child and Adolescent Psychiatry and Mental Health, 16*(1), 1–16. doi:10.118613034-022-00457-y PMID:35346316

Dul, J., & Ceylan, C. (2011). Work environments for employee creativity. *Ergonomics, 54*(1), 12–20. doi:10.1080/00140139.2010.542833 PMID:21181585

Dunk, A. S. (2011). Product innovation, budgetary control, and the financial performance of firms. *The British Accounting Review, 43*(2), 102–111. doi:10.1016/j.bar.2011.02.004

European Commission EU Programme for Employment and Social Innovation (EaSI). (n.d.). Available online: https://ec.europa.eu/ social/main.jsp?catId=1081

European Commission. (2013). *Guide to Social Innovation.* https://ec.europa.eu/growth/industry/innovation/policy/social_en

European Commission. EaSI Call. (2021). Available online: https://ec.europa.eu/info/funding-tenders/opportunities/docs/2021 -2027/esf/wp-call/2021/call-fiche_esf-2021-ag-ncp_en.pdf

Every-Palmer, S., Jenkins, M., Gendall, P., Hoek, J., Beaglehole, B., Bell, C., Williman, J., Rapsey, C., & Stanley, J. (2020). Psychological distress, anxiety, family violence, suicidality, and wellbeing in New Zealand during the COVID-19 lockdown: A cross-sectional study. *PLoS One, 15*(11), e0241658. doi:10.1371/journal.pone.0241658 PMID:33147259

Fasko, D. Jr. (2000-01). Education and Creativity. *Creativity Research Journal, 13*(3-4), 317–327. doi:10.1207/S15326934CRJ1334_09

Foley, S., Badinlou, F., Brocki, K. C., Frick, M. A., Ronchi, L., & Hughes, C. (2021). Family function and child adjustment difficulties in the COVID-19 pandemic: An international study. *International Journal of Environmental Research and Public Health, 18*(21), 11136. doi:10.3390/ijerph182111136 PMID:34769654

Fossey, E., Harvey, C., Mcdermott, F., & Davidson, L. (2002, December 1). Understanding and Evaluating Qualitative Research. *Australian & Newzland Journal of Psychiatry, 36*(6), 717–732. doi:10.1046/j.1440-1614.2002.01100.x PMID:12406114

Fougère, M., & Meriläinen, E. (2021). Exposing three dark sides of social innovation through critical perspectives on resilience. *Industry and Innovation, 28*(1), 1–1844. doi:10.1080/13662716.2019.1709420

Fraunhofer ISI & Nesta. (2016). Cheaper, better, more relevant: Is frugal innovation an opportunity for Europe? *Fraunhofer ISI.* http://www.isi.fraunhofer.de/isiwAssets/docs/p/de/projektberichte/FrugalInnovationSummary_ISI_Nesta_mit-ISI.pdf.

Gallie, W. B. (1955). Essentially contested concepts. *Proceedings of the Aristotelian Society, 56*, 167-198.

Gede Riana, I., Suparna, G., Gusti Made Suwandana, I., Kot, S., & Rajiani, I. (2020, February 12). Human resource management in promoting innovation and organizational performance. *Problems and Perspectives in Management, 18*(1), 107–118. doi:10.21511/ppm.18(1).2020.10

George, G., McGahan, A. M., & Prabhu, J. (2012). Innovation for inclusive growth: Towards a theoretical framework and a research agenda. *Journal of Management Studies, 49*(4), 661–683. doi:10.1111/j.1467-6486.2012.01048.x

Giardino, D. L., Huck-Iriart, C., Riddick, M., & Garay, A. (2020). The endless quarantine: The impact of the COVID-19 outbreak on healthcare workers after three months of mandatory social isolation in Argentina. *Sleep Medicine, 76*, 16–25. doi:10.1016/j.sleep.2020.09.022 PMID:33059247

Gilal, F. G., Gilal, N. G., Channa, N. A., Gilal, R. A., Gilal, R. G., & Tunio, M. N. (2020). Towards an integrated model for the transference of environmental responsibility. *Business Strategy and the Environment, 29*(6), 1–10. doi:10.1002/bse.2524

Gilal, F. G., Gilal, N. G., Gilal, R. G., Gon, Z., Gilal, W. G., & Tunio, M. N. (2021). The Ties That Bind: Do Brand Attachment and Brand Passion Translate Into Consumer Purchase Intention? *Central European Management Journal, 29*(1), 14–38. doi:10.7206/cemj.2658-0845.39

Giusti, L., Mammarella, S., Salza, A., Del Vecchio, S., Ussorio, D., Casacchia, M., & Roncone, R. (2021). Predictors of academic performance during the covid-19 outbreak: Impact of distance education on mental health, social cognition and memory abilities in an Italian university student sample. *BMC Psychology, 9*(1), 1–17. doi:10.118640359-021-00649-9 PMID:34526153

González-Zamar, M. D., Ortiz Jiménez, L., Sánchez Ayala, A., & Abad-Segura, E. (2020). The impact of the university classroom on managing the socio-educational well-being: A global study. *International Journal of Environmental Research and Public Health, 17*(3), 931. doi:10.3390/ijerph17030931 PMID:32028598

Gordon, L., & Hodgson, A. (2017) Doing business at the bottom of the pyramid is not all about low-income countries. *Euromonitor International*. http:// bit. ly/2H6UO Hx

Gordon, L., & Hodgson, A. (2017). Doing business at the bottom of the pyramid is not all about low-income countries. *Euromonitor International*. http:// bit. ly/2H6UO Hx

Govindarajan, V., & Ramamurti, R. (2011). Reverse innovation, emerging markets, and global strategy. *Global Strategy Journal, 1*(3-4), 191–205. doi:10.1002/gsj.23

Govindarajo, N. S., Kumar, D., Shaikh, E., Kumar, M., & Kumar, P. (2021). Industry 4.0 and business policy development: Strategic imperatives for SME performance. *Etikonomi, 20*(2), 239–258. doi:10.15408/etk.v20i2.20143

Graupensperger, S., Benson, A. J., Kilmer, J. R., & Evans, M. B. (2020). Social (un) distancing: Teammate interactions, athletic identity, and mental health of student-athletes during the COVID-19 pandemic. *The Journal of Adolescent Health, 67*(5), 662–670. doi:10.1016/j.jadohealth.2020.08.001 PMID:32943294

Grice, J. C., Davies, A., Robert, P., & Norman, W. (2012). *The Young Foundation social innovation overview. A deliverable of the project: the theoretical, empirical and policy foundations for building social innovation in Europe (TEPSIE). In European Commission-7th framework Programme*. European Commission, DG Research.

Grover, A., Caulfield, P., & Roehrich, K. J. 2014. Frugal Innovation in Healthcare and its Applicability to Developed Markets.

Gul, A., Subhan, S., & Tunio, M. N. (2021). Learning experiences of women entrepreneurs amidst COVID-19. *International Journal of Gender and Entrepreneurship, 13*(2), 1756–6266. doi:10.1108/IJGE-09-2020-0153

Gupta, A.K., 2012. Innovations for the poor by the poor. *Int. J. Technol Learn. Innovat. Dev. 5*(1e2), 28e39

Gupta, V. (2011). Corporate response to global financial crisis: A knowledge-based model. *Glob Econ J, 11*(2), 1850224. doi:10.2202/1524-5861.1706

Hafeez, A., & Amad, E. (2002). Factors determining the labor force participation decision of educated married women in a district of Punjab. *Pakistan Economic and Social Review, 40*(1), 75-88.

Hart, S.L., Christensen, C.M., 2002. The great leap: driving innovation from the base of the pyramid. *MIT Sloan Manag. Rev. 44*(1), 51e56.

Hartley, T. C. (2014). *The foundations of European Union law: an introduction to the constitutional and administrative law of the European Union.* Oxford University Press. doi:10.1093/he/9780199681457.001.0001

Hawkes, S., & Buse, K. (2013). Gender and global health: Evidence, policy, and inconvenient truths. *Lancet, 381*(9879), 1783–1787. doi:10.1016/S0140-6736(13)60253-6 PMID:23683645

Hayran, C., & Anik, L. (2021). Well-being and fear of missing out (FOMO) on digital content in the time of COVID-19: A correlational analysis among university students. *International Journal of Environmental Research and Public Health, 18*(4), 1974. doi:10.3390/ijerph18041974 PMID:33670639

Heeks, R., & Arun, S. (2010). Social outsourcing as a development tool: The impact of outsourcing IT services to women's social enterprises in Kerala. Journal of International Development. *The Journal of the Development Studies Association, 22*(4), 441–454.

Heneman, R. L., & Tansky, J. W. (2002). Human resource management models for entrepreneurial opportunity: Existing knowledge and new directions. In Katz J. and Welbourne T. M. (eds.) Managing people in entrepreneurial organizations. 5, 55–82. JAI Press. doi:10.1016/S1074-7540(02)05004-3

Hindocha, C. N., Antonacci, G., Barlow, J., & Harris, M. (2021). *Defining frugal innovation: A critical review.* Academic Press.

Hoffman, A., & Holzhuter, J. (2012). The evolution of higher education: innovation as natural selection. In A. Hoffman & S. Spangehl (Eds.), *Innovation in Higher Education: Igniting the Spark for Success, American Council on Education,* (pp. 3–15). Rowman & Litttlefield Publishers Inc.

Hossain, D. M. (2007). Social entrepreneurs in Bangladesh. Hossain, DM and Hossain, M.(2012), Social Entrepreneurs in Bangladesh, International Journal of Research in Commerce. *IT & Management, 2*(9), 7–12.

HossainM. (2016). Frugal innovation: a systematic literature review. SSRN 2768254.

HossainM. (2016). Frugal innovation: a systematic literature review. SSRN.

Hossain, M. (2017). Mapping the frugal innovation phenomenon. *Technology in Society, 51*, 199–208. doi:10.1016/j.techsoc.2017.09.006

Hossain, M. (2018). Frugal innovation: A review and research agenda. *Journal of Cleaner Production, 182*, 926–936. doi:10.1016/j.jclepro.2018.02.091

Hossain, M. (2020). Frugal innovation: Conception, development, diffusion, and outcome. *Journal of Cleaner Production, 262*, 121456. doi:10.1016/j.jclepro.2020.121456

Hossain, M., Lev¨anen, J., & Wierenga, M. (2021). Pursuing frugal innovation for sustainability at the grassroots level. *Management and Organization Review, 17*(2), 374–381. doi:10.1017/mor.2020.53

Hossain, M., Simula, H., & Halme, M. (2016). Can frugal go global? Diffusion patterns of frugal innovations. *Technology in Society*, *46*, 132–139. doi:10.1016/j.techsoc.2016.04.005

Hung, J. (2022). Digitalisation, Parenting, and Children's Mental Health: What Are the Challenges and Policy Implications? *International Journal of Environmental Research and Public Health*, *19*(11), 6452. doi:10.3390/ijerph19116452 PMID:35682037

Hunt, C. (2011). *National Strategy for higher education to 2030 report of the strategy group*. Department of Education and Skills.

Hyvärinen, A., Keskinen, M., & Varis, O. (2016). Potential and pitfalls of frugal innovation in the water sector: Insights from Tanzania to global value chains. *Sustainability*, *8*(9), 888. doi:10.3390u8090888

Ilhan, D., & Karatas, H. (2015). An analysis on motivational beliefs and attitudes of undergraduates regarding learning English. *International Journal of Educational Research*, *6*(2).

International Monetary Fund (IMF). (2022) IMF Annual Report. A year like no other. https:// www. imf. org/ exter nal/ pubs/ ft/ ar/ 2022/ eng

International Monetary Fund (IMF). (2022). *IMF Annual Report. A year like no other.* https:// www. imf. org/ exter nal/ pubs/ ft/ ar/ 2022/ eng

Iqbal, Q., Ahmad, N. H., & Halim, H. A. (2021). Insights on entrepreneurial bricolage and frugal innovation for sustainable performance. *Business Strategy & Development*, *4*(3), 237–245. doi:10.1002/bsd2.147

Issa, T., Chang, V., & Issa, T. (2010, August). Sustainable Business Strategies and PESTEL Framework. *GSTF International Journal on Computing*, *1*(1), 73–80. doi:10.5176/2010-2283_1.1.13

Jamshed, K., Shah, S. H. A., Majeed, Z., Al-Ghazali, B. M., & Jamshaid, S. (2022). Role of Green Leadership and Green Training on the Green Process Innovation: Mediation of Green Managerial Innovation. *Journal of Xidian University*, *16*(2), 66–72.

Jejeebhoy, S. J., & Sathar, Z. A. (2001). Women's autonomy in India and Pakistan: The influence of religion and region. *Population and Development Review*, *27*(4), 687–712. doi:10.1111/j.1728-4457.2001.00687.x

Jiang, J., Wang, S., & Zhao, S. (2012). Does HRM facilitate employee creativity and organizational innovation? A study of Chinese firms. *International Journal of Human Resource Management*, *23*(19), 4025–4047. doi:10.1080/09585192 .2012.690567

Jianwu, J; Shuo, W & Shuming, Z. (2012). Does HRM facilitate employee creativity and organizational innovation? A study of Chinese firms. *The International Journal*.

Jones, M. L. (2004, October 07). Application of systematic review methods to qualitative research: Practical issues. *Leading Global Nursing Research*, *48*(3), 271–278. doi:10.1111/j.1365-2648.2004.03196.x PMID:15488041

Kapoor, K., Weerakkody, V., & Schroeder, A. (2018). Social innovations for social cohesion in Western Europe: Success dimensions for lifelong learning and education. *Innovation (Abingdon)*, *31*(2), 189–203. doi:10.1080/13511610.2 017.1419336

Katpar., N. K., Chaudhry, N. I., Tunio, M. N. and Ali, M. A. (2020). Impact of Leadership Style and Organizational Culture on Organizational Commitment. *Sukkur IBA Journal of Management and Business –SIJMB* *7*(1), 92-106.

Katpar., N. K., Chaudhry, N. I., Tunio, M. N., & Ali, M. A. (2020). Impact of Leadership Style and Organizational Culture on Organizational Commitment. *Sukkur IBA Journal of Management and Business, 7*(1), 92-106.

Katper, N. K. Medan, A., Syed, K. B. S., & Tunio, M. N. (2017). Determinants of Debt Maturity Structure in Shariah and Non-Shariah Firms in Pakistan: A comparative Study. *Journal of Applied Economic Sciences, 12*(4), 1210-1225.

Katper, N. K. Medan, A., Syed, K. B. S.., Tunio, M. N. (2017). Determinants of Debt Maturity Structure in Shariah and Non-Shariah Firms in Pakistan: A comparative Study. *Journal of Applied Economic Sciences 12*(4), p1210-1225.

Katper, N. K. Medan, A., Syed, K. B. S.., Tunio, M. N. (2017). Determinants of Debt Maturity Structure in Shariah and Non-Shariah Firms in Pakistan: A comparative Study. *Journal of Applied Economic Sciences 12*(4), p1210-1225. 16.

Khan, A. (2007). *Women and Paid Work in Pakistan.* Retrieved from http://www.researchcollective.org/Documents/Women_Paid_Work.pdf

Khan, S. (2013). Women's empowerment through poverty alleviation: A socio- cultural and politico-economic assessment of conditions in Pakistan. *International Journal of Academic Research and Reflection, 1*(1), 16-40.

Khanna, T., & Palepu, K. G. (2005). Spotting Institutional Voids in Emerging Markets. https://www.hbs.edu/faculty/Pages/item.aspx?num=32645

Khanna, T., & Palepu, K. G. (2005). *Spotting Institutional Voids in Emerging Markets.* Retrieved from https://www.hbs.edu/faculty/Pages/item.aspx?num=32645

Khan, R. (2016). How frugal innovation promotes social sustainability. *Sustainability, 8*(10), 1034. doi:10.3390u8101034

Klaas, B. S., Semadeni, M., Klimchak, M., & Ward, A.-K. (2012). High-performance work system implementation in small and medium enterprises: A knowledge creation perspective. *Human Resource Management, 51*(4), 487–510. doi:10.1002/hrm.21485

Koerich, G. V., & Cancellier, E. (2019). Frugal innovation: Origins, evolution and future perspectives. *Cadernos EBAPE. BR, 17*(4), 1079–1093. doi:10.1590/1679-395174424x

Koster, F. and Benda, L. (2020). Innovative human resource management: measurement, determinants and outcomes. *International Journal of Innovation Science, 12*(3), 287-302.

Kroll, H., & Gabriel, M. (2020). Frugal innovation in, by and for Europe. *International Journal of* Lehtonen, M. The environmental-social interface of sustainable development: Capabilities, social capital, institutions. *Ecological Economics, 2004*(49), 199–214.

Kumar, A. (2016). Improvement of Women Health and Empowerment: A Study of the Self Help Group's (SHG's) Roles in the Patna District of Bihar. *Ind. J. of Applied & Clinical Sociology, 11*(4), 68–71.

Kumar, A., Anand, A., & Kesri, V. (2020). Industry 4.0 to education 4.0: An Indian Student Perspective. *International Journal of Innovative Research in Technology, 6*(12), 417–423. https://www.researchgate.net/publication/341343880

Kwan, B. Y. M., Mbanwi, A., Cofie, N., Rogoza, C., Islam, O., Chung, A. D., Dalgarno, N., Dagnone, D., Wang, X., & Mussari, B. (2021). Creating a competency-based medical education curriculum for Canadian diagnostic radiology residency (Queen's fundamental innovations in residency education)—Part 1: Transition to discipline and foundation of discipline stages. *Canadian Association of Radiologists Journal, 72*(3), 372–380. doi:10.1177/0846537119894723 PMID:32126802

Laeis Stefanie Lemke, G. C. M. (2016). Social entrepreneurship in tourism: Applying sustainable livelihoods approaches. *International Journal of Contemporary Hospitality Management, 28*(6), 1076–1093. doi:10.1108/IJCHM-05-2014-0235

Lamont, J. (2010). The age of 'Indovation' dawns. *The Financial Times.*

Lan, F., & Liu, X. (2017). Business model transformation in digital enablement context through frugal innovation: Learning from Chinese experience. Int. J. Technology. *Policy and Management*, *17*(4), 15. doi:10.1504/IJTPM.2017.087272

Lebni, J. Y., Abbas, J., Moradi, F., Salahshoor, M. R., Chaboksavar, F., Irandoost, S. F., & Ziapour, A. (2020, July). How the COVID-19 pandemic effected economic, social, political, and cultural factors: A lesson from Iran. *The International Journal of Social Psychiatry*, *67*(3), 298–300. doi:10.1177/0020764020939984 PMID:32615838

Leliveld, A., & Knorringa, P. (2018). Frugal innovation and development research. *European Journal of Development Research*, *30*(1), 1–16. doi:10.105741287-017-0121-4

Leong, C., Pan, S. L., Newell, S., & Cui, L. (2016). The Emergence of Self-Organizing E- commerce Ecosystems in Remote Villages of China: A Tale of Digital Empowerment for Rural Development. *Management Information Systems Quarterly*, *40*(2), 475–484. doi:10.25300/MISQ/2016/40.2.11

Lettice, F., & Parekh, M. (2010). The social innovation process: Themes, challenges and implications for practice. *International Journal of Technology Management*, *51*(1), 139–158. doi:10.1504/IJTM.2010.033133

Levänen, J., Hossain, M., Lyytinen, T., Hyvärinen, A., Numminen, S., & Halme, M. (2016). Implications of Frugal Innovations on Sustainable Development: Evaluating Water and Energy Innovations. *Sustainability*, *8*(1), 4. doi:10.3390u8010004

Levänen, J., Hossain, M., & Wierenga, M. (2022). Frugal innovation in the midst of societal and operational pressures. *Journal of Cleaner Production*, *347*, 131308. doi:10.1016/j.jclepro.2022.131308

Lincoln, N. D., Travers, C., Ackers, P., & Wilkinson, A. (2002). The meaning of empowerment: The interdisciplinary etymology of a new management concept. *International Journal of Management Reviews*, *4*(3), 271–290. doi:10.1111/1468-2370.00087

Li, W., Zhao, Z., & Wang, D. (2022). Anxiety, depression and satisfaction with life among college students in China: Nine months after initiation of the outbreak of COVID-19. *Frontiers in Psychiatry*, *2427*, 777190. Advance online publication. doi:10.3389/fpsyt.2021.777190

Lizarralde, I., & Tyl, B. (2018). A framework for the integration of the conviviality concept in the design process. *Journal of Cleaner Production*, *197*, 1766–1777. doi:10.1016/j.jclepro.2017.03.108

Loveys, K., Sagar, M., Pickering, I., & Broadbent, E. (2021). A digital human for delivering a remote loneliness and stress intervention to at-risk younger and older adults during the COVID-19 pandemic: Randomized pilot trial. *JMIR Mental Health*, *8*(11), e31586. doi:10.2196/31586 PMID:34596572

Lüdeke-Freund, F., & Dembek, K. (2017). Sustainable business model research and practice: Emerging field or passing fancy? *Journal of Cleaner Production*, *168*, 1668–1678. doi:10.1016/j.jclepro.2017.08.093

Mackieson, P., Shlonsky, A., & Connolly, M. (2019). Increasing rigor and reducing bias in qualitative research: A document analysis of parliamentary debates using applied thematic analysis. *Qualitative Social Work: Research and Practice*, *18*(6), 965–980. doi:10.1177/1473325018786996

Mahmood, M. A., Irfan, S., Jabeen, N., & Moazzam, A. (2020). Sources of Innovation in Social Enterprises Working in Pakistan. *Journal of the Research Society of Pakistan*, *57*(3), 1.

Mahr, J., & Imhof, M. (2017). *Applying Frugal Innovation to Serve the Bottom of the Pyramid in Germany*. Academic Press.

Maine, E., Lubik, S., & Garnsey, E. (2012). Process-based vs product-based innovation: Value creation nanotech ventures. *Technovation*, *32*(3/4), 179–179. doi:10.1016/j.technovation.2011.10.003

Mair, J., Marti, I., & Ventresca, M. J. (2012). Building inclusive markets in rural Bangladesh: How intermediaries work institutional voids. *Academy of Management Journal*, *55*(4), 819–850. doi:10.5465/amj.2010.0627

Marcén-Román, Y., Gasch-Gallen, A., Vela Martín de la Mota, I. I., Calatayud, E., Gómez-Soria, I., & Rodríguez-Roca, B. (2021). Stress perceived by University Health Sciences Students, 1 year after COVID-19 pandemic. *International Journal of Environmental Research and Public Health*, *18*(10), 5233. doi:10.3390/ijerph18105233 PMID:34069066

McCloskey, D. N. (2010). *The bourgeois virtues: Ethics for an age of commerce*. University of Chicago Press.

McCluskey, G., Fry, D., Hamilton, S., King, A., Laurie, M., McAra, L., & Stewart, T. M. (2021). School closures, exam cancellations and isolation: The impact of Covid-19 on young people's mental health. *Emotional & Behavioural Difficulties*, *26*(1), 46–59. doi:10.1080/13632752.2021.1903182

McDonnell-Naughton, M., & Păunescu, C. (2022). Facets of social innovation in higher education. *Social Innovation in Higher Education*, 9.

Melkas, H., Oikarinen, T., & Pekkarinen, S. (2019). Understanding frugal innovation: A case study of university professionals in developed countries. *Innovation and Development*, *9*(1), 25–40. doi:10.1080/2157930X.2018.1437687

Memon, A.B., Meyer, K. and Tunio, M. N. (2021). Toward collaborative networking among innovation laboratories: a conceptual framework. *International Journal of Innovation Science*. doi:10.1108/IJIS-04-2021-0069

Memon, A. B., Meyer, K., & Tunio, M. N. (2021). Toward collaborative networking among innovation laboratories: A conceptual framework. *International Journal of Innovation Science*.

Memon, A. R., Shaikh, E., & Khan, M. S. (2019). Determination of Customer Satisfaction of Hyderabad Restaurants. *Irish Interdisciplinary Journal of Science and Research*, *3*(3), 11–18.

Michaelis, T. L., Carr, J. C., Scheaf, D. C., & Pollack, J. M. (2020). The frugal entrepreneur: A self regulatory perspective of resourceful entrepreneurial behavior. *Journal of Business Venturing*, *35*(4), 105969. doi:10.1016/j.jbusvent.2019.105969

Miesler, T., Wimschneider, C., Brem, A., & Meinel, L. (2020). Frugal innovation for point- of-care diagnostics controlling outbreaks and epidemics. *ACS Biomaterials Science & Engineering*, *6*(5), 2709–2725. doi:10.1021/acsbiomaterials.9b01712 PMID:33463254

Milley, P., Szijarto, B., Svensson, K., & Cousins, J. B. (2018). The evaluation of social innovation: A review and integration of the current empirical knowledge base. *Evaluation*, *24*(2), 237–258. doi:10.1177/1356389018763242

Ministry of Planning. (2017). Annual Plan 2017-18. Ministry of Planning, Development & Reform.

Mirza, N. (2011). Seven pro-women laws in seven years. *Legislative Watch, 38*.

Morawska-Jancelewicz, J. (2021). The role of universities in social innovation within quadruple/quintuple helix model: Practical implications from polish experience. *Journal of the Knowledge Economy*, 1–42.

Munro, D. (2013). *A guide to financing SMEs*. Palgrave Shaming. doi:10.1057/9781137373786

Mushtaq, T., Tunio, M. N., Akbar, Z., & Jariko, M. (2021). Green Organizational identity: Antecedents and consequences: An Empirical Study. *Contemporary Issues in business and Government, 27*(3), 2056-2069.

Mushtaq, T., Tunio, M. N., Akbar, Z., and Jariko, M. (2021). Green Organizational identity: Antecents and consequences: An Emprical Study. *Contemporary Issues in business and Government, 27*(3), p. 2056-2069.

Nam, V. H., & Luu, H. N. (2021). How Do Human Resource Management Practices Affect Innovation of Small- and Medium-sized Enterprises in a Transition Economy? *Journal of Interdisciplinary Economics*. doi:10.1177/02601079211032119

Naz, A., & Chaudhry, H. R. (2011). Developing gender equality: An analytical study of socio-political and economic constraints in women's empowerment in pakhtun society of Khyber Pakhtunkhwa province of Pakistan. *Indian Journal of Health and Wellbeing*, 2(1), 259–266.

NCSW. (2011). *Assesment of the capacities of women development departments*. Pakistan National Commission on Status of Women.

Niaz, U. (2003). Violence against women in South Asian countries. *Archives of Women's Mental Health*, 6(3), 173–184. doi:10.100700737-003-0171-9 PMID:12920615

Niroumand, M., Shahin, A., Naghsh, A., & Peikari, H. R. (2021). Frugal innovation enablers, critical success factors and barriers: A systematic review. *Creativity and Innovation Management*, 30(2), 348–367. doi:10.1111/caim.12436

North, A. C., Hargreaves, D. J., & McKendrick, J. (1997). In-store music affects product choice. *Nature*, 390(6656), 132–132. doi:10.1038/36484

OECD. (2009). *Globalisation and Emerging Economies*. OECD Publishing.

Pansera, M. (2018). Frugal or fair? The unfulfilled promises of frugal innovation. *Technology Innovation Management Review*, 8(4), 6–13. doi:10.22215/timreview/1148

Pansera, M., & Sarkar, S. (2016). Crafting sustainable development solutions: Frugal innovations of grassroots entrepreneurs. *Sustainability*, 8(1), 51. doi:10.3390u8010051

Partridge, E. (2005). Social sustainability: A useful theoretical framework? In *Proceedings of the Australasian Political Science Association Annual Conference*, Dunedin, New Zealand.

Pathak, R. (2021, February 15). What is PESTLE Analysis? Everything you need to know about it. *Business Analytics*. https://www.analyticssteps.com/blogs/what-pestle-analysis

Pathak, M. (2020). Social, Political and Economic Impact of COVID-19 Pandemic on Assan: A Study. Jouranl if. *Critical Review*, 7(16).

Paul, J., & Rialp-Criado, A. (2020). The Art of Writing Literature review: What do we know and What do we need to know? *International Business Review*, 29(4), 101717. doi:10.1016/j.ibusrev.2020.101717

Pel, B., Haxeltine, A., Avelino, F., Dumitru, A., Kemp, R., Bauler, T., Kunze, I., Dorland, J., Wittmayer, J., & Jørgensen, M. S. (2020). Towards a theory of transformative social innovation: A relational framework and 12 propositions. *Research Policy*, 49(8), 104080. doi:10.1016/j.respol.2020.104080

Peredo, A. M., & McLean, M. (2006). Social entrepreneurship: A critical review of the concept. *Journal of World Business*, 41(1), 56–65. doi:10.1016/j.jwb.2005.10.007

Petrou, A., & Daskalopoulou, I. (2013). Social capital and innovation in the services sector. *European Journal of Innovation Management*, 16(1), 50–69. doi:10.1108/14601061311292850

Phillips, W., Lee, H., Ghobadian, A., O'regan, N., & James, P. (2015). Social innovation and social entrepreneurship: A systematic review. *Group & Organization Management*, 40(3), 428–461. doi:10.1177/1059601114560063

Phills, J. A., Deiglmeier, K., & Miller, D. T. (2008). Rediscovering social innovation. *Stanford Social Innovation Review*, 6(4), 34–43.

Pia, H, Riitta. F, Astikainen, & Kultalahti, S. (2020). Agile HRM practices of SMEs. *Journal of Small Business Management*, 58(6), pp.1291-1306. Routledge. . doi:10.1111/jsbm.12483

Pisanu, F., & Menapace, P. (2014). Creativity and innovation: Four key issues from a literature review. *Creative Education*, *5*(3), 145–154. doi:10.4236/ce.2014.53023

Polese, F., Botti, A., Grimaldi, M., Monda, A., & Vesci, M. (2018). Social innovation in smart tourism ecosystems: How technology and institutions shape sustainable value co-creation. *Sustainability*, *10*(1), 140. doi:10.3390u10010140

Porritt, J. (2005). *Capitalism as if the World Matters; Earthscan.* Sterling.

Porter, M. R., & Kramer, M. R. (2011). Creating shared value. *Harvard Business Review*, *89*(1–2), 1–17.

Pouwels, I., & Koster, F. (2017). Inter-organizational cooperation and organizational innovativeness. A comparative study. *International Journal of Innovation Science*, *9*(2), 184–204. doi:10.1108/IJIS-01-2017-0003

Prabhu, J., & Jain, S. (2015). Innovation and entrepreneurship in India: Understanding Jugaad. *Asia Pacific Journal of Management*, *32*(4), 843–868. doi:10.100710490-015-9445-9

Prahalad, C. K., & Mashelkar, R. A. (2010). Innovation's holy grail. *Harvard Business Review*, *88*(7-8), 132–141.

Qamar, U., Ansari, N., Tanveer, F., & Qamar, N. (2020). Social Entrepreneurship in Pakistan: Challenges and Prospects. *Journal of Management Research*, *7*(2), 1–41.

Qureshi, J. A., Qureshi, M. S., & Qureshi, M. A. (2018). Mitigating risk of failure by expanding family entrepreneurship and learning from international franchising experiences of johnny rockets: A case stu¶#dy in Pakistan. *International Journal of Experiential Learning & Case Studies*, *3*(1), 110–127. doi:10.22555/ijelcs.v3i1.1972

Qureshi, M. A., Qureshi, J. A., Thebo, J. A., Shaikh, G. M., Brohi, N. A., & Qaiser, S. (2019). The nexus of employee's commitment, job satisfaction, and job performance: An analysis of FMCG industries of Pakistan. *Cogent Business & Management*, *6*(1), 1654189. doi:10.1080/23311975.2019.1654189

Radjou, N., Prabhu, J., & Ahuja, S. (2012). Jugaad innovation: Think frugal, be flexible, generate breakthrough growth. Jossey-Bass (first ed.). San Francisco, California, USA, Whiley.

Radjou, N., Prabhu, J., & Ahuja, S. (2012). Jugaad innovation: Think frugal, be flexible, generate breakthrough growth. Jossey-Bass (first ed.). San Francisco, California, USA. Whiley.

Radjou, N., & Prabhu, J. (2015). *The frugal way to grow*. Frugal Innovation Hub.

Radjou, N., Prabhu, J., & Ahuja, S. (2012). *Jugaad innovation: Think frugal, be flexible, generate breakthrough growth.* John Wiley & Sons.

Ragavan, M. I., Culyba, A. J., Muhammad, F. L., & Miller, E. (2020). Supporting adolescents and young adults exposed to or experiencing violence during the COVID-19 pandemic. *The Journal of Adolescent Health*, *67*(1), 18–20. doi:10.1016/j.jadohealth.2020.04.011 PMID:32409152

Rahiem, M. D., Krauss, S. E., & Ersing, R. (2021). Perceived consequences of extended social isolation on mental well-being: Narratives from Indonesian university students during the COVID-19 pandemic. *International Journal of Environmental Research and Public Health*, *18*(19), 10489. doi:10.3390/ijerph181910489 PMID:34639788

Rahman, S. U. (2001). Total quality management practices and business outcome: doi:10.1108/ER-03-2020-0101

Rahman, S.-U. (2001, March). Evidence from small and medium enterprises in Western Australia. *Total Quality Management*, *12*(2), 201–210. doi:10.1080/09544120120011424

Ramírez-Montoya, M. S., Loaiza-Aguirre, M. I., Zúñiga-Ojeda, A., & Portuguez-Castro, M. (2021). Characterization of the Teaching Profile within the Framework of Education 4.0. *Future Internet*, *13*(4), 91. doi:10.3390/fi13040091

Rao, B. C. (2013). How disruptive is frugal? *Technology in Society, 35*(1), 65–73. doi:10.1016/j.techsoc.2013.03.003

Rashid, D. Y., & Abdullah, I. (2013). Women empowerment in the corporate sector of Pakistan. *Interdisciplinary Journal of Contemporary Research in Business, 5*(5), 518–523.

Rasul, S. (2014). Empowerment of Pakistani women: Perceptions and reality. *NDU Journal, 28*, 14.

Ravishankar, M. N., & Gurca, A. (2015). A bricolage perspective on technological innovation in emerging markets. *IEEE Transactions on Engineering Management, 63*(1), 53–66. doi:10.1109/TEM.2015.2494501

Raza, A., Shaikh, E., Tursoy, T., & Almashaqbeh, H. A. (2022). Economics and Business Perspectives of Sustainable HRM. In *Sustainable Development of Human Resources in a Globalization Period* (pp. 36–48). IGI Global. doi:10.4018/978-1-6684-4981-3.ch003

Raza, S. A., Abidi, M., Arsalan, G. M., Shairf, A., & Qureshi, M. A. (2018). The impact of student attitude, trust, subjective norms, motivation and rewards on knowledge sharing attitudes among university students. *International Journal of Knowledge and Learning, 12*(4), 287–304. doi:10.1504/IJKL.2018.095955

Raza, S. A., Qureshi, M. A., Ahmed, M., Qaiser, S., Ali, R., & Ahmed, F. (2021). Non-linear relationship between tourism, economic growth, urbanization, and environmental degradation: Evidence from smooth transition models. *Environmental Science and Pollution Research International, 28*(2), 1426–1442. doi:10.100711356-020-10179-3 PMID:32840747

Redford, A., & Dills, A. K. (2021, January). The Political Economy of Drug and Alcohol Regulation During the CO-VID-19 Pandemic. *Forthcoming Sourthern Economics Journal.* doi:10.2139/ssrn.3728996

Rhyan, C. (2021, April 16). Perspective: Are Rising Health Care Prices Another COVID-19 Side Effect? *Newroom.* https://altarum.org/news/are-rising-health-care-prices-another-covid-19-side-effect

Riana, I. G., Suparna, G., Suwandana, I. G. M., Kot, S., & Rajiani, I. (2020). Human resource management in promoting innovation and organizational performance.

Riffat, H. (2010). Gender and nexus of purdah culture in public policy. *South Asian Studies: A Research Journal of South Asian Studies, 25*(2), 303-310.

Roblek, V., Mesko-Stok, Z., & Mesko, M. Complexity of a sharing economy for tourism and hospitality. In *Proceedings of 23rd International Congress "Tourism and Hospitality Industry 2016 – Trends and Challenges"* (pp. 374-387). Faculty of Tourism and Hospitality Management, University of Rijeka.

Rogers, M., & Greenhalgh, C. (2010). *Innovation, intellectual property, and economic growth.* Princeton University Press.

Rosca, E., Arnold, M., Bendul, J.C., 2017. Business models for sustainable innovationean empirical analysis of frugal products and services. *J. Clean. Prod. 162.*

Rosca, E., Arnold, M., & Bendul, J. C. (2017). Business models for sustainable innovation–an empirical analysis of frugal products and services. *Journal of Cleaner Production, 162,* S133–S145. doi:10.1016/j.jclepro.2016.02.050

RSF. (2020). Social, Political, Economic, and Psychological Consequences of the COVID-19 Pandemic. *Russel Sage Foundation.* https://www.russellsage.org/research/funding/covid-19-pandemic

Saebi, T., Foss, N. J., & Linder, S. (2019). Social entrepreneurship research: Past achievements and future promises. *Journal of Management, 45*(1), 70–95. doi:10.1177/0149206318793196

Sahlberg, P., & Oldroyd, D. (2010). Pedagogy for economic competitiveness and sustainable development. *European Journal of Education, 45*(2), 280–299. doi:10.1111/j.1465-3435.2010.01429.x

Sankofa, N. (2022). Critical method of document analysis. *International Journal of Social Research Methodology*, 1–13. doi:10.1080/13645579.2022.2113664

Sarasvathy, S. D. (2009). *Effectuation: Elements of entrepreneurial expertise*. Edward Elgar Publishing.

Sathar, Z. A., & Kazi, S. (2000). Women's autonoy in the context of rural Pakistan. *Pakistan Development Review*, *39*(2), 89–110. doi:10.30541/v39i2pp.89-110

Sawyer, K. (2012). *Explaining Creativity: the science of human innovation*. Oxford University Press.

Schelhorn, I., Ecker, A., Lüdtke, M. N., Rehm, S., Tran, T., Bereznai, J. L., Meyer, M. L., Sütterlin, S., Kinateder, M., Lugo, R. G., & Shiban, Y. (2021). Psychological Burden During the COVID-19 Pandemic in Germany. *Frontiers in Psychology*, *12*, 640518. Advance online publication. doi:10.3389/fpsyg.2021.640518 PMID:34557124

Schwittay, A. F. (2011). The financial inclusion assemblage: Subjects, technics, rationalities. *Critique of Anthropology*, *31*(4), 381–401. doi:10.1177/0308275X11420117

Serdyukov, P. (2016). Innovation in education: what works, what doesn't, and what to do about it? Journal of Research in Innovative Teaching & Learning, 10 (1).

Shafique, I., Ahmad, B., & Kalyar, M. N. (2019). How ethical leadership influences creativity and organizational innovation: Examining the underlying mechanisms. *European Journal of Innovation Management*, *23*(1), 114–133. doi:10.1108/EJIM-12-2018-0269

Shah, N., Michael, F., & Chalu, H. (2020). Conceptualizing challenges to electronic human resource management (e-HRM) adoption: A case of Small and Medium Enterprises (SMEs) in Tanzania. *Asian Journal of Business and Management*, *8*(4). doi:10.24203/ajbm.v8i4.6066

Shah, S. H. A., Cheema, S., Al-Ghazali, B. M., Ali, M., & Rafiq, N. (2021). Perceived corporate social responsibility and pro-environmental behaviors: The role of organizational identification and coworker pro-environmental advocacy. *Corporate Social Responsibility and Environmental Management*, *28*(1), 366–377. doi:10.1002/csr.2054

Shah, S. M. M., Hamid, K. B. A., Malaysia, U. U., Shaikh, U. A., Malaysia, P. S. U. U., Qureshi, M. A., & Pahi, M. H. (2016). The Relationship between Leadership Styles and Job Performance: The Role of Work Engagement as a Mediator. *International Journal of Scientific Study*, *2*(10), 242–253.

Shahzad, K., Arenius, P., Muller, A., Rasheed, M. A., & Bajwa, S. U. (2019). Unpacking the relationship between high-performance work systems and innovation performance in SMEs. *Personnel Review*, *48*(4), 977–1000. doi:10.1108/PR-10-2016-0271

Shaikh, E., & Tunio, M. N. (2020). Customer satisfaction and Customer loyalty: An empirical case study on the impact of benefits generated through Smartphone applications. *International Journal of Public Sector Performance Management*.

Shaikh, E., Tunio, M. N. (2020). Customer satisfaction and Customer loyalty: An empirical case study on the impact of benefits generated through Smartphone applications. *International Journal of Public Sector Performance Management*.

Shaikh, E., Tunio, M. N., & Qureshi, F. (2021). Finance and women's entrepreneurship in DETEs: A literature review. *Entrepreneurial Finance, Innovation and Development*, 191-209.

Shaikh, E., Tunio, M. N., Khoso, W. M., Brahmi, M., & Rasool, S. (2022). The COVID-19 Pandemic Overlaps Entrepreneurial Activities and Triggered New Challenges: A Review Study. *Managing Human Resources in SMEs and Start-ups: International Challenges and Solutions*, 155-182.

Shaikh, E., Azhar, H., Brahmi, M., & Zehra, N. (2022). The impact of monetary and non-monetary motivation on employees' performance: A case study of Hyderabad Electric Supply Company. *International Journal of Technology Transfer and Commercialisation*, *19*(1), 127–141. doi:10.1504/IJTTC.2022.123088

Shaikh, E., Brahmi, M., Thang, P. C., Watto, W. A., Trang, T. T. N., & Loan, N. T. (2022). Should I Stay or Should I Go? Explaining the Turnover Intentions with Corporate Social Responsibility (CSR), Organizational Identification and Organizational Commitment. *Sustainability*, *14*(10), 6030. doi:10.3390u14106030

Shaikh, E., Khoso, I., & Chandio, F. (2019). Effects of Corporate Social Responsibility on Organizational Performance: A Conceptual and Literature Review. *Journal of Grassroot*, *53*(1).

Shaikh, E., Mishra, V., Ahmed, F., Krishnan, D., & Dagar, V. (2021). Exchange rate, stock price and trade volume in US-China trade war during COVID-19: An empirical study. *Estudios de Economía Aplicada*, *39*(8). Advance online publication. doi:10.25115/eea.v39i8.5327

Shaikh, E., Watto, W. A., & Tunio, M. N. (2022). Impact of Authentic Leadership on Organizational Citizenship Behavior by Using The Mediating Effect of Psychological Ownership. *ETIKONOMI*, *21*(1), 89–102. doi:10.15408/etk.v21i1.18968

Shaikh, S., Sultan, M. F., Mushtaque, T., & Tunio, M. N. (2021). Impact of COVID-19 on GDP: A serial mediation effect on international tourism and hospitality. *International Journal of Management*, *12*(84), 422–430.

Sharif, A., Afshan, S., & Qureshi, M. A. (2019). Acceptance of learning management system in university students: An integrating framework of modified UTAUT2 and TTF theories. *International Journal of Technology Enhanced Learning*, *11*(2), 201–229. doi:10.1504/IJTEL.2019.098810

Shepherd, D. A., Parida, V., & Wincent, J. (2020). The surprising duality of jugaad: Low firm growth and high inclusive growth. *Journal of Management Studies*, *57*(1), 87–128. doi:10.1111/joms.12309

Sigala, M. (2015). From demand elasticity to market plasticity: A market approach for developing revenue management strategies in tourism. *Journal of Travel & Tourism Marketing*, *32*(7), 812–834. doi:10.1080/10548408.2015.1063801

Simoes, L., Garrido, S. R. and Carvalho, A. (2018) Assessing the Social Sustainability of Frugal Products. *Social LCA*, 86. *Technology Management*, *83*(1/2/3), p. 34–54.

Simula, H., Töllmen, A., & Karjaluoto, H. (2015). Facilitating innovations and value co-creation in industrial B2B firms by combining digital marketing, social media and crowdsourcing. In *Marketing Dynamism & Sustainability: Things Change, Things Stay the Same…* (pp. 254–263). Springer. doi:10.1007/978-3-319-10912-1_84

Singh, R. K., Garg, S. K., & Deshmukh, S. G. (2008). Strategy development by SMEs for competitiveness: A review. *Benchmarking*: *An International Journal, 15*(5), 525–547. doi:10.1108/146357708109031

Sivathanu, B., & Bhise, P. V. (2013). Challenges for social entrepreneurship. *International Journal of Application or Innovation in Engineering & Management (IJAIEM)*, 9-10

Slee, B., Lukesch, R., & Ravazzoli, E. (2022). Social Innovation: The Promise and the Reality in Marginalised Rural Areas in Europe. *WORLD (Oakland, Calif.)*, *3*(2), 237–259. doi:10.3390/world3020013

Snyder, H. (2019). Literature review as a research methodology: An overview and guidelines. *Journal of Business Research*, *104*, 333–339. doi:10.1016/j.jbusres.2019.07.039

Solov'eva, T. Y. S., Popov, A. V., Caro-Gonzalez, A., & Hua, L. (2018). Social innovation in Spain, China and Russia: key aspects of development. *Economic and Social Changes: Facts, Trends, Forecast*, *11*(2), 52–68.

Soni, P., & Krishnan, R. T. (2014). Frugal innovation: Aligning theory, practice, and public policy. *Journal of Indian Business Research*, *6*(1), 29–47. doi:10.1108/JIBR-03-2013-0025

Steinfield, L. A., & Holt, D. (2019). Towards A Theory on the Reproduction of Social Innovations in Subsistence Marketplaces. *Journal of Product Innovation Management*, *36*(6), 764–799. doi:10.1111/jpim.12510

Stubbs, W., & Cocklin, C. (2008). Conceptualizing a "sustainable business model. *Organization & Environment*, *21*(2), 103–127. doi:10.1177/1086026608318042

Taghizadeh, S. K., Jayaraman, K., Ismail, I., & Rahman, S. A. (2016). Scale development and validation for DART model of value co-creation process on innovation strategy. *Journal of Business and Industrial Marketing*, *31*(1), 24–35. doi:10.1108/JBIM-02-2014-0033

Tanggaard, L. (2014). Faculty of Humanities, Department of Communication & Psychology, University of Aalborg, Denmark. *European Educational Research Journal*, *13*(1), 2014. www.wwwords.eu/EERJ

The Economic Times. (2021, September). Definition of 'Macroeconomics. The Economic Times. https://economictimes. indiatimes.com/definition/macroeconomics

Tidd, J., & Bessant, J. R. (2018). *Managing Innovation: integrating Technological, Market and Organizational Change.* John Wiley and Sons.

Tiwari, R., & Herstatt, C. (2013). *Open Global Innovation Networks as Enablers of Frugal Innovation: Propositions Based on Evidence from India.* The Hamburg University of Technology, Technology and Innovation Management. Working Paper No. 72

Tiwari, R., Kalogerakis, K., & Herstatt, C. (2016, July). Frugal innovations in the mirror of scholarly discourse: Tracing theoretical basis and antecedents. In *R&D Management Conference,* Cambridge, UK.

Tiwari, R. (2016). Frugal Innovation in Scholarly and Social Discourse. *An Assessment of Trends and Potential Societal Implications.*, *28*, 1–25.

Tunio, M. N., Chaudhry, I. S., Mughal, F., & Shaikh, E. (2022). Marketing Mode and Survival of the Entrepreneurial Activities of Nascent Entrepreneurs. In Big Data Analytics (pp. 1-18). Auerbach Publications. doi:10.1201/9781003307761-1

Tunio, M. N., Shah, S. M. M., Qureshi, M. A., Tunio, A. N., & Shaikh, E. (2022). Career Predilections and Options to Opt Occupation for the Youth in Pakistan. In Developing Entrepreneurial Ecosystems in Academia (pp. 156-170). IGI Global. doi:10.4018/978-1-7998-8505-4.ch009

Tunio, M. N., Soomro, A. A., & Bogenhold, D. (2017). The Study of Self-employment at SMEs Level with Reference to Poverty in Developing Countries. Business and Management Research, 6(2). doi:10.5430/bmr.v6n2p33

Tunio, M. N., Yusrini, L., & Shoukat, G. (2021). Corporate social responsibility (CSR) in Hotels in Austria, Pakistan, and Indonesia: small and medium Enterprise spillover of COVID-19. In Handbook of research on entrepreneurship, innovation, sustainability, and ICTs in the post-COVID-19 era (pp. 263-280). IGI Global.

Tunio, M. N., Yusrini, L., & Shoukat, G. (2021). Corporate Social Responsibility (CSR) in Hotels in Austria, Pakistan, and Indonesia: Small and Medium Enterprise Spillover of COVID-19. In Handbook of Research on Entrepreneurship, Innovation, Sustainability, and ICTs in the Post-COVID-19 Era (pp. 263-280). IGI Global.

Tunio, M. N., Yusrini, L., & Shoukat, G. (2021). Corporate social responsibility (CSR) in Hotels in Austria, Pakistan, and Indonesia: small and medium Enterprise spillover of COVID-19. In Handbook of research on entrepreneurship, innovation, sustainability, and ICTs in the post-COVID-19 era, (pp. 263-280). IGI Global.

Tunio, M. N., Yusrni, L., Shah, Z. A., Katper, N. K., & Jariko, M. A. (2021). How hotel industry cope up with the CO-VID-19: An SME Perspective. *ETIKONOMI, 20*(2).

Tunio, M. N. (2020). ¹. Academic entrepreneurship in developing countries: Contextualizing recent debate. In *Research Handbook on Entrepreneurship in Emerging Economies*. Edward Elgar Publishing. doi:10.4337/9781788973717.00014

Tunio, M. N. (2020). Role of ICT in Promoting Entrepreneurial Ecosystems in Pakistan. *Journal of Business Ecosystems*, *1*(2), 1–21. doi:10.4018/JBE.2020070101

Tunio, M. N., Chaudhry, I. S., Shaikh, S., Jariko, M. A., & Brahmi, M. (2021). Determinants of the Sustainable Entrepreneurial Engagement of Youth in Developing Country—An Empirical Evidence from Pakistan. *Sustainability, 13*(14), 7764. doi:10.3390u13147764

Tunio, M. N., Jariko, M. A., Børsen, T., Shaikh, S., Mushtaque, T., & Brahmi, M. (2021). How Entrepreneurship Sustains Barriers in the Entrepreneurial Process—A Lesson from a Developing Nation. *Sustainability, 13*(20), 1–18. doi:10.3390u132011419

Tunio, M. N., & Shaikh, E. (2020). ((Forthcoming). Nascent entrepreneurs and challenges in digital market in developing countries. *International Journal of Public Sector Performance Management*.

Tunio, M. N., Shaikh, E., Niaz, S., & Katper, N. S. (2021). Multifaceted perils of the Covid-19 and implications: A Review. *Estudios de Economía Aplicada*. doi:10.25115/eea.v39i2.3957

Tunio, M. N., Yusrini, L., Shah, Z. A., Katper, N., & Jariko, M. A. (2021). How Hotel Industry Cope up with the CO-VID-19: An SME Perspective. *Etikonomi, 20*(2), 213–224. doi:10.15408/etk.v20i2.19172

United Nations. (2010). Handbook for legislation on violence against women. United Nations Publications.

Van Mossel, A., van Rijnsoever, F. J., & Hekkert, M. P. (2018). Navigators through the storm: A review of organization theories and the behavior of incumbent firms during transitions. *Environmental Innovation and Societal Transitions, 26*, 44–63. doi:10.1016/j.eist.2017.07.001

van Oort, F. G., & Lambooy, J. G. (2014). *Cities, knowledge, and innovation.* In M. M. Fischer & P. Nijkamp (Eds.), *Handbook of Regional Science* (pp. 475–488). Springer Berlin Heidelberg. doi:10.1007/978-3-642-23430-9_27

Van Wijk, J., Zietsma, C., Dorado, S., De Bakker, F. G., & Marti, I. (2019). Social innovation: Integrating micro, meso, and macro level insights from institutional theory. *Business & Society, 58*(5), 887–918. doi:10.1177/0007650318789104

Vavik, T., & Keitsch, M. (2010). Exploring relationships between Universal Design and Social Sustainable Development: Some Methodological Aspects to the Debate on the Sciences of Sustainability. *Sustainable Development (Bradford), 18*(5), 295–305. doi:10.1002d.480

Vidourek, R. A., King, K. A., Nabors, L. A., & Merianos, A. L. (2014). Students' benefits and barriers to mental health help-seeking. *Health Psychology and Behavioral Medicine, 2*(1), 1009–1022. doi:10.1080/21642850.2014.963586 PMID:25750831

Vieluf, S., Kaplan, D., Klieme, E., & Bayer, S. (2012). *Teaching Practices and Pedagogical Innovation: Evidence from TALIS.* OECD Publishing. www.oecd.org/edu/school/ TalisCeri%202012%20(tppi)–Ebook.pdf doi:10.1787/9789264123540-en

von Zedtwitz, M., Corsi, S., Veng Søberg, P., & Frega, R. (2015). A Typology of Reverse Innovation. *Journal of Product Innovation Management, 32*(1), 12–28. doi:10.1111/jpim.12181

Waheed, A., Xiaoming, M., Waheed, S., Ahmad, N., & Tian-tian, S. (2020). E-HRM implementation, adoption and its predictors: A case of small and medium enterprises of Pakistan. *International Journal of Information Technology and Management, 19*(23), 162–180. doi:10.1504/IJITM.2020.106217

Ward, S. (2020). SMEs: What Are They? *The Balance Small Business.* https://www. The balance smb.com.

WDD-Sindh. (2011). *Provincial Policy for Women Empowerment.* Women Development Department.

Weiss, A. M. (2001). Social development, the empowerment of women and the expansion of civil society: Alternative ways out of the debt and poverty trap. *Pakistan Development Review, 40*(4), 401–432. doi:10.30541/v40i4Ipp.401-432

Weiss, A. M. (2012). *Moving forward with the legal empowerment of women in pakistan.* United States Institute of Peace.

Weyrauch, T., & Herstatt, C. (2017). What is frugal innovation? Three defining criteria. *Journal of frugal innovation, 2*(1), 1-17.

Weyrauch, T., & Herstatt, C. (2016). What is frugal innovation? Three defining criteria. *Journal of Frugal Innovation, 2*(1), 1. doi:10.118640669-016-0005-y

Wierenga, M. (2015). Local frugal innovations: How do resource-scarce innovations emerge in India? https://aaltodoc.aalto.fi:443/handle/123456789/18429

Wierenga, M. (2015). *Local frugal innovations: How do resource-scarce innovations emerge in India?* Retrieved from https://aaltodoc.aalto.fi:443/handle/123456789/18429

Wigboldus, S., & Jochemsen, H. (2021). Towards an integral perspective on leveraging sustainability transformations using the theory of modal aspects. *Sustainability Science, 16*(3), 869–887. doi:10.100711625-020-00851-5

Williams, J. K. (2018). A Comprehensive Review of Seven Steps to a Comprehensive Literature Review. *Qualitative Report, 23*(2). doi:10.46743/2160-3715/2018.3374

Winkler, T., Ulz, A., Knöbl, W., & Lercher, H. (2020). Frugal innovation in developed markets—Adaption of a criteria-based evaluation model. *J Innov Knowl, 5*(4), 251–259. doi:10.1016/j.jik.2019.11.004

Winterhalter, S., Zeschky, M. B., Neumann, L., & Gassmann, O. (2017). Business models for frugal innovation in emerging markets: The case of the medical device and laboratory equipment industry. *Technovation, 66*, 3–13. doi:10.1016/j.technovation.2017.07.002

Zaccaro, S. J. (2007). Trait-based perspectives of leadership. *The American Psychologist, 62*(1), 6–16.

Zahra, S. A., Gedajlovic, E., Neubaum, D. O., & Shulman, J. M. (2009). A typology of social entrepreneurs: Motives, search processes and ethical challenges. *Journal of Business Venturing, 24*(5), 519–532. doi:10.1016/j.jbusvent.2008.04.007

Zeschky, M. B., Winterhalter, S., & Gassmann, O. (2014). From Cost to Frugal and Reverse Innovation: Mapping the Field and Implications for Global Competitiveness. *Research Technology Management, 57*(4), 20–27. doi:10.5437/08956308X5704235

Zhao, Y. (2015). A world at risk: An imperative for paradigm shift to cultivate 21st century learners. *Society, 52*(2), 129–135. doi:10.100712115-015-9872-8

Zhou, L., Ampon-Wireko, S., Brobbey, E., Dauda, L., Owusu-Marfo, J., & Tetgoum, A. (2020). The Role of Macroeconomic Indicators on Healthcare Cost. *Health Care, 8*(123), 123. doi:10.3390/healthcare8020123 PMID:32375346

Zubeida, M. (2011). *Women and devolution, Dawn.* Retrieved from https://www.dawn.com/news/620470/women-and-devolution

204

About the Contributors

Muhammad Nawaz Tunio is Assistant Professor, Department of Business Administration, Mohammad Ali Jinnah University, Karachi, Pakistan. Dr. Tunio is Ph.D. in the Doctoral track Entrepreneurship, Innovation, and Economic Development, Alpen Adria University, Klagenfurt, Austria on the government scholarship of the Higher Education Commission of Pakistan. He was awarded a young scientist research fellowship for Kent State University, Ohio. His fields of research interest are entrepreneurship, CSR, Careers, Youth Development, and Self-employment. He has publications in top-notch research journals, and he has presented papers at international conferences and conducted research workshops. Dr. Tunio has edited several books, contributed chapters in the different book edits by reputable publishers, and edited special issues of the impact factor, and Scopus indexed journals in the field of entrepreneurship. He has conducted several sessions, and workshops. https://orcid.org/0000-0003-1376-5371.

Atia Bano Memon is Assistant Professor in Department of Computer Science at the University of Sindh, Pakistan. She earned her degree of PhD in Computer Science from the University of Leipzig, Germany in 2017. She has also worked as a Postdoctoral Researcher for six months at the Institute for Applied Informatics at the University of Leipzig, Germany. She has published several research publications in well recognized international research journals and conferences. Her research interests include IT-supported service innovation, collaborative innovation, web-based platforms for innovation and collaboration, and social big data analysis and integration for business applications. ORCiD: https://orcid.org/0000-0001-6893-0931.

* * *

Shruti Agarwal is a PhD Scholar, at the Department of Humanities and Social Sciences, Malaviya National Institute of Technology, Jaipur. Shruti has research topics presented in conferences and journals.

Shakeel Ahmed is a Ph.D. Scholar in the Department of Business Administration, at Greenwich University, Karachi, Pakistan. His area of the interest is CSR, Entrepreneurship, ICT, and Innovation.

Luigi Aldieri is Full Professor of Economics at the Department of Economic and Statistical Sciences of University of Salerno. His Ph.D. thesis "Three Essays on Knowledge Diffusion and Firms' Economic Performance" is supervised by Prof. Michele Cincera. His research interests embrace Applied Econometrics, the measurement of knowledge, geographic spillovers and economic performance of large international firms and environmental innovation.

Arslan Asif is a researcher and student in Bahria University Islamabad for research based program. He is having progressive and innovative approach to develop the new strategies that can influence the society in an idealized form. He is passionate about informing people regarding the value of environmental preservation and social sustainability through cohesive approach and empirical research. The author is open to discussion, debates and exploring about the issues and innovation in the fields of Management, HRM and Social Studies to contribute towards development of the society. His insight is to live with informed future.

Mohsen Brahmi is affiliated to the Faculty of FEM, Dept. of Economics, University of Sfax. His PhD thesis "Technological Modernization and Governance of the Mining Industry International Firm Face the Global Competitive Changes'. His research interests embrace Economic performance factors, Innovation, Technology, Corporate governance, Applied Survey, ICT, geographic spillovers, Industry rating International mining Firms and Sustainability.

Vinci Concetto Paolo is Full Professor of Economics at the Department of Economic and Statistical Sciences of University of Salerno. His research interests embrace labor economics; theoretical modelling; environmental economics.

Karambir Singh Dhayal is a PhD Scholar at the Department of Economics and Finance, Birla Institute of Technology and Science, Pilani, Rajasthan, India.

Samreen Fazal is a Ph.D. Scholar in the field of the Management Sciences at the Department of Business Administration, Greenwich University, Karachi, Pakistan. She has participated in different research events, research workshops, and international conferences. Her research interests are Entrepreneurship, Frugal Innovation, and Turnover Intentions.

Farhat Ishaque Ishaque has an MPhil in Management Sciences from Bahira University Islamabad. Have a research article published on Green HRM and Organizational Environmental Performance. Assist a co-author in the book chapter along with Syed Haider Ali Shah. "How frugal innovation, social transition and business sustainability is related, Insights on the contemporary transition towards sustainability in dig: frugal innovation, social transition and business sustainability," which was submitted for inclusion in the title Frugal Innovation and Social Transitions in the Digital Era. Have 15 years of professional experience with international organizations and currently working as an Administration and Human Resources officer with United Nations Pakistan. Completed the certifications of Nature-based Solutions for Disaster and Climate Resilience from the United Nations Environment Programme (UNEP) and the Partnership for Environment and Disaster.

Kamran Jamshed is currently a Ph.D. aspirant and holds a Master's degree in Management Studies from the Business School of Bahria University Islamabad, Pakistan. His published work is on Green Leadership, Green Training, Green Process Innovation, Ethical Leadership, Work Performance, Perceived Organizational Politics, and Political Skills. His current research interests include small businesses, family-oriented businesses, family businesses hotels, travel, and tourism industry, and focusing on GHRM and sustainable development, Human Resource Development, Human trafficking and sustainability in the hospitality industry, strategic management, and organizational behavior and their implications in the industry. He worked in the telecom industry of Saudi Arabia under Mobily (MNC) for more than 7 years in different roles and overall, he was been in the industry for the last 10 years.

Naveeda K. Katper is Assistant Professor at Institute of Business Administration, University of Sindh, Jamshoro, Pakistan. She is PhD in Finance from University of Malaya, Malaysia. She has few publications in good journals, and she is a very active researcher and a very good teacher. She has more than 10 years teaching experience.

Hayfa Kazouz doctoral student in economics at the Faculty of Economics and Management of Sousse, University of Soussem Tunisia, primarily focused on Economics financial issues. Having Publications in FRL Journal and Journal of Sustainable Finance & Investment.

Yogarajah Nanthagopan is teaching at the Department of Project Management, Faculty of Business Studies, University of Vavuniya.

Syed Ali Raza is associated with IQRA University as an Asst. Professor and Deputy Director Research & Publications. His areas of interest include financial economics, energy economics, tourism economics and corporate finance. He has published numerous paper in International Referred Journals including Tourism Management, Energy Policy, Economic Modelling, Social Indicators Research, Current Issues in Tourism, Physical A, Quality and Quantity, International Migration, Total Quality management and Business Excellence, Journal of Business Economics and Management, Studies in Higher Education, Journal of Transnational Management, Transition Studies Review, Global Business Review, Journal of Chinese Economic and Foreign Trade Studies and others.

Syed Mir Muhammed Shah is Vice Chancellor of Sukkur IBA University, Sukkur. He is PhD from Universiti Utara Malaysia at Universiti Utara Malaysia - UUM. He has author many books and book chapters. He has participated in the several international conferences including EURAM2021 and BAM2021. He has contributed extensively in the literature in the form of publications in several impact factor and Scopus indexed journals.

Ramakrishnan Vivek has MBA (Rajarata University), BBA (Jaffna University). He is Assistant Lecturer at Faculty of Business Studies, Sri Lanka Technological Campus.

Eman Zameer Rahman is a research scholar in the Management Sciences Department at Bahria University. A graduate of Masters of Business Administration from COMSATS University. Research interests include green approaches, strategic management, leadership, sustainability, psychological capital, marketing, technology, and innovation.

Index

A

Affordability 6, 42, 44, 108, 137

B

Behavioral Innovation 60-62
Business Impact 35
Business Model Development 167
Business Sustainability 49, 68, 73, 167-168, 172

C

Covid-19 24, 26, 30, 32-40, 69, 103-105, 113, 115-121, 131, 140, 142-143, 145, 153, 157-166, 169
Creative Learning 106-107, 109-110

D

Developing Side of the World 113, 115
Developing Sides 113-114, 177, 179, 181-182
Development 1-2, 4-8, 11, 15, 18, 24, 27, 29-30, 36-37, 41, 44-45, 47, 50-51, 53-58, 61, 65, 67-68, 70, 72, 74-75, 78, 84, 104, 106-107, 110, 112, 114-115, 118, 123-132, 134-135, 138, 140-142, 145-146, 149, 151, 153-156, 158, 164-165, 167-168, 170, 172, 174-175, 177, 179-182
Developments 18, 27, 29, 52, 60, 77, 151
Digital Era 1-2, 17, 67, 73, 167, 172
Digitalization 9, 70, 167, 170

E

Economy 14, 26-29, 32-34, 36-40, 55, 58, 60, 65, 107, 109, 119-120, 122, 136, 145, 151, 155, 157-158, 163, 178-179
Education 6, 18, 22, 28, 34-36, 50, 69, 99, 107-110, 112, 119-122, 124-130, 133-134, 156-166, 169
E-HRM 52, 55-56, 60, 64-66

Emerging Nations 21, 41, 46, 48, 136-137
Empowerment 75, 91, 115, 123-132, 175, 181
Environmental Factors 26, 30, 35, 68, 168
Environmental Issues 30, 144, 148
Environmental Sustainability 6, 67-69, 147, 153, 168-169

F

Frugal Innovation 1-21, 23-25, 41-51, 57, 67-77, 123, 133-138, 140, 144-145, 147-148, 153-156, 167-176

G

Global phenomena 9, 14

H

Health 18, 24, 26-29, 31-38, 40, 42, 49, 53, 66, 74, 107, 110, 116, 121, 124-125, 127, 130-131, 138, 148, 152, 156-158, 161, 164-166, 174
Higher Education 112, 119-122, 128, 159-160, 162-163
Hospitality Industry 144-145, 149, 152, 155
HRM Practices 52-63, 65

I

Impact 1-2, 6, 9, 14, 17-18, 20, 23, 26, 29-33, 35, 38-39, 43, 48, 52, 57, 59, 63-64, 68, 74, 83, 93, 103-104, 114, 116-122, 128, 130, 134, 139-142, 148-151, 157-159, 161-162, 164-165, 168, 174, 181-182
Importance of Social Innovation 119, 121
Innovation 1-9, 11-25, 29, 41-43, 45-51, 53-77, 103-110, 112-123, 130-131, 133-156, 167-171, 173-182
Institutions 7, 13-14, 23, 34, 36, 72, 109, 120, 127, 133, 137-139, 148-149, 155, 158-160, 163, 172, 181-182

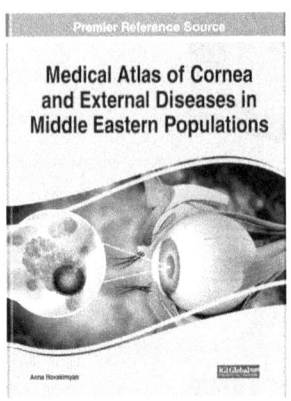

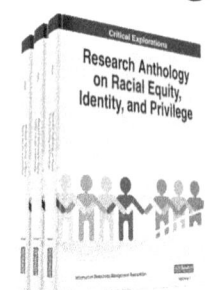

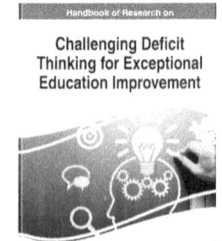

CPSIA information can be obtained
at www.ICGtesting.com
Printed in the USA
BVHW020845081222
653758BV00003B/33